PSYCHOTHERAPISTS IN ACTION

Explorations of the Therapist's
Contribution to the Treatment Process

HANS H. STRUPP

Department of Psychiatry, School of Medicine, University of North Carolina, Chapel Hill

GRUNE & STRATTON NEW YORK LONDON 1960

The research reported in this volume was conducted under grants
M-965 and M-2171 from the National Institute of Mental Health,
U. S. Public Health Service.

LIBRARY OF CONGRESS CATALOG CARD NUMBER: 60-6020
PRINTED AND BOUND IN THE UNITED STATES OF AMERICA

B

CONTENTS

TABLES

FIGURES

PREFACE

For several years I have been engaged in the process of studying the operations of the psychotherapist, with a view toward defining and measuring relevant dimensions of therapeutic technique as well as relating variations in technique to variables in the therapist's personality, training, and experience. This work has been described in a series of publications (see *References*), but from time to time I have received requests from friends and colleagues to see the actual data upon which the quantitative analyses have been based. Their feeling has been that concrete examples might be helpful for training purposes, in addition to giving the reader a more vivid picture of the trends documented by statistical analysis. Thus, publication of this volume was decided upon.

Beginning students of psychotherapy have few opportunities to compare the operations of different psychotherapists, and even if they observe their teachers conducting interviews, the situations and the patients are often far from comparable. It is also true that, typically, at a given point in therapy the therapist formulates one, two, or possibly three hunches of "what is going on," using these working assumptions as a basis for his communications to the patient, and I doubt whether most of us can visualize that vast possibilities for alternative communications exist at a given juncture in therapy. The human brain simply does not function this way. The therapist is more likely to experience considerable certainty and faith in the appropriateness, correctness, and validity of his procedures. The experienced practitioner in particular is not likely to engage in a conscious reasoning process throughout the therapeutic hour; if he did, he would probably be mentally and physically exhausted by the time the next patient presented himself. Economy dictates limitations, and there is nothing wrong with implicit mental processes as long as we keep in mind that there are many alternative ways of proceeding and that we are in no position to assert that one approach is the only "true" and "correct" one. If for no other reason than to catch a glimpse of this diversity, it may be instructive to see how therapists of different backgrounds and levels of experience respond to an experimental situation which appears to bear a fair degree of resemblance to an actual therapeutic situation. The material presented in this volume affords an opportunity to compare the diagnostic formulations, therapeutic conceptions, plans, and communications of a selected sample of therapists who responded as vicarious interviewers to a sound film of an initial interview.

This, however, is only one objective and in itself hardly justifies the effort. Of greater theoretical and practical significance are the substantive research issues which are central to this investigation. Glover's (1955a) survey of British analysts once and for all dispelled the notion (if anyone ever seriously held it) that therapists can be treated as interchangeable units in the sense that their techniques and therapeutic practices are roughly identical. Freud's concept of the countertransference (first published in 1910) at least implicitly makes room for individual differences among therapists. If the person of the therapist is a variable in psychoanalysis and psychotherapy, it follows that we must strive to understand its significance, but even with increasing efforts to study the process and outcome of psychotherapy, research explicitly devoted to elucidating the therapist's part in the process is virtually nonexistent. Frank (1959), in an incisive paper, notes the common failing of research in psychotherapy to define the independent variable, and sums up the issue as follows:

> The most important, and unfortunately the least understood, situational variable in psychotherapy is the therapist himself. His personality pervades any technique he may use, and because of the patient's dependence on him for help, he may influence the patient through subtle cues of which he may not be aware (Frank, 1959, p. 17).

A limited approach to this problem is to inquire, first, what is the process by which the therapist arrives at clinical judgments and evaluations about a patient? How do perceptions, judgments, and evaluations give rise to specific treatment recommendations and planning? How are these conceptualizations reflected in the communications addressed to the patient? How are all these operations influenced by the therapist's training, experience, attitudes, and personality? Surely, the therapist as an observer, or, more correctly, as a participant observer, is subject to influence by the observed (the patient), and this influence may have a considerable bearing on the evolution of the therapeutic relationship and perhaps even the outcome of therapy. These are the major questions to which this investigation attempts to address itself. In the course of this work, attention has been devoted also to the development of a methodologic tool, a system for analyzing therapist communication, which is reported here in some detail.

The potential value of the research results reported in this book obviously hinges on the degree to which they are relevant to the enterprise of psychotherapy and thus can teach us something about the behavior of the psychotherapist. Nobody cares how a psychotherapist plays a game of chess or solves a mechanical puzzle unless this bears a meaningful relationship to relevant aspects of his professional work. As one critic put it: "If you want to study psychotherapy you have to study the actual process of psychotherapy; of course, you are at liberty to study some other kind of game, but let's be clear that the rules of that game are something entirely different." This argument sounds plausible but, I submit, is greatly misleading. The experimental procedure employed in this investigation served the purpose of obtaining comparable data from a fairly large sample of psychotherapists under specified conditions. Like any scientific model, it is useful to the extent that it enables the investigator to learn something about the phenomena under scrutiny and permits inferences which may lead to further hypotheses capable of confirmation or disproof. A model must simplify, objectify, and save research time and effort. If the phenomena were simple to start with, a model obviously would be superfluous; it is the complexity of the naturally occurring events and the human desire to order them which calls for methods to facilitate observation and point the way toward objective and systematic analyses. The process of isolating variables from a welter of complex events is the accepted approach of the scientific method in all disciplines; wherever the scientific method is used, the investigator trades some (and often a great deal) of the richness of the original data for rigor of observation. The value of such schemes is purely heuristic. Once better models have been developed or the inadequacy of previous ones demonstrated, the older model is simply discarded (see Rapoport, 1953).

The experimental situation used in this investigation was not a

therapeutic situation as usually understood. Clearly, no two therapists can interview and interact with the same patient at the same
time. Consequently, it is forever impossible to compare the performance of two or more psychotherapists under strictly comparable
conditions. As a compromise, we constructed a quasi therapeutic
situation, *identical* for all participating therapists, to investigate
similarities and differences in their performance as well as some of
the antecedents of the differences. It is not contended that there is
a one-to-one relationship between any therapist's performance in the
experimental situation and his behavior vis-à-vis a patient. What is
asserted is that the therapist's performance in the experimental
situation bears a meaningful relationship to his ordinary therapeutic
behavior, and that the correlates of his performance (his background,
training, experience, and attitudes) as well as the interrelationships
among diagnostic formulations, treatment plans, and communications may lead to fruitful hypotheses which can be pursued further.
While beset by great methodologic and practical difficulties, a study
of the relationship between the therapist's performance in the experiment and in actual therapy (validity) is not impossible and may
be approached empirically.

Those of us who are connected with the project and studied for
many months the data furnished by over two hundred therapists
felt very keenly that we learned a great deal about the therapists in
our sample as well as about psychotherapy in general. Many therapists gradually began to emerge as persons whose attitudes (toward
the patient in the film, toward the film therapist, the experiment,
the experimenter), therapeutic goals, values, and techniques communicated a great deal to the investigators. We came to respect some
therapists for their unquestionable skill, incisiveness, and penetration. We admired the respect, gentleness, and empathy displayed by
some. There were others who seemed to fall short of the high level
exemplified by the first group. In a few instances, it must be con-
fessed, we became impatient and angry at what appeared a callous,
cold, and rejecting attitude toward a patient who came to seek the
help of a professional person. True, in many instances the therapist's
written comments made it difficult to reconstruct his intonation,
inflection, and other vocal qualities; but many protocols seemed to
convey a great deal of information—sometimes, we suspect, more than
the therapist intended.

While we developed private opinions about "good" and "poor"
therapists, we believe that these opinions did not materially influence

the quantitative results. In analyzing the data, considerable effort was made to minimize the subjectivity of ratings, to spell out criteria on which judgments were based, and to test the agreement among raters. In other words, to quote Professor Edwin G. Boring, we made a serious effort to protect our conclusions from our predictions. Nevertheless, I am fully aware that value judgments dictated parts of the statistical analysis (for example, the explorations of the therapist's empathy). This is perhaps inevitable in any kind of research, and particularly true of research concerned with psychotherapy. The psychotherapist cannot remain indifferent to these issues. The very nature of the activity demands that he take a stand on what is therapeutic (that is, desirable) from his point of view, and what is not. What we can ask is that he be maximally aware of the values he lives by in his therapeutic work.

The organization of the volume is as follows. Part I presents a detailed description of the investigation, together with a discussion of the implications of the findings. Part II contains the records of 40 psychotherapists which are intended to illustrate the statistical trends. These records can be studied independently or in conjunction with the statistical results, with the latter procedure appearing to be the more fruitful one. The editorial comments appended to each case, while based on a knowledge of the quantitative results and the independent judgment of several clinicians (whose agreement was tested), may nevertheless be judged unwarranted from a strictly scientific point of view. It is readily admitted that they go beyond the empirical evidence. It is also envisaged that the reader may possibly come to quite different conclusions or feel that the evidence is insufficient. In short, the reader is cautioned that he is dealing with opinions. Within the framework of the present investigation and my thinking about psychotherapy, I believe them to have heuristic value, but, clearly, they provide no basis for reliably differentiating among "good" and "poor" therapists. At best, they are fairly typical illustrations of statistically significant group trends. I hope that they may serve as a basis for discussion and critical analysis. In this spirit they are offered. Part III includes a description of a system for the comparative analysis of therapist communications, and two applications to therapeutic interviews. Part IV attempts to explore further the implications of the work done so far and point the way toward future research.

If we desire to buy an automobile it is helpful to know something about the various makes and to have a clear concept of the *range* of quality, size, durability, and so on. It is difficult to evaluate car X if it is the only car we have ever seen or driven. It is more useful to inspect a variety of cars, and, better yet, to subject a variety of cars to a road test under comparable conditions. Similarly, one may get a better picture of the psychotherapist (including oneself) if one compares him with others of greater or less experience, greater or less warmth, etc. Knowledge has progressed sufficiently so that experts can reasonably agree on the qualifications and personality characteristics of a "good" therapist (Holt and Luborsky, 1958). There is also some evidence to show that some therapists are more successful than others with certain kinds of patients, and that aspects of the therapist's personality play a part in this (Whitehorn and Betz, 1955). The large task of charting the precise nature of the therapist's influence is still before us. It is my hope that the material presented here will help to sharpen some of the questions we must come to ask and answer about psychotherapy if we desire to increase our scientific understanding of the process.

Chapel Hill, North Carolina   HANS H. STRUPP
July, 1959.

ACKNOWLEDGEMENTS

My greatest indebtedness is to the psychotherapists who collaborated so wholeheartedly in providing the data for this investigation. They gave generously and unstintingly of their time, even those who had some reservations about the worthwhileness of the project. Their readiness to participate is a tribute to a growing awareness among psychotherapists that the time of the psychoanalytic mystique has passed, that the operations of psychotherapy must be subjected to the searching light of objective study if psychotherapy is to become a scientific discipline, and that a willingness to make one's thinking public is a sign of professional honesty, maturity, and integrity—qualities highly becoming to any professional person, but particularly to the psychotherapist, for is it not these very qualities he tries to encourage in his patients? It is noteworthy that the majority of respondents volunteered to sign their names, thus further indicating that they stood firmly behind their ideas and judgments.

To Winfred Overholser, M.D., and Leon Yochelson, M.D., belongs the credit for sponsoring this research proposal and for giving support and encouragement to the project while the author was affiliated with George Washington University.

I also wish to record my gratitude to the National Institute of Mental Health, Public Health Service, for its generous financial support of the project and its faith in the investigator. Special thanks are due Mr. Philip Sapir, who in his capacity as chief of the Research Grants and Fellowships Branch, was ever ready to advise and help.

My friends, Dr. Jack Chassan and Dr. Dorothy E. Green, gave valuable advice on statistical problems, and I am equally grateful to them for many friendly and critical discussions.

Rebecca E. Rieger not only contributed many valuable ideas and suggestions but collaborated faithfully and diligently at many stages. My indebtedness to her friendship and inspiration is very keenly felt.

Louisa Bilon and Dr. Martin Wallach provided research assistance and Elaine Nixon labored arduously over the statistical analyses. To Mrs. Billie Buford I am grateful for her faithful help in typing several revised versions of the manuscript. I wish to thank Mrs. Sophie S. Martin and Dr. Martin Wallach for preparing the index.

I have had the good fortune of benefiting from advice and encouragement of friends and colleagues too numerous to mention; they helped more than they will ever realize.

Finally I wish to record my appreciation to the following organizations and institutions which opened their doors and provided the facilities for carrying out the work: Saint Elizabeths Hospital, Washington, D. C.; Washington Psychiatric Society; Maryland Psychiatric Society; Johns Hopkins Hospital, Baltimore; Postgraduate Center for Psychotherapy, New York; Michael Reese Hospital, Chicago; Chicago Institute for Psychoanalysis; University of Chicago Counseling Center; Veterans Administration Benefits Office, Washington, D. C.; VA Hospital, Perry Point, Md.; and Maryland Psychological Association.

Part of the material included in this volume has previously been published in various journals. Grateful acknowledgment is made to the publishers who have given permission to reprint material copyrighted by them:

Chapters 1, 2, 3, 4, and 6 are based on "The Psychotherapist's Contribution to the Treatment Process,"published in *Behavioral Science,* 1958, 3: 34-67.

Chapter 5 previously appeared as "The Performance of Psychiatrists and Psychologists in a Therapeutic Interview," published in *Journal of Clinical Psychology,* 1958, 14: 219-226.

Chapter 7 was published as "The Performance of Psychoanalytic and Client-Centered Therapists in an Initial Interview in *Journal of Consulting Psychology,* 1958, 22: 265-274.

Chapter 12 was previously published under the title "A Multidimensional System for Analyzing Psychotherapeutic Techniques" in *Psychiatry,* 1957, 20: 293-306.

Chapter 13 was previously published under the title "A Multidimensional Analysis of Technique in Brief Psychotherapy" in *Psychiatry,* 1957, 20: 387-397.

Chapter 14 was previously published under the title "A Multidimensional Analysis of Therapist Activity in Analytic and Client-Centered Therapy" in *Journal of Consulting Psychology,* 1957, 21: 301-308.

Chapter 15 is a reprint of the article "Toward an Analysis of the Therapist's Contribution to the Treatment Process," published in *Psychiatry,* 1959, 22: 349-362.

Chapter 16 is a reprint of an article which appeared under the same title in *Behavioral Science,* 1960.

Gratitude is expressed for permission to quote from other sources cited in the text.

For Lottie

1

INTRODUCTION

Research on psychotherapy may be focused on three broad elements: the therapist, the patient, and the therapist-patient interaction. The present investigation was concerned with the therapist's contribution to the treatment process: what the therapist *does*, and how his procedures are related to and influenced by his background, training, experience, and personality. Research on the therapist's contribution is not, of course, any more important than research on the personality processes which psychotherapy seeks to influence, but it is a necessary link in improving our understanding of what psychotherapy is about. Considering the obvious importance of the therapist variable, it is astonishing how little objective research has been conducted on the problem.

The performance of any two therapists, even in clearly defined and highly specific situations, will reveal differences. It is the antecedents of such differences which constitute the focus of the inquiry. By the same token, there will be similarities, which will be equally important.

Systematic differences in performance may be a function of the therapist's training, experience, and personality, to name a few of the more important variables. The effects may be relatively independent of the particular interpersonal situation (for example, an inexperienced therapist may not interpret at all or too much irrespective of the patient or the situation), or the effects may be highly specific (a therapist may respond to a patient's expression of hostility if it touches, say, his professional status but he may passively accept most other forms of overt hostility). In any case, it is clear that therapeutic techniques are not applied *in vacuo* and that they are differentially affected by factors in the therapist's personality. His performance is determined, in part, at least, by the way in which he perceives the patient's behavior, interprets its meaning in the framework of his clinical experience *and* his own personality, and the way in which this meaning is reflected in his response. It is one of the peculiarities of the therapeutic situation that the therapist's interpersonal perceptions are immediately translated into action deliberately designed to effect a change in the patient's perceptions and behavior.

In a sense, the therapist is a reader of imaginary dials who acts "therapeutically" upon the information indicated by these measuring instruments within himself. When supplied with certain information, say, the behavior of a patient, he will register this information in certain ways and he will react to it in certain other ways. The therapist's theory, experience, and personality determine the kinds of dials he uses as well as their calibration. His therapeutic actions are based on the meanings and implications of these readings.

In order to obtain empirical data on the calibration of the therapist as a clinical instrument, we can supply a certain identical input (patient behavior) and note (a) how this input is perceived and evaluated; (b) what deductions and inferences are drawn from it; and (c) how these processes are translated into therapeutic action. On the hypothesis that this testing procedure will disclose differences among therapists, one can investigate systematic influences which might produce the discrepancies. For example, therapists may use different sets of measuring instruments whose readings have no relation to each other; or they may use similar instruments, but the calibration may differ; or they may interpret differently the meaning of the same pointer reading. Any one of these possibilities and many others may result in divergent therapeutic communications.

This analogy is of course a gross oversimplification of the therapist's activity in the therapeutic situation, but it may help to make explicit the objectives of this investigation. The purpose was to study the therapist's performance in a first interview and to ask: If a group of therapists observe the same patient, how do they perceive the clinical problem? What kinds of evaluations result from their perceptions? How are their perceptions and evaluations related to their communications? And, can differences in their performance be accounted for in terms of common underlying variables?*

We are thus concerned with the problem of the formation of clinical judgments and their impact upon the operations of the psychotherapist.† The therapist must perforce start with activities designed to elicit data from the patient upon which to base clinical judgments which in turn give rise to appropriate therapeutic interventions. (We are excluding here the unlikely possibility of the therapist's blind reliance on the clinical findings of others who may have evaluated the patient and have gone through a similar judgmental process.) This raises the thorny epistemologic question which Bakan (1956), among many others, has considered: How is it possible for the therapist to have any notion at all concerning what is going on in the "mind" of the patient? Furthermore, if psychological experience is essentially private, how can an external observer come to "know" it? Bakan comes to the conclusion that "knowledge

---

*The difficulty of distinguishing between apparent and real differences in clinical judgments and formulations is recognized. Personality being a dynamic constellation, it is possible to focus on a multitude of facets, each of which may be valid in its own right. This problem becomes acute when the respondent (therapist) is given considerable latitude (for example, a question asking him to formulate the dynamics of the patient's difficulties). Such formulations are difficult to compare since there are few criteria for assessing the degree of similarity between two formulations. Even when the respondent's judgments are more clearly channeled (for example, an item asking him to rate the patient's anxiety on a four-point scale) the problem is basically not met. There is probably a "real" difference between two observers, one of whom describes the patient as manifesting "relatively little" anxiety and one who assesses the patient's anxiety as being "a great deal." But, is the difference between "a great deal" and "a fair amount" real or apparent? Does it reflect "true" differences in the assessment of a clinical datum, or is it merely an indication of somewhat discrepant rating standards employed by the clinician? The latter possibility may be suggested particularly when (as in the case of the following study) scale steps are left relatively vague. Where such ambiguities exist, subjective factors in the rater may come into play and fill the gap left by the absence of a highly specific frame of reference. (This may be one explanation to account for the differences which were observed.) Whether a painstaking spelling out of rating criteria would aid in increasing the consensus is a moot question. Certainly, at the present stage of knowledge a high degree of precision is not to be expected, which is not to say that relatively gross judgments are without clinical or scientific value. Obviously, they can be. The point to be made is that subjective elements do enter into clinical judgments; the investigative task then becomes one of making explicit the rater's frame of reference and to account for observed differences.

† The following discussion owes much to an important paper by Helen Sargent (1959).

of the other is somehow to take place by reference to one's own experience" (p. 660), an assumption which becomes meaningful if the dictum is accepted that "after all, we are pretty much alike" (p. 658). This is a cornerstone of Sullivan's theory of interpersonal relations and underlies *pari passu* the psychoanalytic theory of psychotherapy as well as that of other systems of psychotherapy. The question however remains: To what particular experience of his own shall the therapist refer the patient's experience? Bakan gives the following answer:

> What his [the clinician's] education should do is to show him the plausibility, within himself, of alternative behaviors on the basis of given experiences, and the multiplicity of experiences which may give rise to some specific kind of behavior. If . . . the task of the clinical psychologist is that of finding to which experiences within himself he is to refer the given item of behavior which he observes, it is extremely important that his training shall open up to consciousness the wide range of experiences that lie within him. This, of course, is one way of conceiving of the desirability of having psychotherapy for one who is to do psychotherapy (p. 661).

In order to make sense out of the psychological experience of another person it is necessary, then, to refer it to one's own. Thus, Bakan (1954) attempts to reinstate systematic self-observation and introspection as legitimate methods for the clinical psychologist and psychotherapist. But, can we trust the clinician-observer? The history of modern psychology (at least in America) with its emphasis on experimental controls is predicated on a distrust of the observer. It is based on the recognition that observer agreement is a cardinal requirement of the scientific method. Consequently, phenomena concerning which observer consensus is inadequate or absent are *ipso facto* not susceptible to scientific analysis.

To go back to Bakan's argument, what assurance is there that Therapist A refers a patient's psychological experience to the same, or roughly the same, experiences within himself as Therapist B? If the patient's experience means one thing to Therapist A, his inferences may be different from those of Therapist B, and their respective therapeutic interventions may correspondingly diverge even if other variables, such as training, theoretical orientation, etc., are identical. This problem may become particularly serious in the therapeutic situation because every intervention by the therapist may in turn influence the data elicited from the patient, so that, in the extreme case, the therapist cannot be sure whether the patient is merely responding to preconceptions introduced by the therapist. Pertinent examples are Freud's dramatic error regarding patients' reports of seduction in infancy and Stekel's patients who produced dreams "to order." Granted that the patient's productions will only under the most unusual circumstances be *solely* a function of variables introduced by the therapist, the question remains: To what extent do the therapist's perceptions, inferences, and resulting communications influence the data of observation? Commonsense tells us that no two clinicians are so well calibrated that their observations completely coincide. This failure of coincidence would appear to be a function either of the clinician-observer or the process of participant observation, or a combination of both. We may reason that since no two therapists will interact with a given patient in identical ways, the data of their observations must perforce differ. The question for empirical research is to elucidate the reasons for differences among observers. In short, the problem of consensus cannot be sidestepped; by the same token, a fuller understanding of the factors detracting from consensus may contribute to its increase.

To further highlight this problem I should like to refer to an incisive analysis by Lord Russell (1948), quoted by Szasz (1957). Russell suggests a definition of psychology as "the science of those occurrences which, by their very nature, can only be observed by one person" (p. 44). Like Bakan, Russell establishes introspection as a valid method for observing psychological data, feeling that "to a considerable extent [it is] amenable to scientific controls" (Russell, 1948, p. 51). Russell, however, fails to make explicit what these controls are, nor does he come to grips with the possible pitfalls which attend the reliance on observations and inferences by a single person. Similarly, this issue is disregarded in the argument of a physicist quoted by Ruth Tolman (1953):

> The fundamental concepts of psychoanalysis derive from scientific observations in exactly the same sense that concepts in any science are derived. The method of psychoanalysis, free association, is a definite prescribed method which can be used by any qualified experimenter and will, when used, yield consistent results. The experiment is repeatable, by different experimenters, using precisely the same method. Thus findings can be "checked." But the main point of the argument centers about the expression "qualified experimenter." Who *is* a qualified experimenter? That, says the physicist, is the well-trained psychoanalyst and *only* the psychoanalyst. It is folly to expect either to discover or to check psychoanalytic concepts by any other method (Tolman, 1953, p. 726).

We may fully agree that psychoanalytic concepts cannot be verified "independently" and that the use of untrained observers to accomplish this end is ludicrous. The question, however, centers around the consistency of results and the repeatability of the experiment. If two observers, even observers with identical training, do not agree in their observations and resulting inferences, the flaw may lie not in the method but in the person employing it. If two clinician-observers, viewing the same patient, come to different conclusions about the nature of his problem, the meaning of his symptoms, the course of therapeutic action to be followed, etc., the scientist becomes interested in the therapist's inferential processes and the factors affecting them. In the above-quoted argument it is (falsely, I believe) assumed that the method of psychoanalysis (and, by implication, psychotherapy) can be applied impersonally, so that *all* well-trained observers will arrive at highly similar results. It is this assertion (among others) which has been questioned by critics of psycho-analysis, who point to the high degree of subjectivity inherent in the therapeutic procedure as well as the difficulty of demonstrating that a construction based on a set of clinical findings is more than an idiosyncratic interpretation.

It is difficult, and perhaps impossible, to investigate whether a patient interacting with Therapist A would interact in identical or highly similar ways with Therapist B. It seems plausible that per-sonality differences in therapists account for *some* differences in interaction. It may also be conceded that while a patient's trans-ference relationship with any two therapists will not be identical, given carefully trained therapists the patient's significant problems will eventually emerge in much the same manner. Furthermore, prolonged contact with a patient may narrow the gap of disagreement existing among observers on first contact. Reliable empirical evidence on all these points is presently not available, partly because methodologic problems present formidable barriers to their investi-gation.

As already stated, the present investigation has more modest aims. It is essentially an inquiry into the relationships between the inter-viewer's perceptions of a patient and resulting clinical judgments, treatment plans, etc. In addition, it attempts to elucidate in a very preliminary way some antecedents of observer differences. Finally, it seeks to present evidence on the extent to which the foregoing factors may influence the character of the therapist's communications to the patient.

PART I

The Research:
Its Methods and Findings

2

METHOD AND PROCEDURE

If we are interested in comparing the therapeutic behavior of one therapist with that of another, and if we want to study similarities or differences between groups of therapists, we must be able to make specific statements about the conditions which evoke this behavior. This is a basic requirement of any scientific investigation but one which has been extraordinarily difficult to approximate in psychotherapy research. It is impossible to have more than one therapist conduct an interview with the same patient at the same time, nor are we likely to succeed in selecting "comparable" patients. It follows that a compromise must be made. One compromise that has often proved fruitful in science is to sacrifice some of the "realism" of the situation in exchange for improved experimental control.

To study the performance of psychotherapists under comparable controlled conditions, it was decided to use a sound film of an initial interview, to which therapists responded as vicarious interviewers.

The major difference between a "real" interview and the experimental situation is the obvious fact that the interaction is not between the audience therapists and the patient but between the film therapist and the patient. Consequently, the "interventions" of the audience therapist have no effect upon the patient or the course of the interview. Furthermore, the audience therapist's response is not exclusively to the patient, but rather to the totality of the patient-therapist situation as portrayed on the screen. The investigation, then, rests on the assumption that the audience therapist's simulated interview behavior bears a meaningful relationship to his performance as a therapist in similar real-life therapy situations and that valid references can be drawn from this sample of behavior. It is not maintained that the interview between the film patient and any audience therapist would have proceeded exactly as indicated by the therapist's hypothetical responses.

The foregoing assumptions must be made if one wishes to generalize the experimental results, and this, of course, is the purpose of any experiment. Therefore, similar assumptions hold true for the study of the protocols included in these pages. The reader must keep in mind the experimental conditions under which the data were collected and make allowances for possible distortions which the method itself may have induced. Such questions as the following are germane: To what extent was a therapist made uncomfortable by the experimental conditions? To what extent was a reaction of anger or irritation which a respondent may have felt toward the experiment and the experimenter displaced and reflected in the responses to the patient? To what extent was the experimental situation experienced as a "test" and, if so, were the therapist's answers intended as "textbook" answers? Were experienced therapists made more or less insecure by the experimental conditions; in other words, did the experimental situation have differential effects which were systematic? Precise answers to these and related questions cannot be given, but there was some impressionistic evidence that these influences cannot be ruled out completely. The best one may hope is that they were random rather than systematic, and that they did not *materially* affect the statistical findings.

THE SOUND FILM

In an earlier investigation I requested a sample of psychotherapists to formulate hypothetical responses to patients' statements which were printed on cards in an attempt to relate technique differences among therapists to variables such as theoretical orientation, length of experience, personal analysis *vs.* no personal analysis (Strupp, 1955a, 1955b, 1955c). At that time, certain shortcomings in the experimental procedure were noted (lack of context, absence of visual and auditory clues which are usually available to the therapist, etc.). Accordingly, it seemed desirable to provide a more "realistic" situation for the therapist, which would lend itself to the collection of more extensive as well as intensive data.

A sound film of an initial therapeutic interview seemed to meet these requirements. Since lack of facilities and funds precluded the production of such a film, it became necessary to select an existing film and to adapt it for experimental purposes. As it developed, the choice was severely circumscribed in that very few films were either suitable or accessible. Eventually, our choice fell upon the "Psychotherapeutic Interviewing Series," which had been produced for training purposes by the Veterans Administration under the direction of the late Dr. Jacob Finesinger and Dr. Florence Powdermaker. Part V of the series, entitled "A Clinical Picture of Claustrophobia," appealed to us for several reasons, and, permission having been granted by the Veterans Administration, it was used in the study. The film commended itself because (1) it was an unrehearsed initial interview (although it turned out that the patient had been in psychotherapy before with another therapist); (2) the patient as well as the interview seemed reasonably "typical"; (3) the patient communicated freely and eloquently his difficulties in living, so that a great wealth of clinical data was provided in a relatively short time; (4) the interview situation was "provocative" in the sense that it readily stimulated interest and emotional participation in the viewer; (5) the therapist was rather bland and nondescript, so that he might evoke less competition from the film viewer (as it developed, this factor produced other difficulties to be mentioned presently); (6) the technical quality of the film was reasonably adequate.

In its original form the film was a black and white sound film lasting approximately 30 minutes. It was released in 1952. According to a statement by the Veterans Administration, no significant parts of the interview had been deleted.*

The patient's appearance is that of a middle-aged man, presumably in his early forties; he is of medium height, slender, and bald. He appears tense and his movements are often vehement and jerky. His verbalizations are intense, and it is apparent even from the typescript that his anger and hostility build up as the interview progresses.

The interviewer is a young resident in psychiatry. He is tall, light-haired, and conveys the picture of a young and eager professional. He is wearing a white coat. He is evidently ill-at-ease and uncomfortable in his professional role. As a result there is virtually no spontaneity of expression and his communications appear stilted and labored. Occasionally, he busies himself with his pipe in a self-conscious way. He seems remote, distant, and under considerable strain. (This may be accounted for by the presence of the camera

* The film is available on loan from the Veterans Administration Film Library; it may also be purchased from United World Films, 1445 Park Avenue, New York 29, N.Y., at reasonable cost.

as well as two psychiatrist-observers who were watching through a one-way screen.) His facial expressions sometimes convey incredulity or surprise at the patient's communications. He never offers the patient encouragement or reassurance, and generally seems passive. He hides behind a "professional" facade and gives an appearance of complete anonymity. This impression seems corroborated by the divergence of judgments from the audience therapists, some of whom perceived him as moderately "warm," interested, and friendly; others regarded him as wooden, disinterested, and "cold." Similarly, opinions differed widely about the adequacy of his performance, although a majority of respondents judged him to be inexperienced and found fault with his interviewing behavior.

The interview takes place in an office which is furnished conventionally. The interviewer sits behind a desk; the patient, at the side.

A transcript of the sound track follows. The numbers in brackets designate stopping points (see below).

THE FILM

T.: I am Dr. ———.

P.: ——— is my name, doctor.

T.: Won't you sit down?

P.: Thank you. [1]

T.: I wonder if you could tell me a little bit about your troubles, Mr. ———.

P.: Well, this trouble started out with a . . . a sensation; it was a hot and cold sensation that ran over me on a crowded streetcar right in the center of . . . the city. And it was crowded and as I recall vividly we were crossing ——— and going under the viaduct of the railroad there towards Union Station when the streetcar was crowded and swayed, and just as we passed in my line of vision we passed a big truck that was parked double, and when the street car swayed like that . . . a . . . a fear sensation gripped me . . . see . . .

T.: A fear?

P.: A fear, yes. I have always been afraid (T.: Mmm.) because (laughs) of my association with my mother just made me scared to death. I have always been anxious and my association with her the first 20 years of my life has caused my marked anxiety; (T.: Mmm.) and from 20 years from then up to now economic conditions have also caused it. [2]

T.: You say the streetcar swayed?

P.: That's right. The street, it was crowded, and the streetcar swayed and it looked like it was going to bump this truck in my line of vision, and it scared me because the person that was sitting next to me was a large person, and I was crowded, hemmed in; I had my overcoat on, and the streetcar was warm anyway, and when this warm and cold sensation gripped me, it was something that I had never experienced before. It was horrible. And I became scared, afraid; my heart pounded, it raced, it just cut up something awful, and that of course made me more afraid because I thought of a heart attack immediately, and I pulled the cord to get off at the next stop, and of course I wasn't very genteel; I knocked people right and left to get out of there. I was in a hurry.

T.: The person sitting beside you . . .

P.: Was a large woman, with a lot of packages. And I was hemmed in . . . see . . . I never liked to be hemmed in, anyway, in any situation, and . . .

T.: Uhhh.

P.: Sir?

T.: Uhh, never liked to be hemmed in?

P.: No, uhhh. Well, I just never liked to . . . to . . . to be in a position where I could not throw my arms and get out, if I wanted to, and this was one that I could not get out fast enough because I was hemmed in, (T.: Mmmm.) and it caused this panic reaction. (T.: Mmmm.) And when I finally got off the streetcar, as I said a minute ago, it took two blocks to regain my composure, and then I went on to work. [3]

T.: You felt hemmed in by this woman there?

P.: Well, yes, uhhh, you would be hemmed in too if you had your big overcoat on and it was January and the streetcar was crowded, people standing in the aisles and you had a big two-three hundred pound person sitting beside you, you . . . sitting beside you, you, anybody would feel hemmed in there.

T.: Two or three hundred pounds, uhh?

P.: Yes, she was a large woman.

T.: Uhh . . .

P.: And, as I said a minute ago, it started with this horrible sensation and it scared me.

T.: Uhh . . .

P.: So I just got off the streetcar as quickly as I could. But, that was number one.

T.: This feeling of being hemmed in always . . .

P.: Well, I have never liked close quarters. I mean . . . uhh . . . my experience in life has been such that I have been enmeshed in too many things, circumstances that have all been economic, financial. I have had to do things I didn't want to do to make a living (T.: Mmmm.) and it just seems like the whole thing just enveloped me, encased me in something I couldn't get out of. [4]

T.: How do you mean . . . en . . . cased?

P.: Well, uhh . . . let's take economic, for instance. Suppose you never had any free will, suppose you had to do things that you didn't want to do . . . uhh . . . uhh . . . that is, going out and work on a job you didn't like, just to earn a living, just because you had somebody you had to support (T.: Mmmm.) uhh . . . uhh . . . there is no free will there. You just had to do something and . . .

T.: Supporting your mother?

P.: That's correct.

T.: Uhh . . .

P.: I have supported her since 1926.

T.: Uhh . . .

P.: That's correct.

T.: Uhh . . .

P.: And as I said a minute ago, it has been all economic; I have worried and stewed over having to do things. I have wanted to do them but I have wondered why all this should have been dumped in my lap when I had a brother that could have, should have helped if he would have, and that's why I say I have always felt encased in something, enmeshed by unnecessary circumstances, never was allowed to go out and do things I wanted to if I wanted to . . . just got to a stage where I don't know now.

T.: How does it make you feel to be enmeshed?

P.: Well, it is . . . you have heard the expression of a person is feeling cornered, haven't you? [5]

T.: Huh.

P.: Huh?

T.: Feeling cornered?

P.: Yes, in other words, you're . . . you're cornered; you have no other place to go . . . you're just here.

T.: Huh.

P.: Then you become all . . . jumbled up. Then you're thinking.

T.: What do you mean, jumbled?

P.: Well, you become anxious of situations. (T.: Huh.) As I said just a second ago, it's been all economic, and my capacity to earn hasn't been any too great, and if you earn ten cents and you have to spend nine of it before you get it, why, uhh . . . and having had the thing all these years, it is just . . . it is . . . it has always made me feel that is, just hemmed in by unnecessary circumstances until I just got hemmed in once too often. [6] (T.: Uhuh) Uhh . . . of course, it is just a little hard talking about these things, uhh . . . I am beginning to feel a little better and getting a different insight.

T.: Uhh . . .

P.: But I still have . . . since I experienced this panic reaction all over the city; it has just been recently that I have been able to go out of the house by myself, enough to go to the corner a half a block away to buy a newspaper. Heretofore I had to have my wife . . . every place I went . . . I couldn't go alone; I was afraid. I was afraid that I'd get an attack on the street and fall over and who would help me?

T.: You had to have your wife . . . ?

P.: That's correct.

T.: Uhuh . . .

P.: It's just been recently that I have been able to go out on the street. As we gather from my interviews and from a book that I have been reading purporting to this disease, to this ailment, why I . . . I . . . I have gathered sufficient insight now that I am able to go out a little bit but only to a radius of maybe about four or five blocks.

T.: Mmmm . . .

P.: And now the heart action has decreased, and now my trouble, doctor, is I am dizzy. [7]

T.: Huh . . .

P.: I can't walk two blocks without getting so dizzy I feel like I am swaying from right to left. (T.: Mmm . . .) I feel like I'm drunk.

T.: Mmm . . . You were telling me about this being hemmed in. Uuuh . . . Could you tell me a little more how that makes you feel inside?

P.: Yes, it . . . it just causes a very uncomfortable, smothering sensation in my chest, to be hemmed in; it just feels like maybe somebody is sitting on it. You know, just pressing.

T.: Uhh. Just sitting on it, uhh.

P.: Well, (laughs) if you had somebody to put their hand on your chest, you could feel a pressure. (T.: Mmm . . .) Well, that's the way it feels. And then, it keeps my stomach just turning, quivering all the time. It just keeps it, uhh, all upset; and it just makes me so anxious . . .

T.: Uhh . . .

P.: To the point where I become overwhelmed with the anxiety by thinking about it and then I bring on this sensation, and then the sensations bring on my fear.

T.: Mmmm . . .

P.: . . . and then I just keep myself in a circle. [8]

T.: Like someone sitting and twisting . . .

P.: Well, no, that isn't exactly correct, that is only as an example.

T.: Mmmm . . .

P.: You see what I mean? Pressure; put your hand on your other hand; you got pressure.

T.: Mmm . . .

P.: Well, that's just like it feels; that's the sensation of being hemmed in; you're cornered, you don't know which way to go. You are tired of the surroundings you are in and what you have been doing; you can't find anything that takes its place, that seems to be . . . to . . . fulfill the bill for you.

T.: Mmm . . .

P.: But it is the sensations that worry me.

T.: Mmm . . .

P.: This other stuff, huh, I can forget . . .

T.: Mmm . . .

P.: . . . or have to if I want to regain my health.   [9]

T.: Mmm . . .

P.: But . . .

T.: How do you mean, "forget"?

P.: Well, uh . . . as I said a minute ago, I am sort of advanced in this thing, a little bit in . . . in . . . as far as insight is concerned, and I know that anxiety, worry, self-pity and prolonged sorrow are four things that bring on my . . . if I think on any one of those four, and which . . . which prolonged sorrow seems to be my main one now . . .

T.: Mmm . . .

P.: . . . that I can keep myself in a stew . . .

T.: Mmm . . .

P.: And then I can get these feelings . . .

T.: Mmm . . .

P.: And when I get the feelings, they still break over me with such force yet that my heart pounds and that I become dizzy and I even get sick on my stomach after I eat my . . .

T.: Mmm . . .

P.: . . . after I have eaten my dinner, I have full feelings and what not, but it is still my anxiety.

T.: Mmm . . . [10] You've been supporting your mother since . . . ?

P.: Twenty-six.

T.: Mmm . . .

P.: Twenty-six, that's correct.

T.: Mmm . . .

P.: I am still supporting her and I am not working.

T.: You are not working?

P.: I have not worked for two years . . .

T.: Mmm . . .

P.: . . . a year and a half.

T.: Mmm . . . Your father . . . ?

P.: My father is dead.

T.: Mmm . . .

P.: He died in 1926, March 16th.

T.: Mmm . . .

P.: He had pneumonia.

T.: How did it go . . . at home?

P.: Well, I don't . . . my mother lives in H_____. I don't have her with me. She . . . I don't have any . . .

T.: Mmm . . .

P.: I can't . . . I couldn't do that. Her personality is such that it would be impossible. I had her with me for three years here in M———, and it was a source of constant anxiety for me. You see, mother has very, very peculiar traits of character and among others she won't stop talking long enough even to eat her dinner. And when I am at the table, I'd like to eat my dinner in quiet . . . peace. [11]

T.: Mmm . . .

P.: That was one of the bad features. Another was that she just was not interested in enjoying herself at the house—her own room and radio. She bothered my wife. You see, my wife has been ill for the past seven years with chronic encephalitis; that's of course Parkinson's disease . . .

T.: Mmm . . .

P.: And she can't . . . uh . . . it just makes her nervous . . . She is already nervous, you know, from her constant tremors.

T.: Mmm . . .

P.: . . . her inability to use her knife and fork without shaking, and mother just worried her so much, I had to send mother home.

T.: Worried her, huh?

P.: That's right. My wife would be resting in the afternoon; my mother would come barging in with some fool thing she'd heard on the radio which she wanted to tell my wife, well, that wasn't interesting to my wife . . .

T.: Mmm . . .

P.: It was interesting to mother . . . but she is just one of those personalities that never cared about staying put.

T.: Mmm . . .

P.: She was always too interested in the other person . . . too busybody.

T.: Too . . . ?

P.: Busybody. And that . . . it would of course take a long time to get into the history of that, but that's where my terrific marked anxieties come from.

I was always anxious, and I was anxious as hell even before I got out of high school.

T.: Always anxious?

P.: That's correct. Apprehensive. [12]

T.: Mmm . . .

P.: Because I had some unpleasant experiences with mother's personality. After dad died, we moved seven times in four years. That's enough to make a person anxious, isn't it?

T.: Seven times?

P.: That's right. If you work in a bank for the measly sum of $86.66 a month . . .

T.: Mmm . . .

P.: So you see, all my anxieties stem from my economic worries.

T.: Mmm . . .

P.: And of course I developed a lot of antisocial attitudes along the way. [13]

T.: Mmm . . . You say your mother was with you in M——— for three years?

P.: That's correct.

T.: Mmm . . .

P.: And it was very unpleasant. I took advantage of my I-A status in the Army by . . . I told her that perhaps I'd have to go in the Army and that was one good break . . . and from telling her that, I was able to get around sending her home in a more or less dignified manner. Of course, after all, regardless of how many things that I think she has done that I don't like that caused me difficulty, after all, she is still my mother; we can't get away from that. [14]

T.: How? How is that?

P.: Bother me? No, that doesn't bother me . . . uh . . . uh . . . I mean she is my mother, that's all there is to it, but she griped hell out of me for all these years.

T.: Griped, uh?

P.: Griped is an expression of getting mad.

T.: Mmm . . . How did you feel inside when she was here in M———?

P.: Just, oh, gone out, just anxious, just anxious. To a person who has not had any experience with these anxious feelings, it is so hard to describe, but your stomach is all empty, all the time. You're just gone out, you don't . . . it is a hell of a sensation . . . it is hard to explain, but you just don't have anything in there, you're eviscerated.

T.: Nothing in . . . ?

P.: You feel all gone, all washed out all the time, just anxious and then it'd turn . . .

T.: And what would come on?

P.: That was perpetual while she was here.

T.: Mmm . . .

P.: . That was all the time.

T.: Mmm . . .

P.: She just kept me in an anxious stew.

T.: Mmm . . .

P.: That's one . . . There are a lot of them. [15]

T.: Were there any special feelings or thoughts?

P.: Except she hasn't experienced any panic reaction. She is able to go and tell me to do what she pleases . . . I have been confined because I have been afraid that as soon as I walk out in the street my heart will stop beating. I have been afraid of . . . of losing support because of this dizziness that persists. In other words, I've just been afraid. [16]

Pause

T.: You say your mother talks a lot?

P.: Oh yes, it is quite a bit.

T.: Mmm . . .

P.: That is, she is . . . her personality was very peculiar . . . She fought with all the neighbors all the time, and that was embarrassing to me. Of course, I've picked up all her traits of character which I get reminded about now and then from my wife, which makes me mad too. [17]

T.: You picked them up?

P.: Sure, it is only natural. I have associated with her. See, my dad was a civil engineer and was away from work, away from home all the time, and it was by association with my mother in my early life that caused me all my anxieties to begin with. In other words, I was already anxious before I started out. If economic conditions would have been such that I had not been fired from so damn many jobs when I first started out in life . . . for because of economic reasons then I would not have developed to become a professional worrier, and I would not have developed all these symptoms, such as rapid heartbeat and my legs going weak, that I can't cross the street or afraid to ride a streetcar for fear I'd have another heart attack.

T.: Mmm . . .

P.: My inability to go by myself . . . it is just to the point now where I'm just getting tired of it.

T.: Mmm . . .

P.: I want to get well, so I get the hell out of this thing. [18]

T.: You say, anxiety in association with your mother?

P.: Oh yes, yes, I became very anxious; anybody would . . . I would say that anybody who had a mother whose personality was such that she quarreled with the neighbors all the time, or that when she'd go downtown on a Saturday evening you'd be all dressed up, you know when you was a kid, and she'd take you downtown, and every time she'd introduce you, pats you on the head and all that kind of damn foolishness, that doesn't seem to me to be manly, that seems to be artificial. And she had the peculiar character . . . peculiar characteristics of wanting to see what other people had in their houses, in their rooms; if their blinds were up a couple of inches, she would look in to see their rooms . . . what kind of furniture they had, you see. Those things annoyed me. I didn't appreciate it at that early age. [19]

T.: Annoyed?

P.: Uhuh, sure, they annoyed me. That's . . . From that association is where my anxieties begin.

T.: How did you feel when you were annoyed?

P.: Well, I used to get so damn mad I could tear down the house, but I didn't; I suppressed them.

T.: You were . . .

P.: I would get very angry with my mother . . .

T.: Mmm . . .

P.: . . . and I guess I raised a little hell with her, because when I . . . when Dad would come in from . . . from his work over the weekend, or once a month, or once every two months, whenever he would get home, she would tell him on me, so to speak, you know, and my dad wouldn't . . . he would just say, be kindly, and let it go at that. He never reprimanded me.

T.: He . . .

P.: He just told me, "Just be kindly and forget about it." I mean, Dad never reprimanded me. [20]

Pause

T.: He never reprimanded . . .

P.: No. No, never licked me.

T.: Mmm . . .

P.: No, mother did (laughs). Everybody gets licked from my mother. Of course, that is not, that hasn't anything to do with these anxieties; that part doesn't that I have developed, through constant worry and constant thinking about unpleasant things, because it just seems like in my life there hasn't been a damn thing but unpleasant things.

T.: Unpleasant things?

P.: Yes, that's right. Every association that I've had has wound up unpleasantly. Even my work. Either I'd get fired or else I'd quit. So I have just come to the conclusion that I started out with three strikes against me before I came to the plate. It looks like it. [21]

T.: What do you mean, "three strikes"?

P.: Well, my Dad and I . . . didn't have anything.

T.: Mmm . . .

P.: Even though my grandparents were very wealthy. Even though my grand-daddy who was a doctor of medicine and a doctor of divinity . . . he owned and operated a girls' college in H_____.

T.: Mmm . . .

P.: They all had something, this branch of the family. My brother and I, we didn't have anything. Mother made my brother as irresponsible as she made me responsible. He is just irresponsible. He just doesn't give a damn whether school keeps or not. But I do. And when Dad died, we didn't have anything and I took over the head of the family, I worked in the First National Bank for . . . until 1931 where I became involved in . . . probably I got in debt, right after Mother's death, right after Daddy's death, Mother got sick; I had to borrow $300 to pay off the bills and what not. [22]

T.: Right after your . . .

P.: Right after my father's death. That's right. So, when I get fired from the First National Bank in H_____ for writing a little old stinking $35 check on my personal account, and didn't have the money to cover it, I got fired for that . . . see . . . and in my own home town—a thing like that gets around pretty quick, in a small community. I couldn't find a damn job. I didn't have any place to sleep; I didn't have a damn thing to eat. Being an Episcopalian, I went to a person who I knew . . . she ran a boarding house, and I chopped wood at night for my supper, see, to get something to eat. And that was the beginning of all my antisocial attitudes. And if that isn't three strikes against you before you come to bat, I'd like to know what in the hell it is. [23] You just get dumped . . . all these things dumped in your lap, and I wasn't capable emotionally . . . Now I know I wasn't capable of assuming all that responsibility.

T.: Dumped in . . . your lap?

P.: Sure. That's right. All these things just handed to you. What are you going to do? You have to accept them. You don't have to, maybe. Maybe you wouldn't. Maybe somebody else wouldn't, but I did.

T.: How do you mean, "handed you"?

P.: Well, you . . . you . . . you have to take care of your mother . . .

T.: Mmm . . .

P.: You have to try to maintain a little home for yourself . . .

T.: Mmm . . .

P.: You have got a job in a bank which is a nice-sounding proposition but it doesn't pay anything . . . even back in '31 when things were cheap. $86.66 is not very much, particularly if mother wished to live like the Joneses. You see, that's the point there. And I was trying to do my best to fulfill . . . to keep the place . . . and it just got to the point where———(?)—just out from under me. Well, when that went out, I came to M———, and got working in the damn government and got fired from that for getting in debt . . . in trouble financially . . . and so that went out, you see.

T.: You say, after your father died, you took over the . . .

P.: The responsibilities of maintaining a home.

T.: Mmm . . . How was that?

P.: How was it?

T.: How did you feel about that?

P.: Fine. I thought it was all right. I was taught to think that way. Somehow or other, all my relatives said, well, now your dad is dead, you're the head of the family. Well, that . . . I think it propped me up a little bit. You see. But, it would have been perfectly all right to be the head . . . you could have been the head of 100 families if you had some cooperation, perhaps, along the line. [24]

T.: How do you mean, "cooperation"?

P.: Well, for instance, uh . . . I have a brother that, as I said a minute ago, never gave a damn about anything. He would work but he . . . felt like going out on pay night and playing cards, and losing all his money . . . be perfectly all right to him, but he . . . maybe he'd ante up along the line . . . maybe he wouldn't, but I was doing the best I could, and I already had this big $300 debt to start out with. So if that isn't coming to the plate with three strikes, by God, I'd like to know what is. And as a result that . . . that is the beginning . . . just some things to get even along the line. I don't care much about discussing, but it seems to me, hell, . . . you'd want to get even too if you . . . would . . . if all these things . . . you couldn't escape from them it seemed like; it just kept following you no matter where you went.

T.: How do you mean, "get even"?

P.: I mean . . . I figured that the world owed me a living.

T.: Mmm . . .

P.: I still do.

T.: Mmm . . .

P.: And in the long run I'd like to get even with it.

T.: With it?

P.: It, as an entity.

T.: Mmm . . .

P.: But I'm learning that you can't do that. [25]

T.: Tell me about your father's death, uh . . .

P.: You mean, the way it affected me?

T.: Mmm . . .

P.: No, it didn't affect me so much at the time, but in recent years, in the past ten years it has. I mean it is just too bad, you see? It is just too bad that he couldn't stay around here a little longer and make things possible so a fellow wouldn't have had it so damn tough at the beginning . . . at the inception of things. You see what I mean? [26]

T.: You say it affected you?

P.: Well, I thought about it. In other words, I said to myself: "Just why the hell was all this handed to me? Why did I . . . why was I . . . why couldn't it have been Bill Smith over there?" You see?

T.: Mmm . . .

P.: Why was . . . circumstances and life should have picked out me . . . well, hell, I was hardly able to take care of myself.

T.: Mmm . . .

P.: You understand? So, therefore, if my Dad could have lived and still be living, like my mother is, of course, that is thinking in retrospect; you can't do that, but *IF*, I say, probably it would have been different.

T.: Mmm . . .

P.: I probably would not have been rejected from the Army because of psychoneurosis; I couldn't even do my part in the damn war . . . So, you see how it makes you feel like you have struck out even before you come to the plate. Makes me emotional.

T.: Emotional?

P.: Yeah. Makes me . . . fill up even if I think about it.

T.: How do you mean, "fill up"?

P.: Well, just feel like you want to bawl, cry, but I don't want to because . . . reasonable . . . and you don't do that but that's just the way it makes me feel. I just feel . . . I still say: "Why the hell did it happen . . . have to be me? See? I have never been able to live my life. Always had something to cause me to live it some other way, and it has been economic. [27]

T.: Like you want to bawl, huh?

P.: Cry.

T.: Mmm . . .

P.: Oh yeah, I bawl once in a while; you get so damn filled up, I can't take it any more.

T.: Mmm . . .

P.: But getting back to the sensations, that's the bugaboo. I can never go against these things with the assurance. Now I have asked every doctor I have seen the same question. I guess they are getting tired of this by now. But, my question is: "These sensations have been so horrible and they're attacking me so viciously that . . . are they undermining my nervous system, are they going to cause me to have a heart disease, or . . ." see, those are the things that I have never been able to satisfy my mind, doctor, because I experienced a panic reaction all over the city, and ran home where I felt safe.

T.: Mmm . . .

P.: But at home I had these attacks. I didn't have any place to run, so I had to lay there and take it . . . see . . . until I tried to finish my psychology a little bit and then it goes away. That's all I want to ask you. Are they going to kill me? Will they cause me to have . . . will they cause my heart to flop out from under me some day or will they damage my nerve tissues or even my . . . my thinking? [28]

T.: Mmm . . .

While the identity of the interviewer was established, diligent search failed to unearth information about the circumstances which brought the patient to the interview. Similarly, nothing could be ascertained about subsequent events. However, following one of the film showings, a psychiatrist told me that he had seen the patient in psychotherapy for a period of time. The patient had been seen in an outpatient clinic for about two years *prior* to the time the motion picture was made. According to the informant, the patient had subsequently succeeded in finding employment as a restaurant worker and had managed to keep his job. The psychiatrist said that every year he received a Christmas card from him. Unfortunately, very little could be learned about the course of the psychotherapy, techniques employed, problems dealt with, intercurrent events, or outcome.

To prepare the film for audience "participation" it was decided to interrupt the sequence at a number of points interspersed through the interview, thus giving the audience therapist an opportunity to "communicate" to the patient. In selecting points of interruption the following criteria were kept in mind: (1) interruptions should be sufficiently frequent so as to provide a reasonable sample of the respondent's response repertoire, but not so frequent as to disturb the natural sequence unduly; (2) they should precede the film therapist's interventions rather than follow them in order to minimize "contamination"; (3) they should occur at points which might readily evoke a response from the interviewer, but there should also be some interruptions at which the respondent might reasonably be expected to remain "silent"; in other words, an interruption should not convey a strong invitation to respond (although in practice it may have had that effect); (4) they should sample various aspects of the patient's behavior such as complaints about physical symptoms, relationships with significant people in the patient's past and current living, expressions of anger and hostility, disappointment, mourning, work situations, constructive strivings toward health, demands made on the interviewer (pleas for reassurance and help), and resentments against a harsh fate.

Even with these stipulations a choice was often difficult. Several trial runs were conducted in which small audiences were invited to respond and their responses were examined. Subsequently, a group of five psychiatrists considered the proposed choice points in the light of the above criteria as well as their own feelings as they viewed the film. As a result of this discussion the original number of choice points was reduced by more than half, and further consideration by the investigator led to the isolation of 28 points of interruption, which were subsequently used throughout the data collection. A uniform title, "What would you do?" followed by numbers from 1 to 28 was then prepared and inserted into the film sequence to permit continuous projection. Each title appeared on the screen for approximately 30 seconds, which appeared a reasonable but not excessive time span in which to formulate a response and record it on an answer sheet. Moreover, this time limit seemed realistic for the reason that in an actual interview, too, the therapist does not have unlimited time to decide whether to interrupt the patient or to remain silent. Finally, some introductory material contained in the original film, including its title, was deleted. The experimental version of the film, including interruptions, ran for approximately 50 minutes.

THE QUESTIONNAIRE

In order to obtain information concerning the respondent's clinical impressions and proposed treatment plans, a rather comprehensive questionnaire was constructed. It included questions about diagnosis, formulations of the emotional dynamics, clinical impressions and judgments, treatment plans, proposed therapeutic techniques, the therapist's personal attitude toward the patient, possible countertransference reactions, prognosis, possible dangers in therapy, recommendations to the patient, etc. Some of the questions were presented in the form of rating scales; more frequently, they were open-ended items which called for a written statement; sometimes additional open-ended questions were asked to shed further light on a rating. A number of questions were also asked about the respondent's reactions to the film therapist, which, it was thought, in turn, might, provide additional information about the respondent's own techniques and attitudes. A final section of the questionnaire included items about the respondent's professional affiliation, training, experience, theoretical orientation and therapeutic activities.

The length of the questionnaire had to be limited in accordance with the amount of time a respondent might reasonably be asked to devote to the project. Even after several attempts at revision, simplification, and condensation, followed by preliminary trials, the questionnaire seemed inordinately long to some respondents.

The complete questionnaire is as follows:

FORM F
Questions about the Film

The following questions deal with your impressions about the film you just saw. Please answer them as clearly and as completely as you can.

1F. Check one of the following labels to indicate the dominant personality type.

  A. Anxiety   E. Cyclothymic
  B. Hysteria   F. Schizoid
  C. Obsessive   G. Paranoid
  D. Psychopathic   H. Other (specify) _____

2F. What are the major defense mechanisms used by this patient?

3F. How would you formulate the dynamics of his difficulties on the basis of what you have observed during the first interview?

4F. What form of treatment would you recommend to this patient?

5F. If you were to accept this patient for treatment, what therapeutic goal(s) would you set up? If you wish, you may distinguish intermediate and ultimate goals.

6F. If your recommendation were unfeasible for practical reasons (e.g., time, money, etc.), what compromises would you suggest?

7F. If you recommend some form of psychotherapy, how often would you propose to see the patient?

8F. Considering your proposed treatment goals, how many hours of treatment and/or what period of time would you estimate it would require to achieve your objectives? You may again wish to distinguish between intermediate and ultimate goals.

9F. Suppose the patient is primarily interested in symptom relief. How many hours of treatment and/or what period of time would you estimate it would require to achieve this objective?

10F. From what you have seen in the film, what kinds of difficulties would you expect to encounter if you were to undertake psychotherapy with this patient?

11F. Which areas, if any, in the patient's living would you focus on primarily?

12F. Are there any particular dangers you would feel you have to guard against, or any special cautions you would feel you have to observe in dealing with this patient?

13F. Are there any areas in the patient's living that you feel should *not* be dealt with therapeutically—at least, early in therapy?

14F. Are there any attitudes or kinds of behavior you would *en*courage in this patient if you were dealing with him psychotherapeutically? If so, which ones?

15F. Are there any attitudes or kinds of behavior you would *dis*courage in this patient if you were dealing with him psychotherapeutically? If so, which ones?

16F. Would you tend to be strict or permissive with this patient? (check one)
_____I would tend to be no more strict or permissive with this patient than with any other
_____I would tend to be rather permissive
_____I would tend to be rather strict
_____Other (specify):
Why?

17F. How would you deal with this patient's phobic symptoms in therapy? (Check one)
_____I would try to interpret them directly as early as possible
_____I would try to interpret them directly at a much later time
_____I would not interpret them directly at all
_____Other (specify):

18F. Were you impressed by any clues in the patient's verbal or nonverbal behavior which you may not wish to make use of now but which you would keep in mind for possible later use in therapy? If so, which ones?

19F. What form or course would you expect this patient's transference to take?

20F. Do you have any ideas how you would deal with it therapeutically?

21F. Are there any areas or specific problems which, if dealt with therapeutically, might produce a marked improvement in the patient's living? If so, which ones?

22F. Assuming that the patient's behavior during the first hour is rather typical of him, would you tend to be more active (i.e., intervene frequently) or more passive (i.e., intervene infrequently) in subsequent interviews?
_____I would tend to be no more active or passive with this patient than with any other.
_____I would tend to be rather active
_____I would tend to be rather passive
_____Other (specify):

23F. Would you encourage or discourage free association with this patient? (Check one)
_____Would encourage it
_____Would discourage it
_____Would neither encourage nor discourage it
_____Other (specify):
Why?

24F. Do you feel that this patient might engage in much "acting out" behavior? If so, how would you deal with it?

25F. If psychotherapy were undertaken with this patient, in what areas would you expect him to "move"? In what areas would you expect him to remain relatively unchanged?

26F. How much ego strength does this patient seem to have? (Check one)

_____A great deal

_____A fair amount

_____Relatively little

_____Very little

_____Too little evidence to make a judgment at this time

27F. How much anxiety does this patient seem to have? (Check one)

_____A great deal

_____A fair amount

_____Relatively little

_____Very little

28F. How much insight does this patient seem to have into his problem? (Check one)

_____A great deal

_____A fair amount

_____Relatively little

_____Very little

_____Too little evidence to make a judgment at this time

29F. To what extent does the patient appear to be capable of self-observation and self-appraisal as opposed to the tendency to rationalization?

_____Very capable

_____Fairly capable

_____Slightly capable

_____Not at all capable

_____Too little evidence to make a judgment at this time

30F. How would you rate this patient's over-all emotional maturity? (Check one)

_____Very immature

_____Fairly immature

_____Fairly mature

_____Very mature

_____Too little evidence to make a judgment at this time

31F. How would you characterize the patient's social adjustment? (Check one)

_____Very adequate

_____Fairly adequate

_____Fairly inadequate

_____Very inadequate

_____Too little evidence to make a judgment at this time

32F. Considering the entire range of mental disorder, how would you characterize the degree of disturbance in this patient? (Check one)

_____Extremely disturbed

_____Seriously disturbed

_____Moderately disturbed

_____Mildly disturbed

_____Very mildly disturbed

_____Too little evidence to make a judgment at this time

33F. How extensive a change in the patient's character structure would you
      attempt? (Check one)
      _____Very extensive change
      _____Fairly extensive change
      _____Relatively little change
      _____Very little change
            _____Too little evidence to make a judgment at this time
      Why?

34F. Assuming the patient's life situation remained about the same, how would
      you expect him to get along if *no* therapy were undertaken? (Check one)
      _____He would probably get much better
      _____He would probably get a little better
      _____He would probably remain about the same
      _____He would probably get a little worse
      _____He would probably get much worse
            _____Too little evidence to make a judgment at this time

35F. Assuming your recommendations for treatment were followed, how would
      you rate the prognosis for this patient? (Check one)
      _____Very favorable
      _____Somewhat favorable
      _____Neither favorable nor unfavorable
      _____Somewhat unfavorable
      _____Very unfavorable
            _____Too little evidence to make a judgment at this time

36F. Would you make any recommendations to the patient to change his present
      mode of living or his environment? If so, why? If not, why not?

37F. How would you characterize your personal reaction to this patient?
      _____I have a strong positive attitude toward him
      _____I have a somewhat positive attitude toward him
      _____I have a neutral attitude toward him
      _____I have a somewhat negative attitude toward him
      _____I have a strong negative attitude toward him
      Can you state the reason (s) for your reaction?

38F. Do you anticipate any countertransference problems with this patient?
      If so, which ones? How would you handle them?

THE NEXT STEP IS IMPORTANT. PLEASE DO NOT OMIT.

GO BACK AND LOOK OVER THE QUESTIONS YOU HAVE AN-
SWERED SO FAR. PLACE A CHECK MARK IN FRONT OF THOSE
THAT YOU NORMALLY ASK YOURSELF WHEN YOU SEE A PATIENT
FOR THE FIRST TIME. ARE THERE ANY OTHERS, IN THE FILM
INTERVIEW OR GENERALLY, WHICH YOU ASK YOURSELF, BUT
WHICH ARE *NOT* COVERED IN THIS QUESTIONNAIRE? IF SO,
PLEASE LIST THEM BELOW.

The following questions deal with the manner in which the film interview was conducted.

39F. Would you have conducted the interview in a similar or in a different manner? (Check one)

———In a very similar manner
———In a somewhat similar manner
———In a somewhat different manner
———In a very different manner

List the major differences, if any.

40F. Regardless of whether the therapist conducted the interview in a manner similar to yours, how adequate a job did he do? (Check one)

———A very adequate job
———A reasonably adequate job
———A somewhat inadequate job
———A very inadequate job

Please give the reason (s) for your opinion.

41F. Are there any parts of the interview that could have been handled better? If so, which ones?

42F. Was there anything noteworthy about his techniques? If so, what?

43F. How would you characterize the therapist's activity (i.e., the amount of talking he did)? (Check one)

———Much too active
———Somewhat too active
———Neither too active nor too passive; about right
———Somewhat too passive
———Much too passive

44F. How would you characterize the amount of support he gave to the patient? (Check one)

———Much too little support
———Somewhat too much support
———Neither too much nor too little support; about right
———Somewhat too little support
———Much too little support

45F. Would you devote more or less time than is shown in the film to getting facts on the patient's life history in a first interview? (Check one)

———Would devote considerably more time
———Would devote somewhat more time
———Would devote about the same time
———Would devote somewhat less time
———Would devote considerably less time

46F. How would you characterize your personal reaction to the therapist in the film? (Check one)

———I have a strong positive attitude toward him
———I have a somewhat positive attitude toward him
———I have a neutral attitude toward him
———I have a somewhat negative attitude toward him
———I have a strong negative attitude toward him

Can you state the reason (s) for your reaction?

If you have any comments about the film presentation, this questionnaire, or any aspect of this research, please list them below.

FORM B

Biographical Information

1B. Age: _____years   2B. Sex: (Circle one)   M   F

3B. Highest academic degree: _____

4B. Major professional affiliation (Check one)

_____Psychoanalyst   _____Psychologist

_____Psychiatrist   _____Psychiatric Social Worker

_____Psychiatric Resident   _____Other (specify):

5B. Professional activities: (List your major activities and the percentage of your work week devoted to each: (e.g., private practice of psychoanalysis 100%)

_____ _____% of my work week

_____ _____% of my work week

_____ _____% of my work week

_____ _____% of my work week

6B. If you are presently a resident, circle the year of your residency:
1   2   3   4   5

7B. Status of your psychoanalytic training: (Check one and complete question)

_____I have completed my psychoanalytic training and am a member of the American Psychoanalytic Association. Year of completion: 19____

_____I am presently in psychoanalytic training, which started in 19____

_____I plan to enter psychoanalytic training approximately in 19____

_____I have no psychoanalytic training and do not plan to receive any

_____Other (specify):

8B. Have you received any training in psychiatry, psychotherapy, psycho-analysis, etc., *not* listed above? If so, specify; if none, write "NONE."

9B. Present status of your personal analysis: (Check one and complete question)

_____I completed my personal analysis in 19____; it lasted _____ hours

_____I am presently undergoing personal analysis, which started in 19____; I have completed _____ hours. I expect it to last a total of _____ hours.

_____I plan to undertake personal analysis in or about 19____

_____I have had no personal analysis and do not expect to undertake it.

_____Other (specify):

10B. What is (was) your most important reason for undertaking personal analysis? (Check one)

_____Personal

_____Training

11B. How much training have you had in psychoanalytic principles and tech-niques? (Check one)

_____None

_____Very little

_____A fair amount

_____A great deal

12B. How much experience have you had in psychotherapy, not counting your own analysis? (Do not include experience in general psychiatry; check one)

_____None
_____Very little
_____A fair amount
_____A great deal
Approximately how many years: _____ (full-time)

> *Note:* If some of your experience
> has been part-time, convert
> it to full-time experience.

13B. How would you rate your present competence as a psychotherapist? (Check one)
_____Fully competent
_____Reasonably competent
_____Slightly competent
_____Not very competent

14B. What kind (s) of psychotherapy do you practice most typically? (Describe briefly the kind (s) of therapy you do, such as psychoanalysis, analytically oriented therapy, etc.)

15B. What type (s) of patient (s) have you primarily dealt with?

16B. Do you prefer to treat any particular type of patient? If so, which ones?

17B. How long do you see the average patient? (Check one)
_____Less than 3 months   _____Between 1-2 years
_____Between 3-6 months   _____Between 2-3 years
_____Between 6-12 months   _____More than 3 years

18B. How many times per week do you see the average patient? (Check one)
_____Once   _____4 times
_____Twice   _____5 times
_____3 times   _____Other (specify):

19B. If your therapeutic work has been supervised, approximately how many hours of supervision have you had?
_____hours

20B. How would you characterize your own theoretical orientation with respect to your psychotherapeutic work? (From the following list select the orientation which best describes you; it is recognized that influences are usually multiple. *Check one.*)
_____Freudian psychoanalysis   _____Sullivan (Washington School,
(orthodox only)   Wm. A. White Institute)
_____Jung   _____Fromm
_____Adler   _____Alexander (Chicago Institute)
_____Ferenczi   _____Deutsch
_____Rank   _____Rogers (client-centered therapy)
_____Stekel   _____Psychoanalytically oriented
_____Reich   (general)
_____Rado   _____Eclectic (specify):
_____Horney   _____Other (specify):

21B. How would you characterize your training analyst's or supervising therapist's theoretical orientation? (Use one of the above labels and write it below.)

22B. To what extent have your own theoretical orientation and technique been

influenced by those of your training analyst or supervising therapist? Do
your views differ? If so, in what respects? Be specific.

23B. Do you feel that your techniques differ from what is usually described as
"classical analysis"? If so, list the most important differences. What are
your reasons?

24B. What effect, if any, has your personal analysis had on your performance as
a therapist? If you underwent analysis after you had some experience in
psychotherapy, did you behave differently with patients you treated subsequently? What were the most important differences, if any? Be specific.

Name _____

Address _____

_____

PROCEDURE

Therapeutic institutes, hospitals, clinics, and professional organizations in several cities were invited to participate. Perhaps half of
those who were approached replied favorably. Data were collected
in Washington, D.C.; Baltimore, Md.; Chicago, Ill.; New York, N.Y.;
and Perry Point, Md. The only stipulation was that the respondent
should be a psychotherapist; he might be a psychiatrist, a psychologist, or a psychiatric social worker; he might have a great deal or
virtually no experience (a number of residents in psychiatry fell into
the latter category); he might be an analyst in private practice or a
therapist in an outpatient clinic; and so forth. Primary attention,
however, was focused on psychiatrists as probably the most representative group of the psychotherapist population.

The following instructions were given:

The experiment in which you are about to participate is part of a research
project in psychotherapy which is being carried out at The George Washington
University, School of Medicine, under a grant from the National Institute of
Mental Health, of the U.S. Public Health Service. The broad aim of this
research is to obtain objective data on the techniques used by different psychotherapists.

The procedure, which I shall describe in greater detail shortly, consists of two
parts: (1) a sound film of an actual therapeutic interview; and (2) certain
questionnaire materials. Each person should have a work sheet and a booklet.
Please do not open this booklet until you are told to do so.

This is not a "test" in any sense of the word and there are no "right" or
"wrong" answers. You will not be required to sign your name to any of this
material; you may remain completely anonymous if you so desire. In either
event, the information you give will be held in strict confidence and will be
used only for research purposes. We ask you to work independently; please do
not talk to other members of the audience while the experiment is in progress.

You have demonstrated your interest in this research by your willingness to participate. The results may be of great potential value by providing objective information in an area in which so many problems remain to be explored. Your careful attention to every step in the procedure is the most important way in which you can help to insure the worthwhileness of the results. Be sure you give complete and intelligible information.

Your collaboration is sincerely appreciated. We will be grateful for your comments, suggestions, and criticisms at any time.

I now come to the first part of the experiment. This, as I have mentioned, is a sound film of an actual psychotherapeutic interview. You will see and hear a psychiatrist interviewing a male patient. This is a first interview; the doctor and the patient have never met before; we do not know whether they will meet again.

We ask you to make the following assumptions: Imagine that *you* are the therapist and that *you* are interviewing the patient in the film. The patient is not hospitalized, and he is consulting you of his own choosing. You are a professional person, and he is coming to you for help with his difficulties. How are you going to help him? That is the problem. You have agreed to interview him; you may decide to accept him for treatment, or you may not.

In order for you to "participate" in this interview, we have adopted the following procedure. We will start the film and you will meet the doctor and the patient. As usual, the patient will talk, and the doctor will ask questions or make observations. At various points, the interview will be interrupted to give you a chance to tell us what you would do if you were the doctor seeing the patient. At those points you will see on the screen the question: "WHAT WOULD YOU DO?" followed by a number. Now refer to your work sheet. You will see blank spaces numbered 1, 2, 3, etc. These correspond to the numbers you will see on the screen. Put your question or your comments alongside the appropriate number as it appears on the screen. If you have no comment at a particular point, simply write "0" (zero) in the space. If you wish to comment at other points that are not identified by a number, repeat on your work sheet the last few words to which you are responding to help us locate the passage, and write your response.

Let us take an example. Suppose the patient says: "I have been having an awful lot of troubles, doctor." At this point the film interview is interrupted and you see on the screen "WHAT WOULD YOU DO?" followed by a "X". Now refer to your work sheet. The first item is marked " (SAMPLE) X." Suppose your observation of this patient's behavior leads you to say: "Can you tell me more about that?" Simply write this statement opposite the space marked "X". This has been done already. If you had felt like saying nothing, you would have written an "0" (zero) in the space. Suppose there had been no stopping point after the patient's remark, but you had wanted to respond anyway. Suppose further that the last stopping point had been Number 17. In that case, you would have written: ". . . lot of troubles, doctor," after Item 17, and followed this with your comment.

In each instance include such communications as "Uhuh," "Mmmh," and the like, as well as gestures, such as a shrug of the shoulder, raising an eyebrow to indicate disbelief, etc. If there is something unusual about your tone of voice, indicate this, too.

Please write clearly and legibly. You will have 30 seconds at each stopping point.

Please put down on paper what the patient would *see or hear from you.* If, in addition, you wish to record any comments *about* your remarks to the patient, you may do so. Put such comments in parentheses.

Sometimes the stopping points will occur in places where the therapist in the motion picture intervenes; sometimes the patient will go on talking. Therefore, a stopping point does not necessarily mean that you should intervene. You may or you may not respond. Just be sure to indicate what you would do, either by writing your response in the blank space, or by recording a zero.

Try to be as spontaneous as you can. Follow the interview with the usual alertness and attention you give a patient who comes to see you.

Are there any questions about the procedure?

We will now start the film.

(After the film showing.) Now that you have seen the film, we should like to get your impressions of what you have observed. The booklet which is in front of you contains a number of questions which deal with your reactions to the patient, to the therapist in the film, and so on. You will also find some items regarding your own background, training, and experience. Please answer these questions as clearly and as fully as you can; they supplement your responses to the film and will make possible a more meaningful analysis.

The questionnaire, we hope, is self-explanatory. When you have finished, look over your answers to make sure that you have not missed any items. After that, please hand in all papers.

The entire experimental procedure usually required approximately two hours.

3

RESULTS OBTAINED
FROM PSYCHIATRISTS

The experimental procedure yielded two kinds of data: comments directed to the patient portrayed in the film (techniques) and responses to the questionnaire. The second group may be subdivided into diagnostic impressions and evaluations, treatment plans and goals, including technique problems, and biographical data which served as reference variables.

THE SAMPLE

Complete data were collected from 237 therapists representing these professional groups:

Psychiatrists (including 32 analysts)	91	
Residents in psychiatry	43	
Total (medical training)..................................	—	134†
Psychologists		79
Psychiatric social workers		17‡
Others		7
Total sample		237

---

* The distributions of responses to all questionnaire items have been deposited as Document number 6225 with the ADI Auxiliary Publications project, Photoduplication Service, Library of Congress, Washington 25, D. C. A copy may be secured by citing the Document number (ADI Doc. No. 6225) and by remitting $7.50 for photoprints, or $2.75 for 35 mm. microfilm. Advance payment is required. Make checks or money orders payable to: Chief, Photoduplication Service, Library of Congress.

† Unless otherwise indicated, the results reported in this chapter are based on this group.

‡ Because of its smallness this group has largely been disregarded in subsequent analyses.

Statistics on age, experience, and personal analysis are presented in Table 1. Additional information may be gleaned from the following distributions:

Status of psychoanalytic training:

	N	%
Completed psychoanalytic training (Member of the American Psychoanalytic Association, N=21)	33	25
In training	18	13
Plans	25	19
No psychoanalytic training	47	35
No answer	11	8

Status of personal analysis:

	N	%
Completed personal analysis	49	37
Presently undergoing analysis	39	29
Plans	15	11
No personal analysis	25	19
No answer	6	4

Amount of training in psychoanalytic principles and techniques (self-estimate):

	N	%
None	13	10
Very little	27	20
A fair amount	54	40
A great deal	34	25
No answer	6	5

Amount of experience in psychotherapy, not counting personal analysis (self-estimate):

	N	%
None	11	8
Very little	22	17
A fair amount	55	41
A great deal	40	29
No answer	6	5

Present competence as a psychotherapist (self-estimate):

	N	%
Fully competent	31	23
Reasonably competent	67	50
Slightly competent	17	13
Not very competent	17	13
No answer	2	1

Theoretical orientation:

	N	%
Freud (orthodox)	13	10
Sullivan	27	20

Alexander 8   6
Psychoanalytically oriented (general) 75   56
Eclectic 10   7
Meyer 9   7
Miscellaneous 13   10
No answer 15   11
                                                          ——
                                                          170*

TABLE 1

SUMMARY STATISTICS OF AGE, EXPERIENCE, PERSONAL ANALYSIS

	N	Mean	SD
Age...................................	131	38.25 years	10.67
Experience in therapy...................	131	6.78 years	7.22
Personal analysis.......................	74†	384.19 hours	245.22

† Includes respondents who responded affirmatively and indicated the number of hours.

Quantative analysis and statistical treatment

Quantative analysis of therapists' communications. The systematic analysis of several thousand comments given by over 200 therapists required some method of quantification. A system of analysis was employed whose development and operational characteristics are described in greater detail in Chapter 12. The system yields five measures for any therapist communication. There are two sets of categories (*Type of Therapeutic Activity* and *Dynamic Focus*) and three intensity scales (*Depth-Directedness, Initiative,* and *Therapeutic Climate*). The components are as follows:

Type of Therapeutic Activity specifies the outer form or structure of a therapeutic intervention and provides a gross analysis of the therapist's techniques. The major categories are:

Facilitating communication (minimal activity)
Exploratory operations
Clarification (minimal interpretation)
Interpretive operations
Structuring
Direct guidance
Activity not clearly relevant to the task of therapy
Unclassifiable

Certain subcategories serve to refine the primary ratings.

Depth-Directedness is based on the conception that inference is an integral

* Exceeds number of cases since there were some multiple responses.

part of all therapeutic communications and that it is always present to some degree. Each communication is rated by means of an eight-point scale:*

0	1	2	3	4	5	6	7	8
Non-inferential		Mildly inferential		Moderately inferential			Highly inferential	

Dynamic Focus refers to the frame of reference adopted by the therapist at a particular juncture and characterizes the manner in which he focuses the therapeutic spotlight. Two major sectors are used to differentiate whether the therapist "goes along" with the patient (A) or whether he introduces a different focus (B). Sector A includes silences, passive acceptance, simple reflections of feeling, and minimal questions. Sector B is analyzed in terms of the following five categories:

Requests for additional information
Focus on dynamic events in the *past*
Focus on dynamic events in the *present*
Focus on the dynamics of the therapist-patient relationship (analysis of the transference)
Focus on the therapist-patient interaction in terms of the therapist's role as an expert, authority, etc.

Initiative measures the extent to which the therapist assumes responsibility for guiding the patient's communications in a given channel. Seven degrees are distinguished:†

0	1	2	3	4	5	6	7
Absence of initiative		Mild initiative		Moderate initiative		Strong initiative	

Therapeutic Climate or emotional overtones discernible in a communication are quantified by means of a bipolar scale:

−2	−1	0	+1	+2
Coldness, rejection	Milder degrees of −2		Milder degrees of +2	Warmth, acceptance
		Neutrality		

Rater agreement. To estimate the reliability of the system, a random sample of 20 answer sheets was selected and scored independently by two raters.‡ The indices presented in Table 2 are based on a unit-by-unit analysis.

---

* This scale is identical to the four-point scale described in Chapter 12. The expansion of the scale merely represents the introduction of "half-steps" which have been found useful. The original conception remains unchanged.

† See preceding footnote. In this case, the original scale consisted of four major scale steps.

‡ Reliability data for typescript of actual interviews are reported in Chapter 13.

TABLE 2
AGREEMENT BETWEEN TWO INDEPENDENT RATERS

System Component	Agreement on 20 cases (number of judgments = 1,673)
Type	86.9%
Depth-Directedness	94.7%
Dynamic Focus	77.9%
Initiative	96.0%
Therapeutic Climate	17 nonzero judgments were made, of which 4 were disagreements.

Note: All percentages are significant beyond the .01 level.

Agreement on a unit (therapist communication) means that both raters assigned it to the same category, or that they gave it an intensity score no more than one-half step apart. It was difficult to test rater agreement on *Therapeutic climate* because of the relative infrequency of nonzero scores. There is reason to believe that scores on this dimension are heavily influenced by voice inflections and other nonverbal clues that are inevitably lost in written materials. Since the evidence in many instances was insufficient so that a "neutral" (zero) score had to be assigned, it may be assumed that the scores on this component almost certainly represent a gross underestimate.

The over-all disagreement was 11.2 per cent, which is considered acceptable. Since most ratings were made jointly by two raters, thus permitting discussions and resolutions of disagreements, the stability of the ratings used in the subsequent analyses is probably greater.

Statistical treatment. The statistical analyses, for the most part, were concerned with the systematic comparison of therapists' response distributions grouped according to one or more independent variable. While all analyses imply at least a general hypothesis, the fact remains that the work is to a large extent exploratory. For this reason, it appeared important to accept conservative standards; accordingly, the .05 level of probability (two-tailed test) has been used as a minimum level for rejecting the null hypothesis. Since the system components are correlated, the danger of compounding statistical significance when comparing the results on the various components has also been kept in mind. In view of the crudeness of the measurements, it seemed prudent to avoid the assumptions underlying such statistical techniques as the *t* test and analysis of variance and to use instead their nonparametric counterparts (Siegel, 1956).

More specifically, comparisons were performed separately on each component of the system. In the case of categories, analyses were based on the distribution of frequencies within a category. For example, a therapist giving 10 "silent" responses was given a score of 10, etc. In the case of the continua, the hypothesis was tested that the more intense scores discriminated between groups of therapists. To maintain the ordinal character of the scale, we compared by the chi square technique the proportion of therapists who obtained *any* scores of 5 or above on these scales. A similar procedure was followed for scores on *Therapeutic climate,* where greater importance was assigned to nonzero scores. Negative ("cold," rejecting) scores were judged particularly critical. Consequently, the comparisons involve the proportion of therapists in a given group who gave negative or positive scores respectively, the two kinds of scores being treated independently.

The major statistical techniques were the Mann-Whitney *U* test (when two independent samples were being compared) and the Kruskal-Wallis one-way analysis of variance (when more than two independent samples were being tested).

Finally, to quantify therapists' questionnaire reponses, many of which were of the free-answer type, it was necessary to develop content codes after surveying the range of response for each item. All free-answer questions were then scored jointly by two trained raters.

Diagnostic and prognostic evaluation

Diagnosis. This was the first item in the questionnaire, and required the respondent to indicate the patient's dominant personality type. As shown in Figure 1, eight precoded alternatives, taken from an article by Raines and Rohrer (1955), were listed. "Anxiety" was the preferred label, given by almost 40 per cent of the respondents. Actually, this is no more than a phenomenologic description since the patient had mentioned the word on numerous occasions. Multiple diagnoses tended to include "Anxiety" in most instances. "Hysteria" and "Paranoid" were chosen with almost equal frequency, followed by "Obsessive," "Character Disorder," "Psychopathic," and some minor ones.

Defense mechanisms. Most prominently mentioned were projective tendencies, including paranoid trends. Rationalization and intellectualization ranked next, followed by somatization, etc. On the average, two or more defense mechanisms were mentioned, the nomenclature itself showing wide variations.

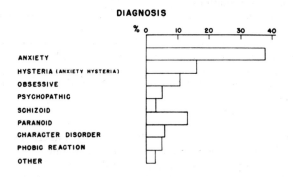

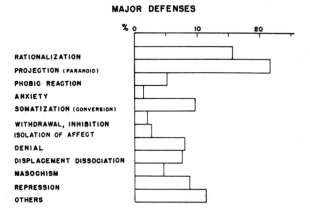

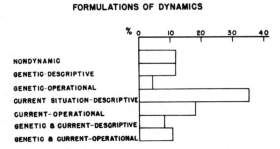

FIG. 1. Diagnoses, Defense Mechanisms, and Formulations of Dynamics.

Formulations of dynamics. In this free-response item, respondents were requested to formulate the dynamics of the patient's difficulties. Four major classes were defined, as illustrated by the following examples:

1. Nondynamic formulations

He is a dependent person who feels not adequate to cope with his problems.

Dynamics formulated around family interpersonal relationships.

The patient has never matured emotionally beyond the point of infancy or early childhood.

Hostile dependency. Symptoms probably a reaction to rejected need for dependency.

2. Genetic formulations

a. Descriptive

Seductive, dominating mother; weak, ineffectual father. Very dependent male with difficulty in identification with either parent.

Unresolved oedipal conflicts and guilt in death of father.

Patient lost capacity for healthy self-assertiveness or appears to have been incapable of changing direction. He was thoroughly castrated by mother. Dad?

b. Operational

An older indulged son feels displaced by a younger sibling, reacts with anger at being no longer the baby, but is forced to repress his anger.

The patient probably felt rejected by his mother and identified with his father who left him "to hold the bag" so to speak, and brother, identified with mother, was accepted.

His identity as a male is seriously disturbed, marked by fixation at an infantile level, marked castration anxiety, assumption of narcissistic feminine identification with a castrating mother.

3. Emphasis on current situation

a. Descriptive

Obsessive-compulsive character traits with self-defeating operations and self-burdening; strong guilt feelings over responsibility toward mother and wife.

Never freed himself from mother. His aggression is tremendous but can't find acceptable expression.

Chronic, morbid, resentment state based on unsatisfied dependency needs: "the world owes me a living."

b. Operational

Intense hostility toward a domineering mother, who expected a strong sense of responsibility which he must defeat in his neurotic actions.

The patient's anxiety attack started with his being thrown against a "fat woman," which caused a "warm feeling." The following phenomena represent his attempt to defend himself against awareness of longing for dependency on his mother, which he felt momentarily satisfied in contact with the fat woman.

Onset situation incomplete. Rage at mother and wife; impulse to hurt leads to rising titre; resentment at woman hemming him in on streetcar; streetcar almost hits truck equated with his almost out-of-control impulses leading to panic.

4. Formulations combining genetic and current emphases

a. Descriptive

Domineering, manipulative, phobic mother with passive father. Patient feels many unsatisfied dependency needs which he tries to wring from the environment.

A closely bound-to-mother individual who has had difficulty in reaching any degree of maturity and is angry at the deprivation of his dependent needs. Considerable secondary gain, anger repressed and related to his cardiac symptoms; dependent need related to dizziness.

Passive orientation to father, ambivalence to mother. Easily corruptible superego, with many dependency strivings.

b. Operational

Intense rage at the enveloping mother and the abandoning father, handled by developing anxiety to keep him away from situations in which he could directly express his feelings . . . Underlying love for mother beneath the rage.

Guilt and anxiety leading to incorporative attitudes. Regressive oral demanding attitudes toward mother repressed because of fear. Illness of his wife followed by mother's leaving home left patient without fulfillment of dependent needs. This resulted in insecurity and phobic mechanisms to get support. (Symbolic expression of fragmentary incorporative attitude toward mother in G.I. symptoms.)

Hostile identification with mother is basic issue; underlying depression in relation to father's death with suppressed rage and acting out as alternative defenses against passive (homosexual) trends. Suspect patient is hypertensive.

Most likely dynamics is rage at father (seen as a maternal but absent person), defended by phobic displacement, obsessive-compulsive mechanisms, etc. These are not sufficient to ban anxiety, and he feels anxiety directly.

The major categories are arranged approximately in order of increasing complexity, although no prejudgment was made about the relative positions of genetic and current formulations. Within the categories, an "operational" statement probably makes greater demands on the respondent's ability to make inferences than a "descriptive" one, which remains closer to observable events.

It seemed desirable, therefore, to judge formulations by an overall criterion which came to be known as "Dynamic Quality." This rating was made on a four-point scale, ranging from 1 (low) to 4 (high). In arriving at this global judgment, the following criteria were kept in mind:

a. Complexity. Does the formulation attempt to explain one or several facets of the patient's problem? Does it integrate a number of seemingly disparate manifestations? Is it a "rich" or a "meager" formulation?

b. Degree of inference. Is the formulation inferential or does it remain at a descriptive level? Does it state or imply a hypothesis which may have a bearing on therapy?

c. Precision. Is the language precise or is it "loose"? Are technical terms used in a strict sense or is technical language used as a jargon? Does a formulation seem to apply to the patient specifically or is it worded so generally that it might apply to anyone?

d. Operational aspects. Does the formulation indicate how the patient "handles" his conflict or does it describe a state? Is the conflict set forth in terms which are at least potentially verifiable or is the likelihood of verificaion virtually nonexistent?

Rater agreement on the over-all rating, between two independent raters, was 88 per cent (disregarding discrepancies of one scale step). Some examples follow:

Quality level 1

The patient feels that he never had a chance and he seems to believe that he could have done well if he did. His belligerence seems to cover dependent longings (to be cared for, not depended upon).

Could see clearly only the frustration at time of father's death. Mother further frustrated his passive and dependent longings. Hostility noted, probably, was reaction to this.

Domineering and doting mother. Inadequate father.

Father's death = desertion. Strong attachment to mother.

Immature, unassertive personality who was overly conscious about the responsibilities thrust upon him.

Hostile dependency with maternal domination.

Quality level 2

Loss of father or inability to strongly identify with father because of his absence. Hostile integration with mother but no channel for expression.

Conflict between dependency and independency. Confusion about handling of his hostility.

A rather infantile personality with phobias and periodic anxiety reactions. Also with rationalization of his antisocial acts which fulfill dependent needs.

Passive individual, hostile dependency on mother, sustaining inadequate mastery situations.

A passive inhibited character neurosis resenting being called upon to be active and responsible man and regressing to the agoraphobic and claustrophobic state.

Hostility to an overprotective and domineering mother with ambivalent attitudes toward dependency needs.

Quality level 3

1. Strong constitutional element. 2. Intense unresolved conflict with a neurotic mother. 3. Inadequate ego formation.

Maternal overprotection and rejection. Remote father with misidentification (leads to) marked dependency, hostile, rigid superego.

Feels conflicts are genital in orientation judged by anxiety-hysteric-peeping-mother focus, etc. Passive orientation; no evidence of psychotic processes.

Wishes for revenge, actual acts of revenge and revenge fantasies have resulted in a need for punishment partly satisfied by anxiety feelings.

Narcissistic anxiety on a deeply repressed sexual conflict with much rivalry and hostile retreat.

Intense rage at the enveloping mother and the abandoning father, handled by developing anxiety to keep him away from situations in which he could directly express his feelings. Underlying love for mother beneath the rage.

Hostile, controlling individual, "world owes me a living." Panics based on fear of loss of control of everything.

Quality level 4

Exceptionally marked positive oedipal relationship to an over-seductive mother. Fear of loss of control of incestuous and destructive impulses.

Frustration handled by repression, with repressed hatred of mother, revenge through masochism and spiteful acting out.

A closely bound-to-mother individual who has had difficulty in reaching any degree of maturity and is angry at the deprivation of his dependent needs. Considerable secondary gain, anger repressed and related to his cardiac symptoms. Dependent need related to dizziness.

Guilt, anxiety leading to incorporative attitudes. Regressive, oral, demanding attitudes toward mother repressed because of fear. Illness of his wife followed by mother's leaving home left patient without fulfillment of dependent needs. This resulted in insecurity and phobic mechanisms to get support. (Symbolic expression of fragmentary incorporative attitude toward mother in G.I. symptoms.)

Onset situation incomplete. Rage at mother and wife; impulse to hurt, rising titre; resentment at woman hemming him in on streetcar; streetcar almost hits truck equated with his almost out-of-control impulses (leading to) panic. No genetic formulation because of lack of material.

Deep dependent attachment to an overpowering mother, with sibling rivalry toward both brother and father leading to failure of normal resolution of oedipal phase and unstable regression to preoedipal relationship to mother, with constant efforts to regain the oedipal position.

Other diagnostic evaluations. Reference to the questionnaire shows that several diagnostic assessments were obtained through precoded items. Each item was followed by a four-point intensity scale, and the added alternative: "Too little evidence to make a judgment at this time." Response distributions are presented in Figure 2. (In some cases, categories containing very small frequencies were combined with the adjoining one.) The alternative, "Too little evidence," actually lies outside the scale continuum and signifies a respondent's refusal to make a judgment. It may also indicate the degree of inference involved in a rating, as perceived by the respondents. Thus, Ego Strength shows 16.5 per cent of the responses in that category, whereas Disturbance discloses less than 1 per cent. By this standard, therapists by and large thought there was sufficient evidence on such items as Anxiety, Insight, Self-observation, Emotional Maturity, and Disturbance but they expressed greater tentativeness on Ego Strength, and Social Adjustment. Relatively few respondents refused to commit themselves.

The distributions disclose fair agreement among the respondents on the relative intensity of the variable being rated. The quantifications are, of course, crude, and part of the agreement is accounted for by the small number of available scale steps. For example, the subjective difference between "a great deal" of anxiety and a "fair amount" of anxiety may be slight, but the discrepancy between "a great deal" and "relatively little" anxiety seems considerable. In this case, 85 per cent of the respondents agreed that the patient experienced at least a fair amount of anxiety, but 11 per cent judged it to be "relatively little." The distributions on the other items are comparable, except for Emotional Maturity and Social Adjustment where the divergent minorities of about 10 to 15 per cent observed on other items dwindled to about 1 per cent.

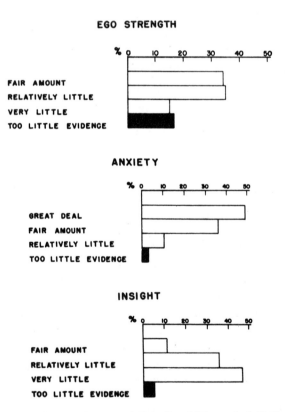

Fig. 2. Ego Strength, Anxiety, Insight, Capability of Self-Observation vs. Tendency for Rationalization, Emotional Maturity, Social Adjustment, and Disturbance.

CAPABILITY OF SELF-OBSERVATION
VS. RATIONALIZATION

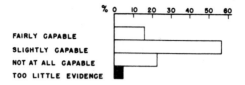

EMOTIONAL MATURITY

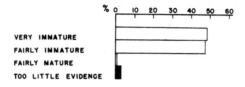

SOCIAL ADJUSTMENT

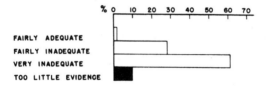

DISTURBANCE

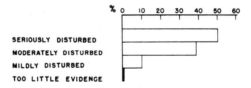

FIG. 2. Continued.

Prognosis. The question on prognosis was worded as follows: "Assuming your recommendations for treatment were followed, how would you rate the prognosis for this patient?" Responses were made on five-point scales, to which the alternative, "Too little evidence," was appended.

Figure 3 shows that more than half of the respondents thought

PROGNOSIS WITHOUT THERAPY

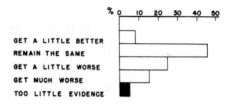

PROGNOSIS WITH THERAPY

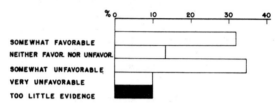

ATTITUDE TOWARD PATIENT

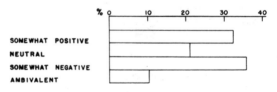

REASONS

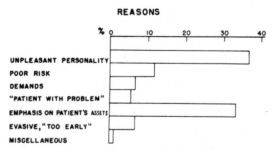

FIG. 3. Prognosis without Therapy, Prognosis with Therapy, Attitude toward the
Patient, and Reasons for the Attitude.

that the patient would remain "about the same" or even "get a little better" without therapy, but 40 per cent thought he would "get a little worse" or "much worse." With therapy, the prognosis was seen as favorable by about a third and unfavorable by 45 per cent. These ratings involve relatively complex predictions so that the absence of a consensus is not startling. Also, favorableness of the prognosis partly depends on the respondent's frame of reference, treatment goals, etc. Even if the crudeness of the judgment is conceded, the fact remains that a notable percentage of the respondents took an optimistic view, whereas a somewhat more sizable group was pessimistic about the prospects.

Attitude toward the patient. Figure 3 indicates that the proportions of positive and negative attitudes were almost equal; about a fifth professed a neutral attitude, and the reaction of a tenth was ambivalent. When asked for the reasons for their reactions, 43 respondents left the question blank. Of those who replied, 36 per cent referred in one form or another to the patient's "unpleasant personality characteristics"; an almost equal percentage stressed his personality assets, often with some expression of empathy. It is worth noting that 11 per cent disliked him on what might be called "technical grounds," i.e., poor risk or poor motivation for therapy.
  Here are some of the "reasons" given:

> He appears helpless, relatively (attitude positive).
> I feel he is suffering and needs help and is asking for it (attitude positive).
> I can feel sympathy for his problems, but I also realize that others have no "the world owes me a living" with the same problem (attitude neutral).
> Patient blames everything and everyone else for his troubles (attitude neutral).
> Believe he would be very difficult for me to work with unless his coming to interview was motivated by some real desire to change (attitude somewhat negative).
> Don't know him very well (attitude neutral).
> I can empathize with some of his feelings; I had similar ones in adolescence (attitude somewhat positive).
> Martyred self-justification usually seems to strike me as "deception, dishonesty, shirking," etc. (attitude strongly negative).
> [The reason can be given] more easily than what it [attitude] is: he needs help and can benefit from it, but his form of defense against his anxieties is one of the least appealing from a human as well as a therapist's viewpoint (attitude neutral).
> His manner of attempting to control the situation (somewhat negative).
> Probably related to statement and attitude "the world owes me a living" (attitude somewhat negative).

I find it hard to be objective about this. I would say I'm ambivalent, probably negative from my own denial of or attempts to repress dependency desires (attitude neutral).

I've tried working with several persons of this type; my success has been negligible (somewhat negative).

Excessive amount of self-pity (somewhat negative).

The world is full of injustice; therefore, I feel quite sympathetic, but "there ain't no justice nohow so quit the griping" (attitude ambivalent from very strong positive to very strong negative).

His tendency to rationalize, his unwillingness to assume responsibility for his troubles, his cry of "Why did it have to happen to me?"; his desire to get even (attitude somewhat negative).

Hostility and paranoid components (attitude somewhat negative).

His resentful self-pity, routinized statement of his illness (attitude somewhat negative).

I like him because of his strong determination and wish to see things through. He has some "guts" and a right therapist could help him. He is on his way (attitude somewhat positive).

I'd like to see what could be done about his difficulties; on the other hand, he seems rigid in a somewhat irritating way (attitude neutral mixed).

One doesn't like in the outsider what he knows to exist in himself (attitude somewhat negative).

So hostile (strong negative attitude).

Talks freely; seems to have some insight; some sincerity (attitude somewhat positive).

Interesting patient; beautiful nonverbal material; can get some help (attitude somewhat positive).

I feel I can understand what a fix he is in (attitude somewhat positive).

I do not enjoy a stubborn negativism with the hostility so close to the surface (attitude somewhat negative).

True suffering is not colored by marked hostility (somewhat negative).

Related to his persistent demand for others to take care of him (somewhat negative).

Hard to restrain myself from resenting his self-deprecating attitude (attitude somewhat negative).

I think I could soon understand what he's trying to communicate and help him (somewhat positive).

I feel sorry for anyone who feels wretched with such a background (attitude somewhat positive).

Because of my relatively poor record of therapeutic success with patients of this type. My reaction seems partly rational and partly associated with ego defeat. My attitude is one of considerable discouragement rather than simple hostility. I have not lost faith in the possibility of worthwhile therapeutic achievement in such a case (attitude somewhat negative).

Afraid his manipulative, distorted demands would make me anxious (somewhat negative).

I think he would be a difficult patient to treat; he would be markedly resistive, antagonistic. He makes me feel inadequate to be able to do much for him (attitude somewhat negative).

Too many "quicky" explanations of pseudo-scientific quality (attitude some-what negative).

I respond positively to his helplessness; I respond negatively to his defensive-ness (attitude quite strongly ambivalent).

He is not interesting; his rationalization, lack of any aesthetic sensitivities, some paranoid tendencies make him not very likeable (attitude somewhat negative).

Irritating, controlling, petulant and whiny (attitude strongly negative).

He seems willing to look at himself to some degree and seek help (attitude somewhat positive).

Too many people with greater potential and better ego structure in need of help to spend time and effort on such patients (attitude strongly negative).

He wants to be helped and has a need to get a chance (attitude somewhat positive).

Don't know him well enough to react (attitude neutral).

Seems very much like so many patients like him that I see diagnostically and treat in practice (attitude neutral).

He does not impress me as sincere. Unless hospital facilities are near at hand, psychotherapy, here, would be largely on the research basis because of patient's poor capacity for reality testing. He doesn't seem sincerely to want to look within (attitude somewhat negative).

Formulations of therapeutic plans, goals, and techniques

Therapeutic goals and approaches (Fig. 4). More than half the respondents set rather modest goals consisting of some form of symptom-relief. This was true particularly when a distinction was made between intermediate and ultimate goals. Even those thera-pists who described their goal as "a certain amount of insight" gen-erally regarded this as the ultimate objective. Virtually no therapist indicated that he would strive for extensive personality reorgani-zation. Only three therapists refused to accept the patient for treatment.

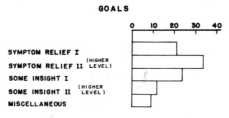

Fig. 4. Therapeutic Goals and Approaches.

If we consider areas in which therapists expected the patient to "move" and areas in which they expected him to remain relatively unchanged, practically no one expected any basic personality change,

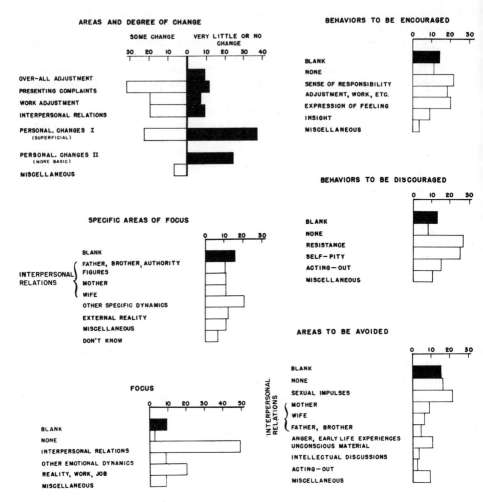

FIG. 4. *Continued.*

whereas the possibility of more superficial change was conceded by a fair proportion. However, a slightly larger proportion did not foresee even this as a likely occurrence. The greatest improvements, relatively speaking, were expected with regard to symptoms, work adjustment, and interpersonal relations, but minorities specified that little or no movement was to be anticipated in these areas. Many therapists took a rather pessimistic view of the patient's disturbance and of his capacity to profit from psychotherapy.

Asked to specify areas or problems which might be most ame-

nable to therapy, therapists mentioned three major areas: (a) interpersonal relations (mostly with mother and wife, to a lesser extent
with father, brother, and authority figures), (b) specific emotional
dynamics (self-destructive tendencies, etc.), (c) external reality
(work, jobs, living arrangements, etc.).

A similar question, designed to elicit information on areas in the
patient's living which might receive primary focus, produced a shift
in the response pattern: interpersonal relations and external reality
were named more frequently and emotional dynamics less frequently. The differences may be a function of the wording of the
two questions.

Closely related to the questions of focus were two items pertaining to attitudes or kinds of behavior which the therapist would
encourage (or discourage) in therapy with this patient. Encouraged
were: (a) a sense of responsibility, feelings of worthwhileness, self-
esteem, independence, and the patient's masculine role; (b) increased socialization, gainful employment, "living in the present";
(c) the expression of feelings without guilt; (d) the development
of insight. Discouraged were: (a) intellectualization, obsessive
ruminations (resistances); (b) self-pity, self-deprecation, helplessness, demands; (c) acting out of antisocial impulses.

Among areas to be avoided (early) in therapy, the following were
mentioned: sexual and homosexual impulses, oedipal material, and
the patient's concept of his own masculinity. Next in frequency
ranged interpersonal relations with his mother and wife. Small frequencies were accumulated under the headings of intellectual discussions, anger, hostility, death wishes, early life experiences,
unconscious material, fantasies, dreams. Twenty-six respondents
specifically indicated, however, that no areas should be avoided.
Some therapists counseled the avoidance of certain areas (e.g., interpersonal relations with mother and wife) which were singled out
for therapeutic focus by others. It is conceivable that the time stipulation ("early in treatment") may have been the cause for these
apparent contradictions.

Problems of therapeutic technique (Fig. 5). In order to explore
the interrelationships between perceptions, evaluations, and treatment plans, a question was included concerning clues in the
patient's behavior which the therapist might not wish to use in an
initial interview but which he might keep in mind for later reference. Such clues might facilitate inferences concerning the nature

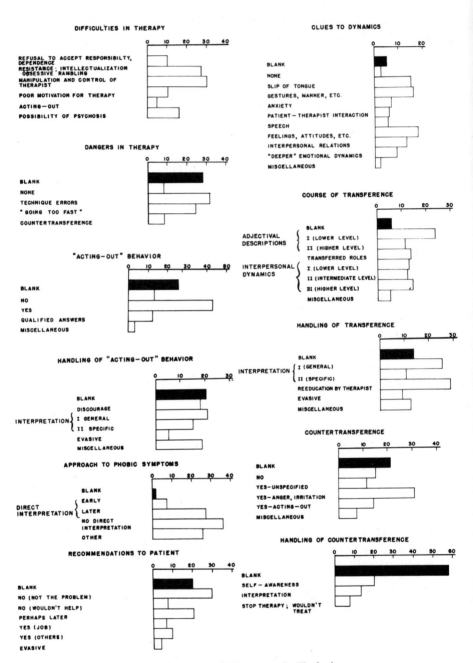

Fig. 5. Problems of Therapeutic Technique.

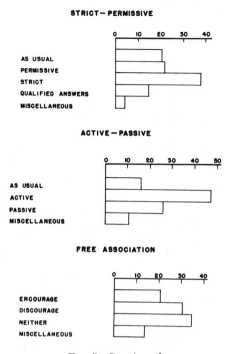

FIG. 5. Continued.

of the patient's emotional conflict and generate hypotheses to be tested in subsequent therapeutic sessions.

The majority of the 200 clues referred to observations about the patient's feelings and attitudes (anger, hostility, "the world owes me a living") with frequent elaboration of their dynamic significance. Another cluster dealt with nonverbal clues (gestures, manner, bodily movements, etc.). A relatively large number referred to a slip of the tongue occurring in the interview (speaking about his father's death, the patient substituted the word "mother"). References to "deeper dynamics," i.e., highly inferential statements, were comparatively infrequent.

Responses relating to the course of the transference seemed to fall into three major categories: (a) adjectival descriptions, (b) statements in terms of transferred roles (often tautologic), and (c) statements in terms of interpersonal dynamics. This sequence implies a hierarchy of increasing complexity and specificity; the kind of formulation chosen was found to be associated with the respondent's

length of experience in therapy (see below). The following examples
illustrate responses assigned to the major scoring categories:

(a) *Adjectival Descriptions*
Negative
Resentful, complaining
First positive, then negative.
(b) *Transferred Roles*
[Course of the transference is that of] the relationship with his mother. With
me, I would expect him to be a child with father, wanting help with wife
and mother.
[He would see me as] Mother, with expectations of being smothered by
therapist, too.
(c) *Interpersonal Dynamics*
[Transference] Probably would be fairly quickly established and therapist
would probably first be the good father. Later, his [patient's] need for dependency gratification would make things stormy.
Possibly anxiety about possible illnesses in therapist. Hostile defensiveness if
pressed.
I would expect him to develop hostile feelings which he would not be able
to express but which would cause him to have symptoms and perhaps to stay
away.

Two principal methods for handling transference problems were
suggested: one is best described as interpretive, i.e., pointing out
the distortive elements in the patient's manuevers; the other refers
to a skillful use of the therapist's role in changing the patient's attitudes and actions, by firmness, reassurance, or other re-educative
techniques. In the latter method, interpretations are not necessarily
excluded, but the major emphasis is upon the therapist as a person,
authority figure, or reality model.

A patient who is very demanding, aggressive, and manipulative
is likely to evoke emotional reactions from the therapist. More than
half of the respondents expected to get involved in countertransference reactions with this patient. Most frequently mentioned
were anger, annoyance, irritation, and impatience. Less often mentioned was the danger of acting out in response to the patient's
manipulative and controlling tendencies, which might lead the
therapist to abdicate his therapeutic role. More than 20 per cent of
the therapists failed to answer this question. Almost three times as
many therapists did not answer the second part of the question asking for specific statements about the "handling" of possible countertransference reactions. Those who replied stated they would try to
be aware of the problem and act accordingly. A smaller number
said they would discuss it with the patient or interpret it.

Related to questions about transference and countertransference were several items concerning difficulties and/or dangers that might arise in the therapy. With regard to difficulties, respondents mentioned prominently the patient's attempt to manipulate and control the therapist. Of equal magnitude was resistance, intellectualization, and obsessive rambling. Akin to the foregoing were comments about the patient's refusal to accept responsibility, his dependence and parasitic trends, his projections of blame, and his poor motivation for therapy. The possibility of a psychotic episode was also anticipated by a fair number of therapists.

The question about dangers elicited responses which tended to be centered around techniques, with a variety of problems that could not easily be subsumed under common denominators. Frequent comments referred to an incorrect handling of the transference relationship, and an appreciable number cautioned against the therapist's "going too fast." They suggested the need for a sympathetic and understanding attitude to prevent the patient from becoming too anxious or developing a psychosis.

Three items dealt with more specific technique problems. The first asked whether the respondent expected the patient to engage in much acting-out behavior, and, if so, how he would deal with it. The preferred methods for handling the problem were to be interpretation and control, by firmness, strictness, or setting limits. Miscellaneous recommendations were made for supportive measures, including reassurance, focus on the patient's personality assets, and re-education.

Considerable divergence of opinion was expressed regarding the optimal method for dealing with the patient's phobic symptoms. The majority considered direct interpretation of these symptoms contraindicated at any time; a somewhat less sizable group thought interpretation should occur at a much later time; another group advocated more or less idiosyncratic approaches; and a small minority thought that the therapist should interpret them as early as possible.

A similarly divergent distribution was obtained on the question of recommendations to the patient to change his present mode of living or his environment. About one-third of the responses were in the negative, with most members of this group pointing out that recommendations were outside the therapist's province and unrelated to the therapeutic problem. Twenty per cent of the respondents qualified their replies, counseling deferment of a decision. Certain respondents indicated a willingness to make recommendations, primarily with respect to the patient's job, living arrangements for his mother, wife, etc.

Another set of questions sought to explore further the therapist's approach to therapy, and to determine the extent to which the therapist's "usual" techniques might be modified by or adapted to the particular set of problems presented by this patient. One out of five therapists indicated that they would be no more strict or permissive with this patient than with any other. A like number preferred permissiveness. Forty per cent, however, voted for strictness, basing their judgment mostly on technical requirements. A minority qualified their responses by stating they would be strict in some areas, permissive in others, etc.

A question about the therapist's level of activity was worded as follows: "Assuming that the patient's behavior during the first hour is rather typical of him, would you tend to be more active (i.e., intervene frequently) or more passive (i.e., intervene infrequently) in subsequent interviews? Here the division of opinion appeared even more pronounced than in the preceding item: Almost 50 per cent said they would tend to be rather active; a quarter said "rather passive"; others qualified their response or gave a noncommittal answer.

Free association was discouraged by a third; encouraged by a fifth; neither encouraged or discouraged by another third.

Form of therapy, frequency of sessions, and length (Fig. 6). The preferred method of treatment was described simply as "psychotherapy." Thirty respondents qualified their responses by adding such terms as "intensive," "insight," "uncovering," or "analytically oriented." It is not certain, however, that those respondents who failed to define "psychotherapy" more closely did not in fact refer to more intensive therapy. Psychoanalysis, as the most extensive and intensive form of therapy, was recommended by less than 10 per cent. Other minorities recommended supportive therapy, group therapy, and various combinations.

Further information on the method of treatment—at least on its external aspects—is provided by the frequency of weekly sessions suggested by the respondents. The modal response was 1-2 times per week. Almost equally preferred, however, were interviews at the rate of 2-3 times per week. A sizable minority thought the patient should be seen only once a week. Therapists who voted for three or more sessions per week comprised only 10 per cent.

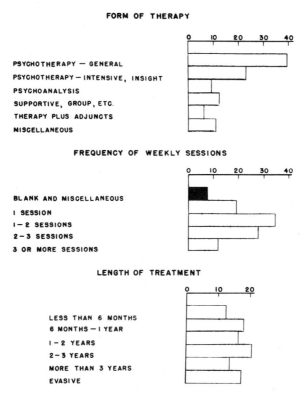

FIG. 6. Form of Therapy, Frequency of Sessions, and Length of Therapy.

Considering the divergence of goals and modes of treatment, it is not surprising that the length of therapy was estimated quite differently. Therapists who distinguished between intermediate and ultimate goals expected to achieve the former in one year or less, whereas the latter were estimated more prominently in the two to three year range. As many therapists anticipated the treatment to last six months or less, as three years or more. An appreciable proportion gave evasive answers.

A more specific question dealt with the length of time required to relieve the patient's symptoms. The majority estimated that this could be done in one year, a fair percentage being even more optimistic. To the extent that the therapist views symptoms as rooted in the patient's personality structure, the modification of which is the more important task of psychotherapy, he might feel reluctant to

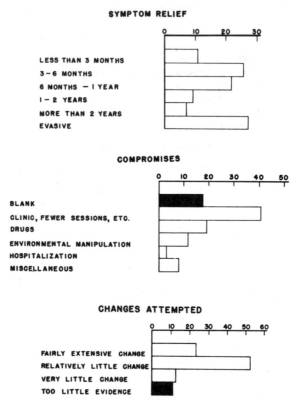

FIG. 6. Continued.

take a stand on a question which might strike him as thoroughly nondynamic. The large percentage of abstentions or noncommittal answers on this item may be partly explained by this reasoning.

In view of the patient's poor economic condition, his wife's invalidism, etc., it appeared appropriate to consider the possibility of compromises in case the recommendations for treatment were unfeasible for practical reasons. The most frequent response concerned changes in external arrangements of therapy, such as fewer sessions per week, referral to a clinic, or less intensive treatment. A moderate proportion suggested such adjuncts as tranquilizing drugs. It is noteworthy that negligible minorities recommended hospitalization or electric shock therapy.

As a global estimate of the kinds of changes in the patient's personality structure the respondents would attempt, the following responses appear instructive: A quarter of the responding therapists described their over-all goals as a fairly extensive change; more than half contented themselves with relatively little change; and 12 per cent said they would strive for very little change.

Analysis of systematic differences

Variability as a function of experience. In view of the wide range of professional experience among the therapists, analyses were performed to determine the degree of association between length of experience and the various questionnaire items. The sample was divided into three groups: Group I included psychiatrists having 0 to $1\frac{3}{4}$ years of experience in therapy; Group II, 2 to 5 years of experience; and Group III, 6 years or more. Responses to each questionnaire item were then broken down in terms of this grouping, and the chi square technique applied to test the significance of the differences in the three groups.

The results can be summarized by the statement that length of professional experience seemed to have a negligible bearing upon therapists' diagnostic and prognostic evaluations. In the case of continuous variables, product-moment coefficients of correlation were also computed. These are presented in Table 3.

The significant correlation between Ego Strength and experience as well as age indicates that, with increasing experience, therapists tended to judge the patient's ego strength to be *less*. Similarly, older therapists evaluated the prognosis *without* therapy as less favorable than younger therapists. However, on both items the evidence was inconsistent and tentative. With respect to formulations of the patient's dynamics, experienced therapists contributed a larger number of "superior" formulations (the correlation, not shown in Table 3, was $r = .22$).

These results are plausible if it is recalled that many of the questionnaire items called for relatively simple judgments and predictions, so that an inexperienced therapist—or even a layman—might make a more or less informed guess. On the other hand, certain items, like formulation of the patient's emotional dynamics, made considerably greater demands on the therapist's technical knowledge; hence the experienced therapist was at an advantage. There was no conclusive evidence that experienced therapists preferred a particular kind of formulation, as measured by the classifications mentioned.

These tests also proved nonsignificant almost without exception on questions dealing with therapeutic plans, goals, and techniques.

A parallel analysis comparing analysts (mean experience 13.7 years), psychiatrists (mean experience 7.3 years), and residents (mean experience .9 years), was likewise inconclusive except that analysts tended to judge the length of therapy to be longer than either psychiatrists or residents (who did not seem to differ significantly) and analysts preferred three or more weekly sessions, in contrast to psychiatrists who preferred one or two weekly interviews.

In both analyses, the more experienced therapists, irrespective of whether they described themselves as analysts, tended to state the course of the transference in terms of interpersonal dynamics, whereas inexperienced respondents tended to prefer descriptions in terms of transferred roles.

TABLE 3

PRODUCT-MOMENT COEFFICIENTS OF CORRELATION BETWEEN ATTITUDINAL AND
BIOGRAPHICAL VARIABLES

(Average N = 115)

Variable	Prognosis with Therapy	Attitude toward Patient	Experience (in years)	Experience (self-estimate)	Competence as Therapist (self-estimate)	Age
Ego Strength	.37**	.15	.20*	.07	.03	.23**
Anxiety	.08	.20*	−.09	−.03	.00	−.12
Insight	.38**	.33**	.12	.11	−.05	.03
Self-Observation vs. Rationalization	.36**	.35**	−.10	−.02	.04	−.09
Emotional Maturity	−.41**	−.20*	.05	.04	.03	.03
Social Adjustment	.28**	.21*	.15	.08	−.09	.10
Disturbance	−.17	−.04	−.07	−.10	.02	−.05
Prognosis without Therapy	.05	−.11	.14	−.01	.08	.21*
Prognosis with Therapy	—	.39**	.16	.07	−.08	.06
Attitude toward Patient	—	—	.02	.05	−.09	−.11
Experience (in years)	—	—	—	.72**	−.65**	.85**
Experience (self-estimate)	—	—	—	—	−.80**	.64**
Competence as Therapist (self-estimate)	—	—	—	—	—	−.56**

* Significant at the .05 level.
** Significant at the .01 level.

Variability as a function of attitude toward the patient. The next analysis concerned a breakdown of responses to each questionnaire item in terms of the therapist's attitude toward the patient.

Table 3 shows a positive correlation between prognosis and attitude. It is not surprising that prognosis is correlated with diagnostic evaluations, but it is noteworthy that most of the relationships shown in Table 3 are paralleled by the therapist's attitude toward the patient. A slightly different method of analysis lends greater concreteness to these findings (see Fig. 7). In each instance, chi

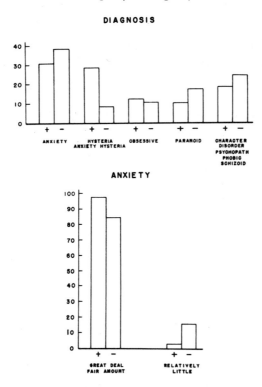

FIG. 7. Clinical Evaluations in Terms of Therapist's Attitude Toward the Patient, Based upon Statistically Significant Chi Squares. Each bar indicates the percentage of therapists choosing a particular response alternative depending upon their attitude toward the patient. (+ = positive attitude, $N = 40$; — = negative or ambivalent attitude, $N = 65$; neutral attitude, $N = 28$, omitted.)

squares were computed for the distributions of the positive and negative groups; the small ambivalent group was included in the negative group; the neutral group, because of its relative smallness, was omitted. The results were significant at least at the .05 level, and usually at the .01 level or beyond.

Therapists indicating a negative attitude toward the patient were more likely to choose such diagnostic labels as psychopath, character

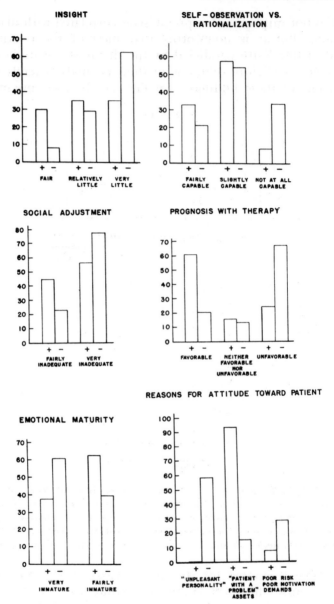

FIG. 7. Continued.

disorder, paranoid, and phobic; tended to see the patient as less anxious, having less insight, being less capable of self-observation, more immature emotionally, and more poorly adjusted socially. A negative attitude toward the patient was associated with significantly poorer prognosis, and therapists responding in this manner were more likely to comment about the patient's "unpleasant personality charateristics."

Of the 27 chi squares relevant to therapeutic goals and techniques, 6 were significant at or beyond the 5 per cent level. It will be seen from Table 4 that the number of significant chi squares is almost doubled when the statistic is computed on the full sample of therapists (psychiatrists, psychologists, and social workers). Since the

TABLE 4

COMPARATIVE DATA ON PROBABILITY LEVELS OF CHI SQUARE FOR FULL SAMPLE
AND PSYCHIATRIST SAMPLE

Topical Area and Questionnaire Items	Full Sample ($N=168$)*	Psychiatrists only ($N=105$)**
Goals and Approaches		
Areas to be Avoided..........................	.01	NS
Problems of Therapeutic Technique		
Dangers in Therapy...........................	.02	NS
Handling of Counter-transference...............	.05	NS
Recommendations to Patient...................	.001	.02
Strict-Permissive.............................	.001	.05
Active-Passive................................	.05	.01
Free Association..............................	.01	NS
Form of Therapy, Frequency, Length		
Form of Therapy..............................	.05	.05
Frequency of Sessions.........................	.05	.05
Symptom Relief (time estimate)................	.001	.05
Changes Attempted...........................	.05	NS

* "Neutral" group omitted; "ambivalent" group omitted.
** "Neutral" group omitted.
NS = Not significant.

direction of change is quite consistent, it may be assumed that the trends are attenuated when the size of the sample is reduced. It appears less likely that the observed trends are more pronounced in the nonpsychiatrist groups.* While greater confidence, obviously,

* The experience levels of the various attitudinal groups, on the other hand, are more sharply differentiated for psychiatrists than for the full sample. In the former group, therapists professing a positive attitude had a mean experience of 4.72 years; neutral, 8.46 years; negative and ambivalent, 6.55 years. Analysis of variance yielded an F of 15.74, which is significant at the .001 level. For the full sample, the mean differences were statistically nonsignificant.

can be placed in those results which are significant in both samples, it seemed justifiable to present·graphically the results for the full sample. This has been done in Figure 8.

Only one of the questions pertaining to therapeutic goals and approaches yielded a significant chi square, and this may be due to the particular grouping of responses. This result indicated (full

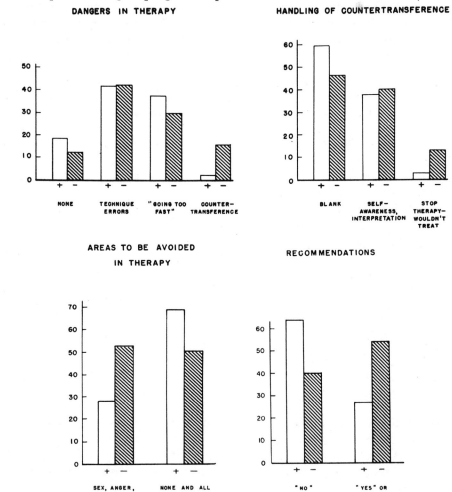

Fig. 8. Responses in Terms of Therapist's Attitude Toward the Patient, Based upon Statistically Significant Chi Squares. Each bar indicates the percentage of therapists (full sample) choosing a particular response alternative depending upon their attitude toward the patient. (+ = positive attitude, $N = 75$; — = negative attitude, $N = 93$; neutral attitude, $N = 45$, and ambivalent attitude, $N = 21$, omitted.)

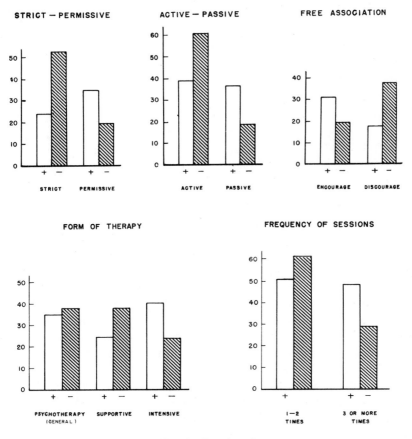

FIG. 8. Continued.

sample only) that therapists whose attitude toward the patient was negative were more likely to suggest avoidance of certain areas in therapy, such as: the patient's relationship with his wife, sexual impulses, hostility, anger, death wishes, unconscious material, fantasies, and dreams.

Under the heading, "Problems of Therapeutic Technique," the null hypothesis was rejected for several questionnaire items. Descriptively, these results may be stated as follows: Therapists expressing a negative atttitude toward the patient were more likely to anticipate dangers to successful therapy from the therapist's anger, irritation, and other countertransference reactions (full sample only). On the other hand, therapists holding a positive attitude were more likely to mention the danger of pressing the patient too hard in therapy and recommended a sympathetic and understanding attitude by the

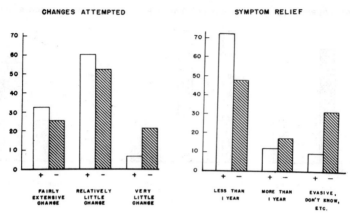

FIG. 8. Continued.

therapist. While there was a slight (but inconclusive) trend for the "dislike" group to expect more countertransference reactions, this group was more likely to discontinue therapy if the therapist became aware of countertransference, or not to accept the patient for treatment in the first place. Therapists admitting a negative attitude were more likely to make recommendations to the patient concerning changes in his mode of living, an approach often strongly disadvised by the "like" group.

The evidence was clear-cut that therapists whose attitude toward the patient was positive tended to characterize their proposed techniques as permissive, whereas a significantly larger proportion of the "dislike" group voted for strictness.

Similarly, with respect to the therapist's activity or passivity, a positive attitude toward the patient was associated with passivity, a negative attitude with activity.

Free association tended to be encouraged by the therapist feeling positively about the patient, but was discouraged by those holding a negative attitude (full sample only).

With regard to the form of therapy, frequency of sessions, etc., a positive attitude was associated with the more intensive forms of treatment, including psychoanalysis, whereas therapists feeling negatively toward the patient were more likely to recommend supportive therapy or other adjuncts. A positive attitude was correlated with more frequent weekly visits, fewer evasive answers about symptom-relief, and plans for more extensive change in the patient's character structure (full sample only). Responses to the last item indicated that, compared to therapists expressing a positive attitude, four times as many therapists holding a negative attitude planned for "very little change."

Attempts were also made to explore the possible influences of *theoretical orientation* and *personal analysis* upon therapists' response patterns. With respect to theoretical orientation, it proved difficult to isolate "pure" groups since respondents often acknowledged multiple influences. Several criteria were used to define "orthodox" and "neo-Freudian" groups, but these were so small as to preclude the application of rigorous statistical techniques. The results of this analysis must therefore be regarded as inconclusive. Similar difficulties were encountered with regard to personal analysis. Here an attempt was made to match a sample of psychiatrists whose training had included personal analysis with a comparable nonanalyzed group, experience, age, and sex being held constant. Even with an N of 28 in each group it proved impossible in most instances to test for the significance of differences on the various item responses. While the evidence must be judged indeterminate, it may be worth mentioning that the observed differences appeared small for the most part.

Analysis of therapists' communications to the patient

Over-all response distributions. Table 5 presents frequencies and percentages of therapists' responses, as distributed within each system component. As might be expected in a first interview, many communications were designed to obtain a fuller picture of the patient's person and problem. Highly inferential communications as well as comments revealing a high level of initiative were relatively rare.

TABLE 5

SUMMARY DISTRIBUTIONS OF PSYCHIATRISTS' RESPONSES, QUANTIFIED BY A
MULTIDIMENSIONAL SYSTEM OF ANALYSIS
(N = 126 Psychiatrists)

System Component	Responses	
	N	Per Cent
Type		
Silence..	975	27.3
Passive Acceptance.......................................	169	4.7
Exploratory Operations..................................	1,689	47.3
Clarification...	128	3.6
Interpretive Operations..................................	175	4.9
Direct Guidance..	302	8.5
Miscellaneous and Unclassifiable........................	134	3.7
Total..	3,572	100.0

TABLE 5.   *Continued.*

System Component	Responses N	Per Cent
Depth-Directedness		
Level 1 Mildly inferential...............................	202	8.2
2	459	18.6
3	1,125	45.4
4	495	20.0
5 Moderately inferential...........................	104	4.2
6	60	2.4
7	20	.8
8 Highly inferential...............................	9	.4
Total*..	2,474	100.0
Dynamic Focus		
No Change in Focus.................................	510	20.6
Reflections of Feeling...............................	116	4.7
Requests for Additional Information.................	1,092	44.2
Dynamic Events—Past...............................	151	6.1
Dynamic Events—Present............................	288	11.6
Therapist as Expert.................................	284	11.5
Analysis of Transference............................	33	1.3
Total*..	2,474	100.0
Initiative		
Level 1 Mild.......................................	170	6.9
2	387	15.6
3	1,086	43.9
4 Moderate.......................................	514	20.8
5	175	7.1
6	65	2.6
7 Strong..	77	3.1
Total*..	2,474	100.0
Therapeutic Climate		
−2..	5	.2
−1..	31	1.2
0..	2,326	94.0
+1..	108	4.4
+2..	4	.2
Total*..	2,474	100.0

* Excludes silences and unclassifiable responses.

Experience in psychotherapy. It seems reasonable to hypothesize that a highly experienced therapist will conduct an initial interview differently from an inexperienced resident. Table 6 shows the reŝults of the analysis of variance which may be summarized as follows: *

1. Inexperienced psychiatrists tended to ask more exploratory questions than experienced therapists.
2. Experienced psychiatrists tended to give a larger number of interpretive responses than inexperienced psychiatrists. These communications tended to be more inferential, and their dynamic focus concerned dynamic interpersonal events in the patient's past and present life.
3. Experienced therapists showed a higher degree of initiative in their communications than inexperienced practitioners.
4. Experienced therapists tended to change the dynamic focus of their communications more than the less experienced respondents.
5. Experienced therapists tended to be slightly "warmer."
The above changes appeared to be progressive with increasing experience.

Analysts, psychiatrists, residents. A parallel analysis was performed on a somewhat different criterion: the respondent's self-description of his status within the profession. The analysis is analogous to the first one because the three groups were markedly divergent in terms of professional experience: Analysts' mean experience was 13.7 years; psychiatrists', 7.3 years; residents', 0.9 years. However, the variable of personal analysis and analytic training seems to enter more prominently into this grouping. The first group (with one exception) had both personal analysis and analytic training; the third group, for the most part, had neither; the middle group was divided. (On an over-all basis, the correlation between professional experience and personal analysis was .43.)

The following differences were statistically significant:

1. The number of interpretive communications given by analysts was proportionately larger than that of residents. As expected, such communications tended to be more inferential.
2. The relative degree of initiative shown by analysts was greater than that of residents.
3. Analysts tended to shift the dynamic focus from passive acceptance to past and current interpersonal events more than psychiatrists and residents.
4. While the over-all comparison was nonsignificant, the relative frequency of responses whose emotional tone was judged "cold" was greater among analysts than among residents (ratio of 3:1). Differences among "warm" responses were not statistically significant.

---

* Unless otherwise indicated, the reference to statistical results in this section is Table 6. The descriptive statements are based on statistically significant group comparisons, as shown in that Table. When more than two groups were involved, an attempt was made to "locate" the significant over-all difference by comparing subgroups with each other. Such references in the text describe subsidiary comparisons which were statistically significant at an acceptable level. Occasional exceptions to this procedure are specifically noted.

TABLE 6
THERAPIST COMMUNICATIONS—SUMMARY OF STATISTICAL ANALYSES*

Variable	Silence	Ex-plora-tions	Inter-preta-tions	Direct-Guid-ance	Depth-Direct-edness	Main-tain focus	Addit. Info.	Dy-namic Events	Therap. as Expert	Ini-tia-tive	"Cold"	"Warm"	Subgroups	N
		Type					**Dynamic focus**				**Climate**			
Experience	—	.05	.01	—	.01	.05	.05	.02	—	.01	—	.09	0–1.75 yrs. / 2–9 yrs. / 10–30 yrs.	40 / 53 / 34
Grouping within Profession	—	.06	.01	—	.01	.001	—	.01	—	.02	—	—	Analysts / Psychiatrists / Residents	30 / 57 / 43
Personal Analysis†	.02	.02	—	—	—	—	—	—	—	—	—	—	Personal Analysis / No Personal Analysis	28 / 28
Membership in Amer. Psy. Ass'n.	—	—	—	—	—	—	—	—	—	—	—	—	Members / Non-Members	18 / 14
Length of Analysis	—	—	—	—	—	—	—	—	—	—	—	—	More than 500 hours / Less than 500 hours	22 / 13
Theoretical Orientation†	—	—	—	—	—	—	—	—	—	—	—	—	Orthodox Freudians / Neo-Freudians	16 / 16
Attitude toward Patient	—	—	—	—	—	—	.03	—	—	—	.07	.05	Positive (+) / Neutral (0) / Negative (−) / Ambivalent (±)	39 / 26 / 51 / 13
Prognosis	.01	—	—	—	.05	.05	—	—	—	.05	.05	.05	Favorable (+) / Non-committal (0) / Unfavorable (−)	41 / 17 / 58
Attitude-Prognosis (Jointly)	—	—	—	—	—	—	.05	—	—	—	.05	—	Att.: ±; Prog.: + / Att.; −; Prog.: −	22 / 33

* Significance levels (two-tailed tests) are based on the Mann-Whitney U test (comparisons of two groups) or the Kruskal-Wallis one-way analysis of variance (comparisons of more than two groups). Probabilities of .10 or less are given in the table; p values greater than .10 have been omitted (indicated by a dash). The statistic used for *Depth-Directedness, Initiative,* and *Climate* (over-all comparisons) was chi square.
† Matched samples.

5. The decline of exploratory communications with experience, reported above, was significant at the .06 level for the present grouping. The direction of change was identical.

Personal analysis. While the foregoing results suggest that the observed differences are primarily a function of experience, it is possible that personal analysis might make a contribution of its own. In order to explore this question, two samples were equated in terms of experience, and at each experience level a therapist with a personal analysis was matched with a therapist without this training. The matched samples are described in Table 7. The results indicate that the only significant differences concern the relative frequency of silent responses and exploratory questions: analyzed therapists give a significantly larger number of silent responses, this difference being achieved at the expense of exploratory questions.

TABLE 7

SUMMARY OF BIOGRAPHICAL VARIABLES FOR TWO MATCHED SAMPLES OF PSYCHIATRISTS

($N = 28$)

Variable	Personal Analysis	No Personal Analysis
Age (mean)	38.4 years	38.2 years
Experience in therapy (mean)	6.4 years	6.4 years
Personal Analysis (mean)	458.8 hours	—
Analysts	10	1
Psychiatrists	10	17
Residents	8	10
Total Sample (M.D. degree)	28	28
Theoretical Orientation:		
Psychoanalytically oriented—general	19	15
Freud—orthodox	1	0
Sullivan	2	3
Meyer	0	3
Miscellaneous	6	7
Male--Female	24–4	25–3

To learn whether these differences might be more pronounced at the high or the low end of experience, the matched samples were equally divided into a high and low experience group. Comparisons showed that the difference in silent responses was particularly prominent among inexperienced therapists, suggesting that personal analysis might have a greater influence at the lower end of the experience continuum. These results are supported by another analysis in which 18 members of the American Psychoanalytic Association were compared with 14 nonmembers (both groups had a mean experience of approximately 14 years but most members of the second group had no personal analysis.) No statistically significant differences were observed in these highly experienced groups. Nor did therapists whose analyses exceeded 500 hours differ in their responses from therapists whose personal therapy was relatively less extensive.

Theoretical orientation. Despite the difficulties of isolating "pure" groups, an attempt was made to match two presumably divergent samples: those who subscribed to an "orthodox Freudian" orientation and those who might be called "neo-Freudians." Each group included 16 therapists, all of whom had undergone personal analysis. The orthodox Freudians' median experience level was 8.5 years, median length of personal analysis 650 hours; the neo-Freudians had a median experience of 7.0 years, and the median length of their analyses was 250 hours. Statistical comparisons failed to reveal any reliable differences between these groups.

Attitude toward the patient. It was shown in the preceding section that the therapist's conscious attitude toward the patient tended to be correlated with his clinical evaluations as well as his treatment plans, goals, and proposed techniques. This finding suggested the hypothesis that the therapist's self-rating of his conscious attitude might carry over to his communications; specifically, that therapists expressing a negative attitude would tend to be "colder," that is, more rejecting in their communications, than therapists professing a positive attitude.

Comparisons between groups of therapists professing a positive, neutral, negative, or ambivalent attitude disclosed a statistically significant difference relative to exploratory questions; however, since this finding was not corroborated on related system components, it may be considered due to chance.

With regard to *Therapeutic Climate,* chi square for "cold" responses was significant at the .07 level of confidence; for "warm" responses it was significant at the .05 level. Therapists indicating a negative attitude gave three times the number of "cold" responses as therapists having a positive attitude. The "ambivalent" attitude group was differentiated reliably from each of the remaining groups by giving the largest proportion of "warm" responses. The positive attitude group did not differ significantly from the negative one in terms of "warm" responses.

Prognosis. In view of the correlation between therapists' self-estimates of their attitude toward the patient and their prognostic ratings, a parallel analysis was conducted by grouping respondents according to their prognostic estimates. The results may be summarized as follows:

1. Statistically significant group differences were observed with regard to silent responses. Therapists expressing a noncommittal prognostic estimate tended to give the smallest number of silent responses.

2. Respondents giving a favorable prognosis were more likely to accept the patient's focus without attempting to shift it.

3. Therapists giving a noncommittal prognosis tended to show more initiative in their communications than the other two groups.

4. Therapists whose prognosis was unfavorable gave more than four times as many "cold" responses than respondents who considered the prognosis favorable. (The noncommittal group appeared closer to the "favorable" one.)

5. The relative frequency of "warm" responses was greatest among therapists whose prognosis was noncommittal, and relatively low (one-half or less) in both the "favorable" and the "unfavorable" groups.

Attitude and prognosis considered jointly. To cast further light on the above findings, two extreme groups were isolated and compared. The first group included therapists whose attitude toward the patient was positive and whose prognosis was favorable (mean experience = 5.6 years), the second those whose attitude was negative and whose prognosis was unfavorable (mean experience = 6.6 years).* The group comparisons revealed few technique differences, except that the second group tended to change the focus by asking significantly more exploratory questions. In terms of *Climate,* however, the differences reported separately for Attitude and Prognosis were accentuated. Only one therapist in the first group obtained a "cold" response, in contrast to 10 in the second group, a ratio of almost 1:7. "Warm" responses revealed a small difference in the predicted direction which was not statistically significant.

It may be appropriate to reiterate the earlier statement that the scores on *Climate* represent almost certainly a gross underestimate, so that many potentially "positive" or "negative" responses had to be treated as "neutral" for lack of sufficient evidence. Consequently, the frequencies involved in these comparisons are relatively small, but the relationships between film responses and therapist's attitude and prognosis nevertheless emerge as quite consistent. "Cold" responses, by this evidence, appear to be a more sensitive indicator of the therapist's conscious attitude than "warm," empathic ones.

---

* The mean difference was statistically nonsignificant.

4

EXPLORATION OF
THE EMPATHY VARIABLE

The findings highlighting the interrelationships between the emotional tone of therapists' communications, conscious attitude, and clinical evaluations led to further explorations. In scoring the responses to the points of interruption in the film, our* attention was called early to marked qualitative differences in terms of responses to particular choice points (some of which appeared especially critical) as well as the over-all response patterns. As we developed a greater appreciation for the range of responses, we became increasingly impressed by differences in the therapists' underlying attitudes toward the patient, their willingness or unwillingness to engage in a therapeutic relationship, and their empathy. To be sure, some protocols did not lend themselves to this kind of analysis, mostly because the respondent had been unable or unwilling to make his stand sufficiently explicit, so that his written statements, which at best conveyed only a pale impression of the sound of his voice, left the question indeterminate. But a substantial number of protocols did provide sufficient evidence, and often very clear-cut evidence.

Responses to selected choice points. Before dealing with certain global impressions gained from complete protocols, I should like to present some examples of responses to "critical" choice points. Often, there seemed to be a noteworthy consistency between therapists' responses to several of these choice points.

One of the most controversial and seemingly most diagnostic

---

* I wish to take this opportunity to reiterate my sincere appreciation to Mrs. Rebecca E. Rieger, my research associate, who made a vital contribution to this phase of the work.

passages occurred at the end of the interview. Somewhat unexpectedly perhaps, the patient makes an impassioned plea for reassurance by expressing concern about his anxiety symptoms which, he fears, might lead to a heart attack. The question expresses both his obsessive ruminations and his intense anxiety. It may be a "loaded" question in the sense that his unconscious objective is to put the therapist "on the spot," to force him to commit himself. It also expresses the patient's dependency needs, his demands for a magical protector, and his passive-aggressive submission to an authority figure. The passage ends with the question:

> That's all I want to ask you. Are they [these attacks] going to kill me? Will they cause me to have . . . will they cause my heart to flop out from under me some day or will they damage my nerve tissue or even my . . . my thinking?

Here are some typical examples of therapists' responses:

> I feel that your emotional difficulty is really more important than any heart disease you might have. We can have you checked physically to determine your physical health.
>
> You prefer to talk of your symptoms, not your feelings. They are not the real problem.
>
> You must be convinced by now that they won't damage you after all these years. Tell me, how would your life be different if you didn't have them?
>
> No; but the attacks are causing you a lot of distress.
>
> No; these are only the effects of things you don't understand within yourself. What we can do here is see what we can find out about the attacks, what sets them off.
>
> No, your physical symptoms will not harm you. But it is important to understand what they do for you.
>
> No, this will not happen.
>
> I seem to feel that you know there is a connection between how you feel and the way you think life has treated you.
>
> Naturally, you are concerned about yourself.

In the following replies the therapist sidesteps the issue. He may feel that by doing so he is avoiding a trap, but in any event he is deliberately or unknowingly neglecting the patient's feelings. It is predictable that this evasion would be experienced by the patient as a rejection or at least as a "letting down." If it is kept in mind that the interview is drawing to a close, the possibility of increasing rather than allaying the patient's anxiety should be a matter of serious concern to the therapist. Operationally, such therapists either subtly changed the focus by asking a related question, or they threw the question back. The latter maneuver, used quite frequently by inexperienced therapists, appeared to be an evasion because the patient had talked about his feelings at some length.

You say you have these attacks at home now?
Even your thinking, huh?
Why should they damage you?
These are things you fear?
I'd like to discuss the types of work that you have done, for a while.
What did the other doctors tell you?
How do you feel when you feel "safe"?
What do you think?
Do you think they will?

There was a small group of therapists who decided either to make no reply at all or to launch a frontal attack upon the patient's neurotic defenses:

With your good luck, you're going to live and suffer.
Do you want to be a chronic invalid and be taken care of?
What difference would it make if I said yes or no? (Perhaps I might go on, not antagonistically, to explain that's not the problem.)
They might.
I don't know.

The following responses reflect the therapist's desire to avoid an authoritative answer and yet to give a forthright reply which may have the effect of allaying the patient's anxiety, at least temporarily:

As far as I know, that will not cause a heart attack or damage your nerve tissue, but you surely want more than this. You want help for these symptoms, and I'll have to know more.

I know these feelings are very uncomfortable. I can't answer your question completely. I feel it's something that should be looked into.

That's a very important question, of course, but something we'll have to go into fully later. First, we need a fuller understanding of you and your problem. I'd like to talk with you again and go into everything in more detail. Let's make another appointment if it's all right with you.

These examples may convey something of the wide range of responses and their individual flavor. They also show how different therapists attempted to meet the problem inherent in the patient's concluding question. Apart from the patient's needs at the moment, it was clear that certain therapists emerged as persons, as individuals, as human beings who were not averse to using the pronoun *I*, whereas others considered it important to remain anonymous. It was our impression that some of the most highly experienced therapists appeared most clearly as persons, both in an accepting and a rejecting sense; conversely, inexperience tended to go together with anonymity.

An interesting difference in responses was observed with regard to a passage in which the patient mentions a constructive striving toward health which, to the superficial viewer, might easily be considered subordinate to his recital of symptoms, etc. After detailing a number of symptoms, the patient says:

> P.: You see what I mean? Pressure. Put your hand on your other hand; you got pressure. (T.: Mmm.) Well, that's just like it feels; that's the sensation of being hemmed in; you're cornered; you don't know which way to go. You are tired of the surroundings you are in and what you have been doing; you can't find anything that takes its place, that seems to be . . . to . . . fulfill the bill for you. (T.: Mmm.) But it's the sensations that worry me. (T.: Mmm.) This other stuff, huh, I can forget . . . (T.: Mmm.) . . . or have to if I want to regain my health.

The "obvious" thing to do at this point is to ask for further information:

> Forget what?
> What other stuff?

It seems to require greater alertness and self-awareness to focus on the patient's striving for health, which appears heavily overlaid by his emphasis on symptoms:

> You feel as if you'd like to be healthier, too?
> You really want to get over these feelings?
> How do you feel you can regain your health?
> What kind of help might you expect from me?

Among therapists whose conscious attitude toward the patient (expressed independently in the questionnaire) was positive and who gave a favorable prognosis ($N = 22$), 32 per cent focused on the "health" aspect, whereas among the negative attitude—unfavorable prognosis group ($N = 33$), only one therapist (3 per cent) took this approach. Among the latter group, 12 therapists included the phrase "other stuff" in their responses, whereas, in the former group only two therapists did, one of whom combined the remark with a reference to the patient's health. This piece of evidence suggests that the second group tended to be more preoccupied with "pathology" than the first one.

An illuminating contrast in approach is provided by therapists' responses to an episode in which the patient relates an experience of being discharged from a job. Comments encompassed empathic remarks about the patient's misfortune, his underlying feelings, requests for further information, and moral judgment or condemnation.

> . . . So, when I got fired from the First National Bank in H—— for writing a little old stinking $35 check on my personal account and didn't have the money to cover it, I got fired for that . . . see . . . And in my home town, a

thing like that gets around pretty quick, in a small community. I couldn't
find a damn job. I didn't have any place to sleep. I didn't have a damn
thing to eat. Being an Episcopalian, I went to a person who I knew . . . she
ran a boarding house, and I chopped wood at night for my supper, see, to
get something to eat. And that was the beginning of all my antisocial attitudes. And if that isn't three strikes against you before you come to bat, I'd
like to know what in the hell it is.

    You seem to have had a hard time of it, especially after your father died.
    You feel badly about that time in your life.
    I can see things were pretty rough for you.
    You seem angry when you talk of this.
    Tell me about these antisocial attitudes.
    Despite the rough time, you seemed to know how to get work and take
care of yourself.
    How do you think the bank manager should have handled the situation?
    How did the bank happen to fire you for what seemed like just an error?
    Fired for writing a bad check, huh?
    What would you have the bank do?
    You did write the check and expected to get away with it?
    You feel sorry for yourself; no one seemed interested.

Comparisons of responses to single items (stopping points) were
often less revealing of the therapist's attitude toward the patient, but
the totality of the response pattern frequently provided important
clues. On the basis of these observations it was decided to attempt
an over-all evaluation of the protocols.

    Over-all evaluation of protocols. The objective of arriving at a
global judgment of the degree of empathy shown by therapists was
to determine whether such ratings could be made reliably, that is,
whether independent raters could agree on the evaluation, and to
explore the relationships between over-all ratings to other relevant
therapist variables. Considering the exploratory character of this
analysis, we restricted ourselves to a few gross categories. The major
criteria are given below:

    Score +: Therapist recognizes the existence of an emotional problem and
communicates such understanding to the patient somewhere in the interview.
Such communications may convey reassurance but this may not necessarily be
the case.

    Therapist recognizes that the patient is seeking help, that he is in need of
help, that psychotherapy can help him, that there may be a relationship between patient's physical symptoms and his emotional conflicts, and that
insight or understanding of the latter may alleviate the former.

    Therapist communicates that he understands that the patient is suffering,
that he is anxious and in a state of discomfort.

    Therapist attempts to alleviate the patient's discomfort in the interview by
putting him at ease, by trying to alleviate his anxiety, by instilling some hope

for the future, by recognizing his past accomplishments despite difficulties, by raising his self-esteem.

Therapist feels the need to communicate to the patient something about treatment plans, referral, etc., that is, he recognizes that the patient has a right to expect a statement or recommendation from the interviewer as an expert, that the interview must serve a useful purpose to the patient, either by opening further possibilities or by making certain that the present experience is a constructive one.

Therapist gives evidence of listening to the patient's story, either by pertinent remarks or questions or by respectful silence. There should be no evidence that therapist changes a topic in order to impose his own frame of reference or trend of thought (especially in the beginning), nor should he respond with silence to urgent pleas from the patient.

The phrasing of comment should be respectful, nonderogatory, sympathetic, noncritical, nonjudgmental. There should be a complete absence of communications which by themselves would be assigned a score of —.

Score —: Therapist is cold, distant, unperceptive, unfeeling, and impersonal. Such attitudes would be inferred from a total absence of communications receiving a score of + or, more directly, from overt evidence: communications which seems to imply derogation, criticism, antagonism, hostility, disrespect, moral judgment, condemnation, accusation, impatience, punishment, nonacceptance of the patient as a person, or rejection. Included also would be communications by which the therapist implies or states openly that the patient is malingering, that he is antisocial, lazy, derelict in his duties to his family, exploiting, manipulating, sponging on others, psychopathic, unconventional, "crazy," ridiculous, silly, exaggerating, falsely accusing others or imposing on the interviewer in any manner.

Therapist devotes large portions of the interview to gathering facts about the patient's life history. The interview resembles a cross-examination.

Therapist "gives" nothing to the patient such as: recommendations for treatment, recognition that a problem exists, that psychotherapeutic help is available, that problems like his can and have been helped by psychotherapy; reassurance; acknowledgment that the patient is having a hard time, that his emotional and/or reality problems complicate his living.

Therapist responds with silence to patient's plea for reassurance, or uses rote devices to throw back the question. Therapist fails to respond to patient's underlying feelings throughout the interview.

Therapist gives interpretations which in the context of an initial interview and the patient's emotional state seem premature, inappropriate, etc. This judgment would apply with particular force to interpretations which are given very early in the interview, confront the patient directly with an important aspect of his problem, are not stated tentatively, but rather authoritatively; which because of their directness would be experienced by the patient as an attack on his self-esteem and consequently rejected; interpretations which seem "over the patient's head."

Score 0: The record provides insufficient evidence to warrant either a score of + or —, either because communications are minimal or because their emotional tone is "neutral." Therapist does not emerge sufficiently to be judged on the aforementioned criteria. (Records receiving a score of 0 tend to lean

toward the — side, principally because there is an absence of positive
indicators.)

Score ±: The record gives evidence of both + and — indicators, as previously defined, and it is difficult to determine which of these preponderate.

Rater agreement. Two successive ratings were made by two
trained raters working independently. Rater agreement is reported
in Table 8. Since there were indications of a certain affinity between
+ and ± ratings, and between 0 and — ratings, differences within
these groupings were counted as "partial agreement." It is believed
that sound recordings of the therapist's voice would have substantially increased the reliability of the judgments.

TABLE 8

AGREEMENT WITHIN AND BETWEEN TWO INDEPENDENT RATERS
(N = 131)

	Full Agreement*	Partial Agreement**	Disagree-ment
Rater 1: Rating 1 vs. Rating 2.............	69 (53%)	35 (27%)	27 (20%)
Rater 2: Rating 1 vs. Rating 2.............	52 (40%)	38 (29%)	41 (31%)
Rater 1 vs. Rater 2: Rating 1..............	51 (39%)	33 (25%)	47 (36%)
Rater 1 vs. Rater 2: Rating 2..............	57 (44%)	28 (21%)	46 (35%)

  * Using four categories: +, —, 0, and ±.
 ** Combining categories + and ±, and 0 and —.

Relationships of empathy ratings to other variables. It was found
that almost two-thirds of the therapists expressing a positive attitude
toward the patient received positive empathy ratings; a negative
attitude tended to be related to negative empathy ratings in approximately the same manner. The result was again paralleled by prognosis, the more favorable prognostic estimates being associated with
greater empathy. There was a slight tendency for therapists having
ten or more years of experience to achieve a larger proportion of
positive empathy ratings than less experienced therapists.

When empathy ratings were studied in relation to personal analysis, the results were strongly in favor of the analyzed group (Table
9). Experienced therapists whose training had included personal
analysis greatly exceeded the matched group whose training had not
included personal analysis.

A further breakdown in terms of the therapist's self-rating of his
attitude was undertaken in order to explore possible relationships

between empathy and attitude. The results indicated that on an over-all basis the nonanalyzed group somewhat exceeded the analyzed group in terms of negative attitudes, but the difference was not statistically significant. In the less experienced group, analyzed therapists tended to have a more positive attitude; however, in the more highly experienced group the trend appeared to be almost reversed. Although these findings must be considered highly tentative because of the small size of the sub-samples, in the experienced, analyzed group a conscious *negative* attitude appeared to be associated more often with a *positive* empathy rating, whereas in the nonanalyzed group there appeared to be greater congruence between negative attitude and lack of empathy. Moreover, no experienced, analyzed therapist having a positive attitude obtained a negative empathy rating; in contrast, such a discrepancy was observed among four members of the nonanalyzed group.

TABLE 9

DISTRIBUTIONS OF EMPATHY RATINGS AND SELF-RATINGS OF ATTITUDE IN TWO GROUPS OF PSYCHIATRISTS MATCHED IN TERMS OF PERSONAL ANALYSIS

Experience in Therapy	Attitude toward Patient	Personal Analysis Empathy Rating			No Personal Analysis Empathy Rating		
		+	−	Total	+	−	Total
0–3 years...............	+	3	6	9	2	2	4
	−	4	1	5	4	6	10
Total...............		7	7	14	6	8	14
3.5–30 years............	+	4	0	4	2	4	6
	−	7	3	10	2	6	8
Total...............		11	3	14	4	10	14
Combined..............	+	7	6	13	4	6	10
	−	11	4	15	6	12	18
Total...............		18	10	28	10	18	28

The data suggest that at the higher levels of experience a therapist whose training had included personal analysis was better able to empathize with the patient regardless of his (the therapist's) conscious attitude, or perhaps in spite of a conscious (negative) attitude. Contrariwise, a nonanalyzed therapist having a negative conscious attitude toward his patient was more likely to communicate this attitude to the patient. Furthermore, experienced, nonanalyzed therapists were more prone to profess a positive attitude even though their communications to the patient revealed a lack of empathy, while no experienced, analyzed therapists claimed a positive attitude that was not associated with empathy. In other words, personal analysis seemed to have little effect on the therapist's conscious attitude toward the patient—a majority in both groups admitted a negative reaction—but it had a differential effect upon the degree of empathy communicated to the patient.

5

COMPARISONS BETWEEN
PSYCHIATRISTS AND PSYCHOLOGISTS

This chapter presents comparisons between 55 psychiatrists and 55 psychologists, matched on the basis of length of experience in psychotherapy and personal analysis (Table 10). In addition, reference will be made to certain parallel analyses performed separately for psychiatrists and psychologists.*

TABLE 10

SUMMARY OF BIOGRAPHICAL VARIABLES FOR MATCHED SAMPLES OF PSYCHIATRISTS AND PSYCHOLOGISTS

	N	Length of Experience (years)		Personal Analysis (hours)		Age (years)	
		M	S.D.	M	S.D.	M	S.D.
Psychiatrists—Analyzed	32	4.5	3.5	322	228	34.4	6.2
Psychologists—Analyzed...	32	4.6	3.5	319	210	38.4	8.6
Psychiatrists—Nonanalyzed	23	2.3	2.4	—	—	32.5	5.4
Psychologists—Nonanalyzed	23	2.3	2.1	—	—	30.8	6.2
All Psychiatrists..........	55	3.7	3.3	(322)	(228)	33.7	6.0
All Psychologists..........	55	3.7	3.2	(319)	(210)	35.2	8.5

To facilitate comparisons between the results obtained for psychiatrists and psychologists, the order of presentation follows that of the preceding chapter.

Diagnosis, prognosis, clinical evaluations, and attitude toward patient

Diagnosis. Like psychiatrists, analytically oriented psychologists

---

* See footnote on p. 33 regarding auxiliary publication of complete response distributions.

chose a variety of diagnostic labels, "anxiety" being the preferred
diagnosis. The response distributions of the matched samples did
not differ significantly.

Defense mechanisms. Psychologists mentioned almost the same
number of defense mechanisms as psychiatrists (an average of about
3). Chi square did not indicate statistically significant differences
between the two samples.

Formulation of dynamics. The kinds and quality of dynamic
formulations, as defined previously, did not differentiate the matched
samples. In fact, the distributions disclosed a marked degree of
similarity.

Other diagnostic evaluations. A number of diagnostic assessments
were obtained through precoded items. These included: Ego
Strength, Anxiety, Insight, Capability of Self-Observation and Self-
Appraisal as opposed to the Tendency for Rationalization, Emotional
Maturity, Social Adjustment, Disturbance. The evaluations of psychiatrists and psychologists appeared to be very similar. No chi
square value was significant to an acceptable level.

Prognosis. While respondents differed in their prognostic estimates, differences between psychiatrists and psychologists were statistically nonsignificant.

Attitude toward the patient. The matched samples were undifferentiated in terms of their attitudes toward the patient (self-ratings
on a five-point item); nor did psychiatrists differ from psychologists
regarding the reasons given for their professed conscious attitude.

Analysis of systematic differences. In order to investigate further
the possible reasons for differences in therapists' evaluations the full
psychiatrist sample ($N = 134$) was successively broken down according to a number of therapist variables. In order to determine the
extent to which these relationships were paralleled in the sample of
psychologists, it would have been desirable to conduct the analyses
on the matched samples. Unfortunately, the relatively small size of
these samples rendered this unfeasible. As a compromise, the *full*
sample of psychologists was used. In evaluating the results it must
be kept in mind that the psychiatrist sample was notably larger
(134 vs. 64), more experienced (mean of 6.8 years vs. 3.1 years),
and somewhat older (38.2 years vs. 35.6 years). In addition, the
range of experience, as indicated by the standard deviation, was twice
as great for psychiatrists as for psychologists. Despite these shortcomings it seemed appropriate to report the results for two rea-

sonably large groups of therapists participating in this investigation. The layout of Table 11 is directly comparable to the one presented earlier for the full psychiatrist sample.

TABLE 11

PRODUCT-MOMENT COEFFICIENTS OF CORRELATION BETWEEN
ATTITUDINAL AND BIOGRAPHICAL VARIABLES
Average N (psychologists) = 55

Variable	Prognosis with Therapy	Attitude toward Patient	Experience (in years)	Experience (self-estimate)	Competence as Therapist	Age
Ego Strength...........	.26*	.08	.31*	.23	−.09	.19
Anxiety...............	.24	.23	.23	.16	−.06	.10
Insight...............	.27*	.18	.24	.29*	−.22	.12
Self-Observation vs. Rationalization....	.29*	.28*	.15	.13	.07	−.02
Emotional Maturity.....	−.13	−.11	−.11	−.05	.00	−.19
Social Adjustment......	.17	−.06	.30*	.26*	−.01	.27*
Disturbance...........	−.31*	.10	−.21	−.33**	.18	−.27*
Prognosis without Therapy	−.18	−.16	.23	.35**	−.20	.23
Prognosis with Therapy..	—	.42**	.17	.19	−.08	.03
Attitude toward Patient..	—	—	.25*	.17	−.11	.08
Experience (in years) ...	—	—	—	.73**	−.57**	.66**
Experience (self-estimate)............	—	—	—	—	−.64**	.60**
Competence as Therapist (self-estimate)........	—	—	—	—	—	−.41**

* Significant at the .05 level.
** Significant at the .01 level.

The results for the full psychologist sample may be summarized as follows:

1. As in the psychiatrist sample, length of experience was significantly correlated with Ego Strength, and quality of dynamic formulation (chi square significant at the .01 level). In addition, however, experience correlated significantly with Social Adjustment and Attitude toward the Patient. If self-estimates of experience rather than number of years were taken as the reference variable, Insight, Disturbance and Prognosis without Therapy also disclosed significant correlations. Increasing experience tended to correlate with the more unfavorable estimates.

2. Therapists' age correlated significantly with estimates of the

patient's Social Adjustment and Disturbance, the direction of the
correlation being similar to that reported in the preceding
paragraph.

3. Breakdowns in terms of personal analysis and theoretical orientation were unfeasible for the psychologist sample as well.

4. Correlations between therapists' attitude and clinical evaluation appeared to be of a somewhat lower order than that reported
for psychiatrists. Statistical significance was obtained in the case of
Self-Observation vs. Rationalization and quality of the dynamic
formulation.

5. As in the case of psychiatrists, prognosis correlated significantly
with therapists' attitude ($r = .42$). Prognostic estimates were also
found to be significantly correlated with such clinical evaluations as
Insight, Self-Observation vs. Rationalization, and Disturbance.

While the correlations for psychologists did not disclose a one-to-
one relationship to those reported for psychiatrists, the pattern
must be judged rather similar if allowance is made for inevitable
sampling fluctuations and the sample differences already mentioned.

Therapeutic goals and approaches

The distributions of responses given by the matched samples of
psychiatrists and psychologists differed significantly in terms of
therapeutic goals ($p < .01$). Psychiatrists tended to specify more
modest goals, such as symptom relief, whereas a larger proportion
of psychologists stressed greater insight, greater self-acceptance, etc.
Virtually no member in either group envisaged an extensive reor-
ganization of the patient's personality.

Responses did not differ significantly on the following questionnaire items: Areas in which therapists expected the patient to
"move" and areas in which they expected him to remain relatively
unchanged; areas or problems which might prove most amenable to
therapy; areas in the patient's living which might receive primary
focus in treatment; attitudes or kinds of behavior which the therapist would encourage (or discourage) in therapy with this patient;
areas which should be avoided (early) in therapy.

Problems of therapeutic technique

Psychiatrists appeared to differ very little from psychologists on
a number of questions including: clues derived from the patient's
behavior during the interview; descriptions of the course of the
transference and its technical handling; anticipation of countertrans-

ference reactions and methods of dealing with them; difficulties and/or dangers which might arise in the course of therapy; approach to the patient's phobic symptoms; the desirability of making recommendations to the patient to change his present mode of living or his environment; therapist's activity or passivity.

The matched samples diverged significantly with regard to their expectations of acting out behavior and its therapeutic handling. A larger proportion of psychiatrists expected the patient to engage in this form of transference reaction ($p < .02$); they were also more likely to state that they would actively discourage its development by firmness, strictness, setting limits, etc. ($p < .05$).

Responses to a question dealing with the desirability of strictness or permissiveness very probably reflected the same line of thinking in that psychiatrists advocated strictness more than their psychologist colleagues ($p < .01$).

Similarly, psychiatrists tended to be more outspoken about discouraging free association with this patient, in contrast to a larger proportion of psychologists who explicity encouraged free association ($p < .05$).

Form of therapy, frequency of sessions, and length

Comparisons of the response distributions for the matched samples indicated that psychologists tended to advocate the more intensive forms of psychotherapy with this patient than psychiatrists ($p < .05$). There was no statistically significant difference regarding the frequency of weekly sessions, but the trend was for psychiatrists to prefer one weekly interview.

There was a slight tendency for psychiatrists to estimate the duration of psychotherapy to be shorter than psychologists ($p < .10$); more psychiatrists than psychologists estimated the length of treatment to be less than one year.

The distributions did not differ significantly regarding the time required to achieve symptom-relief.

A question relating to possible alternatives to the respondent's first choice of treatment elicited a somewhat larger proportion of recommendations for pharmacologic therapy (presumably tranquilizing drugs) from psychiatrists, but differences in the over-all distributions were nonsignificant. Comparable analyses, for the full psychologist sample, disclosed the following results:

1. A breakdown in terms of experience produced very few statistically significant differences, with one notable exception: experi-

enced therapists were *less* likely to recommend the more intensive forms of psychotherapy ($p < .05$).

2. Attitude toward the patient was significantly associated with strictness vs. permissiveness; anticipation of acting out; and discouragement of certain attitudes and behaviors. Stated otherwise, therapists expressing a negative attitude toward the patient tended to advocate strictness on the therapist's part ($p < .01$); were more likely to expect acting-out behavior ($p < .09$); and were more likely to discourage self-pity, self-deprecation, self-punishing behavior, refusal to accept responsibility, and projections of hostility ($p < .06$).

3. Therapists giving a negative prognosis were more likely to expect the patient to act out than therapists whose prognosis was favorable.

Therapists' communications (film responses)

Matched sample over-all comparisons. Therapists' communications to the patient (film responses) were quantified by the system of analysis described in Chapter 12. The distributions obtained under the various components (type of therapeutic activity, depth-directedness, dynamic focus, initiative, and therapeutic climate) were then compared by means of the nonparametric Mann-Whitney U test to determine the degree of divergence between the two matched samples. These results may be summarized as follows:

1. Psychiatrists differed from psychologists by asking a significantly larger number of exploratory questions ($p < .01$).

2. Psychologists in turn showed a relatively greater preference for the reflection-of-feeling technique usually associated with Rogers' client-centered theory ($p < .001$).

3. Psychologists tended to change the dynamic focus less than psychiatrists and were more likely to accept the patient's frame of reference ($p < .002$).

4. The two matched samples were not differentiated in terms of the relative frequency of "silent" responses, communications in which the therapist emerges as an expert or an authority, highly inferential communications, communications changing the dynamic focus to interpersonal events of the present or the past, communications showing a high level of initiative, and "warmth" or "coldness" of emotional tone.

Analysis of systematic differences

Level of experience. As in the preceding sections, the results obtained from breakdowns of the full psychiatrist sample were compared with corresponding analyses based on the full psychologist sample. For the psychiatrist sample, the following findings appeared to be attributable to length of experience in psychotherapy:

1. Inexperienced psychiatrists tended to ask more exploratory questions than experienced therapists.

2. Experienced psychiatrists tended to give a larger number of interpretive responses than inexperienced practitioners. Related analyses disclosed that these communications were more inferential, and that their dynamic focus concerned dynamic interpersonal events in the patient's past and present life.

3. Experienced therapists showed a higher degree of initiative in their communications than inexperienced practitioners.

4. Concomitant with the above findings, experienced therapists tended to change the dynamic focus of their communications more than the less experienced respondents.

5. Experienced therapists tended to be slightly "warmer."

Most differences between inexperienced and experienced psychologists were statistically nonsignificant. However, communications in which the therapist emerged as an expert or as an authority tended to increase with experience ($p < .05$), and "warm" responses showed increments in the same direction ($p < .05$).

Personal analysis. Psychiatrists whose training had included a personal analysis differed from nonanalyzed psychiatrists, with whom they were matched in terms of experience (N in each sample was 28), by giving a significantly larger number of silent responses at the expense of exploratory questions. This difference appeared to be more pronounced at the lower end of the experience continuum.

Two similarly matched samples of psychologists (N in each sample was 33) were statistically undifferentiated in terms of their film response distributions on all components of the system of analysis.

However, comparable analyses between psychiatrists and psychologists (see Table 10) disclosed that analyzed psychiatrists tended to exceed analyzed psychologists in "silent" responses ($p < .11$) and exploratory questions ($p < .09$). Psychologists, on the other hand, showed a consistent preference for reflections of feeling. A comparison between nonanalyzed psychiatrists and nonanalyzed psychologists corroborated the differences regarding explorations and reflections of feeling, but not regarding silence. This suggests that analyzed psychiatrists tended to be the relatively most "silent" of the samples, and that the other variations between psychiatrists and psychologists do not seem to be a function of the personal analysis variable.

Theoretical orientation. A comparison between two samples of psychiatrists whose respective theoretical orientations were orthodox Freudian and neo-Freudian failed to disclose any statistically reliable differences in their film responses. A similar comparison for psychologists proved unfeasible because of small N's for "pure" subgroups. (Certain differences between analytically oriented psychologists and those following the client-centered theory of Rogers are reported in Chapter 7.

Attitude toward the patient. A breakdown of the psychiatrist sample in terms of the therapist's expressed conscious attitude toward the patient revealed no notable differences in techniques per se, but disclosed that therapists indicating a negative attitude gave a significantly larger number of responses whose emotional tone was rated "cold"; "warm" responses did not suffer significantly.

Psychologists, in contrast, did not reveal statistically reliable differences in terms of therapeutic climate, but certain technique differences were observed:

1. Psychologists expressing a "neutral" attitude toward the patient asked a significantly larger number of exploratory questions ($p < .02$).

2. Concomitantly, those expressing a neutral attitude tended to accept the patient's focus least; on the other hand, psychologists professing a positive attitude were more likely to accept the patient's focus ($p < .02$).

Prognosis. The following statistically reliable differences were observed when the psychiatrist sample was broken down in terms of the respondents' prognostic estimates:

1. Psychiatrists expressing a noncommittal prognostic estimate tended to give the smallest number of silent responses.

2. Respondents giving a favorable prognosis were more likely to accept the patient's focus.

3. Therapists giving a noncommittal prognosis tended to show more initiative in their communications than the favorable or unfavorable groups.

4. Therapists whose prognosis was unfavorable gave more than four times as many "cold" responses than respondents who considered the prognosis favorable.

5. The relative frequency of "warm" responses was greatest among therapists whose prognosis was noncommittal and relatively low in both the favorable and unfavorable groups.

The analysis for psychologists was not directly comparable because the number of respondents giving a noncommittal prognosis was too small. Results based on a comparison between respondents giving a favorable and an unfavorable prognosis showed that the latter group exceeded the former in the relative frequency of exploratory questions ($p < .05$).

Empathy

The criteria for judging the degree of empathy communicated by the therapist have been described in the preceding chapter. It will be recalled that the judgment was a simple over-all rating of the therapist's response behavior at the 28 choice points in the film. If the respondent appeared to empathize with the patient, he was given an over-all rating of plus; if there was evidence of coldness, aloofness, rejection, etc., a rating of minus was assigned; if the record provided insufficient evidence to warrant either a score of plus or minus, a "neutral" rating (0) was given; if the record contained both plus and minus indicators, an "ambivalent" rating ($\pm$) resulted. Conceptually, there appeared to be an affinity between ratings of + and $\pm$, on the one hand, and between — and 0, on the other, so that for most subsequent analyses a plus-minus dichotomy was used.

Despite the crudeness of these measures it was possible to demonstrate fair rater agreement. Successive ratings by each of two raters showed a consistency ranging from 69 per cent to 85 per cent; interrater agreement ranged from 64 per cent to 72 per cent. These indices were similar for the psychiatrist and nonmedical therapist samples, which were judged separately. The results for the latter sample (including 15 psychiatric social workers) are presented in Table 12.

TABLE 12

AGREEMENT WITHIN AND BETWEEN TWO INDEPENDENT RATERS
ON OVER-ALL RATINGS OF EMPATHY

($N = 93$)

	Full Agreement*	Partial Agreement**	Disagreement
Rater 1: Rating 1 vs. Rating 2	72 (77%)	7 (8%)	14 (15%)
Rater 2: Rating 1 vs. Rating 2	60 (65%)	13 (14%)	20 (21%)
Rater 1 vs. Rater 2: Rating 1	47 (51%)	14 (15%)	32 (34%)
Rater 1 vs. Rater 2: Rating 2	40 (43%)	27 (29%)	26 (28%)

Note: N comprises 64 psychoanalytically oriented psychologists, 14 Rogerians, and 15 psychiatric social workers.
* Using four categories: +, —, 0, and $\pm$.
** Combining categories + and $\pm$, and 0 and —

In the psychiatrist sample, empathy ratings showed statistically significant associations with therapists' conscious attitude and prognosis, indicating that positive empathy tended to co-vary with positive attitude and favorable prognosis. For the nonmedical therapist sample, comparable analyses revealed a similar trend, but chi square was not significant at an acceptable level ($.20\ p < .15$).

There was a slight tendency for experienced psychiatrists to have higher empathy ratings ($p = .13$); for nonmedical therapists, chi square was significant at the .09 level.

When the empathy ratings of psychiatrists whose training had included personal analysis were compared with nonanalyzed psychiatrists of comparable professional experience, the results were in favor of the analyzed group ($p < .07$). At the lower experience levels (less than three years), there appeared to be no difference between analyzed and nonanalyzed therapists in terms of empathy ratings; however, at the higher levels of experience, analyzed therapists obtained a larger proportion of positive empathy ratings. For a similarly matched sample of nonmedical therapists ($N = 33$ in each group, including 29 psychologists and 4 psychiatric social workers), the over-all results statistically nonsignificant, but at the higher levels of experience the above mentioned trend appeared to be in evidence (Table 13).

TABLE 13

DISTRIBUTIONS OF EMPATHY RATINGS AND SELF-RATINGS OF ATTITUDE IN TWO GROUPS OF PSYCHOLOGISTS MATCHED IN TERMS OF PERSONAL ANALYSIS

Experience in Therapy	Attitude toward Patient	Personal Analysis Empathy Rating			No Personal Analysis Empathy Rating		
		+	−	Total	+	−	Total
0–2 years..................	+	2	5	7	5	5	10
	−	2	7	9	3	3	6
Total....................		4	12	16	8	8	16
2.5–12 years...............	+	6	3	9	3	3	6
	−	4	4	8	3	8	11
Total....................		10	7	17	6	11	17
Combined.................	+	8	8	16	8	8	16
	−	6	11	17	6	11	17
Total....................		14	19	33	14	19	33

A further breakdown in terms of the therapist's conscious attitude toward the patient showed that in the experienced, analyzed group of psychiatrists, a negative attitude appeared to be associated more often with a positive empathy rating, whereas in the nonanalyzed, experienced group there seemed to be greater congruence between negative attitude and lack of empathy. No corroboration for this finding was found in the nonmedical therapist sample.

It is apparent that the results pertaining to the relationships between empathy ratings, personal analysis, and conscious attitude must be viewed with considerable caution, first, because of the very small size of the subsamples, and, second, because the error of measurement in each variable is undoubtedly compounded when these variables are considered jointly.

With respect to interprofessional differences, the most important single observation suggested by the data is their relative absence, that is, in many of their clinical evaluations, including diagnosis, prognosis, and numerous other judgments, psychiatrists as a group appeared to be highly similar to psychologists as a group, when level of professional training and experience were held relatively constant. It should be stressed that within each group of therapists there was considerable variation, which has been discussed in greater detail in the earlier chapter devoted to the data obtained from psychiatrists. In this connection, it is important to reiterate that therapists generally diverged considerably in their perceptions of the patient's problem, diagnosis, prognosis, etiology, severity, and so on. However, psychiatrists appeared to be as divided in their opinions as psychologists, nor did greater experience as a therapist seem to produce greater agreement. It may be noted that psychoanalysts, the most highly experienced group of therapists represented in this study, were no exception in this regard.

As a group, psychologists differed from psychiatrists by advocating somewhat more ambitious therapeutic goals and more intensive (insight-producing) therapy, whose duration was judged longer. Psychiatrists, on the other hand, were more likely to expect the patient to engage in acting-out behavior, a development they hoped to discourage by strictness and by imposing controls upon free association.

It is difficult to offer an explanation for these differences, but it is possible that they reflect differences in the background training of

psychiatrists and psychologists. Psychiatrists, by this evidence, appear
to be more in the medical tradition of taking charge or instituting a
regimen, as opposed to the psychologists who appear to advocate
more prominently an attitude of passive expectancy, of letting the
patient work out his own problem. While speculative, this explanation fits in with the psychologists' preference for the reflection-of-
feeling technique (see below).

Attempts to account for differences in therapists' perceptions and
evaluations led to the systematic exploration of a number of therapist
variables. These analyses, performed separately for psychiatrists and
psychologists, disclosed that with increasing experience in psychotherapy, respondents in both groups produced characterizations of
the patient's emotional dynamics which were more complex, more
specific, and apparently more knowledgeable. This finding is hardly
surprising if one considers that this formulation made considerably
greater demands on the respondents than many of the simple judgments (e.g., level of anxiety, degree of disturbance, etc.) on which
even an inexperienced therapist could offer a more or less informed
guess. It seems more important that both experienced psychiatrists
and psychologists tended to judge the patient's ego strength to be
less and the prognosis without therapy to be more unfavorable.
Psychologists provided further substantiation for the impression that
increments in experience seemed to lead to more unfavorable
clinical evaluations, including a more negative attitude toward the
patient. It remains an open question whether this reflected the
experienced therapist's greater realism or his disillusionment.

On the whole, the relationships between experience and clinical
evaluations appeared to be more tenuous, however, than those between clinical evaluations and the therapist's attitude toward the
patient, expressed in a self-rating. Among psychiatrists, as well as
among psychologists, a negative attitude toward the patient was
significantly associated with an unfavorable prognosis and vice versa
(r's in the neighborhood of .40). While the results for psychiatrists
and psychologists, respectively, were not entirely congruent, there
was little doubt that the therapist's clinical judgments were influenced by his prognosis and/or his attitude toward the patient. In
both samples, too, a negative attitude was significantly associated with
a recommendation for greater strictness on the therapist's part.

Furthermore, psychiatrists admitting to a negative reaction toward
the patient and giving an unfavorable prognosis tended to be

"colder" in the communications. No support for this result was found for the psychologist sample. However, in both groups a positive attitude toward the patient and a favorable prognosis seemed to lead to greater acceptance of the patient's focus and fewer exploratory questions. Contrariwise, a relative preference for exploratory operations and changes in dynamic focus may refer, at least within this context, to the therapist's concern with strictness and control, which were shown to be correlates of a negative attitude and unfavorable prognosis.

The attempt to assess the degree of empathy communicated by the therapist led to the tentative conclusion that a negative attitude toward the patient did not necessarily result in an absence of empathy. Rather, experience combined with personal analysis appeared to facilitate the therapist's empathy irrespective of his conscious attitude.

The implications of these results will be considered in the following chapter. For the present, it suffices to mention that the results presented for psychologists generally corroborated those reported for psychiatrists; the clinical evaluations of both groups of therapists, treatment plans, techniques, etc., appeared to be influenced by emotional reactions to the patient. Therapists were frequently aware of their own feelings of anger, irritation, and impatience, which they considered a response to the patient's hostility, demandingness, and dependency. They seemed to be less aware of the possibility that their own emotional reaction might color their clinical evaluations, diagnoses, and prognostic estimates.*

With regard to therapists' communications, psychologists showed a relative preference for the reflection of feeling technique which has become most prominently associated with the client-centered approach of Rogers. (Psychiatrists tended to prefer exploratory questions.) Since Rogers' influence is more pervasive in psychological than in psychiatric circles, this result may reflect the unacknowledged influence of his doctrine.

Experienced psychiatrists tended to have a larger number of interpretive comments and displayed greater initiative than inexperienced practitioners within the profession. They also tended to be "warmer." The communications of experienced psychologists did

---

* It is possible that in some instances hostility felt by the respondents toward the experimental procedure and/or the experimenter colored their evaluations and judgments. It is doubtful, however, that this represents a major influence.

not differ significantly from those of their less experienced colleagues (although weak trends followed the pattern reported for psychiatrists) except in terms of "warmth."

Analyzed psychiatrists tended to use silence more freely than either nonanalyzed psychiatrists or psychologists irrespective of whether they had been analyzed. These results may reflect certain basic differences in the training of psychiatrists and psychologists for psychotherapy. It is likely that the variable "years of experience in psychotherapy" is not equivalent for the two professional groups. At the lower extreme of the experience continuum, psychologists in view of their more extensive training in psychology probably are a more sophisticated group than first-year residents in psychiatry. On the other hand, a psychiatrist having five or more years of experience in psychotherapy on a full-time basis is usually more experienced than a psychologist whose duties often include many other facets besides psychotherapy. It is, of course, a matter of speculation whether the significant differences reported for psychiatrists are in fact attributable to the greater discrepancy between experienced and inexperienced therapists. The passive-expectancy hypothesis, already mentioned, may provide an alternate explanation.

6

IMPLICATIONS

The findings appear to have numerous implications for psychotherapy; however, the importance one attaches to them is, of course, contingent upon the extent to which one can generalize from an experimental situation to the "naturally occurring" events in the interview process. It is not contended that the behavior of the psychotherapist in an initial interview with a "real" patient bears a one-to-one relationship to his performance in the experiment—an objection sometimes raised by respondents. What is asserted is that the evaluative processes, as they were studied under experimental conditions, are sufficiently similar to the "normal" behavior of the therapist to generate fruitful hypotheses about his behavior in a first interview. Such hypotheses may raise a variety of new questions for research and lead to additional observations in the therapeutic situation.

On the basis of the results which have been reported, two broadly defined groups of therapists appear to emerge whose attitudes and approach may be characterized schematically in this manner:

Group I	Group II
Therapist's Attitude toward Patient	
Somewhat Positive	Somewhat Negative
"Reason"	
"He is suffering and needs help."	"Unpleasant personality characteristics," poor risk, poor motivation for therapy

Group I	Group II
Diagnosis: (Preferred)	
Hysteria (anxiety hysteria)	Paranoid, character disorder, psychopath, anxiety
Clinical Evaluation:	
A great deal of anxiety	Slightly less anxiety
Relatively more insight	Relatively less insight
Relatively more capable of self-observation vs. rationalization	Relatively less capable of self-observation vs. rationalization
More mature emotionally	Less mature emotionally
Fairly inadequate social adjustment	Very inadequate social adjustment
Prognosis with Therapy:	
Favorable	Unfavorable
Treatment Plans:	
	Avoid dealing with sexual impulse, hostility, anger, death wishes, unconscious material.
Danger in "pushing" patient too fast. Therapist must be sympathetic, understanding.	Danger of therapist's irritation, anger, impatience, other countertransference reactions.
Handle countertransference by being aware of it or handle in therapy.	Handle countertransference by discontinuing therapy or not accepting patient at all.
Would not make recommendations to the patient about his mode of living. This is not the problem in therapy.	Might make recommendations to the patient to change his present mode of living or his environment.
Would tend to be permissive with patient.	Would tend to be strict with patient.
Would tend to be passive in therapy.	Would tend to be active in therapy.
Would encourage free association.	Would discourage free association.
Recommend intensive (insight) therapy.	Recommend supportive therapy, group therapy, drugs, other adjuncts.
3 or more weekly interviews.	1 or 2 weekly interviews.
Symptom-relief expected in 1 year or less.	Evasive about length of time needed to accomplish symptom-relief.
Would attempt relatively greater changes in patient's character structure.	Would attempt relatively little change in patient's character structure.
Therapist's experience:	
Relatively low	Relatively high
"Communications"	
Emotional tone relatively "warm"	Emotional tone relatively "cold"
Empathy rating positive	Empathy rating negative

The above relationships are by no means invariant; we are dealing with *statistical trends,* and there were many subgroups of therapists who did not follow the pattern. However, the conclusion is suggested that clinical impressions and therapeutic planning are influenced by attitudinal variables within the therapist. Group I therapists appear to be more tolerant, more humane, more permissive, more "democratic," and more "therapeutic." Group II therapists emerge as more directive, disciplinarian, moralistic, and harsh. This contrast suggests the hypothesis that Group I therapists are "warmer" in their communications to the patient and that "cold," rejecting comments will be less frequent.

What is meant by this distinction? On the one hand, it is a basic attitude of understanding, respect, and compassion—what Albert Schweitzer calls "reverence for life." It is the ability to listen without preconception, prejudgment, or condemnation. It is the ability to pierce the neurotic distortions, the socially unacceptable attitudes and acts, the more unsavory aspects of the personality, and to see behind it a confused, bewildered, and helpless individual trying to shape his destiny, hampered and hindered by his neurotic conflicts and maladaptations. On the other hand, it is an attitude of coldness, calculation, "clinical evaluation," distance, "objectivity," aloofness, moral judgment, and condemnation. It is a readiness to take the neurotic defenses and the patient's character structure at face value and to react to them with irritation, impatience, annoyance, and anger. It is also an attitude of forming a moral judgment about the patient's illness from the beginning of the interview.

On another level, we seem to be dealing with groups of therapists whose philosophical orientation differs about determinism and free will. The prevalent view of emotional disturbances in contemporary Western culture—certainly since the time of Freud—lays heavy emphasis upon man's impotence in coming to terms with unconscious forces by which he is lived, and for whose existence and influence he bears no greater personal responsibility than for the rising of the sun. On the other hand, the data reveal another group of therapists who seem to be more deeply imbued with the traditional, moralistic position which identifies neurotic conflicts and resulting attitudes and actions with a "weakness of character," lack of moral fiber, laziness, and laxity. Accordingly, the way to "improve" is by an act of will, not through self-understanding and insight. It is astonishing to encounter the moralistic view with such frequency among professional therapists, unless one is willing to assume that this particular patient's seeming unreasonableness, demandingness, and hostility led to a momentary abandonment of the "therapeutic" position.

Thus we see that some therapists are willing and even eager to help the patient through long-term intensive psychotherapy, realizing that the acceptance of a patient for therapy constitutes an important decision to invest significant amounts of one's time, energy, and emotional resources, whereas others disclosed a marked distaste for this possibility. It seemed that occasionally this "avoidance" reaction was couched in such phraseology as: the patient is not going to get better anyway; certainly he will not get worse without treatment; he is a chronic complainer; he is generally "no good"; his motivation for therapy is poor. There were very few practitioners who explicitly recognized personal limitations in treating such a patient, suggesting that they would prefer to send him to a colleague. As one might suspect, such a recommendation would come from experienced therapists who had treated a wide variety of patients.

It must also be recognized that oftentimes the more favorable estimates of prognosis and recommendations for long-term intensive psychotherapy came from rather inexperienced therapists. As a matter of fact, there was a tendency for older and more experienced therapists to have more negative attitudes toward the patient and to be less sanguine about the course of therapy. Several writers have called attention to the observation that analysts sometimes seem to achieve their greatest successes when they are beginners, and that increasing experience (which may be assumed to be correlated with greater theoretical sophistication) seems to lead neither to a greater rate of therapeutic success nor to a more precise understanding of how success is achieved. Whether this result is attributable to a youthful enthusiasm on the part of beginning therapists which they succeed in communicating to their patients or whether more experienced therapists are "realistically" more cautious in their statements, we are left with the question about the therapeutic value of the therapist's attitude irrespective of the technical operations of psychotherapy to which therapeutic progress is usually ascribed. Frank (1958) has recently called renewed attention to the potential effects of "nonspecific" factors in psychotherapy which it shares with faith healing and other forms of religious experience.

To some extent at least, therapists who participated in this investigation were aware of their positive or negative reactions to the patient and their willingness or unwillingness to enter into a therapeutic relationship with him. Undoubetdly, they were less aware of the manner in which their attitudes interacted with (and perhaps influenced) their clinical evaluations. In the light of this evidence, we must consider the possibility that the therapist's attitudes, as conveyed by his communications to the patient, tend to bring about a realization of the therapist's expectations. For psychotherapy, the crux of the matter is not the perceptions and clinical evaluations or even the therapist's conscious attitude toward the patient; it is the manner in which these variables influence and help to structure the therapeutic relationship. Does a "positive" attitude on the part of the therapist in and of itself provide a powerful impetus to the patient's striving for self-help, self-realization, and constructive moves? Contrariwise, does a "negative" attitude lead to corresponding self-evaluations in the patient? This formulation is undoubtedly too simple to explain therapeutic success or failure, but the progress of therapy may well be facilitated or impeded depending upon the therapist's feelings about the "case."

The danger of countertransference reactions was recognized early by Freud and a considerable body of literature has been devoted to this problem. However, most of these writings have dealt with more specific, intercurrent events in therapy which cause a more or less temporary disruption of the therapeutic process. Much less attention has been paid to *global* negative reactions on the part of the therapist, which are more germane to this discussion. Similarly, the psychoanalytic literature reveals a paucity of publications dealing with constructive influences resulting from *positive* attitudes on the part of the therapist. Here, I do not mean positive attitudes per se, but positive attitudes in the context of the therapist's total personality whose maturity, strength, and integrity may provide a new model of reality to the patient.* If this is so, then *per contra* a persistent "avoidance reaction" on the part of the therapist is bound to have deleterious effects on the course of therapy, if indeed it does not lead to premature termination. One may wonder to what extent the explanation of "negative therapeutic reaction" or "poor motivation for therapy" often pinned on a patient who leaves therapy after a few interviews may be a function of the therapist's unwillingness or inability to create a more benevolent therapeutic atmosphere, so that therapeutic failure is not so much due to limitations in the patient as it is a function of limitations in the therapist.

On this basis, the therapist's contribution to the treatment process may be conceived as a dual one: it is personal and technical. His

* This problem will be considered in Chapter 15.

personal attributes (maturity, warmth, acceptance) enable him to create the kind of interpersonal relationship in which constructive personality change can take place; his knowledge of psychodynamic principles and techniques permits him, in and through this relationship, to initiate the kinds of emotional unlearning and learning experiences that are considered necessary to the alleviation or resolution of neurotic conflicts. The latter would be impossible without the former; the former, by itself, would never be sufficient. To recast this, in the form of a hypothesis:

A. Psychotherapy is maximally effective when the therapist is able (a) to relate to the patient in a warm, empathic manner, so that the person of the therapist, as revealed in this relationship, will in time serve as a new, more mature, and more desirable model of reality than past interpersonal relationships which have distorted the patient's perceptions of himself and others; and (b) by appropriate technical devices (interpretations, etc.) to demonstrate clearly and effectively the self-defeating character of the patient's previous patterns of interpersonal behavior.

B. Psychotherapy is less effective when only the first condition is met.

C. Psychotherapy is least effective when the first condition is lacking, irrespective of the status of the second condition.

If it is granted that the therapist's personal attitudes toward a patient *may* influence and even warp his clinical judgments, what are the criteria for deciding that one kind of judgment is largely a projection of the therapist's inner needs and another kind is consonant with the clinical evidence? Consider the patient portrayed in the film interview. Were those therapists "realistic" who judged him to be severely disturbed but were hopeful about the prognosis? Were those who regarded him as equally disturbed but who were pessimistic about the prognosis swayed by their emotional reactions? The diagnosis assigned to the patient undoubtedly bore a relationship to prognostic estimates, but the choice of a diagnostic label in itself may have been prompted or influenced by the therapist's attitude. Was a diagnosis of character disorder or psychopath more "correct" than hysteria or obsessive-compulsive neurosis? It may be objected that all therapists were forced to base their judgments on very limited clinical evidence, but would more complete information about the patient's background, previous and current difficulties in living, etc., have resulted in greater agreement?

The evidence thus highlights the unsatisfactory state of contemporary nosologic classifications as well as the momentous difficulties of arriving at a meaningful diagnosis. For example, a patient may be diagnosed in terms of specific symptoms which he manifests. Such a diagnosis may or may not give clues to the dynamics or the etiology of the disturbance. Usually, the problem is complicated because, like everyone, the patient uses a variety of psychic mechanisms, and a diagnosis based on symptoms may be grossly misleading. A primary problem is that we are faced with exaggerations, inhibitions, and distortions of mental processes which are common to everyone so that frequently it becomes a matter of predilection which facets of the personality are singled out. Classifications based on "symptoms" are generally regarded as unsatisfactory but continue to be used. As Szasz (1957) points out, the problem of psychiatric nosology and diagnosis is still in a state of confusion, one of the major reasons being that we do not specify whom we study, where, and with what methods. Furthermore, assumptions about "disease entities" (following the medical model) still pervade psychiatric thinking, although few therapists take them seriously. Thus, we see respondents focus on symptoms (anxiety), personality "types" (schizoid), judgments in terms of nonconformance to cultural norms (psychopathic personality), and "disease entities" (hysteria).*

In the context of this investigation, what consequences might be expected to ensue from a diagnosis of "anxiety" as opposed to "hysteria" or "paranoid"? For one thing, it was shown that prognostic and other clinical estimates tended to co-vary with diagnosis. Similarly, treatment plans and therapeutic techniques differed. In view of the fact that the interrelationships were paralleled by the therapist's attitude toward the patient, the question arose—but could not be answered conclusively—to what extent the therapist's attitude toward the patient shaped his clinical evaluations, plans, and predictions. In other words, the therapist's emotional reaction might partly dictate the diagnostic label as well as the proposed treatment plans and therapeutic techniques. Since it was also found that therapists who professed a negative attitude toward the patient and/or gave an unfavorable prognostic estimate tended to exhibit a lack of empathy in their communications, a more serious eventuality must be envisaged, namely, that the character of the therapist's communications might secondarily conduce to the very conditions he predicted. For instance, if the therapist's attitude subtly conveys a sense of hopelessness or futility to the patient, a reciprocal attitude

---

* Admittedly, the wording of the question asking the respondent to specify the "dominant personality type" followed by a number of choices, which was taken over—uncritically, as it turned out—from another study (Raines & Rohrer, 1955), evidently served to perpetuate and compound the confusion.

on the part of the patient might be less a function of the alleged "severity" of his disorder than a specific response to a particular therapist. The latter may remain unaware of the self-realizing character of his expectations, and in fact regard the patient's performance as confirmation for his prediction.

This possibility may be greater for inexperienced therapists than, say, for a seasoned analyst. However, there was as much disagreement among analysts with respect to diagnosis and clinical evaluations of the patient in the film as there was among less experienced therapists. Therapists, for whatever reasons, focused on different aspects of the patient's behavior and drew divergent, sometimes diametrically opposed, inferences. Certainly, their differential attention to symptoms, defense mechanisms, social behavior, etc., partly accounts for the variety of diagnostic formulations. But the differential focus also reflects the therapist's interests, preoccupations, and areas of sensitization. Thus, the therapist is faced not only with the difficulty of abstracting from the welter of behavioral and attitudinal phenomena a diagnostic formulation which makes precise assertions about etiology, "disease entities," or proposed treatment; he must also consider and adjust for the subjective elements within himself which may suffuse his observations, evaluations, judgments, and therapeutic operations. All sciences strive to expand "objective" knowledge and to reduce subjective factors. Here it seems reasonable to postulate: the less precision there is in our conceptions about psychopathology, nosology, and therapy, the greater will be the influence of personal, subjective factors; conversely, an increase in knowledge will inevitably lead to their diminution.

The question, "What was the patient's 'real' diagnosis?" raises the problem of whose judgment is to be taken as the ultimate criterion. A group of clinicians having access to more complete clinical data than the respondents in this study might pool their judgments, or psychologists might contribute independent evaluations based on psychological tests; however, in the final analysis it is always the clinical judgment of some person or persons to which we must have recourse. This would be true even if we were willing to suspend judgment for the moment and have the patient undergo intensive psychoanalytic treatment, which, it might be expected, would illuminate the dynamics of his personality more thoroughly than any other method. If, after the end of several years of analytic therapy, we approached the analyst and asked for an evaluation, he, too, would from the very start have been influenced by the theoretical assumptions and preconceptions which he brought to bear on the situation and subsequent therapeutic operations might have served to corroborate his initial judgments. It has long been known that patients produce dreams that "fit" the analyst's theoretical framework, and they may equally focus on those aspects of their life experience in which they sense the analyst is particularly interested. It is partly for these reasons that orthodox Freudians, Adlerians, Jungians, and others each discover evidence which seems to corroborate their theoretical preconceptions.

It is widely recognized today that every scientist to a greater or lesser degree influences by his very presence the phenomena under investigation. In psychotherapy, this problem is particularly serious because many times during each therapeutic hour the therapist goes through the process of superimposing his own theoretical framework upon the clinical data (the patient's productions and behavior) and communicates to the patient in terms of this framework. Since the conception of the analyst as a mirror which merely reflects the patient's thoughts, ideas, wishes, and feelings represents at best an unrealizable ideal, we must consider the possibility that the person of the therapist exerts an influence—and perhaps a very considerable one—at every point in treatment. The important question is whether he recognizes this influence, its extent and character, and succeeds in adjusting for it. It seems safe to say that very few, if any, therapists ever fully succeed. This influence may be less in the case of Freud's "primary model" technique than in other forms of psychotherapy, but it would be greatly misleading to conclude that the former technique completely or even largely excludes it. One of the important functions of research in this area consists in identifying the nature of the therapist's influence and making it available to his awareness and potential control, if indeed it cannot be eliminated.

How to control subjective biases is a difficult question which may not be answered for some time. Maximal self-awareness on the part of the therapist through personal analysis and intensive supervision have traditionally been advocated and undoubtedly will go a long way, but it may not be sufficient. Perhaps more specific adjuncts must be developed. I am thinking of such teaching devices as clinical demonstrations (by means of sound film or electronic recordings) of specific consequences of the therapist's attitudes and actions upon the patient's behavior and performance in therapy. In some measure, perhaps, the data of this investigation may serve to alert the therapist to a few potentially serious pitfalls associated with subjective factors and forestall incipient, narcissistic beliefs in true "objectivity" or the infallibility of clinical judgments.

7

THE PERFORMANCE
OF CLIENT-CENTERED
THERAPISTS

The therapist's theoretical orientation has long been considered a key to the understanding of his therapeutic formulations and techniques. The followers of Freud who subsequently evolved their own schools of thought differed with the originator of psychoanalysis on questions of theory as well as practice, although the most heated battles have been fought over theoretical issues (e.g., the libido theory, the death instinct, etc.). Numerous differences are still unresolved today, and competing schools continue to diverge in their approaches to theory and therapeutic practice. From the operationist point of view, it is fruitful to inquire about the empirical counterparts of theoretical differences; if operational differences between competing theoretical viewpoints cannot be specified, their supposed uniqueness becomes suspect. So far, it has proved exceedingly difficult to subject competing therapeutic theories to a thorough empirical analysis, the major obstacle being the lack of comparability between therapist-patient pairs and the absence of adequate methods of analysis. In the present investigation, comparisons between therapists adhering to variants of the psychoanalytic viewpoint were inconclusive, which, as has been pointed out, is no demonstration that theoretical differences fail to influence therapeutic operations; it may merely prove that the method was not sufficiently sensitive to capture such differences. However, there was one notable exception to these findings. This exception concerned the performance of therapists who adhered to the theory of client-centered therapy advanced by Carl Rogers (1951, 1957). Since these respondents differed in numerous important respects from therapists subscribing to the psychoanalytic point of view, it is considered appropriate to discuss their performance in some detail. To lend greater comparability to the statistical analysis, Rogerian therapists (all of whom were psychologists) will be compared with psychologists following the psychoanalytic orientation broadly defined. The comparisons are based on data from 64 psychologists following the psychoanalytic orientation and 14 psychologists who described their orientation as unqualifiedly Rogerian (8 were affiliated with the Counseling Center of the University of Chicago).

Summary statistics on age, experience, and personal analysis are presented in Table 14. The following data shed some further light on the composition of the samples:

Two-thirds of the psychoanalytically oriented psychologists (Sample A) held the Ph.D. degree, as compared with 36 per cent of the psychologists who followed Rogers' theory (Sample R).

Sixty per cent of the members in both groups said they had a fair amount or a great deal of experience in therapy, and considered themselves competent therapists. All members of Sample R said they practiced client-centered therapy exclusively. Sample A showed a wider distribution, but most replies fell within the broad category of psychoanalytically oriented psychotherapy. Most Rogerians indicated that they had received very little training in psychoanalytic principles and techniques; 69 per cent of Sample A claimed "a fair amount" or "a great deal."

TABLE 14

SUMMARY STATISTICS OF AGE, EXPERIENCE, PERSONAL ANALYSIS

	N†	Sample A* Mean	S.D.	N†	Sample R ** Mean	S.D.
Age................	65	35.6 years	8.7	13	33.4 years	6.4
Experience in therapy.	62	3.3 years	3.1	12	3.0 years	2.4
Personal analysis	33	291 hours	198	9	142 hours	101

* Psychoanalytically oriented psychologists.

** Rogerian psychologists.

† Fluctuations reflect absence of complete information and/or not having had personal analysis.

Sixty-four per cent of Sample R had received their personal analysis within the client-centered framework. The responses of members of Sample A who indicated that they either had completed

See footnote on p. 33 regarding auxiliary publication of complete response distributions.

or were in the process of undergoing personal analysis (more than half the group) suggested that their analyses were based upon psychoanalytic theory.

Approximately one-half of the members in both groups stated that they devoted more than 25 per cent of their time to the practice of psychotherapy. Almost two-thirds of Sample R specified their therapy as being primarily with neurotic patients. Thirty-eight per cent of Sample A responded similarly, but another third said that their patients represented a wider range of personality disorders.

Sample A appeared to treat their "average patient" for longer periods than Sample R: 38 per cent of the former group described the length of therapy as exceeding one year, as contrasted with 14 per cent in the latter. On the other hand, Rogerians predominantly saw the "average patient" twice a week, whereas the model frequency for Sample A was closer to one weekly session.

RESULTS

The data were quantified in the manner previously described. In view of the small size of Sample R, response categories within an item had to be combined. Typically this resulted in 2 x 2 tables which were tested by means of chi square, corrected for continuity (see Table 15; chi squares were based on the frequencies).

TABLE 15

RESPONSE DISTRIBUTIONS OF PSYCHOANALYTIC AND CLIENT-CENTERED THERAPISTS

Questionnaire Item	Sample A $N = 64$ %	Sample R $N = 14$ %	Chi square* p
Diagnosis: Anxiety	39	57	
All others	61	43	—
Defenses: Rationalization, projection, conversion	53	68	
All others	47	32	—
How would you formulate the dynamics of his difficulties on the basis of what you have observed during the first interview?			
Low quality formulation	70	89	
High quality formulation	30	11	—
How much ego strength does this patient seem to have?			
A fair amount	44	64	
Relatively little, very little	56	36	—
How much anxiety does this patient seem to have?			
A great deal	65	85	
All others	35	15	—

TABLE 15 Continued.

Questionnaire Item	Sample A $N = 64$ %	Sample R $N = 14$ %	Chi square* p
How much insight does this patient seem to have into his problems?			
A fair amount, relatively little...............	67	92	
Very little.................................	33	8	——
How would you characterize the patient's social adjustment?			
Fairly inadequate..........................	40	60	
Very inadequate...........................	60	40	——
Considering the entire range of mental disorder, how would you characterize the degree of disturbance in this patient?			
Seriously disturbed........................	53	33	
Moderate and all others...................	47	67	——
Assuming your recommendations for treatment were followed, how would you rate the prognosis for this patient?			
Favorable.................................	60	100	
Unfavorable...............................	40	0	.05
How would you characterize your personal reaction to this patient?			
Positive..................................	30	69	
Neutral, negative, ambivalent..............	70	31	.02
If you were to accept this patient for treatment, what therapeutic goal(s) would you set up? If you wish, you may distinguish between intermediate and ultimate goals.			
No goals or blank.........................	5	64	
All others................................	95	36	.001
Considering your proposed treatment goals, how many hours of treatment and/or what period of time would you estimate it would require to achieve your objectives? You may again wish to distinguish between intermediate and ultimate goals.			
Less than 2 years..........................	53	87	
More than 2 years.........................	47	13	——
Suppose the patient is primarily interested in symptom-relief. How many hours of treatment and/or what period of time would you estimate it would require to achieve this objective?			
Less than 6 months........................	53	86	
More than 6 months.......................	47	14	——
From what you have seen in the film, what kinds of difficulties would you expect to encounter if you were to undertake psychotherapy with this patient?			

Table 15 Continued.

Questionnaire Item	Sample A $N = 64$ %	Sample R $N = 14$ %	Chi square* p
Parasitic attitudes, poor motivation for therapy, acting out, psychosis	49	8	
Resistance, manipulation of therapist, others....	51	92	.02
Are there any particular dangers you would feel you have to guard against, or any special cautions you would feel you have to observe in dealing with this patient?			
None or blank	38	85	
All others	62	15	.01
Do you anticipate any countertransference problem with this patient? If so, which ones? How would you handle them?			
No	21	55	
Yes	79	45	.07
Be aware of problems	42	20	
All others	58	80	——
Are there any areas in the patient's living that you feel should *not* be dealt with therapeutically—at least early in therapy?			
None or blank	32	100	
All others	68	0	.001
Which areas, if any, in the patient's living would you focus on primarily?			
None or blank	8	62	
All others	92	38	.001
Are there any attitudes or kinds of behavior you would *en*courage in this patient if you were dealing with him psychotherapeutically? If so, which ones?			
Blank, none, or feelings	54	88	
All others	46	12	.02
Are there any attitudes or kinds of behavior you would *dis*courage in this patient if you were dealing with him psychotherapeutically? If so, which ones?			
Blank or none	19	71	
All others	81	29	.001
Would you tend to be strict or permissive with this patient?			
Strict (with or without qualifications)	37	0	
All others	63	100	.02
Assuming that the patient's behavior during the first hour is rather typical of him, would you tend to be more active (i.e., intervene frequently) or more passive (i.e., intervene infrequently) in subsequent interviews?			
Active	52	38	
All others	48	62	——

TABLE 15   Continued.

Questionnaire Item	Sample A $N = 64$ %	Sample R $N = 14$ %	Chi square* p
Would you encourage or discourage free association with this patient?			
Discourage...............................	30	0	
All others................................	70	100	.06
Were you impressed by any clues in the patient's verbal or nonverbal behavior which you may not wish to make use of now, but which you would keep in mind for possible later use in therapy? If so, which ones?			
None.....................................	0	27	
All others................................	100	73	.001
What form or course would you expect this patient's transference to take?			
Adjectival or role descriptions.................	60	91	
Interpersonal dynamics......................	40	9	——
Do you have any ideas how you would deal with it therapeutically?			
Corrective emotional experience or wouldn't handle as such.........................	9	82	
Discourage development, interpretation, or active re-education............................	91	18	.001
Do you feel that this patient might engage in much "acting out" behavior? If so, how would you deal with it?			
No.......................................	34	14	
Yes, or qualified...........................	66	86	——
Wouldn't handle or corrective emotional experience.....................................	12	78	
Other therapeutic measures..................	88	22	.001
Would you have conducted the interview in a similar or in a different manner?			
Similar or somewhat different................	72	31	
Very different.............................	28	69	.02
Regardless of whether the therapist conducted the interview in a manner similar to yours, how adequate a job did he do?			
Adequate or somewhat inadequate............	95	58	
Very inadequate...........................	5	42	.01
How would you characterize the therapist's activity (i.e., the amount of talking he did)?			
About right...............................	51	56	
Too passive...............................	49	44	——
How would you characterize the amount of support he gave to the patient?			
About right...............................	61	58	
Too little.................................	39	42	——

TABLE 15 (concluded)

Questionnaire Item	Sample A $N = 64$ %	Sample R $N = 14$ %	Chi square* p
Would you devote more or less time than is shown in the film to getting facts about the patient's life history in a first interview?			
Same or more time........................	84	25	
Less time................................	16	75.	.001
How would you characterize your personal reaction to the therapist in the film?			
Positive or neutral........................	76	23	
Negative................................	24	77	.001

Note: The response dichotomies reported for each questionnaire item represent a sharp condensation of the original multiple scoring. For this reason, N for each sample fluctuates from item to item; total N's range from 36 to 213, with typical values in the 70's.

* p values of .10 and above not reported.

Clinical evaluations and therapist attitudes

Responses to the question of diagnosis revealed no significant differences. It seems noteworthy, however, that no member of Sample R chose such labels as psychopath, schizoid, paranoid, or character disorder, which were used by appreciable minorities of Sample A, as well as by psychiatrists. Asked to state the patient's major defense mechanisms, Sample R named a relatively smaller number than Sample A (ratio of 1:3), but the distributions did not appear to differ significantly. Nor did the samples differ in terms of qualitative descriptions of the patient's emotional dynamics.

Evaluations of the degree of ego strength, anxiety, insight, social adjustment, and disturbance disclosed no statistically significant differences.

The members of Sample R judged the prognosis with therapy to be more favorable than the members of Sample A ($p = < .05$); no Rogerian therapist considered it unfavorable. By contrast, an unfavorable prognosis was given by 40 per cent of the therapists in Sample A, who were in closer agreement with the predictions made by psychiatrists.

A larger proportion of Rogerian therapists professed a positive attitude toward the patient than analytically oriented psychologists ($p = < .02$). Members of the University of Chicago Counseling Center unanimously described their attitude as positive. Those responding negatively often stated that their attitude was influenced by the patient's hostility, anger, and dependency; those responding positively stressed his personality assets or saw him as "a patient with a problem," a response often given with some empathy.

Plans, goals, and difficulties in therapy

Sample R showed greater reluctance to set up therapeutic goals than Sample A ($p = < .001$), but the two samples did not differ significantly as to estimated length of treatment or time needed to accomplish symptom-relief. It seems pertinent to note that psychoanalysts were less optimistic than either of the psychologist groups.

Concerning difficulties expected in treatment, Sample R therapists were significantly less likely to mention: the patient's parasitic attitudes, poor motivation for therapy, acting out, or the possibility of psychosis ($p = < .02$). Nor were countertransference or problems of technique mentioned with any degree of frequency by Sample R ($p = < .01$). One-half of Sample R anticipated countertransference problems with this patient, as compared with almost 80 per cent in Sample A; twice as many Rogerians answered the question in the negative ($p = .07$). No Rogerian mentioned areas in the patient's living which should be avoided at least early in therapy, whereas numerous areas were mentioned by Sample A therapists ($p = < .001$). Similarly, Rogerians were less likely to name areas in the patient's living which should be singled out for focus in therapy ($p = < .001$).

Rogerians either declined to specify attitudes or behaviors the therapist would encourage in therapy with this patient, or stressed the expression of feelings. Sample A therapists were more likely to emphasize a sense of responsibility, increased socialization, relating feelings and symptoms to interpersonal situations, etc. ($p = < .02$).

Conversely, Sample A therapists were more likely to discourage attitudes and behaviors, such as: intellectualization, obsessive ruminations, self-pity, self-deprecation, helplessness, refusal to accept responsibility, demanding attitudes, and acting out; Rogerians, by comparison, tended to say they would discourage nothing or leave it to the patient ($p = < .001$).

No member of the Rogerian group advocated strictness by the therapist, as contrasted with more than a third of the members of Sample A who considered strictness therapeutically desirable ($p = < .02$). A question about the therapist's activity or passivity did not differentiate the two groups, possibly because the terms of reference were not clearly defined. Free association was discouraged by an appreciable proportion of Sample A therapists, but not by Sample R ($p = < .06$).

A question was asked about clues in the patient's verbal or nonverbal behavior which might not be used immediately but kept in mind for possible later reference. All members of Sample A who answered the question (85 per cent) mentioned one or more clues. Four Rogerians specifically stated "none" ($p = < .001$). Rogerians commented about the patient's feelings and attitudes but, in contrast to Sample A, paid less attention to such clues as: gestures, bodily movements, manner of speaking, the patient's past or present interpersonal relations with his mother, wife, brother, or father—with or without inference about their dynamic significance.

Descriptions of the course of the transference did not diverge significantly, but members of the two samples disagreed about approaches to the problem ($p = < .001$). Rogerians predominantly encouraged or fostered a "corrective emotional experience" by conveying respect or by clarifying feelings. Members of Sample A, on the other hand, tended to advocate interpretation and other procedures, such as reassurance and firmness, in which the therapist uses his role to induce changes in attitudes and actions.

Responses to a question dealing with "acting out," an aspect of the transference problem, revealed a similar pattern: no statistically significant differences with respect to its occurence, but divergence in terms of "handling." Here, too, Rogerians recommended understanding, clarification, and reflection; analytically oriented therapists preferred an interpretive approach ($p = < .001$).

Evaluation of and attitude toward the film therapist

A number of questions were included to study similarities or differences between the film therapist's and the respondent's approaches to interviewing. It was hoped in this way possibly to obtain a clearer picture of the respondent's own procedure.

Sample R therapists were more definite in their assertion that they would have conducted the interview "in a very different manner" ($p = < .02$). They dissociated themselves from his approach and tended to evaluate his performance as "a very inadequate job"; the majority of therapists in Sample A considered his performance reasonably adequate ($p = < .01$).

Within each sample, there was notable disagreement as to whether the therapist had been too passive or had given insufficient support, but the intersample comparisons were nonsignificant.

Rogerians and psychoanalytically oriented therapists disagreed very markedly about the amount of time they would have devoted to obtaining data on the patient's life history; 75 per cent of Sample R stated that they would have spent somewhat less or considerably less time than the film therapist; almost one-half of Sample A said they would have devoted somewhat more or considerably more time ($p = < .001$). (The transcript shows that about 10 per cent of the therapist's interventions can be construed as case history questions in the usual sense. These questions were usually asked in the context of the patient's story and attempted to clarify a time, place, or interpersonal event. On the other hand, the therapist frequently repeated a word or phrase in a questioning tone of voice, apparently to obtain further data on a feeling or attitude.)

The two samples revealed a statistically highly significant difference in terms of their attitude toward the therapist. The majority of Rogerian therapists described their attitude as negative, whereas most analytically oriented therapists professed a positive or neutral attitude ($p = < .001$). The respondents' criticisms were directed at the film therapist's techniques as well as at his person. Prominently mentioned by both samples were the following objections: Therapist was not in control of the situation, engaged in too much activity but not of the "right" kind or not at the "right" time, too much interference with patient's talk, too much "accenting" (repeating last word), wrong emphasis, no plan. Rogerians criticized him especially for failing to focus on the patient's feelings and attitudes, and for a lack of empathy.

DISCUSSION

The results showed a number of pronounced differences in approach which highlighted discrepancies between therapists subscribing to psychoanalytic principles and the client-centered framework. Both positions are too well known to require exposition. It seems appropriate, however, to quote what Rogers (1956) considers to be the distinctive emphases of client-centered therapy:

> A second distinctive aspect [the first is the emphasis on research] is the deep confidence in the capacity of the individual, which client-centered therapists have found to be justified by their experience. Rather than seeing man as essentially a destructive animal [the reference is evidently to the death instinct postulated by Freud late in his career, one of the most disputed and least accepted tenets in contemporary analytic thinking], with the primary problem of the control of his impulses, we have found man to be essentially constructive, if he can be released from his defensiveness. Our experience is that, to the extent that he can fully accept his experience and himself, he becomes satisfactorily self-controlled. Our view of the basic nature of man differs sharply from those of most therapeutic orientations, which believe that guidance and control must be arranged by the expert.
>
> A third point of difference relates to a difference in theory. The theory of

therapy which is developing in client-centered therapy stresses the importance of the immediate moment of experience in the relationship, not the genetic causation of behavior in the client, nor the formulation of some theoretic picture in the mind of the therapist.*

* It is difficult to see how the terms "guidance and control" in the sense that Rogers seems to use them do, in fairness, characterize the mainstream of contemporary psychoanalytic thinking. A semantic confusion seems to arise from the conception that the psychotherapist who functions in the role of a professional expert *ipso facto* manipulates the patient or controls him, and that guidance in the educational sense is synonymous with authoritarianism. Compare, in this connection, the formulations of a prominent psychoanalyst regarding therapeutic goals and the part played by the therapist:

"Treatment, of course, is aimed at the solution of the patient's difficulties in living and the cure of his symptomatology. Ideally these therapeutic goals will be reached by the growth, maturation, and inner independence of the patient . . . . This goal will also be actualized by the development of his capacity for self-realization, his ability to form durable relationships of intimacy with others, and to give and accept mature love" (Fromm-Reichmann, 1950, p. 34).

". . . security and inner independence of the authoritarian values attributed to the conventional requirements of our culture are indispensable for the therapist who wants to guide his patients successfully toward finding out about the degree of cultural adjustment which is adequate to their personal needs" (Fromm-Reichmann, 1950, p. 33).

"The psychiatrist's respect for his patients will also help him to safeguard against the previously mentioned mistake of assuming an attitude of personal "irrational authority" instead of listening and conducting therapy in the spirit of collaborative guidance. This irrational authoritarian behavior will be harmful not only because it interferes per se with the patient's tendency toward growth and maturation but also, and more important, because it constitutes a traumatic repetition of the authoritarian aspects of the cultural pattern of behavior in general and of the parental pattern in particular, to which most mental patients have been harmfully subjected in their past" (Fromm-Reichmann, p. 17).

In his third point of difference, Rogers asserts that the experimental element of the psychotherapeutic situation is more important than the formulation of some theoretic picture in the mind of the therapist. This statement carries with it the implication that the therapist cannot adequately empathize with the patient, thereby helping to actualize the immediate moment of experience, if he attempts to understand rationally what is going on. Rogers has elaborated on this alleged dilemma in another paper (Rogers, 1955). I, for one, know of no evidence that the therapist's private thoughts about the nature of the patient's emotional problem, its severity, etiology, etc., in and of themselves preclude or interfere with empathy, nor that the exclusion of the therapist's rational processes assure it. I feel that any psychotherapist does more than empathize with his patient; whether he interprets a feeling of attitude in terms of current or past interpersonal relationships, or whether he selects a particular feeling or attitude for reflection, he seems to follow a design for action dictated by his theory.

Psychotherapy based on psychoanalytic principles does differ from other forms of psychotherapy in its emphasis on giving the patient a rational understanding of his interpersonal processes as they emerge in the therapeutic relationship. The emotional experience remains uppermost, but in addition the patient gains a conscious appreciation of his own contribution to his difficulties.

Rogers' conception of the "ideal" therapist is that of a participant in an interpersonal situation whose primary function is to empathize with and understand the patient within his (the patient's) frame of reference. From this vantage point, the therapist is imposing an external frame of reference if he attempts to diagnose, assess, or prognosticate. The same dictum would apply to hypotheses or hunches the therapist may have about the etiology of the patient's conflict or how best to help him through psychotherapy. By this definition, the therapist who explicitly or implicitly goes beyond the patient's phenomenologic self-descriptions is not client-centered. Certain objections voiced by Rogerian therapists regarding the experimental procedure are understandable from this point of view. While they cooperated willingly, they made it clear that ordinarily they do not work this way.

On this basis, too, the following results are consistent with the client-centered viewpoint: a reluctance to make a diagnosis beyond the general label "anxiety," to formulate therapeutic goals, to mention dangers that might be encountered in therapy or cautions that would have to be observed, to encourage or discourage specific attitudes or behaviors in the patient, to treat him with strictness, to discourage the free expression of feelings (free association), or generally to consider problems of technique or "handling." Rogerians were also disinclined to make inferences about the patient's behavior in the interview situation, the etiology of his disturbance, or the dynamic import of his behavior. Finally, they de-emphasized case history questions.

One of the sharpest discrepancies between client-centered and analytically oriented therapists related to the question of prognosis: *no* Rogerian gave an unfavorable estimate, whereas 40 per cent of Sample A took a pessimistic view. How can this finding be explained?

First, it must be considered that our knowledge of neurotic disorders and psychotherapy is not sufficiently developed to permit specific predictions about the outcome of treatment even when a great deal is known about the patient. Such predictions undoubtedly become increasingly accurate as therapy progresses and the therapist comes to learn more about the nature of the conflict, its ramifications, its history, and the patient's current level of functioning. Thus, a prognostic estimate based on a single interview may be little more than a guess, and it may reveal more about the therapist than about the patient.

Second, the key issue in this comparison seems to be the high degree of uniformity among Rogerians which was not paralleled by the analytically oriented therapists whose responses appeared to be more "normally" distributed. If therapists were talking about a specific event, the predictions of some respondents obviously must be right and the predictions of others must be wrong. Unquestionably, therapists were not talking about a specific event but about a therapeutic outcome concerning which a wide range of ideas and opinions were entertained.

In an attempt to shed some light on this result, I propose to examine the following alternatives: (a) Rogerians gave a more favorable prognosis because they perceived the patient as less disturbed; (b) Rogerians planned for more modest therapeutic goals and therefore gave a more optimistic prognostic estimate; (c) prognostic estimates may be relatively unrelated to the presenting problem or the therapist's past successes with similar patients, but reflect more directly the therapist's attitude, his theoretical orientation, or combinations of these.

(a) The available evidence indicates that therapists in both samples tended to regard the patient as seriously disturbed. They were also reasonably agreed that he suffered a great deal of anxiety, that he was emotionally immature, socially maladjusted, and that he had relatively little insight. There is no reason to believe, therefore, that Rogerians judged the patient's difficulties as less severe.

(b) It is difficult to judge similarities or differences in therapeutic goals because of the vagueness of the terms of reference. Rogerians tended to advocate greater self-acceptance; analytically oriented therapists tended to strive for some insight. However, the latter group generally did not recommend the more intensive form of psychotherapy usually associated with psychoanalysis. On this basis, it seems fair to say that the Rogerians' more favorable prognostic estimates were not a function of more limited therapeutic goals.

(c) It will be recalled that there was a highly significant statistical relationship between psychiatrists' prognostic estimates and their self-ratings of their conscious attitude toward the patient ($r = .39$). For psychoanalytically oriented psychologists the correlation was $r = .42$). Among Rogerians the invariance between attitude and prognosis was almost complete (8 therapists at the University of Chicago Counseling Center expressed a positive attitude and rated the prognosis favorable).

In the case of psychiatrists it was found that both attitude and prognosis were significantly associated with other clinical evaluations and treatment plans. In addition, therapists' attitudes tended to be reflected in the emotional tone and the degree of empathy of their communications. These findings suggested the interpretation that clinical assessments tended to reflect, in part at least, the therapist's emotional reaction to the patient.* On the other hand, if the therapist had undergone personal analysis, his empathy tended to be greater irrespective of his conscious attitude. In other words, personal analysis seemed to introduce some distance between a negative reaction to the patient and the therapist's ability to empathize with him. It is possible, then, that the therapist's conscious attitude toward the patient is less important than what he does about it.†

To integrate a workable therapeutic relationship the therapist, according to psychoanalytic theory, must convey an attitude of acceptance, patience, respect, etc. He must also be able to empathize (Fenichel, 1945). This does not mean that he must have or should have a positive attitude toward *all* aspects of the patient's behavior. Rather, it is recognized that the therapist, like other people, may experience emotional reactions. However, he is enjoined to be vigilant to make sure that they do not interfere with the therapeutic

---

* It seems reasonable to assume that clinical evaluations, treatment plans, and goals are a function of the diagnosis. Comparisons of therapists (based on the total sample) giving a "pure" diagnosis of Hysteria, Obsessive-Compulsive, Paranoid, and Anxiety showed a number of statistically significant differences in terms of clinical evaluations, etc. It was pointed out in the same connection that the choice of certain diagnostic labels (paranoid, psychopath) may signify a subtle value judgment which in turn may be determined by the therapist's attitude toward the patient. The data seemed to favor this conclusion.

† It should be recalled that the operational definition of therapist's conscious attitude toward the patient, as used in this investigation, was a self-rating on a five-point scale. Apart from considerations of reliability, this rating was undoubtedly influenced by therapists' willingness to express their genuine conscious attitude, unconscious distortions, etc. It is difficult to say to what extent such ratings represent countertransference reactions even if there were greater agreement about the term (Orr, 1954). It seems that Gitelson's (1952) description of reactions to the patient as a whole, which he terms transferences of the analyst as distinguished from reactions to partial aspects of the patient (countertransference), fits the present ratings reasonably well:

"It is my impression that total reactions to a patient are transferences of the analyst to his patients and are revivals of ancient transference potentials. These may be manifested in the over-all attitude toward patients as a class or may exacerbate in the "whole response" to particular patients. These attitudes may be positively or negatively toned. They are likely to manifest themselves early in the contact with a patient and determine the tendency of the analyst toward the whole case" (Gitelson, 1952, p. 4).

process, and if they do, to seek clarification through self-analysis or other means.

The emphasis on diagnosis and etiology, according to analytic theory, determines at least partially the therapist's approach to therapy. Reich (1949) says:

> It should be clear that one approaches an aggressive patient unlike a masochistic one, a hyperactive hysteric unlike a depressive one, that one changes one's attitude to one and the same patient according to the situation, that, in brief, one does not behave neurotically oneself, even though one may have to deal with some neurotic difficulties in oneself.
>
> One cannot give up one's own individuality, a fact which one will consider in the choice of patients. But one should be able to expect that this individuality is not a disturbing factor and that the training analysis should establish the necessary minimum in plasticity of character (Reich, 1949, p. 139).

From these considerations it would follow that ideally the prognosis for any one patient represents a realistic assessment of the severity of the disturbance and reflects clinical experience regarding the response of similar patients to psychotherapy.

While evidence has been presented that a prognostic estimate *may* be based on the therapist's emotional reaction to the patient rather than on the clinical evidence, it does not follow that an unfavorable prognosis is *ipso facto* proof of a rejecting attitude on the therapist's part. It may well be a realistic assessment of the clinical picture.

It appears that the results obtained from client-centered therapists must be explained on different grounds. First, one of the most important conditions for constructive personality change postulated by Rogers (1957) is the therapist's "unconditional positive regard" for the patient. This means a "prizing" of the person, the absence of *conditions* of acceptance and of a selective evaluating attitude. Unconditional positive regard appears closely related to empathy, another of Rogers' key postulates, which is defined as the therapist's "experiencing an accurate, empathic understanding of the client's awareness of his own experience" (Rogers, 1957, p. 99).

Second, in explicitly rejecting the usefulness of diagnosis for psychotherapy, Rogers denies that the therapist's approach or operations should be influenced or modified by the type of patient and disturbance. This would also imply that prognostic estimates, to the extent that they attempt to take into account the severity or chronicity of the patient's disturbance, are pointless.

Thus, it appears logical that the client-centered therapist who fully accepts the theory must (a) describe his attitude toward the patient as positive and (b) give a favorable prognosis. The ratings under discussion seem to reflect very clearly the respondent's theoretical orientation and are perhaps best explained on this basis.

Whether a conscious attitude toward the patient is a more or less individual expression of the therapist's emotional reaction or whether the attitude is an intrinsic part of the therapist's theoretical framework, or both, the more important question relates to the manner in which this attitude is expressed in the therapeutic situation. Some evidence has been adduced to show that there is in fact a carry-over. It remains to be demonstrated to what extent the therapist's initial attitude toward the patient influences the course and outcome of therapy, but there seems to be a very real possibility that the therapist making a negative evaluation and/or reacting negatively to the patient may unwittingly contribute to the realization of the events he diagnoses or predicts. Contrariwise, the therapist who brings a genuinely positive approach to bear upon the relationship may thereby promote a more favorable outcome.* Both psychoanalytic and client-centered theory emphasize that the person of the therapist, as revealed in this relationship, will in time serve as a new, more mature, and more desirable model of reality than past interpersonal relationships which have distorted the patient's perceptions of himself and others. From different vantage points, the following quotations both seem to support this conclusion:

> What is curative in the [therapeutic] process is that in tending to reconstruct with the analyst that atmosphere which obtained in childhood the patient actually achieves something new. He discovers that part of himself which had to be repressed at the time of the original experience. He can only do this in an interpersonal relationship with the analyst, which is suitable to such a rediscovery . . . Thus, the transference phenomenon is used so that the patient will completely re-experience the original frames of reference, and himself within those frames, in a truly different relationship with the analyst, to the end that he can discover the invalidity of his conclusions about himself and others (Rioch, 1943, p. 151).

Rogers puts it this way:

> In a minimal way, the client may perceive from the first the unconditional positive regard of the therapist for him. The perception is continually strengthened as he discovers that each facet of himself which is exposed—contradictions, weaknesses, strengths, abnormal feelings, tender feelings, vicious attitudes, antisocial behaviors, fears and despairs—are all met with equal positive regard, because each of these elements is a part of him, and he is prized

---

* If it turns out that the therapist's personality—his dedication, faith, belief—is indeed a primary force in modern psychotherapy, painstaking research may give a still clearer picture of the components. (See in this connection Frank, 1958, and Chapter 15.)

unconditionally. The client then gradually takes in the experience of being loved—a love which is nonpossessive and nondemanding, warm but not over-solicitous. As he lives for a sequence of hours in this atmosphere, the experience has two primary results. It permits him to relax the tight defensive structure of his concept of himself and to admit into awareness and fully experience attitudes which previously he had found too threatening. . . . In the second place, the attitude of the therapist toward him is gradually inter-nalized so that he can take the same attitude toward himself. He comes to prize himself, to feel that he *is* of value (Rogers, 1956, p. 204).

PART II

Selected
Protocols of Therapists

A NOTE ON

SELECTED PROTOCOLS

OF THERAPISTS

The protocols included in Chapters 8, 9, and 10 represent psychiatrists as the major professional group which formed the basis for extensive statistical analyses. The protocols are arranged by level of experience in psychotherapy. While experience failed to account for most differences in terms of diagnostic, prognostic, and other clinical evaluations as well as treatment plans and proposed techniques, it will be seen that the *communications* of experienced therapists often disclose greater succinctness, penetration, and planfulness than those of less experienced practitioners. It will also be noted that attitudinal variables (attitudes toward the patient, degree of empathy, etc.) cut across the lines of experience. Thus, the arrangement by experience was considered convenient, without implying a value judgment of its importance.

With regard to psychologists following psychoanalytic principles, there were few differences which set them apart from psychiatrists; for this reason, examples from this group are omitted.

Psychologists following the "client-centered" theory of Carl Rogers were the most homogeneous single group which sharply diverged from all other respondents. These differences emerged with regard to clinical judgments as well as communications. Ten cases representing this group follow the protocols by psychiatrists (Chapter 11).*

---

* Various analyses designed to explore differences attributable to theoretical orientation (orthodox Freudians vs. neo-Freudians) led to inconclusive results. This is not equivalent to saying that theory makes no difference as far as clinical judgments, diagnosis, and communications are concerned; it seems important to keep in mind the limitations of this investigation, particularly the fact that it dealt with an initial interview rather than therapy over an extended period of time. The reader can judge for himself whether he can detect differences between, say, a Sullivanian, a Meyerian, or an orthodox Freudian.

.A word of caution should accompany the editorial comments following each psychiatrist record. The selection of this illustrative material was guided by the desire to include reasonably representative records at various levels of experience. Secondly, since all records were given an over-all rating of degree of empathy communicated by the therapist (see ch. 4 for criteria), only protocols were chosen concerning which two expert raters expressed unanimous agreement on two separate occasions. Thirdly, another independent judge* studied all records and prepared brief characterizations of his impressions, without knowledge of the empathy ratings previously assigned. The author's comments represent his own impressions, aided by the over-all ratings and characterizations. It will be apparent to the reader that the comments appended to some records are favorable to the therapist whereas others are more critical. Under no circumstances is the conclusion warranted that the experimental situation is considered a crucial test of the therapist's competence. I have attempted to make explicit the reasons for my evaluations as well as the bases of judgment. There is reason to believe that these judgments are not wholly idiosyncratic; however, the reader is advised to arrive at his own evaluations. It is hoped that the records will aid in providing a frame of reference within which an individual protocol can be judged. The value of this illustrative material is believed to lie primarily in the strict comparability of the data.

---

* I am greatly indebted to Dr. Martin Wallach for his assistance in this phase of the work.

8

GROUP I: PSYCHIATRISTS
EXPERIENCE LEVEL:
LOW

BIOGRAPHICAL INFORMATION

Code:	1
Age:	33 years.
Sex:	Female.
Professional affiliation and status:	Psychiatric resident, second year.
Psychoanalytic training:	Plans.
Personal analysis:	Plans.
Experience in psychotherapy:	½ year.
Type of therapy:	Analytically oriented therapy.
Type of patients:	Military; neurotics and personality disorders.
Theoretical orientation:	Analytically oriented.

CLINICAL ASSESSMENTS

Diagnosis

Dominant personality type:	Anxiety; inadequate personality.
Formulation of dynamics:	Unresolved oedipal and sibling rivalry.

Treatment plans

Form of treatment:	Analytically oriented psychotherapy but not analysis to start with.
Treatment goals:	Initial goal would be to bring patient to some awareness of his own role.
Frequency of sessions:	1-2 times a week to start.
Length of treatment:	

Intermediate goals:	0
Ultimate goals:	Suspect this patient would drop therapy before initial goal achieved. Think this alone would take 3-6 months.
Symptom-relief:	Can't estimate. From interview we still don't know what precipitated patient's attack on bus or if that was what brought him to treatment.
Difficulties expected:	Hours of rationalization; acting out in terms of lateness and missed appointments and somatic complaints.
Focus:	Initially the here-and-now daily incidents; source of support; household arrangements; wife, etc.
Dangers:	Prevent his provoking a strong countertransference to be defensive against.
Areas to be avoided:	Would depend—would tend to let patient set his own pace.
Behaviors to be encouraged:	Would try to get him to work or to doing something.
Behaviors to be discouraged:	Would discourage tendency to dwell on somatic symptoms and his past problems.
Strictness vs. permissiveness:	Rather strict.
Clues:	His tremendous hostility.
Course of transference:	Marked dependence with increasing testing demands.
Approach to transference:	This is why I'd tend to be firm to try to avoid patient's getting into situation where he'd feel rejected.
Activity vs. passivity:	No more active or passive (but fewer interruptions to begin with).
Free association:	Don't think patient could or would profitably.
Ego strength:	Too little evidence.
Anxiety:	A great deal.
Insight:	Very little, if any.
Emotional maturity:	Very immature.
Social adjustment:	Too little evidence (probably very inadequate).
Degree of disturbance:	Seriously disturbed.
Degree of therapeutic change attempted:	Too little evidence.
Prognosis without therapy:	Would remain about the same.
Prognosis with therapy:	Too little evidence (somewhat unfavorable).
Recommendations:	Would question his means of support.
Attitude toward patient:	Somewhat negative.
Reasons:	Believe he would be very difficut for me to work with unless his coming to interview was motivated by some real desire to change.

EVALUATION OF FILM THERAPIST

Adequacy:	Reasonably adequate.

Reason: Believe an initial interview should clarify the
                           questions I ask above unless further evaluation
                           possible.
Activity vs. passivity: Somewhat too active.
Support: Neither too much nor too little.
Life history data: Somewhat more time.
Attitude toward therapist: Somewhat negative.
Reason: He looked so very puzzled.

FILM RESPONSES

1. 0 (unless patient remained silent).
2. 0 (let patient go on).
3. 0 (but look interested).
4. 0
5. (Don't know now; would not have interrupted this patient so many times to begin with.)
6. (If no interruption previously, would inquire regarding "economic problems.")
7. (Didn't hear patient's last comment; probably would say "oh?" if anything.)
8. 0 (not look as puzzled as the interviewer looks to me).
9. Other stuff?
10. 0 (unless patient remains silent).
11. (If patient paused and expected comment) Yes?
12. 0 (let patient go on).
13. (Didn't hear comment completely —think he used this word "antisocially?")

14. Oh? (or) Um?
15. (If patient remained silent) One of a lot of things?
16. This keeping you from work?
17. (Couldn't hear patient's comment; 0 probably.)
18. (Let patient go on if he does.)
19. (If anything) Didn't appreciate it?
20. Dad home how much? ("Else I quit . . . " Quit?)
21. ?
22. Brother?
23. (Think I'd have interrupted a bit sooner with) Fired for writing a bad check, huh?
24. Cooperation?
25. 0 (now).
26. Too bad he couldn't have stayed around?
27. 0
28. Seems like you've felt more or less this way for a long time.

COMMENT

Clinical Assessments: The second part of the diagnosis, "Inadequate personality," implies opprobrium and is consonant with the therapist's admitted negative attitude toward the patient. According to accepted psychiatric classification, such patients are not "ill," they are simply "no good" because they fail to measure up to the norms of adult behavior expected by the culture.* In this case, the respondent questions the patient's motivation for therapy. The dynamic formulation ("Unresolved oedipal and sibling rivalry") is little more than a cliché; its generality is so great as to be almost completely useless. It

---

* Compare, in this connection, the "official" description: "'Such individuals are characterized by inadequate response to intellectual, emotional, social, and physical demands. They are neither physically nor mentally grossly deficient on examination, but they do show inadaptability, ineptness, poor judgment, lack of physical and emotional stamina, and social incompatibility." (American Psychiatric Association. Diagnostic and Statistical Manual of Mental Disorders, p. 35.)

shows the respondent's familiarity with professional jargon, which may gloss over her ignorance or inability to think about a patient in individual and specific terms.

Her recommendation for strictness and firmness is explained by reference to possible dangers in the transference situation ("to avoid patient's getting into a situation where he'd feel rejected"). On several questions she feels there is too little evidence to make a judgment. However—and this is in contrast to her diagnosis of inadequate personality—she sees the patient as seriously disturbed and suffering from a great deal of anxiety, usually considered a symptom pointing to a *neurotic* disorder. This may be a reflection of the therapist's intrinsic uncertainty.

Film Responses: Her communications are exceedingly minimal: either she remains silent or asks rather brief questions. It is difficult to see how the patient could form any reasonable surmise about the person of the therapist or how psychotherapy with her could be helpful. There is no evidence that the therapist recognizes the patient's needs or feelings or that she responds to them in any way. The patient's striving for improvement (Response 18) is ignored, as is his plea for reassurance (Response 28). The latter response, in its absence of support, appears particularly incongruous with the intensity of the patient's feelings expressed at this point. The response to item 23 ("Fired for writing a bad check, huh?") seems consistent with the therapist's judgment of the patient as an antisocial individual who already stands "convicted" before the "trial" has barely begun. Note the complete absence of communications expressing understanding or human warmth. One wonders about the respondent's conception of the role and function of a psychotherapist. Certainly, she is hostile toward the patient.

CODE: 2

BIOGRAPHICAL INFORMATION

Code:	2
Age:	31 years.
Sex:	Male.
Professional affiliation and status:	Psychiatric resident, second year.
Psychoanalytic training:	Undecided.
Personal analysis:	Group psychotherapy (2½ years as medical student, 1 year as resident).
Experience in psychotherapy:	¼ year; very little.
Type of therapy:	Analytically oriented therapy.
Type of patients:	Psychotics.
Theoretical orientation:	Somewhat analytical.

CLINICAL ASSESSMENTS

Diagnosis

Dominant personality type:	Anxiety.
Formulation of dynamics:	He appears to be a person who has by force of circumstances and early conditioning experiences denied his own needs, with conflict over this denial.

Treatment plans
    Form of treatment: Intensive psychotherapy.
    Treatment goals: Resolution and recognition of his underlying
                                 conflicts and ability to gain greater satisfac-
                                 tions out of his living without such gross
                                 anxiety.
    Frequency of sessions: 3 times weekly at first, if feasible, but this might
                                 be altered depending on developments in
                                 therapy.
    Length of treatment:
        Intermediate goals: 0
        Ultimate goals: Probably at least 6 months, perhaps longer,
                                 perhaps shorter.
    Symptom-relief: 2 months (?) or about 25 hours of treatment.
    Difficulties expected: Frequent telephone calls by patient in anxiety
                                 attacks, expectation by patient of advice.
    Focus: His feelings, primarily about wife, mother and
                                 deceased father.
    Dangers: No.
    Areas to be avoided: No.
    Behaviors to be encouraged: No, not knowingly.
    Behaviors to be discouraged: No, not knowingly.
    Strictness vs. permissiveness: No more strict or permissive than with others.
    Clues: Obvious anxiety nonverbally when discussing
                                 certain topics.
    Course of transference: First postitive, later much negative trans-
                                 ference.
    Approach to transference: Clarification of the feelings involved, partially.
    Activity vs. passivity: No more active or passive than with others.
    Free association: Encourage it.
    Ego strength: A fair amount.
    Anxiety: A great deal.
    Insight: Relatively little.
    Emotional maturity: Fairly immature.
    Social adjustment: Too little evidence.
    Degree of disturbance: Moderately disturbed.
    Degree of therapeutic change
        attempted: Fairly extensive change.
    Prognosis without therapy: Probably get a little worse.
    Prognosis with therapy: Somewhat favorable.
    Recommendations: No, detrimental to investigative therapy.
    Attitude toward patient: Somewhat positive.
    Reasons: 0. Not exactly.

EVALUATION OF FILM THERAPIST
    Adequacy: Reasonably adequate job.
        Reason: The patient was able to relate his problems
                                 satisfactorily.
    Activity vs. passivity: Somewhat too passive.

Support:	Somewhat too little.
Life history data:	About the same time.
Attitude toward therapist:	Somewhat positive.
Reason:	0

FILM RESPONSES

1. (Couldn't hear the initial statements by patient.)
2. Um, hum.
3. You say you regained your composure?
4. Could you explain that feeling more?
5. I'm not sure just what you mean when you say cornered?
6. Um, hum.
7. Dizzy? (questioning attitude nonverbally)
8. Sounds like a vicious cycle, doesn't it?
9. You feel as if you'd like to be healthier then.
10. You mentioned prolonged sorrow as one of the main things that brings this feeling on.
11. And your mother talks when you want quiet and peace?
12. Then this has been developing over a long period of time.
13. You say all your difficulties stem from economic worries? (questioning nonverbal attitude)
14. But you do feel, I gather, resentful of your mother's attitudes and actions.
15. Um, hum.
16. Sounds like a paralyzing kind of fear.
17. Mad?
18. I can understand your desire to, as you put it, to "get well."
19. Annoy you?
20. You felt he wasn't much help to you then?
21. Been pretty unhappy, then?
22. Felt burdened down by all that?
23. Um, hum.
24. Cooperation?
25. I don't understand what "it" is that you're trying to get even with.
26. Um, hum.
27. You feel then you would have liked for things to have been different?
28. These things worry you a great deal.

COMMENT

Clinical Assessments: Considering his level of experience, this therapist shows a fair understanding of the patient's problems and succeeds to some extent in integrating his clinical impressions to form a somewhat coherent picture of the patient and his problems. He seems open-minded, interested, and willing to enter into a therapeutic relationship. Like many inexperienced therapists, he is hopeful about the prognosis and anticipates therapeutic success in a relatively short time; at the same time, he is not oblivious to difficulties which might be expected in treatment. He is eager to help, respectful toward the patient, and his attitude is positive.

Film Responses: The general tenor of communications is warm and empathic. There are no incisive comments, pointed questions, or interpretations; rather, the therapist evinces an intuitive understanding of the patient's suffering and difficulties and manages to communicate something about his willingness to "give." He never takes issue with or argues about the patient's complaints and often accepts them in a nonjudgmental manner (see, for example, responses 20,

21, 22, 27). He supports the patient's striving for "health" (response 18) and thereby attempts to instil some hope. While sympathetic, response 28—often a key item—fails to meet the patient's challenge for reassurance and help. The therapist manifests a measure of spontaneity and warmth, uncontaminated by technical considerations, which was often found lacking in more sophisticated and more experienced respondents.

CODE: 3

BIOGRAPHICAL INFORMATION

Code:	3
Age:	34 years.
Sex:	Male.
Professional affiliation and status:	Psychiatrist.
Psychoanalytic training:	Presently in training.
Personal analysis:	Started 1954; has had 110 hours; expects to complete 300 hours.
Experience in psychotherapy:	Fair amount; 1 year.
Type of therapy:	Analytically oriented.
Type of patients:	Psychotics; phobic and anxiety reactions.
Theoretical orientation:	Analytically oriented and Sullivanian.

CLINICAL ASSESSMENTS

Diagnosis

Dominant personality type:	Anxiety; obsessive.
Formulation of dynamics:	Obsessive-compulsive characteristics with self-defeating operations and self-burdening; strong guilt feelings over responsibility toward mother and wife.

Treatment plans

Form of treatment:	Psychotherapy.
Treatment goals:	Intermediate: Body symptoms as reflection of living troubles and easing of body symptoms. Ultimate: Relaxation of obsessivity and compulsivity.
Frequency of sessions:	3 times weekly.
Length of treatment:	
Intermediate goals:	5-6 hours.
Ultimate goals:	150 hours.
Symptom-relief:	5-6 hours.
Difficulties expected:	Clinging to body symptoms, intellectualizations.
Focus:	His relations with mother and wife, obsessive patterns.
Dangers:	Too rapid working through of defenses.
Areas to be avoided:	Not aware of any.
Behaviors to be encouraged:	Expression of his feelings toward wife and mother.
Behaviors to be discouraged:	0

Strictness vs. permissiveness:	Rather permissive.
Clues:	Fidgeting, mentioning money matters, medical sophistication (terminology).
Course of transference:	The therapist is like my mother. The therapist is like the world, demanding a lot, giving little.
Approach to transference:	0
Activity vs. passivity:	Rather passive.
Free association:	Neither encourage or discourage it.
Ego strength:	A fair amount.
Anxiety:	A fair amount.
Insight:	A fair amount.
Emotional maturity:	Very immature.
Social adjustment:	Fairly inadequate.
Degree of disturbance:	Moderately disturbed.
Degree of therapeutic change attempted:	Relatively little change.
Prognosis without therapy:	Probably get much worse.
Prognosis with therapy:	Somewhat favorable.
Recommendations:	Live with wife only.
Attitude toward patient:	Somewhat positive.
Reasons:	He appears helpless, relatively.

EVALUATION OF FILM THERAPIST

Adequacy:	Very adequate.
Reason:	He followed closely and asked not too many and not too few questions.
Activity vs. passivity:	Neither too active nor too passive.
Support:	Neither too much nor too little.
Life history data:	About the same time.
Attitude toward therapist:	Neutral attitude.
Reason:	0

FILM RESPONSES

1. 0
2. What is there about this fear that brings you to the doctor?
3. You sound like you were distressed by something that day, perhaps culminated by these feelings.
4. Any idea about what was happening in your life that made you feel hemmed in?
5. What's cornering you?
6. Money matters trouble you?
7. Dizzy?
8. Do you feel that this series of body feelings are started by things or events outside you or physical illness?
9. Forget what?
10. 0
11. 0
12. About what? The situation in the house?
13. You suggested money troubles before.
14. 0
15. Does she get you into this stew?
16. Afraid of losing support?
17. 0
18. 0
19. 0
20. This was your father's attitude about this in particular?
21. 0

22. You became head of the family.
23. 0
24. You feel it's a lonely struggle?
25. 0
26. 0

27. Some other way?
28. Perhaps it would be useful to hear what you feel will be the result of these feelings.

COMMENT

Clinical Assessments: This therapist is one of the few respondents who is impressed by obsessive features in the patient's personality. He considers the prognosis somewhat favorable and describes his attitude as somewhat positive. He seems to have formed a definite impression of the patient and shows faith in his clinical judgments. He sees the patient as a person in need of professional help and is willing to extend it. He appears to be capable of objectivity and is not becoming emotionally involved with the patient from the outset. One may wonder how he expects to achieve symptom relief in five to six hours. He appears earnest, straightforward, and comfortable in his professional role. (The professional experience of one year with which he credits himself may be an underestimate.)

Film Responses: The tone of his communications is friendly and he probably can establish a good working relationship with this patient. His responses seem appropriate, respectful, and empathic. He stays close to the patient's verbalizations and is attentive. There is no evidence of preconceived notions, moral judgments, or unwarranted intrusions. It is noteworthy that he is able to remain silent (passively expectant and accepting), but he is also capable of alternating silences with mildly investigative questions. Responses 24 and 28, while neither strongly supportive nor reassuring, indicate that he is empathizing with the patient's feelings and is cognizant of his struggle.

CODE: 4

BIOGRAPHICAL INFORMATION

Code:	4
Age:	26 years.
Sex:	Male.
Professional affiliation and status:	Psychiatric resident, second year.
Psychoanalytic training:	No training; no plans.
Personal analysis:	Completed 125 hours; expect to complete 250 hours.
Experience in psychotherapy:	1 year, very little.
Type of therapy:	Analytically oriented.
Type of patients:	Psychotics.
Theoretical orientation:	Neo-Freudian.

CLINICAL ASSESSMENTS

Diagnosis

Dominant personality type:	Anxiety.

Formulation of dynamics:	He lost capacity for healthy self-assertiveness and appears to have been incapable of changing direction. He was thoroughly mistreated by mother—dad?

Treatment plans

Form of treatment:	Intensive, analytically oriented psychotherapy.
Treatment goals:	Intermediate: give him some hope or rather some substance to the hope he has.
	Ultimate: capacity for hopeful change under influence of environment.
Frequency of sessions:	At least 3 times weekly.
Length of treatment:	0. (Can't estimate.)
Intermediate goals:	
Ultimate goals:	
Symptom-relief:	25-50 hours maybe.
Difficulties expected:	1. Too much projection. 2. A passive-aggressive anger rather than aggression heading to appropriate activity. 3. Somatic preoccupation.
Focus:	Therapeutic situation.
Dangers:	1. Avoid arguments. 2. I doubt if patient could have psychotic break, but would watch for it.
Areas to be avoided:	No.
Behaviors to be encouraged:	Encourage any behavior; anything is better than this paralysis, unless it is obvious running away.
Behaviors to be discouraged:	Discourage placing blame on mama. Focus on some positive aspects she has.
Strictness vs. permissiveness:	Would vary depending upon content and affect.
Clues:	At times he was rather graphic both verbally and nonverbally, which as a general attribute should be encouraged and made use of (e.g., eviscerate. . . .)
Course of transference:	Usual positive and then negative, but probably basically negative throughout.
Approach to transference:	Use it, interpret it late.
Activity vs. passivity:	Very dependent on patient's needs.
Free association:	Neither encourage nor discourage.
Ego strength:	Relatively little.
Anxiety:	A great deal.
Insight:	Very little.
Emotional maturity:	Very immature.
Social adjustment:	Very inadequate.
Degree of disturbance:	Seriously disturbed.
Degree of therapeutic change attempted:	Very extensive change but would settle for much less.
Prognosis without therapy:	Remain about the same.
Prognosis with therapy:	Too little evidence (depends upon therapist).
Recommendations:	No; more running away.

Attitude toward patient: Somewhat positive; somewhat negative.
    Reasons: I'm ambivalent.

EVALUATION OF FILM THERAPIST
    Adequacy: Reasonably adequate (good job).
      Reason: Plenty of material for diagnosis and evaluation
                                  of treatment.
    Activity vs. passivity: Somewhat too passive.
    Support: Neither too much nor too little.
    Life history data: Somewhat more time.
    Attitude toward therapist: Somewhat positive.
      Reason: 0. No.

FILM RESPONSES

1. 0
2. Have you seen someone else re-
    garding these problems?
3. 0 (I wouldn't harp on the hemmed
    in so much in the first interview).
4. I'd like to hear some more.
5. 0
6. Uhhm.
7. Can you tell me something about
    your wife?
8. Uhhm.
9. *Forget?*
10. You said you were married?
11. *Yes.*
12. Uhhm.
13. *Yes.*
14. That somewhat depends on what
    you mean.
15. *Yes.*

16. When was your mother here ex-
    actly?
17. I didn't hear that.
18. What do you mean by, "Well" ...
19. Did she do this here also? "I sup-
    pressed it" . . . Too bad (smile).
20. What about Dad?
21. *You quit? Why?*
22. *Yes.*
23. Antisocial attitudes? (I would go
    slow here.)
24. 0
25. How do you mean?
26. Not quite.
27. This would be an appropriate
    place to cry.
28. (Answer depends on knowledge of
    patient's physical condition and
    would be factual, although ob-
    viously a loaded question.)

COMMENT

Clinical Assessment: While inexperienced and uncertain, this therapist appears
eager to answer the questions propounded in the questionnaire and reveals some
familiarity with patients and their problems (personal analysis—he has completed 125 hours—may have helped). He is respectful, alert, and reflective
(notice his mention of the possibility of a psychotic break). He is also aware
that therapy may be difficult and that a scaling down of therapeutic goals may
be necessary. The description of his attitude seems disarmingly honest.

Film Responses: The therapist's lack of experience is borne out by his
responses: they are minimal, unincisive, and fairly "routine." At the same time,
he is not hiding behind a professional screen and is quite direct. Response 27
("This would be an appropriate place to cry.") reveals a higher level of sophistication, almost like a response his analyst may have made to him or one he picked

up from a more experienced colleague. Nonetheless, it seems appropriate and communicates a great deal of understanding and warmth. The patient's plea at the end of the interview (Item 28) evidently finds the therapist off-guard and unable to cope with it directly. On the whole, he seems well-meaning but inexperienced.

CODE: 5

BIOGRAPHICAL INFORMATION

Code:	5
Age:	29 years.
Sex:	Male.
Professional affiliation and status:	Psychiatric resident, first year.
Psychoanalytic training:	Plans.
Personal analysis:	Plans.
Experience in psychotherapy:	None.
Type of therapy:	0
Type of patients:	0
Theoretical orientation:	0

CLINICAL ASSESSMENTS

Diagnosis

Dominant personality type:	Obsessive.
Formulation of dynamics:	0

Treatment plans

Form of treatment:	Psychotherapy, not necessarily analytic.
Treatment goals:	Intermediate: supportive via individual psychotherapy. Ultimate: self-esteem.
Frequency of sessions:	3 times per week.
Length of treatment:	Probably 100 plus.
Intermediate goals:	0
Ultimate goals:	0
Symptom-relief:	Few hours. However, would recur as another symptom.
Difficulties expected:	Patient probably would keep retreating behind various symptom defenses.
Focus:	Early adjustment. Relationship to father and mother.
Dangers:	Allowing patient to use therapist as permanent crutch.
Areas to be avoided:	0
Behaviors to be encouraged:	Outgoing activities.
Behaviors to be discouraged:	Staying at home, never going out.
Strictness vs. permissiveness:	Rather strict.
Clues:	0
Course of transference:	Therapist given father role.

Approach to transference:	Use it to build ego strength and self-esteem.
Activity vs. passivity:	Rather passive.
Free association:	Neither encourage nor discourage it.
Ego strength:	Relatively little.
Anxiety:	A fair amount.
Insight:	A fair amount.
Emotional maturity:	Too little evidence.
Social adjustment:	Very inadequate.
Degree of disturbance:	Mildly disturbed.
Degree of therapeutic change attempted:	Fairly extensive change.
Prognosis without therapy:	Get much worse.
Prognosis with therapy:	Somewhat favorable.
Recommendations:	No. Better to work it through where he is.
Attitude toward patient:	Somewhat positive.
Reasons:	0

EVALUATION OF FILM THERAPIST

Adequacy:	Reasonably adequate.
Reason:	0
Activity vs. passivity:	Neither too active nor too passive.
Support:	Neither too much nor too little.
Life history data:	Somewhat more time.
Attitude toward therapist:	Somewhat positive.
Reason:	I suppose it is because he acted about the way I would.

FILM RESPONSES

1. (Make patient comfortable.) Will you tell me what brought you here?
2. 0
3. You say you felt hemmed in.
4. (Nod head understandingly.)
5. Yes.
6. How have you responded to that hemmed in feeling before?
7. 0
8. (With understanding nod.)
9. What other stuff?
10. 0
11. 0
12. 0
13. Antisocial attitudes?
14. 0
15. How else did she make you feel?
16. 0
17. 0
18. Tell me more about this anxiety.
19. 0
20. How did you feel about your father's ideas: "Just forget it"?
21. 0
22. 0
23. 0
24. Cooperation?
25. 0
26. Umhmm (nod).
27. Did you ever let this anger explode outwardly?
28. What do you feel about this?

COMMENT

Clinical Assessments: The responses are fairly typical of a completely inexperienced therapist. His lack of knowledge is evidenced by his inability (unwillingness?) even to attempt a formulation of the emotional dynamics; he is cautious to the point of self-effacement. He really does not know where to start and makes no pretense that he does. He is a beginner in every sense of the word.

Film Responses: His lack of familiarity with patients suffering from emotional difficulties is clearly reflected in his communications. He sees but two alternatives: either to remain silent or to ask for elaborations. His response to Item 27 sounds like naive curiosity; his final comment ("What do you feel about this?") is inept.

This record is illustrative not only of an inexperienced therapist; it reveals a rather immature individual whose marked inhibitions prevent him from responding to another person even on a simple human level. One gets the impression that this respondent is utterly overwhelmed by the task and the demands made on him. He is unsure of what he is supposed to do, and—what is more important—he seems to view the patient as a "stranger" whose inner experiences are somehow mysterious and beyond the ken of human understanding. He is unable to communicate anything about the commonality of human experience or, to use Sullivan's phrase, that we are all much more simply human than otherwise.

CODE: 6

BIOGRAPHICAL INFORMATION

Code:	6
Age:	38 years.
Sex:	Male.
Professional affiliation and status:	Psychiatric resident, first year.
Psychoanalytic training:	Have none and am uncertain.
Personal analysis:	Completed 100 hours, continuing.
Experience in psychotherapy:	½ year, very little.
Type of therapy:	Meyerian (?)—attempting mutually to recognize and resolve issues.
Type of patients:	Psychotics.
Theoretical orientation:	Eclectic. Too early to even recognize significant differences in the list.

CLINICAL ASSESSMENTS

Diagnosis

Dominant personality type:	Anxiety. Psychopathic.
Formulation of dynamics:	Unfulfilled dependency needs concurrent with over-protection and constant relegation to infantilism which he alternately rejects and requires.

Treatment plans

Form of treatment:	Psychotherapy.
Treatment goals:	Relief of symptoms, classification of issues, minimum insight.
Frequency of sessions:	In my present setting, 1 time a week.

Length of treatment:	1 year.
Intermediate goals:	0
Ultimate goals:	0
Symptom-relief:	2-3 months.
Difficulties expected:	The prognosis is not too good; his hostility at times would be immense, and he offers less intrinsic interest than many patients.
Focus:	The present, the time of onset and present symptoms, and childhood. Especially work.
Dangers:	Any interpretation should be delayed until the facts are very certain and he is about to do it himself, or is doing it. His extreme dependency needs and hostility would have to be handled gradually.
Areas to be avoided:	Sexual.
Behaviors to be encouraged:	Expression of emotions, the threatened crying and angry outbreaks.
Behaviors to be discouraged:	The self-pity, hostile acts.
Strictness vs. permissiveness:	Rather strict.
Clues:	1. The check-writing episode.
	2. The 300 pound woman.
Course of transference:	Varying between morbid hostility and dependence, probably in that order.
Approach to transference:	Attempt to make it as overt and as recognized as possible.
Activity vs. passivity:	No more active or passive than with others.
Free association:	Neither encourage nor discourage.
Ego strength:	Relatively little.
Anxiety:	A fair amount.
Insight:	Relatively little.
Emotional maturity:	Very immature.
Social adjustment:	Fairly inadequate.
Degree of disturbance:	Moderately disturbed.
Degree of therapeutic change attempted:	Relatively little.
Prognosis without therapy:	Get a little worse.
Prognosis with therapy:	Somewhat unfavorable.
Recommendations:	Not at present. I actually don't know what they are yet.
Attitude toward patient:	Neutral.
Reasons:	More easily than what it is: he needs help and can benefit from it. But his form of defense against his anxieties is one of the least appealing from a human as well as therapist viewpoint.

EVALUATION OF FILM THERAPIST

Adequacy:	Reasonably adequate.

Reason:	Much of the essential matter for evaluation was obtained; there could have been more; and he ended with a potential therapeutic relation.
Activity vs. passivity:	Somewhat too passive.
Support:	Somewhat too much.
Life history data:	Somewhat more.
Attitude toward therapist:	Neutral.
Reason:	I think the strain of the movie situation told on him to his disadvantage; hence, feel any defects should be weighed with this fact.

FILM RESPONSES

1. 0
2. You say your association with your mother has always caused you fear?
3. You've never had an experience like that before . . . you said?
4. 0
5. Yes. "Jumbled up in my thinking . . ." What happens when you're jumbled up?
6. When did you first begin to have this sensation of being hemmed in?
7. "Help me . . ." How long have you felt that way?
   (Same) When did this start?
   (Doctor's question regarding "hemmed in"—I would rather follow above.)
8. (Again—ask for time and circumstances of beginning of this reaction.)
   "Fill the bill . . ." What do you feel like doing at such times?
9. (Same as 8) (I cannot hear some of patient's words too well through here.)
10. (I would ask or have asked the above, i.e.) When and with what circumstances did it begin? How often and under what circumstances does it occur? What do you feel like doing at such times?
11. (Describing wife's illness) How do you feel about your wife's disease?
12. How did your anxiousness show itself then?

13. Were you troubled with economic worries when you were living home?
14. What things that she's done do you refer to?
15. "Churned . . ." And what do you feel like doing at such times? (Or, if that were pursued already . . .) There were others?
16. "Afraid . . ." Afraid of what? (or) Afraid that you might . . . ?
17. (I just couldn't hear what the patient said at this point.)
18. You say your anxiety began in your relation with your mother?
19. What other things did she do to you that seem disturbing? "Suppress them . . ." What would you actually do?
20. When you felt like tearing down the house, what would you do?
21. In what way have your relationships with other people been unpleasant for you?
22. 0
23. Your antisocial attitudes?
24. You didn't get cooperation?
25. You wanted to get even . . .
26. (I didn't hear that again.) "War . . ." How do you feel about that?
27. 0
28. What do you want to do during these spells?

COMMENT

Clinical Assessments: Here is another inexperienced therapist who, by his own admission, is a beginner. He is impressed by the patient's hostility and dependency and reacts negatively to them. This therapist is an instructive example of a respondent whose reaction to the patient is essentially negative, but who registers his attitude as "neutral." In his elaboration of this rating, he explains that he is repelled by the patient's defenses (hostility and dependency) but he is not really able to plumb the depth of his attitude or recognize his true character. Nevertheless, he marshals sufficient objectivity to view the patient as a person in need of help rather than a parasitic member of society who is beyond the pale. His dynamic formulation discloses a certain pompousness, which was often found to be associated with inexperience. On the other hand, he has some ideas how to proceed and seems eager and alert. Probably as a function of his negative—or better, perhaps, ambivalent—attitude he regards the patient as offering "less intrinsic interest than many patients."

Film Responses: This respondent structures the therapeutic task as one of getting facts about the patient's feelings and life history—as many as possible in as short a time as possible (misapplication of Meyerian teachings?). Thus, he misses no opportunity to pursue this goal rather relentlessly. This form of questioning may convey to the patient that the therapist is interested, but he may miss empathic understanding. Undoubtedly, the patient's discursiveness acts as a strong invitation to the therapist to fix time, dates, events, onset, and establish other facts, as well as to discourage rambling accounts, but one may question whether this therapist's technique will be effective in penetrating the verbal fog, at least in a first interview. On a deeper level, this overactivity may represent a reaction-formation against the therapist's own hostility and discomfort.

CODE: 7

BIOGRAPHICAL INFORMATION

Code:	7
Age:	31 years.
Sex:	Male.
Professional affiliation and status:	Psychiatric resident, first year.
Psychoanalytic training:	Plans open.
Personal analysis:	Plans.
Experience in psychotherapy:	½ year; very little.
Type of therapy:	Analytically oriented psychotherapy.
Type of patients:	Depressive reactions.
Theoretical orientation:	Psychoanalytically oriented (general).

CLINICAL ASSESSMENTS

Diagnosis

Dominant personality type:	Anxiety.
Formulation of dynamics:	He is a dependent person who felt not adequate to deal with his problems.

Treatment plans

Form of treatment:	Psychotherapeutic out-patient interviews.
Treatment goals:	Intermediate: getting a job.
	Ultimate: insight into emotional immaturity.
Frequency of sessions:	Once a week.
Length of treatment:	
Intermediate goals:	3 months.
Ultimate goals:	Perhaps a year or more (1-1½ total).
Symptom-relief:	One hour weekly for 6 months.
Difficulties expected:	The patient would develop deep dependency relationship and needs.
Focus:	His dependency. Bitterness to society and why antisocial behavior.
Dangers:	No.
Areas to be avoided:	His antisocial behavior might be a sensitive spot in guilt—to be delayed.
Behaviors to be encouraged:	Less sensitivity to domination, to learn more delay in seeking revenge on society. Then to learn to accept himself and society.
Behaviors to be discouraged:	Less aggressive defense (and see above).
Strictness vs. permissiveness:	Rather strict.
Clues:	Apparent anxiety in talking with the therapist; apparently fearing criticism for his antisocial behavior.
Course of transference:	Negative at first seeing the therapist as scolding society or parent.
Approach to transference:	Discuss the resistance as such with the patient.
Activity vs. passivity:	Rather passive—to listen at first.
Free association:	Neither encourage nor discourage.
Ego strength:	Relatively little.
Anxiety:	A great deal.
Insight:	A fair amount.
Emotional maturity:	Very immature.
Social adjustment:	Very inadequate.
Degree of disturbance:	Moderately disturbed.
Degree of therapeutic change attempted:	Too little evidence.
Prognosis without therapy:	Get a little better.
Prognosis with therapy:	Neither favorable nor unfavorable.
Recommendations:	No; patient would resent any domination and being somewhat psychopathic would discontinue therapy most likely.
Attitude toward patient:	Somewhat positive.
Reasons:	I feel sympathy for this patient's emotionally sick status.

EVALUATION OF FILM THERAPIST

Adequacy:	Very adequate.
Reason:	Allowed the patient to tell his problems without interference and picked up cues.

Activity vs. passivity: Neither too active nor too passive.
Support: Neither too much nor too little.
Life history data: Somewhat less time.
Attitude toward therapist: Somewhat positive.
Reason: Calm, relaxed manner, sympathetic nonverbal
                               transference (physical appearance and manner
                               resemble a psychiatrist friend).

FILM RESPONSES

1. 0
2. How can I help you?
3. You relate this with something you don't quite feel you understand?
4. 0
5. Covered by what?
6. Do you relate economic circumstances to being hemmed in?
7. What insight?
8. Hmm?
9. What would a person have to do to fill the bill?
10. You seem anxious here?
11. Hm?
12. About what?
13. What economic worries? How family supported now?
14. Get away?
15. 0
16. What do you think we can do about this?
17. Didn't hear the question. What makes mad?
18. You think your feelings may have some relation to your situation?
19. What your mother did annoyed you?
20. Did your father understand and appreciate your situation?
21. Maybe you are sensitive to domination? (mother and work)
22. Involved?
23. You have problems (sympathetically here).
24. Cooperation?
25. Learning how?
26. Yes. You need a father?
27. You mean you aren't satisfied the way you are now?
28. These symptoms come from emotional problems. Solving them will relieve the symptoms.

COMMENT

Clinical Assessments: This therapist, too, has had little experience in psychotherapy, but he conveys the impression of an open-minded and level-headed person who has considerable intuitive understanding of the patient's plight, the deficiencies in his technical knowledge notwithstanding. Notice the absence of jargon and pseudo-sophistication. His technical formulations are kept simple, unpretentious, and unassuming; yet, they betray keen observational powers and a good understanding of the ways in which a person like the patient might interact with a therapist (see his comment about the patient's probable reaction to domination and his behavior in the transference). Personal prejudices and moral considerations do not impede the therapist's ability to see the patient as a disturbed person in need of help, and he sympathizes with his "sick status." Nevertheless, he recommends strictness (a recommendation more frequently made by therapists having a negative attitude toward the patient). His prognosis is guarded. It is also instructive to note his interpretation of the patient's behavior vis-à-vis the therapist as fear of criticism for antisocial behavior, as compared with many respondents who felt the patient was parading his antisocial tendencies in a shameless manner.

Film Responses: There can be little doubt about the therapist's ability to communicate empathically. Response 2 ("How can I help you?") is as human, unvarnished, and straightforward as any that was encountered. It helps to establish a productive therapeutic relationship from the beginning, by recognizing that the patient comes for help, that he has a right to expect it from a professional person, that he is in the "right" place. Simultaneously, it conveys interest in the patient as a person, and yet it poses a useful question because it discourages the possible notion of the therapist as a sponge which passively soaks up the patient's complaints, feelings of injustice, etc.

In Response 6, a preliminary attempt is made to establish connections. In Response 10 the therapist recognizes the patient's discomfort in the here-and-now. Response 21 ("Maybe you are sensitive to domination?") may be somewhat premature, but it recognizes an important attitude explicitly and concisely. Response 23 is a warm, supportive statement, which can come only from a mature person who is capable of "giving." In his final response, the therapist succeeds in communicating with admirable parsimony the essence of psychotherapy. The statement is appropriate, meets the patient's plea for reassurance without holding out unrealistic hopes, commensurate with the patient's level of education and understanding, and its veracity is unexceptional. It also establishes the therapist as an expert in human relations who is prepared to guide the patient along the path of insight. Thus, it outlines a therapeutic plan, even though the patient is almost certainly unable to comprehend its full implications, and it inspires hope. At least, the patient will come away with the feeling that he has been listened to attentively and respectfully, and that there are techniques by which he can be helped.

CODE: 8

BIOGRAPHICAL INFORMATION

Code:	8
Age:	30 years.
Sex:	Male.
Professional affiliation and status:	Psychiatric resident, second year.
Psychoanalytic training:	No plans.
Personal analysis:	No plans.
Experience in psychotherapy:	1 year; very little.
Type of therapy:	Mildly analytically oriented therapy with emphasis on current situations.
Type of patients:	Psychotic and psychoneurotic.
Theoretical orientation:	Whitehornian.

CLINICAL ASSESSMENTS

Diagnosis

Dominant personality type:	Anxiety.
Formulation of dynamics:	This patient has never matured emotionally beyond the point of infancy or early childhood.

Treatment plans

Form of treatment:	Psychotherapy 1-2 times weekly, plus group

	therapy with a mixed group of neurotics. Would also try reserpine or thorazine.
Treatment goals:	The goals would have to be quite limited. They would consist of covering the anxiety to the point where he can function, at least minimally, socially.
Frequency of sessions:	1-2 times weekly.
Length of treatment:	2 years.
Intermediate goals:	0
Ultimate goals:	0
Symptom-relief:	A moderate degree of symptom-relief would probably occur within several months.
Difficulties expected:	Getting caught up in the patient's obsessive discussion of his symptoms.
Focus:	His occupational history and how, in some detail, he spends his time.
Dangers:	Very definitely. This man is not too far removed from a frank psychotic break.
Areas to be avoided:	Would stay away from sex and sex identification.
Behaviors to be encouraged:	Yes. Would encourage reality testing; dealing with practical problems, etc.
Behaviors to be discouraged:	Would discourage excessive rumination, and fascination with his symptoms.
Strictness vs. permissiveness:	Rather strict.
Clues:	Antisocial attitudes; "getting even"; "that wasn't manly."
Course of transference:	Hostile dependence.
Approach to transference:	Would tend, at least for a period, to be rather dominating.
Activity vs. passivity:	Rather active.
Free association:	Discourage.
Ego strength:	Very little.
Anxiety:	Relatively little.
Insight:	Very little.
Emotional maturity:	Very immature.
Social adjustment:	Very inadequate.
Degree of disturbance:	Seriously disturbed.
Degree of therapeutic change attempted:	Very little.
Prognosis without therapy:	Get much worse.
Prognosis with therapy:	Somewhat unfavorable.
Recommendations:	Yes. His present mode of living borders on the psychotic.
Attitude toward patient:	Somewhat negative.
Reasons:	Excessive amount of self-pity.

EVALUATION OF FILM THERAPIST

Adequacy:	Reasonably adequate.
Reason:	A fair amount of information was obtained;

patient was satisfied and is ready to go along with therapeutic suggestions for the future.

Activity vs. passivity: Somewhat too passive.
Support: Neither too much nor too little.
Life history data: Considerably more time.
Attitude toward therapist: Neutral.
Reason: 0. No specific reasons.

FILM RESPONSES

1. Could you tell me what it was that brought you here to see me?
2. 0
3. 0
4. Would you tell me about some of these situations that you are referring to?
5. (Affirmative but questioning gesture. No comment.)
6. Once too often?
7. (Encouraging grunt. No comment.)
8. How long has it been that you have had symptoms of the sort that you are mentioning?
9. (Same comment as #8.)
10. When were you last able to work?
11. Would you tell me a little about your wife?
12. Then you would date this difficulty back to the time you got out of high school?
13. Antisocial attitudes?
14. Have you always had this difficulty with her?
15. What type of work were you doing most recently?
16. 0 (bland expression).
17. You have children, Mr. _____?
18. I'm not quite clear as to why you seek help now after all these years of difficulty.
19. You said, "That's not manly"? (questioning expression).
20. Do you have children of your own?
21. Could you tell me more about the jobs that you have held?
22. Was this the only source of the debt?
23. Antisocial attitudes?
24. What sort of cooperation?
25. What specific measures did you employ to get even?
26. (Puzzled look. No comment.)
27. Economic?
28. I'd like to discuss the types of work that you have done for a while.

COMMENT

Clinical Assessments: This therapist views the patient as seriously disturbed, near a psychotic break, and the prognosis is somewhat unfavorable. He would strive for quite limited goals, and is not averse to using ataractic drugs. His formulations and judgments indicate a higher level of training and experience, and he has rather definite ideas about managing the case. He reacts negatively to the patient, basing his reaction upon the "excessive amount of self-pity" displayed. He would be strict, active, and discourage free association as well as "excessive rumination and fascination with his symptoms." Evidently, this therapist does not like the patient, and he states this dislike in terms of technical considerations. An aseptic, distant tone pervades his comments: he is clearly talking about a "case," not a person.

Film Responses: As might be expected, his questioning is matter-of-fact, "clinical," cool, and aloof. He may be interested in the patient's account, but he gives no indication that he understands his suffering or his desire for help.

The patient is a specimen. The therapist's distance is epitomized in his final response ("I'd like to discuss the types of work that you have done for a while"). In the context of the patient's intense feelings, his plea for help, and the approaching end of the interview, the therapist's question must inevitably be experienced as extraordinarily callous, unfeeling, and even cruel. (Can this response be considered "reality-oriented" or suitable for a person who is perceived as close to a psychotic break?)

CODE: 9

BIOGRAPHICAL INFORMATION

Code:	9
Age:	28 years.
Sex:	Male.
Professional affiliation and status:	Psychiatric resident, third year.
Psychoanalytic training:	Plans to enter.
Personal analysis:	Completed 230 hours; plans to have 450 hours.
Experience in psychotherapy:	2½ years; a fair amount.
Type of therapy:	Analytically oriented therapy.
Type of patients:	Both neurotic and psychotic.
Theoretical orientation:	Psychoanalytically oriented (general).

CLINICAL ASSESSMENTS

Diagnosis

Dominant personality type:	Obsessive.
Formulation of dynamics:	Not enough data to formulate well. Most likely dynamic is rage at father (seen as a maternal but absent person) defended by phobic displacement, obsessive-compulsive mechanism, etc. These are not sufficient to bind anxiety and he feels anxiety directly.

Treatment plans

Form of treatment:	Psychotherapy.
Treatment goals:	Initially—to support defenses and lessen anxiety. Later goals to be set after more information is available.
Frequency of sessions:	2 times a week to start; later must be geared to patient's needs.
Length of treatment:	
Intermediate goals:	Initial goal—6-8 weeks; beyond this time cannot be determined since goals are quite uncertain with available data.
Ultimate goals:	0
Symptom-relief:	6-8 weeks for some slight relief as above. I do not know what you refer to as "symptoms."
Difficulties expected:	1. Getting involved in obsessive system. 2. Possibly permitting too much dependence on therapist; this should be watched.
Focus:	Not enough data.

Dangers:	Not enough data to estimate ego strength. This must be evaluated as soon as possible.
Areas to be avoided:	Not enough data.
Behaviors to be encouraged:	1. Less concern over somatic symptoms. 2. Less concern with obsessive rumination. 3. More active, capable behavior.
Behaviors to be discouraged:	Would discourage concern with past and childhood and deal with present.
Strictness vs. permissiveness:	Rather strict.
Clues:	Reaction to father's death. Avoidance of discussing father.
Course of transference:	Hostile dependent.
Approach to transference:	Limit dependence—at least early.
Activity vs. passivity:	Rather active—at least early.
Free association:	Discourage it.
Ego strength:	Too little evidence.
Anxiety:	A fair amount.
Insight:	Very little
Emotional maturity:	Very immature.
Social adjustment:	Very inadequate.
Degree of disturbance:	Seriously disturbed.
Degree of therapeutic change attempted:	Too little evidence.
Prognosis without therapy:	Probably get a little better.
Prognosis with therapy:	Somewhat favorable.
Recommendations:	No; do not believe this is the way to help him.
Attitude toward patient:	Somewhat negative.
Reasons:	Difficulty in working with a severely obsessive and immature patient.

EVALUATION OF FILM THERAPIST

Adequacy:	Somewhat inadequate.
Reason:	Much left unanswered which could have been explored. Leads furnished by patient were not followed up. Interviewer much too passive.
Activity vs. passivity:	Much too passive.
Support:	Somewhat too little support.
Life history data:	Somewhat more time.
Attitude toward therapist:	Somewhat negative.
Reason:	Above; do not think he interviewed well.

FILM RESPONSES

1. Tell me what brought you here.
2. 0
3. Um-huh.
4. Tell me more about it.
5. (Called out of room.)
6. (Called out of room.)
7. You say you had some other interviews?
8. 0
9. When did these sensations first begin?
10. When did this start?
11. "Movement worked in two fears . . ." How do you live? "Busybody . . ." Just what kind of person is she?

12. What made you anxious then?
13. Such as?
14. 0
15. Can you tell me some of the others?
16. What kind of person was your father?
17. Such as?
18. You said "another heart attack"— (raise eyebrow).
19. What's the earlies thing you remember?
20. What was he like?
21. Tell me what happened on some of your jobs.

22. 0
23. How did the bank happen to fire you for what seems like just an error?
24. Cooperation? (raise eyebrow quizically).
25. What would you do?
26. Not quite. Can you clarify it a little?
27. Do you dream much? What was the last dream you can remember? (Interview almost over—would like this material.)
28. You said you tried to "change your psychology." Can you tell me what this involved?

COMMENT

Clinical Assessments: This resident, clearly, has had more extensive training (notice his departure from a static, descriptive level) and experience, as evidenced by his dynamic formulation, treatment plans, and clinical judgments. If his self-assurance and self-confidence in his evaluations can be taken at face value— and there appear to be no counterindications—he has had experience with patients. Similarly, he has had occasion to observe experienced interviewers, as documented by his critical comments about the film therapist's technique. He has a frame of reference, which serves him to order his observations and to make sense of them.

He, too, is a member of a minority group who accorded primary attention to the obsessive features in the patient's functioning. Also, he runs counter to the group trend by viewing the prognosis as somewhat favorable while professing a somewhat negative attitude. He is able to give reasons for his attitude, which sound plausible. Possibly as a reaction to the patient's hostility and dependency, which may have rung a familiar note in the therapist in the sense that he may have to suppress and deny similar tendencies within himself, he recommends strictness and activity on the therapist's part, and he discourages free association. The latter would appear reasonable in terms of his emphasis on obsessive preoccupations.

Film Responses: The tone of clinical "objectivity" which suffuses the therapist's clinical judgments finds clear expression in his communications as well. His goal is to establish facts and gather data. Warmth, reassurance, empathy are completely lacking. On the other hand, he refrains from moralistic judgments. (Compare Response 23: "How did the bank manager happen to fire you for what seems like just an error?" with the response given by Case 1: "Fired for writing a bad check, huh?" In the latter, the patient has already been proven "guilty"). In Response 28 he, too, disregards the urgency of the patient's plea and fails to respond to the feelings.

CODE: 10

BIOGRAPHICAL INFORMATION

Code:	10
Age:	30 years.
Sex:	Male.
Professional affiliation and status:	Psychiatric resident, second year.
Psychoanalytic training:	Plans to enter.
Personal analysis:	In analysis, 500 hours so far.
Experience in psychotherapy:	1½ years; very little.
Type of therapy:	Dynamic psychotherapy.
Type of patients:	Schizophrenic; character disorders.
Theoretical orientation:	Psychoanalytically oriented (general).

CLINICAL ASSESSMENTS

Diagnosis

Dominant personality type:	Hysteria.
Formulation of dynamics:	A dependent man who is too fearful of being frustrated by those on whom he depends and feels hostile toward, to express his demands directly. Instead he is "using" his illness to gain dependent gratification and express hostile feelings.

Treatment plans

Form of treatment:	Psychotherapy.
Treatment goals:	Intermediate: to get back on his feet working, etc.
	Ultimate: to feel confident enough to express feelings more directly and relate positively to other people.
Frequency of sessions:	2-3 times a week.
Length of treatment:	
Intermediate goals:	1-2 years.
Ultimate goals:	Several years.
Symptom-relief:	Once a week for a few months (say 6) of supportive treatment.
Difficulties expected:	Refusal to keep appointments if insight is pushed.
Focus:	Working inabilities, i.e., reasons for treatment.
Dangers:	No.
Areas to be avoided:	Avoid repetition of old difficulties.
Behaviors to be encouraged:	Encourage him to intellectualize, figure things out and make formulas for living to help himself. This, especially in short therapy.
Behaviors to be discouraged:	The attitude that circumstances run his life.
Strictness vs. permissiveness:	I would encourage him at first to "make sense" of his life and insist on this strictly. I would be permissive about failures of his.
Clues:	No.
Course of transference:	Like to mother: openly friendly, secretly hostile.

Approach to transference:	Reassurance indirectly.
Activity vs. passivity:	Rather active.
Free association:	Discourage it.
Ego strength:	Relatively little.
Anxiety:	Relatively little.
Insight:	Relatively little.
Emotional maturity:	Fairly immature.
Social adjustment:	Very inadequate.
Degree of disturbance:	Seriously disturbed.
Degree of therapeutic change attempted:	Too little evidence.
Prognosis without therapy:	Probably remain about the same.
Prognosis with therapy:	Somewhat favorable.
Recommendations:	No; that isn't the problem.
Attitude toward patient:	Somewhat positive.
Reasons:	He seems to be at a point of thinking about trying to do something constructive after years of unsuccessful and miserable defending.

EVALUATION OF FILM THERAPIST

Adequacy:	Very inadequate.
Reason:	Poor historical data. No discussion about what's to be done.
Activity vs. passivity:	Much too passive.
Support:	Somewhat too little support.
Life history data:	Considerably more time.
Attitude toward therapist:	Strongly negative.
Reason:	He seems to me to be looking sort of pompous but doing nothing.

FILM RESPONSES

1. You have asked to see me. What is the difficulty which you want help with?
2. Tell me some more about this incident on the streetcar.
3. How has this incident continued to bother you so that you came to see me today?
4. 0
5. Do you have any feeling or idea about what was cornering you or forcing you to do as you have done?
6. You feel then that the circumstances are what hemmed you in?
7. When did all these symptoms, fear, dizziness, and so on, all start?
8. When did this inability to go out of the house begin?
9. So it's really the sensations that concern you more than the streetcar incident.
10. You say you can think about certain things and cause your symptoms. Why do you choose to think about these if you have control over it?
11. 0
12. Tell me about some earlier anxieties, in childhood.
13. Such as?
14. 0
15. What kinds of things would mother do that upset you?
16. During the time you've been incapacitated who has supported the family?
17. What traits for example?

18. You say you're getting "tired" of these symptoms?

19. Tell me something more about father and other family members, please.

20. 0

21. Could you tell me something about wife and your adult life more . . .

22. 0

23. Did you expect when you wrote the check that it would be held against you?

24. Well, you have had many difficulties, as you describe. What do you want to do about these now?

25. What now?

26. 0 (nodding "yes").

27. So you've felt that circumstances prevented your doing better. Do you see any solutions now?

28. No, but they do handicap your enjoyment of living.

COMMENT

Clinical Assessments: With relatively little experience, this therapist succeeds in formulating a reasonably clear picture of the patient as a person and his difficulties in living. His empathic understanding of the patient enables him to perceive him as a person in need of help, and he focuses on the constructive aspects of the patient's strivings, without losing sight of the therapeutic problem. This is consonant with his diagnosis of "Hysteria." His proposed therapeutic approach is supportive and re-educative rather than investigative or analytical. Apparently, his focus is on getting the patient back on his feet in the shortest possible time by encouraging constructive moves. (One may question whether it can be done in this fashion.) His attitude is somewhat positive (notice the absence of defeatist statements, often encountered in other protocols!), his outlook favorable, and one gathers that he sees no reason why the patient cannot or should not be helped. For his part, he seems willing to lend his resources.

Film Responses: Here, again, we observe a notable concomitance between the therapist's formulations and the focus of his communications. He is interested, wide-awake, and takes advantage of openings to stimulate constructive moves (see Responses 10, 24, 25, 27, and 28). Similarly, he wishes to establish the purpose of the interview—why the patient has elected to seek help at this particular time (Responses 1 and 3). His response to the final item is unequivocal and responsive to the patient's insistent demand for a definite answer. There may be some doubt about its potential value to the patient at this juncture, but it cannot fail to communicate that the therapist is "with" him. In sum, the therapist accomplishes at least the following: he seeks elaboration and documentation of the patient's difficulties without subjecting him to the "third degree"; he reinforces his desire to change; he works toward clarifying the purpose of the interview and the patient's motivation for therapy; he communicates that help is available, that he is willing to give it, and that the past need not completely determine the future. He succeeds in this task without showering the patient with reassurance or instilling extravagant hopes. His approach is thoroughly pragmatic and reality-oriented. He says in effect: Here is a problem; it is not insoluble; let's see what you and I can do about it.

9

GROUP II: PSYCHIATRISTS

EXPERIENCE LEVEL: INTERMEDIATE

BIOGRAPHICAL INFORMATION

Code:	11
Age:	40 years.
Sex:	Male
Professional affiliation and status:	Psychiatrist.
Psychoanalytic training:	In training.
Personal analysis:	Completed analysis; 700 hours.
Experience in psychotherapy:	3½ years; a fair amount.
Type of therapy:	1. Analytically oriented psychotherapy. 2. Psychoanalysis.
Type of patients:	Out-patients; neurotics and "borderline"; "psychosomatic" patients.
Theoretical orientation:	Psychoanalytically oriented (general).

CLINICAL ASSESSMENTS

Diagnosis

Dominant personality type:	Anxiety; phobic reaction.
Formulation of dynamics:	Hostile identification with his mother as basic issue; underlying depression in relation to father's death with suppressed rage and acting out as alternative defenses against passive (homosexual) trends. Suspect patient is hypertensive.

Treatment plans

Form of treatment:	Would like more data. Question of psycho-therapy alone or combined with some newer drugs (to be given by internist).
Treatment goals:	Some reduction in anxiety and improvement in life situation would be maximum goals. Would be pessimistic about results.
Frequency of sessions:	2-3 times a week.
Length of treatment:	6 months to 1 year for improvement (sympto-matic).
Intermediate goals:	0
Ultimate goals:	0
Symptom-relief:	6 months to 1 year (if it can be done at all).
Difficulties expected:	1. Acting out, including possibility of anti-social behavior, missing appointments, "forget-ting to come," etc.
	2. Anxiety in patient, with passive and aggres-sive feelings toward therapist.
	3. Question of psychotic episode.
Focus:	Day-to-day events, job difficulties and getting back to work.
Dangers:	Psychotic reaction not impossible; further evalu-ation of paranoid trends desirable.
Areas to be avoided:	Questions about homosexuality, i.e., patient's view of himself.
Behaviors to be encouraged:	Looking at current issues in living more real-istically.
Behaviors to be discouraged:	Would discourage acting out as much as possible and getting a job.
Strictness vs. permissiveness:	Firm about our conditions for work and that he stick to them.
Clues:	1. Aggressive trends (regarding father's death and it all fell on him).
	2. Tremendous rage—anxiety in film—regarding mother.
	3. Possible criminal record and prison record.
Course of transference:	1. Passivity and demandingness and complaint of not being helped.
	2. Acting out of hostility rather than expression.
Approach to transference:	Only with firmness, allowing myself expression of arrogance under provocation.
Activity vs. passivity:	Active-passive doesn't suit me as alternatives. He would need firmness as indicated above about
	1. Frankness regarding past antisocial behavior.
	2. Containment of it in therapeutic situation.
Free association:	Neither encourage nor discourage.
Ego strength:	Very little.
Anxiety:	A great deal.

Insight: Very little.
Emotional maturity: Very immature.
Social adjustment: Very inadequate.
Degree of disturbance: Seriously disturbed.
Degree of therapeutic change
    attempted: Very little change.
Prognosis without therapy: Too little evidence.
Prognosis with therapy: Very unfavorable (but willing to be surprised).
Recommendations: Not yet; with more evidence of feasibility,
                                  would recommend that he go to work.
Attitude toward patient: Somewhat negative.
    Reasons: Probably related to statement and attitude
                                  about "the world owes me a living."

EVALUATION OF FILM THERAPIST

    Adequacy: Somewhat inadequate.
    Reason: More specific history; more "structuring" of
                                  certain reasonable expectations that he would
                                  have of initial interview.
    Activity vs. passivity: Somewhat too passive.
    Support: Neither too much nor too little; about right.
    Life history data: Considerably more time.
    Attitude toward therapist: Somewhat positive.
    Reason: Seemed to be doing well enough and amiably
                                  disposed to his patient.

FILM RESPONSES

1. 0 (sit down myself and give attention).
2. 0
3. Mm (with some sort of nod).
4. Tell me more about that.
5. 0
6. In a general way I understand
   you have been anxious and upset
   at times, but I would like to hear
   a great deal more about it—how it
   started and how you've noticed it
   since.
7. 0
8. Um (and nod).
9. This other stuff?
10. Anxiety, fear, self-pity and pro-
    longed sorrow?
11. At this point it might be a good
    idea for you to tell me about
    yourself, your parents, brothers
    and sisters if any, your experience
    in growing up—a sort of history
    of yourself from the beginning.

12. 0 (in relation to having said 11).
13. Your antisocial attitude?
14. 0
15. I didn't get that (I didn't, in fact,
    hear patient's last remark starting
    with: that's one . . .).
16. By the way, have you ever sought
    help before from a doctor for
    these matters, had a physical
    check-up, seen a psychiatrist be-
    fore?
17. So? (with questioning inflection).
18. 0
19. Tell me more about the early ex-
    periences and feelings.
20. Um?
21. Tell me more about difficulties on
    the various jobs.
22. 0
23. Let's see, you were how old when
    father died?
24. 1931, those were depression times?

25.· As long as we're talking because
you come to me for some recommendations, you might as well tell
me about that too.
26. Not entirely; tell me more.

27. 0
28. Have you had any physical check-
ups and what have you been told
of the results?

COMMENT

Clinical Assessments: This therapist regards the patient as very anxious and
seriously disturbed, and he would strive for very little change in therapy. The
latter judgment is in keeping with a very unfavorable prognostic estimate,
although he declares a willingness "to be surprised." He feels that the film
therapist failed to structure the interview sufficiently and thereby to obtain a
more specific case history. The possibility of a psychosis is envisaged, and he is
impressed with underlying homosexual trends. He displays some eagerness to
get the patient back to work, but this is more in the spirit of buckle-down-and-
quit-the-griping than therapy. According to his own statement, he would not be
averse to responding to the patient's hostility and demandingness with arrogance.
The formulations are thoroughly "professional," cold, and distant. The patient's
expectation that the world owes him a living seems to trigger a hostile, negative
reaction in the therapist, of which he seems to be partially aware.

Film Responses: The questions are case-history oriented, factual, and coolly
investigative. He wants to get the facts, "the whole truth and nothing but the
truth." There is no glimmer of understanding or empathy. Response 28 is
especially revealing of this basic orientation; he sidesteps the immediacy of the
patient's feelings and treats the problem "medically."

One might venture the prediction that if the patient were to enter therapy
with this therapist, treatment would soon founder and the patient might leave
in disillusionment (unless a more serious eventuality supervened). It is also
predictable that such outcomes would be attributed to the patient's poor motivation for therapy, negative therapeutic reaction, or psychopathic tendencies.

CODE: 12

BIOGRAPHICAL INFORMATION

Code:	12
Age:	46 years.
Sex:	Male.
Professional affiliation and status:	Psychiatrist.
Psychoanalytic training:	Some.
Personal analysis:	Completed analysis; 600 hours.
Experience in psychotherapy:	7 years; a fair amount.
Type of therapy:	Analytically oriented.
Type of patients:	Neurotics.
Theoretical orientation:	Sullivan.

CLINICAL ASSESSMENTS
Diagnosis

Dominant personality type:	Anxiety.

Formulation of dynamics:	Chronic morbid resentment based on unsatisfied dependency need: "the world owes me a living."
Treatment plans	
Form of treatment:	Intensive psychotherapy.
Treatment goals:	Awareness of relation of his symptom to the intolerability of his living situation as he sees it, then exploration of how it may be modified. A major goal would be getting him back to work.
Frequency of sessions:	2 a week.
Length of treatment:	At least a year, 100 hours (2 a week).
Intermediate goals:	0
Ultimate goals:	0
Symptom-relief:	I do not believe this could be achieved without modification of patient's attitudes and his life situation.
Difficulties expected:	Constant reversion to symptoms, resentment toward me if prompt relief weren't forthcoming.
Focus:	Marriage, work.
Dangers:	No; he is extremely well-defended.
Areas to be avoided:	No.
Behaviors to be encouraged:	Self-reliance. I'd hunt hard for successes he has had, however small.
Behaviors to be discouraged:	Resentment, self-pity (though how to do this I'm not quite clear).
Strictness vs. permissiveness:	Rather strict.
Clues:	His continual shift to blame others, crouching posture, angry tone.
Course of transference:	Never very positive, increasingly hostile when therapist does not solve his problem for him.
Approach to transference:	I would point this out repeatedly.
Activity vs. passivity:	Rather active (but not more than was in the first one).
Free association:	Discourage.
Ego strength:	Relatively little.
Anxiety:	A fair amount.
Insight:	A great deal (of intellectual, cannot judge emotional).
Emotional maturity:	Fairly immature.
Social adjustment:	Very inadequate.
Degree of disturbance:	Moderately disturbed.
Degree of therapeutic change attempted:	Relatively little.
Prognosis without therapy:	Would remain about the same.
Prognosis with therapy:	Somewhat unfavorable.
Recommendations:	Inadequate information as to what his present mode of living is.
Attitude toward patient:	Somewhat negative.
Reasons:	His resentful self-pity, routinized statement of his illness.

EVALUATION OF FILM THERAPIST

Adequacy: Very inadequate.

Reason: 1. I would have followed through leads which kept things moving, not returned to earlier areas.

2. I would have tried to get him to be more specific, and keep him more on the present.

Activity vs. passivity: Somewhat too passive.

Support: Somewhat too little.

Life history data: Considerably more time.

Attitude toward therapist: Somewhat positive.

Reason: I felt sorry for him; he was so uneasy and at sea.

FILM RESPONSES

1. (Sit down and look pleasantly expectant.)
2. 0
3. 0
4. Can you give me an example?
5. (Nod slightly.)
6. You feel that being hemmed in on the streetcar was the same as being hemmed in by life?
7. (Look disinterested.)
8. What helps you to feel better? (I would be trying to steer him back to concrete examples and interpersonal issues.)
9. What other stuff?
10. You feel prolonged sorrow about something?
11. You find your mother's talking hard to take?
12. How did you attempt to deal with your mother?
13. (Look expectant and interested.)
14. It *is* hard to speak up to one's mother.
15. 0
16. Have you noticed what helps you to feel less anxious?
17. What do you do when you feel mad?
18. You were anxious for economic reasons? Did your brother ever offer to help?
19. How did you handle your annoyance?
20. (Couldn't quite hear. I would make some comment to keep him on Dad.)
21. (Look sympathetic.)
22. 0
23. What do you do to get your mind off these feelings?
24. How about your wife? Does she cooperate with you? (Again trying to get him into here and now, also to search for some assets in the situation.)
25. Perhaps that has something to do with your feeling anxious.
26. You found you couldn't get away with trying to get even? (trying to get back to a potentially fruitful lead).
27. 0
28. You must be convinced by now that they won't damage you, after all these years. Tell me, how would your life be different if you didn't have them?

COMMENT

Clinical Assessments: This therapist seems impressed by the patient's anxiety, but he reacts negatively, as did many others, to the patient's attitude that the world owes him a living; yet his clinical judgments do not seem appreciably influenced by his own negative attitude. He recommends intensive psychotherapy, which, however, is directed less at emotional insight than at getting the patient back to work; this he sees as a major goal. Unlike a number of his colleagues who envisioned the possibility of a psychotic break, this therapist considers the patient "extremely well defended." Probably as a result of his exposure to psychoanalytic thinking (and therapy?) he does not believe that symptoms can be relieved without a modification of the patient's attitudes and his life situation (?). He seems to know what is transpiring in the interview, and sticks to observables. Notice the absence of analytic jargon. While he has little sympathy for the patient ("resentful self-pity, routinized statement of his illness") he pities the film therapist for the difficulty of his task.

Film Responses: His communications appear appropriate and adequate. His Sullivanian orientation seems evidenced by his desire to obtain concrete examples and to deal with interpersonal issues (Responses 8, 12, 18, 24). He supports the patient by saying that it *is* hard to speak up to one's (domineering) mother (Response 14). Furthermore, he responds to the patient's feelings (Response 28), and, rather skillfully, quickly shifts to another, but highly pertinent, question, thereby evading the patient's attempt to "rope in" the therapist. On the whole, he stays close to the patient's feelings. He seeks to clarify feelings rather than facts, and manages to communicate a measure of interest and warmth. He is rather gentle and avoids direct confrontations, which, at this time, would probably give rise to a verbal barrage. One may speculate that his approach may be quite successful in allaying the patient's anxiety in the interview situation and increase his comfort. At the same time, the patient may be expected to start working on his problem.

CODE: 13

BIOGRAPHICAL INFORMATION

Code:	13
Age:	34 years.
Sex:	Male.
Professional affiliation and status:	Psychiatrist.
Psychoanalytic training:	Plans.
Personal analysis:	Completed 400 hours; is continuing to 1,000 or more hours.
Experience in psychotherapy:	3 years; a fair amount.
Type of therapy:	Analytically oriented treatment.
Type of patients:	Psychoneurotic and borderline psychotic.
Theoretical orientation:	Sullivan.

CLINICAL ASSESSMENTS

Diagnosis

Dominant personality type:	Psychopathic.
Formulation of dynamics:	I wouldn't formulate dynamics from this limited amount of material.

Treatment plans

Form of treatment:	Psychotherapy, probably modified by use of

drugs (nonbarbiturate) for purpose of helping patient get over disorganizing anxiety.

Treatment goals:	The goal of relief from anxiety that is disabling, return to some form of work. Would not consider him for truly reconstructive psychotherapy.
Frequency of sessions:	1 time per week.
Length of treatment:	30-40 hours.
Intermediate goals:	0
Ultimate goals:	0
Symptom-relief:	30-40 hours.
Difficulties expected:	Excessive dependency demands and retreat from therapy when those demands couldn't be met.
Focus:	Current relationship to wife.
Dangers:	(Dangers? What do you mean?) Dependency demands as a risk to therapy.
Areas to be avoided:	Sexual attitudes of a passive nature.
Behaviors to be encouraged:	The expression of positive feelings toward any accomplishment.
Behaviors to be discouraged:	Any agreement which might implicitly or explicitly support the idea "three strikes against me."
Strictness vs. permissiveness:	Rather strict.
Clues:	Death of father. Feelings following his death.
Course of transference:	Passive dependent with hostile outbursts when frustrated.
Approach to transference:	One or two but they aren't clear at this time.
Activity vs. passivity:	Rather active.
Free association:	Discourage.
Ego strength:	Relatively little.
Anxiety:	A fair amount.
Insight:	Relatively little.
Emotional maturity:	Fairly immature.
Social adjustment:	Fairly inadequate.
Degree of disturbance:	Mildly disturbed.
Degree of therapeutic change attempted:	Very little change.
Prognosis without therapy:	Get a little better.
Prognosis with therapy:	Neither favorable nor unfavorable.
Recommendations:	No; this would encourage dependency attitudes.
Attitude toward patient:	Somewhat negative.
Reasons:	One doesn't like in the outsider what he knows to exist in himself.

EVALUATION OF FILM THERAPIST

Adequacy:	Reasonably adequate.
Reason:	He learned of pathology, something of defenses, and he probably got some idea of dynamics.
Activity vs. passivity:	Somewhat too passive.
Support:	Neither too much nor too little.

Life history data: About the same.
Attitude toward therapist: Neutral.
    Reason: He mumbled; wasn't sharp.

FILM RESPONSES

1. (Pause. Wait for patient to say something.)
2. (Listen for short while longer. Focus back to initial statements about onset of anxiety in car.)
3. (Stay with feelings about this particular anxiety attack for further elaboration of feelings.)
4. (Focus on some other setting of "being hemmed in.") Tell when another time you had this kind of feeling.
5. Yes—and your feelings. Tell me about another time.
6. You said you felt *anxious?*
7. (Focus on *wife*) She goes every time.
8. (Back to) Like someone sitting on it.
9. 0
10. Sorrow—prolonged?
11. Yes, go on.
12. In high school?

13. Antisocial?
14. 0
15. More some time than others?
16. Something would happen?
17. Mad?
18. (To mother or wife. Cut through defensive use of economics.)
19. (Focus on patient-mother relationship. Avoid the "gossipy aspects of mother.")
20. (Back to anger.)
21. Tell me about one unpleasant work experience.
22. 0
23. There were other antisocial acts?
24. You felt bucked up, good?
25. What did you do?
26. No, I don't see what you mean.
27. (More about the "filled up" feeling.)
28. What thoughts have you had about this?

COMMENT

Clinical Assessments: This therapist declines to formulate a statement about emotional dynamics on the basis of limited evidence and, in general, seems riled by the questions posed to him ("Dangers? What do you mean?") Although he perceives a fair amount of anxiety in the patient, he considers him a psychopath who is only mildly disturbed and essentially unsuited for psychotherapy. He says he would not consider him for "truly reconstructive" psychotherapy, but one wonders whether he would be willing to enter into any therapeutic relationship with him. This disinclination to treat the patient may also be reflected in the judgment that he would get a little better without treatment, possibly a rationalization. The recommendation for drug therapy is in keeping with the foregoing. While he asserts a noncommittal attitude with respect to prognosis, the inference that he regards it as basically unfavorable seems well supported. His comment, "One doesn't like in the outsider what he knows to exist in himself" in support of his negative attitude reveals a certain insight, but his responses give little evidence that he is capable of counteracting his rejecting impulses, at least in this context. Little perspicacity is needed to perceive that this therapist has little use for the patient.

Film Responses: The therapist's apparent lack of understanding for the patient's discomfort is borne out by his minimal communications. There appears to be an inherent reluctance to say anything, and each word seems like a concession. He makes no pretense of being warm, friendly, or sympathetic, and apparently considers the patient an unwanted intruder or an imposing bore. Response 26 seems coldly rejecting even if true, and Response 28 at best redundant, considering that the patient has put forth considerable effort (however defensive and distorted) to detail his feelings.

CODE: 14

BIOGRAPHICAL INFORMATION

Code:	14
Age:	35 years.
Sex:	Male.
Professional affiliation and status:	Psychoanalyst.
Psychoanalytic training:	In training (?).
Personal analysis:	Completed 600 hours; completed analysis.
Experience in psychotherapy:	7 years; a fair amount.
Type of therapy:	Mainly psychoanalysis.
Type of patients:	Neurotics and character disorders.
Theoretical orientation:	Psychoanalytically oriented (general).

CLINICAL ASSESSMENTS
Diagnosis

Dominant personality type:	Character disorder.
Formulation of dynamics:	Frustration handled by repression, with repressed hatred of mother, revenge through masochism and spiteful acting out.

Treatment plans

Form of treatment:	Intensive psychotherapy.
Treatment goals:	Freedom from anxiety attacks and organ preoccupation, job stability, enlargement of social contacts.
Frequency of sessions:	2 or 3 times a week.
Length of treatment:	2-3 years.
Intermediate goals:	
Ultimate goals:	
Symptom-relief:	2 hours per week for 1½ years.
Difficulties expected:	Intellectualization, rivalry in the hour, dependency demands outside the hour.
Focus:	Need for attention, loneliness, emptiness, avoidance of intimacy.
Dangers:	Over-intellectualizations and premature interpretations.
Areas to be avoided:	0
Behaviors to be encouraged:	Less self-disgracing and more simple situational assessments.

Behaviors to be discouraged: Corollary of above.
Strictness vs. permissiveness: No more strict or permissive than with others.
Clues: 0
Course of transference: Hostile dependency.
Approach to transference: Interpret it as it appears in the transference.
Activity vs. passivity: No more active or passive than with others.
Free association: Neither encourage nor discourage it.
Ego strength: Too little evidence.
Anxiety: A fair amount.
Insight: A fair amount.
Emotional maturity: Fairly immature.
Social adjustment: Fairly inadequate.
Degree of disturbance: Moderately disturbed.
Degree of therapeutic change
  attempted: Too little evidence.
Prognosis without therapy: Remain about the same.
Prognosis with therapy: Too little evidence.
Recommendations: Prefer to analyze than to "direct."
Attitude toward patient: Somewhat negative.
  Reasons: Too many "quickie" explanations of pseudo-scientific quality.

EVALUATION OF FILM THERAPIST

Adequacy: Somewhat inadequate.
  Reason: Lopsided interview.
Activity vs. passivity: Somewhat too passive.
Support: Somewhat too little support.
Life history data: Considerably more time.
Attitude toward therapist: Somewhat negative.
  Reason: Too much hiding behind his pipe and being at his desk.

FILM RESPONSES

1. 0
2. You have an idea as to the cause of your fear?
3. These thoughts come quickly to you . . .
4. 0
5. 0
6. 0
7. You've grown to be more conscious of yourself?
8. And you've gotten so you're quite suggestible?
9. What else has been troubling you lately?
10. I notice you know some medical terms!?
11. Uh huh.
12. Uh huh.
13. You're apt to have an explanation ready for everything?
14. 0
15. Empty! Apparently you don't feel as if you've got some solidity of your own?
16. In spite of how you feel about her, you lean on your mother for support?
17. In spite of everything you've gotten to be a lot like her?
18. Uh huh!
19. 0 (make mental note that he wants "all" the attention).

20. Not much attention from your father?
21. Uh huh (mental note: about time to find out his awareness of wanting attention from me).
22. What's that . . . (slip)?
23. You feel sorry for yourself. No one else seemed interested.
24. 0
25. Get even . . . for others not showing more interest in your problems?
26. 0 (denial of realistic dependency need, hostile dependency).
27. 0
28. You want my interest and attention but you don't expect to get it unless you're seriously ill ("heart drops out").

COMMENT

Clinical Assessments: Here is a therapist with a good deal of training and experience, including psychoanalysis. He views the patient as suffering from a character disorder, and recommends intensive psychotherapy for a period of two to three years. He is noncommittal about the prognosis, and describes his attitude as somewhat negative. His reason is that he does not like the patient's particular defenses ("Too many 'quickie' explanations of pseudo-scientific quality"). On the whole, his evaluations seem sensible and perceptive. He anticipates a good many intellectualizations, and rivalry with the therapist, who is in danger of making premature interpretations. Expressions of any positive feelings for the patient are conspicuous by their absence.

Film Responses: Without seeing the need to make an introductory statement or to clarify the purpose of the interview, he assumes an expectant attitude and proceeds to ask investigative questions. Response 8 may have a tinge of sarcasm, although one cannot be sure. This impression is reinforced by Responses 13, 15, 23, and 28. The therapist's statements are undoubtedly correct as far as the patient's dynamics are concerned, but in the context of the patient's mounting anger they probably fuel his resentment and hostility, which thus may become directed against the interviewer. From the patient's point of view, he may experience the comments as a cold, unsympathetic attack against which he would have to defend himself more vehemently. If this is true, the confrontations must be considered premature and out of place in an initial interview. This suggests the possibility that the therapist is riding roughshod over the patient's feelings, which he fails to recognize or chooses to disregard, and that he is ignoring the patient's subjective frame of reference at the expense of his own preconceived plan of procedure. Instead of succeeding in establishing a common ground upon which future collaboration may be possible, the therapist may drive the patient away. The latter may feel that he has been punished and criticized again, which can hardly be regarded as a therapeutic desideratum.

CODE: 15

BIOGRAPHICAL INFORMATION

Code: 15
Age: 37 years.
Sex: Male.

Professional affiliation and status:	Psychoanalyst.
Psychoanalytic training:	In training.
Personal analysis:	Completed analysis of about 1,200 hours.
Experience in psychotherapy:	8 years; a fair amount.
Type of therapy:	Psychoanalysis, analytic psychotherapy.
Type of patients:	Severe neurotics.
Theoretical orientation:	Psychoanalytically oriented (modified Freudian).

CLINICAL ASSESSMENTS

Diagnosis

Dominant personality type:	Anxiety; hysteria; paranoid; agoraphobia.
Formulation of dynamics:	Exceptionally marked positive oedipal relationship to an over-seductive mother. Fear of loss of control of incestuous and destructive impulses.

Treatment plans

Form of treatment:	If he could afford it, he should have a one year period of psychoanalysis, 4-5 times a week. If not, once a week psychotherapy of a supportive nature.
Treatment goals:	If for psychoanalysis, the goal of course would be the evolvement of a transference neurosis with eventual de-repression following the regressive reliving of the oedipal relationships. Freeing of the patient from his anarchistic reenactment of past emotional ties.
Frequency of sessions:	(See form of treatment.)
Length of treatment:	(See form of treatment.)
Intermediate goals:	0
Ultimate goals:	0
Symptom-relief:	I would not treat him for this.
Difficulties expected:	Denial, intellectualization, rationalization, marked transference, resistance, positive and negative. Intensification of phobia and panic.
Focus:	None in analysis.
Dangers:	Doctor's over-concern about symptoms of patient and over-solicitude.
Areas to be avoided:	1. Areas involving symptoms. 2. Incest. 3. Destructiveness except in terms of derivatives or defenses against these impulses.
Behaviors to be encouraged:	Focusing on his part in the creation of the crisis.
Behaviors to be discouraged:	Intellectualization, universalization and self-exculpation.
Strictness vs. permissiveness:	If in analysis, I would do whatever was necessary to keep the analysis going. If in psychotherapy, my strictness and permissiveness would vary according to the patient's defenses.

Clues:	His slips of speech. His gestures and mannerisms.
Course of transference:	Strong positive concealing latent negative. Later, strong negative in the form of more symptoms, more acting out outside, and more paranoia.
Approach to transference:	Systematic interpretation of defenses and resistances and transference and repetition-compulsion.
Activity vs. passivity:	No more active or passive than with others.
Free association:	If in analysis, of course encourage free association; no other way of getting to unconscious material.
Ego strength:	Too little evidence.
Anxiety:	A fair amount.
Insight:	Very little.
Emotional maturity:	Very immature.
Social adjustment:	Very inadequate.
Degree of disturbance:	Moderately disturbed.
Degree of therapeutic change attempted:	Fairly extensive.
Prognosis without therapy:	Remain about the same.
Prognosis with therapy:	Too little evidence.
Recommendations:	Don't know enough about his present living to say. But I wouldn't want him living with his mother now if he were in analysis.
Attitude toward patient:	Somewhat positive.
Reasons:	0 (yes).

EVALUATION OF FILM THERAPIST

Adequacy:	Very inadequate.
Reason:	He prepared the patient for non-directive therapy. He interrogated too often. He did not show interest in longitudinal dynamics.
Activity vs. passivity:	Much too active in a purposeless way.
Support:	Somewhat too little support at close of interview.
Life history data:	Somewhat more time.
Attitude toward therapist:	Strongly negative.
Reason:	He seemed wishy-washy and interested in getting only definitions.

FILM RESPONSES

1. 0
2. 0
3. Panic reaction.
4. 0
5. 0
6. Hemmed in all these years and this is your first attempt to seek help?
7. 0
8. 0
9. 0
10. 0
11. 0
12. 0
13. 0

14. When was the first time you
    feared going out on the street
    alone and what were the circum-
    stances?
15. 0
16. When did it all begin?
17. 0 (made a slip: daddy away from
    work instead of home). I'd repeat
    "daddy away from home."
18. 0
19. 0
20. Home alone with mother most of
    the time.

21. What contacts have you had with
    psychiatry?
22. After *mother's* death.
23. 0
24. 0
25. What do you hope to gain from
    treatment?
26. 0
27. 0
28. How do you feel you can be
    helped here?

COMMENT

Clinical Assessments: This is the record of an experienced analyst whose technical command of the situation is unexceptional. His dynamic formulation seems to capture the essence of the patient's conflict and provides a concise statement of the opposing emotional forces. His proposed treatment of choice is psychoanalysis, although one may wonder whether an estimate of one year's intensive therapy is not overly optimistic. From the recommendation of psycho-analysis follow his comments about free association, symptom-relief, focus of therapy, etc., which hew close to psychoanalytic thinking. He is noncommittal about prognosis, and describes his attitude as somewhat positive; evidently he is also able to give the reason(s) for his attitude, but seems to prefer to keep them to himself. His evaluation of the film therapist is highly critical, but probably correct. It seems noteworthy, however, that the latter is condemned not only for his technical deficiencies, but he is disliked, and even hated, on more personal grounds.

Film Responses: Communications are exceedingly sparing, which was true of analysts as a group. The few comments that are made are kept concise, and no words are wasted. One surmises that the interviewer is carrying out the role of the classical analyst who attempts to present himself as a mirror which only reflects the patient's productions. Unlike most interviewers, he focuses on slips of the tongue in Responses 17 and 22. The first slip was very rarely singled out by other respondents; the second, while of the utmost dynamic significance, was noted by a good many therapists, but was rarely taken up, undoubtedly because the time was considered. Inasmuch as the slip reveals the patient's unconscious death wishes for his mother, clear awareness of which would surely give rise to intense anxiety, a direct attack would probably be exceedingly disturbing. The advisability of such a procedure, especially in an initial interview, seems open to serious question. The tone of his communications is at best business-like, but more often it seems cold, unfriendly and even hostile.

Too, there are certain contradictions which deserve comment. The therapist mentions in his clinical impressions that, among others, the area of incest should be avoided, at least early in therapy; yet, in Response 20 he alludes to this problem ("Home alone with mother most of the time?"). He criticizes the film therapist for somewhat too little support, mentioning specifically the close of the interview; however, he refrains from giving support to the patient at any point in the interview, and at the end, rather than responding to the patient's urgent feelings, advances another direct confrontation. One wonders about the nature of the therapist's professed positive attitude; he certainly fails to communicate it, either in his clinical assessments or in his proposed communications to the patient.

CODE: 16

BIOGRAPHICAL INFORMATION

Code:	16
Age:	29 years.
Sex:	Male.
Professional affiliation and status:	Psychiatrist.
Psychoanalytic training:	In training; started 1955.
Personal analysis:	Presently undergoing analysis; started 1955; completed 60 hours.
Experience in psychotherapy:	A fair amount; 4.0 years.
Type of therapy:	Analytically oriented.
Type of patients:	Neurotics.
Theoretical orientation:	Psychoanalytically oriented (general).

CLINICAL ASSESSMENTS

Diagnosis

Dominant personality type:	Obsessive.
Formulation of dynamics:	By placing blame externally, he refuses all responsibility for his condition. The load is on the therapist and not himself. Very difficult to help.

Treatment plans

Form of treatment:	Supportive therapy—in which you make yourself available but do not take responsibility for his decisions.
Treatment goals:	Minimal support until he can find some work. Can be done 1 time per week.
Frequency of sessions:	Once a week.
Length of treatment:	Minimum 2 years.
Intermediate goals:	0
Ultimate goals:	0
Symptom-relief:	3 months—but in need of continual support.
Difficulties expected:	All responsibility for failure would be on the therapist. Hostility and verbiage may block therapy.
Focus:	Feelings.
Dangers:	Assuming the load.
Areas to be avoided:	No intensive probing should be attempted— follow his lead.
Behaviors to be encouraged:	Expression of feeling.

Behaviors to be discouraged:	Making the therapist God.
Strictness vs. permissiveness:	Rather permissive.
Clues:	Muscular tensions, body attitudes, mother-father relationship.
Course of transference:	Maternal.
Approach to transference:	Realistic; break through this transference.
Activity vs. passivity:	Rather passive.
Free association:	Neither encourage nor discourage.
Ego strength:	A fair amount.
Anxiety:	A fair amount.
Insight:	A fair amount.
Emotional maturity:	Fairly immature.
Social adjustment:	Very inadequate.
Degree of disturbance:	Seriously disturbed.
Degree of therapeutic change attempted:	Relatively little change.
Prognosis without therapy:	Probably remain the same.
Prognosis with therapy:	Somewhat favorable.
Recommendations:	No, that's his problem.
Attitude toward patient:	Mixed feelings.
Reasons:	0

EVALUATION OF FILM THERAPIST

Adequacy:	Reasonably adequate.
Reason:	For some types of handling this case, it was handled fairly well.
Activity vs. passivity:	Somewhat too passive.
Support:	Somewhat too little support.
Life history data:	Would devote somewhat less time.
Attitude toward therapist:	Somewhat negative.
Reason:	Seemed cold.

FILM RESPONSES

1. 0
2. 0
3. 0
4. Could you go on?
5. Yes . . .
6. It seems as if that's made you quite uncomfortable.
7. Seems as if one thing follows another.
8. You seem to feel all your tensions in your muscles and stomach.
9. You feel the answer to your problem is in your feelings.
10. You seem to be feeling some now!
11. Oh!
12. The way you describe it you seem to be carrying a large load.
13. You mean withdrawing helps you deal with your tensions.
14. 0
15. You seem to have a lot of feelings about your mother?
16. 0
17. A lot of pressure . . . and a lot of feelings.
18. And you feel I can be of some help.
19. From what you say, it's been a life full of annoyances.
20. (Nod of encouragement.)

21. You present things as if everything and everybody are against you.
22. 0
23. Despite the rough time, you seemed to know how to get work and take care of yourself.
24. Quite a load!
25. And you feel I can be of help somehow.
26. Um. How do you think I can help?
27. The world has been quite hard, and you blame it all for your tensions.
28. I don't know. In the past you say you've never got any help from anyone.

COMMENT

Clinical Assessments: This young therapist, having more than a minimum of experience, is impressed with the patient's obsessive mechanisms and recommends supportive therapy. While he views the prognosis as somewhat favorable, he strives for relatively little change and feels that a minimum of two years is required. He describes the treatment goals as minimal and considers the patient a difficult one. He believes the therapist should be rather passive, encourage the expression of feelings, but refuses to take responsibility for decisions which are rightfully the patient's. Apparently, he also anticipates attempts to maneuver the therapist into a position of omnipotence which would then give the patient an opportunity to act out his intense dependency needs. The therapist describes his attitude toward the patient as "mixed feelings." His formulations do not appear hostile or rejecting per se, but evidently he regards the patient as a considerable potential threat to the therapist (himself?), and he plans to be on his guard.

Film Responses: In contrast to the film therapist, who is criticized for too much passivity, too little support, and a cold attitude, this therapist attempts to respond to the patient's feelings rather systematically (Responses 6, 8, 9, 10, 12, etc.); simultaneously, he communicates a measure of warmth and gives a fair amount of support (for example, Responses 23 and 24). In Response 10 he focuses on the patient's feelings in the interview situation (a Sullivanian emphasis). He directs the patient's attention to ways and means in which the interviewer might be of help, thereby establishing the purpose of the interview, clarifying the position of the therapist, and exploring the patient's motivation for therapy (Responses 18, 25, and 26). Response 28, however, seems unnecessarily ambiguous and defensive, as though the interviewer were getting a little tired of the patient. Also, to be consistent with his diagnosis of obsessionalism, he might have preferred to give the patient less ammunition for his defenses than is implied in his rather weak comment, "I don't know."

CODE: 17

BIOGRAPHICAL INFORMATION
Code: 17
Age: 46 years.
Sex: Male.
Professional   affiliation   and

status:	Psychoanalyst.
Psychoanalytic training:	Completed training; member APA.
Personal analysis:	Completed analysis 1949; lasted 600 hours.
Experience in psychotherapy:	A fair amount; 9.0 years.
Type of therapy:	Psychoanalysis and analytically oriented therapy.
Type of patients:	All kinds.
Theoretical orientation:	Sullivan.

CLINICAL ASSESSMENTS

Diagnosis

Dominant personality type:	Obsessive; paranoid.
Formulation of dynamics:	Hostile, controlling individual: "World owes me a living." Panic based on fear of loss of control of everything.

Treatment plans

Form of treatment:	Prolonged psychotherapy.
Treatment goals:	Intermediate: recognition of his prevailingly hostile, demanding, petulant, childish attitudes. Ultimate: resolution of chronic struggle with mother.
Frequency of sessions:	3 times weekly.
Length of treatment:	
Intermediate goals:	6 months.
Ultimate goals:	3 to 5 years.
Symptom-relief:	Don't know.
Difficulties expected:	Marked power struggle. Great need to intellectualize and run the show. Total lack of humility.
Focus:	Warfare with mother and ultimately illusory attitude to father.
Dangers:	Stopping therapy.
Areas to be avoided:	Sexual problem.
Behaviors to be encouraged:	Need to see other side of picture.
Behaviors to be discouraged:	Acting out.
Strictness vs. permissiveness:	Rather strict.
Clues:	No.
Course of transference:	Very slow development; excessive superficiality but no real interaction for long time.
Approach to transference:	Maintain therapeutic role; not identify or feel sorry for him.
Activity vs. passivity:	Rather active.
Free association:	Neither encourage nor discourage.
Ego strength:	A fair amount.
Anxiety:	A great deal.
Insight:	Very little.
Emotional maturity:	Very immature.
Social adjustment:	Very inadequate.
Degree of disturbance:	Moderately disturbed.

Degree of therapeutic change
   attempted: Fairly extensive change.
Prognosis without therapy: Probably get a little worse.
Prognosis with therapy: Somewhat unfavorable.
Recommendations: No; irrevelant to his problem.
Attitude toward patient: Strong negative.
   Reasons: Irritating, controlling, petulant, and whining.

EVALUATION OF FILM THERAPIST

   Adequacy: Somewhat inadequate.
   Reason: Very little got formulated for the patient. He got no benefit from interview.
   Activity vs. passivity: Much too passive.
   Support: Much too little support.
   Life history data: Would devote same time.
   Attitude toward therapist: Somewhat negative.
   Reason: His approach was too naive, yet too smug.

FILM RESPONSES

1. (Escort him to the seat.)
2. What do you mean, fear with mother (ask for detail).
3. (I would ask when it happened before.)
4. Mm-mm— (quizzical look and grunt).
5. Mm-mm.
6. You feel quite aggravated, don't you? Life has mistreated you, eh?
7. What do you mean by insight? (Dr. merely repeats last words of patient's, doesn't lead the interview.)
8. (I would go back at this point and ask when first time panic occurred.)
9. 0
10. (I would again try to lead him back to tell me the beginning, first time in detail.)
11. ("Don't work." I would ask,) "How do you support her? You feel she's a nuisance?"
12. (I would ask him if he gets openly angry at his mother at any time.)
13. (I would direct inquiry to show not only economic.)
14. You mean, you must do the right thing? (and show contradiction with previous expressions).
15. Do you mean angry or anxious?
16. 0
17. (Here I would say) You get mad a whole lot, don't you? (and try to follow lead of his being angry).
18. (Try to get him off symptoms by directing it, express disinterest in symptoms recital.)
19. Lots of things annoyed you?
20. (I would ask) What would you do when you got angry at mother?
21. 0 (or) Life has treated you roughly (sarcastically).
22. (I would pick up the slip of the tongue "mother's" death instead of "father's" death.)
23. (Grunt) What would you have the bank do?
24. What did you like about being the head of the family (therapist getting more irritating to patient all the time).
25. What did you do to get even?
26. No, I don't. What did you feel was coming to you?
27. You seem to blame everything and everyone for your difficulties. Do you think you play a role in your difficulties?
28. What do you think? (Throw the question back.)

COMMENT

Clinical Assessments: An experienced therapist who has completed analytic training and is a member of the American Psychoanalytic Association, this respondent is impressed by the obsessive and paranoid features in the patient's defenses, views the prognosis as somewhat unfavorable, and recommends prolonged psychotherapy, which he sees as a protracted task. His recommendations for therapy appear to be formulated within the psychoanalytic framework (see his comments about treatment goals, course of and approach to transference, therapeutic change to be attempted, and recommendations). He expects a marked power struggle in therapy, which he would discourage by strictness and maintenance of the therapeutic role, concomitant with a refusal to identify with the patient or feel sorry for him. The possibility of the patient's discontinuing therapy is seen as a danger. He describes his attitude as strongly negative and states the "reasons" rather emphatically ("irritating, controlling, petulant, and whining"). One wonders whether this reaction would occur in a therapist who regarded the patient's attitudes as an integral part of his problem. The question may be raised whether the therapist's task is to work toward a resolution of the patient's problem or to indulge in the luxury of reacting to symptoms in terms of cultural stereotypes. The therapist may counter this argument by saying that he has a clear conception of his role and that he foresees no difficulty in carrying it out, even though he may react emotionally to the patient's behavior; in fact, he might say that the very admission of his feelings helps him to control them and that he might be worse off if he deluded himself that any human being in our culture will ever succeed in completely divesting himself of punitive reactions to unreasonable demands, expectations, and attitudes in another person. Nevertheless, the danger that such emotional reactions influence and possibly impede the therapeutic operations must be faced.

Film Responses: The therapist assumes a very active role almost from the beginning, leaving no doubt that he, rather than the patient, is directing the interview. It is also clear that he would early discourage the patient's excursions into lengthy descriptions of his symptoms (Response 18); similarly, he would confront him with contradictions (e.g., Response 14). He endeavors to penetrate the patient's rationalizations (e.g., Responses 15, 23, 26, and 27) by disagreeing or questioning his formulations. These operations would undoubtedly jolt him, but it is uncertain whether they would achieve their objective in the context of this interview. In Response 23 ("What would you have the bank do?") the possibility of a misunderstanding or error is resolved in the bank's favor, with the implication that the patient was at fault. Response 21 ("Life has treated you roughly"), whose tone of sarcasm is highlighted, is predictably associated with an outburst of rage by the patient.

On the whole, it seems that the therapist is intent upon mobilizing the patient's anger, which may be highly therapeutic where a good working relationship has been established, but which cannot fail to be disruptive in its absence; in a first interview, it seems premature. One gets the impression that the therapist becomes increasingly impatient with and hostile toward the patient as the interview progresses. Like some other respondents who felt negatively toward the patient, he fastens upon the slip of the tongue in Response 22. In Response 26 ("No, I don't. What did you feel was coming to you?") he communicates his disinclination to sympathize with the patient; Response 27, even if factually true, sounds like the punitive evaluation of an exasperated parent whose patience has been strained beyond endurance. Response 28, made in the same vein, seems unduly evasive since the patient has explicated at some length what he thinks. These comments, while clearly made by a person who has a specific objective, document ill-concealed irritation, anger, and hostility, qualities hardly reconcilable with the psychoanalytic approach.

CODE: 18

BIOGRAPHICAL INFORMATION

Code:	18
Age:	34 years.
Sex:	Male.
Professional affiliation and status:	Psychoanalyst.
Psychoanalytic training:	Completed training.
Personal analysis:	Completed analysis of 450 hours.
Experience in psychotherapy:	5 years; a fair amount.
Type of therapy:	Psychoanalysis and analytically oriented therapy.
Type of patients:	Psychoneuroses and psychosomatic disorders.
Theoretical orientation:	Freudian psychoanalysis, and Alexander.

CLINICAL ASSESSMENTS

Diagnosis

Dominant personality type:	Schizoid.
Formulation of dynamics:	I would not attempt a formulation on the basis of such incomplete information about past personal history.

Treatment plans

Form of treatment:	Psychotherapy (cautiously uncovering type).
Treatment goals:	Symptom remission.
Frequency of sessions:	Once a week to start with.
Length of treatment:	1-2 years.
Intermediate goals:	
Ultimate goals:	
Symptom-relief:	1 a week for 50-100 weeks.
Difficulties expected:	Paranoid break a danger to be avoided.
Focus:	Don't know yet.
Dangers:	Avoid too rigid exposure of fear and shame about underlying passive homosexual trends, which might lead to paranoid break.
Areas to be avoided:	Don't know yet.
Behaviors to be encouraged:	Don't know yet.
Behaviors to be discouraged:	Don't know yet.
Strictness vs. permissiveness:	Don't know yet.
Clues:	His change in posture, sitting up erectly, banging fist on desk, when he spoke of having to take over as head of family.

Course of transference:	Passive, compliant, disguisedly homosexual (to a male therapist).
Approach to transference:	Probably not interpret it, but encourage him to speak out.
Activity vs. passivity:	Don't know yet.
Free association:	Don't know yet.
Ego strength:	Relatively little.
Anxiety:	A fair amount.
Insight:	Too little evidence.
Emotional maturity:	Fairly immature.
Social adjustment:	Fairly inadequate.
Degree of disturbance:	Moderately disturbed.
Degree of therapeutic change attempted:	Relatively little change.
Prognosis without therapy:	Get a little worse.
Prognosis with therapy:	Somewhat unfavorable.
Recommendations:	No, not yet; not enough diagnostic and dynamic understanding of case.
Attitude toward patient:	Neutral.
Reasons:	Seems very much like so many patients like him that I see diagnostically and treat in practice.

EVALUATION OF FILM THERAPIST

Adequacy:	Somewhat inadequate.
Reason:	Interview bogged down and patient had feeling doctor didn't understand.
Activity vs. passivity:	Much too passive.
Support:	Somewhat too little.
Life history data:	Considerably more time.
Attitude toward therapist:	Somewhat negative.
Reason:	He seemed so tense, self-conscious, with shocked, amazed expression on face at certain things patient said.

FILM RESPONSES

1. What can I do for you?
2. What did you mean about your mother?
3. Do you feel that way in closed rooms or elevators?
4. What do you mean about always being enmeshed financially or economically?
5. Do you think you have anything to do with getting yourself into such situations, or do these things just happen to you?
6. How have you been since that first spell you had?
7. Tell me more about that.
8. How has your health been otherwise?
9. Could you tell me now the story about your whole life, beginning with when you were born and coming up to the present?
10. (Same as 9.)
11. (Same as 9.)
12. Could you tell me more about your wife's condition?
13. What do you mean by *that*?
14. 0
15. 0

16. 0
17. (Nod—encouragement to go on, plus indication of understanding.)
18. Do you feel ashamed of these symptoms?
19. (Nod, as 17.)
20. 0
21. 0
22. (Nod, as 17.)
23. 0
24. Who didn't cooperate?
25. What do you feel you *can* do about it?

26. 0
27. How old were you when your father died? How old are you now?
28. Well, aside from how it affects your health, it does sound as though these symptoms cause you enough distress that I think it would be worthwhile going into the matter more thoroughly. Would you like to come back for another diagnostic interview?

COMMENT

Clinical Assessments: This therapist considers schizoid features as being most prominent in the patient's personality structure and recommends psychotherapy initially on a once a week basis. He expects treatment to last one to two years. He is cautious in his formulations and would guard against the emergence of underlying passive homosexual trends which in his judgment might lead to a paranoid break. He also cautions against premature interpretations. One gathers that the therapist desires to obtain a great deal of additional information before committing himself on a number of the questions posed to him. He seems impressed by the patient's weak ego structure (notice the contrast to other respondents who launch frontal attacks upon the patient's defenses!). He regards the prognosis as somewhat unfavorable and describes his attitude as neutral. He seems to be saying, there is nothing unusual or remarkable about this patient; he is in need of help, to which he is entitled, and it isn't my job to say whether the symptoms are "good" or "bad," although as a private citizen I may have opinions whether such a person is likable or not.

Film Responses: The therapist offers a spontaneous greeting, which is no more than a common courtesy, but many respondents failed to extend it. Compare Sullivan's pithy remarks on this point:

> May I suggest that a stranger is fully as bothered about meeting the interviewer as the interviewer would be in a similar situation. Thus, while I don't try to show a great welcome to the patient, I do try to act as if he were expected, that is, I try to know the name of the person who makes an appointment to see me for the first time, and to greet him with it, relieving him of any morbid anxiety as to whether he came on the wrong day, and so on. And I suggest that he come in, which is a form of hospitality that extends to many branches of civilization. . . . Once he is in, I indicate where he should sit. I think most of us have experienced the relief, in a difficult situation, of having someone indicate where we may sit; it relieves us of all the wondering about where the other person intends to sit, where it is proper to sit, and so on. (Sullivan, H. S.: The Psychiatric Interview. New York, Norton, 1954, pp. 60-61.)

He then proceeds to ask a few questions designed to provide fuller information about the patient's complaints (Responses 2, 3, and 4), and in Response 5 ventures a clarifying comment which may prove quite thought-provoking to the patient. Note that it does *not* meet his defenses head-on. It may also anticipate and possibly preclude the later accusations against his brother and "the world," which emerge so prominently in the second half of the interview. Responses 6 and 8 convey simple human and therapeutic interest. The interviewer attempts to obtain a fuller statement about the patient's background and past difficulties in Responses 9, 10, and 11. Response 12 centers around the current situation. As the interview proceeds, the interviewer gives encouragement to proceed, endeavoring to communicate understanding and interest. Response 18, inquiring about feelings of shame, indicates sensitivity to the patient's subjective experience. Response 25 ("What do you feel you *can* do about it?") is a challenge. It says in effect: "All right, this was the past; it cannot be changed; but perhaps there is something you can do about the future." Notice the constructive element in this formulation. In his final comment the therapist recognizes the patient's distress, without showering him with reassurance, and outlines the next steps, as he sees them. This statement seems honest, friendly, and sincere.

These communications are characterized by respect for the patient's difficulties and suffering; they convey an interest in his problem and a willingness to help; they are sober, reality-oriented, and business-like, and they inform the patient that the therapist is conversant with such problems and that he knows his business. He has also delineated what is to be done next, but he has also steered clear of emotional involvements in the patient's dependency needs and hostile demands.

CODE: 19

BIOGRAPHICAL INFORMATION

Code:	19
Age:	52 years.
Sex:	Female.
Professional affiliation and status:	Psychiatrist.
Psychoanalytic training:	No training, no plans for training.
Personal analysis:	Completed analysis; lasted 100 hours.
Experience in psychotherapy:	2½ years; a fair amount.
Type of therapy:	Analytically oriented.
Type of patients:	Psychotics (schizophrenics) and neurotics.
Theoretical orientation:	Analytically oriented.

CLINICAL ASSESSMENTS

Diagnosis

Dominant personality type:	Anxiety.
Formulation of dynamics:	Never freed himself from mother. His aggression is tremendous but can't find acceptable expression.

Treatment plans

Form of treatment:	Interview therapy.
Treatment goals:	A comfortable functioning.
Frequency of sessions:	Twice weekly.

Length of treatment: ?
   Intermediate goals: 0
   Ultimate goals: 0
Symptom-relief: 0
Difficulties expected: Attempts at intellectualization, a working out of his great dependency needs.
Focus: 0
Dangers: Letting him become over-anxious. Handling the transference.
Areas to be avoided: I couldn't answer such a question. I wait until the interviews unfold and don't introduce the topics.
Behaviors to be encouraged: Accepting himself.
Behaviors to be discouraged: Projecting, but this would not be handled directly.
Strictness vs. permissiveness: Rather permissive.
Clues: Lots of them—his irritation, anger.
Course of transference: Dependent, with some hostility.
Approach to transference: 0
Activity vs. passivity: Rather passive.
Free association: Neither encourage nor discourage it.
Ego strength: A fair amount.
Anxiety: A great deal.
Insight: Relatively little.
Emotional maturity: Very immature.
Social adjustment: Fairly inadequate.
Degree of disturbance: Seriously disturbed.
Degree of therapeutic change
   attempted: Too little evidence.
Prognosis without therapy: Probably get much worse.
Prognosis with therapy: Neither favorable nor unfavorable.
Recommendations: If he could have, he would have made changes. Therefore I would not make suggestions.
Attitude toward patient: Somewhat positive.
Reasons: 0

EVALUATION OF FILM THERAPIST

Adequacy: Reasonably adequate.
   Reason: 0
Activity vs. passivity: Neither too active nor too passive.
Support: Somewhat too little.
Life history data: About the same time.
Attitude toward therapist: Somewhat negative.
   Reason: Seemed rather self-absorbed.

FILM RESPONSES

1. 0 (appear attentive).
2. 0 (appear attentive).
3. 0 (appear attentive).

4. (Ask about "being encased.")
5. Yes, cornered (then I'd see what happened).

6. 0

7. 0

8. (Ask regarding fear.)

9. (Ask regarding "*have* to forget.")

10. Anxiety?

11. 0 (See where he goes from there.)

12. Can you tell me more about the apprehension?

13. (Just give come on) Umm (to see if he continues with antisocial).

14. It was hard to have such feelings about mother?

15. (Didn't catch what he said. Would let him go on with, "One of a lot of them.")

16. (Some reassurance with) Fears show themselves in different ways.

Could you tell me more about your fears?

17. (Couldn't understand the recording.)

18. These feelings must be distressing.

19. 0

20. That would be pretty hard for a kid to do?

21. *Always* three strikes against you.

22. You took the responsibility.

23. 0

24. Need of cooperation.

25. This is something you tried?

26. 0

27. That you couldn't live your way.

28. This has been a big worry.

COMMENT

Clinical Assessments: The therapist is a woman, aged 52, who has had some personal analysis but relatively little experience in psychotherapy. Her approach is straightforward and more intuitive than technical. She gives anxiety as her diagnosis and says she feels somewhat positively toward the patient; no reasons are given. She advocates permissiveness and passivity for the therapist. She is sensitive to the patient's anger, hostility, and dependency, but does not appear to react to them defensively. She is noncommital about the prognosis, but feels he would get much worse if no therapy were undertaken.

Film Responses: The therapist asks some exploratory questions, but maintains an expectant silence at many points in the interview. Her occasional supportive statements (Responses 14, 18, 20, etc.) reveal a maternal concern. She maintains this attitude in Response 28, which, however, seems a bit weak and does not fully meet the patient's challenge.

In sum, she conveys interest and understanding, support and appreciation for the patient's difficulties. She is warm and protective but not effusive. There is a unique quality of motherliness and friendliness in her comments, but she remains fully attuned to the seriousness of the patient's problem. She is realistic, and apparently quite capable of evaluating the implicit meanings of the patient's behavior and communications. She may be expected to initiate a warm, comfortable, and good working relationship with the patient, within which her therapeutic aims may be furthered.

CODE: 20

BIOGRAPHICAL INFORMATION

Code:	20
Age:	31 years.
Sex:	Male.
Professional affiliation and status:	Psychiatrist.
Psychoanalytic training:	In training.
Personal analysis:	In analysis (completed 450 hours, will complete about 1,000 hours).
Experience in psychotherapy:	2½ years; a fair amount.
Type of therapy:	Analytically oriented therapy.
Type of patients:	Psychotics in institution and out-patient neurotics at clinic or private practice.
Theoretical orientation:	Freudian psychoanalysis, Sullivan, Deutsch.

CLINICAL ASSESSMENTS

Diagnosis

Dominant personality type:	Schizoid.
Formulation of dynamics:	The patient's dependency was never resolved; he never became a separate individual. He is angry at his mother, at the whole world for not providing him with satisfaction of his needs.

Treatment plans

Form of treatment:	Psychotherapy.
Treatment goals:	Intermediate: expression of his resentment, rage, with development of sense of support from therapy and probable cessation of symptoms. Ultimate: acceptance of the fact that "unpaid bill" will never be paid.
Frequency of sessions:	Twice a week.
Length of treatment:	
Intermediate goals:	6-9 months.
Ultimate goals:	2-3 years.
Symptom-relief:	6-12 months.
Difficulties expected:	1. Acting out by leaving treatment. 2. Over-dependency upon treatment.
Focus:	Relationship with wife and mother.
Dangers:	If therapist is too strict he might leave treatment. If therapist is too concerned and sympathetic, patient may become over-dependent and get satisfaction directly out of therapy.
Areas to be avoided:	I would deal with present difficulties; would not deal too much in past at first.
Behaviors to be encouraged:	Expressing resentment and rage.
Behaviors to be discouraged:	I would discourage self-pity, although I would be sympathetic.
Strictness vs. permissiveness:	No more strict or permissive than with others.

Clues:	Verbal: "Hemmed in," "gripped with fear" . . . His tendency to sob to therapist, How would you feel? Nonverbal: pushing away with hands, making fist with hands.
Course of transference:	At first, positive transference till symptoms are rid of. The negative transference after symptoms gone; act out negatively by leaving therapy.
Approach to transference:	I would interpret his negative transference in terms of his desire to leave treatment.
Activity vs. passivity:	Rather passive.
Free association:	Discourage.
Ego strength:	A fair amount.
Anxiety:	A great deal.
Insight:	Relatively little.
Emotional maturity:	Very immature.
Social adjustment:	Very inadequate.
Degree of disturbance:	Seriously disturbed.
Degree of therapeutic change attempted:	Fairly extensive as ultimate goal.
Prognosis without therapy:	Remain about the same.
Prognosis with therapy:	Somewhat unfavorable.
Recommendations:	No; he has too strong a tendency for dependency which he would use rather than look into it. Satisfied directly in treatment.
Attitude toward patient:	Somewhat positive.
Reasons:	He is having it pretty rough.

EVALUATION OF FILM THERAPIST

Adequacy:	Reasonably adequate.
Reason:	0
Activity vs. passivity:	Neither too active nor too passive.
Support:	Somewhat too little.
Life history data:	About the same time.
Attitude toward therapist:	Somewhat negative.
Reason:	Probably because of circumstances (filming, etc. . . .). He was too cold and aloof.

FILM RESPONSES

1. (Show him the chair and sit down.)
2. 0 (Look attentive.)
3. And that fear *gripped* you?
4. Hemmed in? Forced to do things you did not want to do?
5. Hemmed in?
6. That's a pretty bad feeling, huh?
7. Dizzy?
8. Overwhelmed, smothered . . .
9. 0
10. Prolonged sorrow? (trying to get background to the symptoms).
11. No quiet. No peace? Uh?
12. Always? (Again trying to trace the pattern back.) (I might try to ask) Where are you between your wife and your mother?
13. Antisocial?
14. We can't "get away" from that (emphasizing *get away* vs. hemmed in).

15. That's one?
16. Afraid of losing support?
17. 0
18. You want to get out of it. You don't like to be hemmed in.
19. It "embarrassed" you? (emphasizing "embarrassed" because I think it made him mad). You could get angry at your mother?
20. (I was daydreaming—missed last few seconds. I would investigate why I lost the thread.)

21. Three strikes against you?
22. You did not have anything? (I would not pick on his lapses.)
23. I can see things were pretty rough for you! (He is asking for sympathy.)
24. And you did not get any cooperation?
25. Uh-uh.
26. Uh-uh!
27. Hemmed in, uh?
28. Even your thinking, uh?

COMMENT

Clinical Assessments: This young psychiatrist, aged 31, claims only two and a half years of experience but seems to possess skill and maturity beyond his years. He is sensitive to the patient's intense anxiety, which also determines his diagnosis. His statement of the emotional dynamics is couched in nontechnical language and seems adequate as a beginning working hypothesis. His response to the question dealing with possible dangers appears perceptive and sound. As he sees it, the therapist has to steer a precarious course between the Scylla of therapeutic strictness and the Charybdis of sympathetic concern; the treatment may founder on either. His treatment goals are fairly ambitious but he is somewhat pessimistic about the prognosis. His attitude toward the patient is warm and sympathetic; while his thinking on technical questions seems clear and objective, he never loses sight of the patient's suffering. Similarly, he does not fully agree with the film therapist's technique but he empathizes with the difficulties of his task and does not condemn him for his shortcomings. He appears to have an appreciation for the range of human experience (via his own analysis?): resentment and rage are no monstrous emotions which are to be suppressed; rather, he would encourage their expression in therapy.

Film Responses: The therapist seems more concerned about recognizing, acknowledging, and working with the patient's feelings than in establishing "facts." He and the patient are integrated in a situation; he is interacting, not merely responding, even under the difficulties of the experimental situation! Support is given throughout but reassurance is tendered sparingly (Response 23: "I can see things were pretty rough for you."). This, one surmises, is the therapist's genuine feeling. He fails, however, to establish the purpose of the interview, and responds to Item 28 as though he expected the session to continue. Perhaps as a result, Response 28 seems rather bland.

On the whole, the therapist stays nicely with the patient and seems to know where he is and why. He seems to place adequate emphasis on feelings and conveys his understanding of the patient's plight. Without being mothering or "mushy," he manages to give support and some reassurance.

10

GROUP III: PSYCHIATRISTS

EXPERIENCE LEVEL:

HIGH

BIOGRAPHICAL INFORMATION

Code:	21
Age:	60 years.
Sex:	Male.
Professional affiliation and status:	Psychiatrist.
Psychoanalytic training:	No training; no plans.
Personal analysis:	Completed 150 hours.
Experience in psychotherapy:	15 years; a great deal.
Type of therapy:	Some radical, some supportive.
Type of patients:	Schizophrenic, neurotic, depressed.
Theoretical orientation:	Eclectic.

CLINICAL ASSESSMENTS

Diagnosis

Dominant personality type:	Anxiety, paranoid.
Formulation of dynamics:	0

Treatment plans

Form of treatment: Prolonged psychotherapy (preferably for a time in psychiatric clinic) might help him get "unlearned" and oriented to life; prospects of help only moderate; a little psychotherapy is likely to be (1) ineffective or (2) upsetting.

Treatment goals: Long-term re-evaluation of life.

Frequency of sessions: At minimum, 2 times per week for some months, then adapt to indications.

Length of treatment:	Three years, and a lifetime of occasional contacts.
Intermediate goals:	
Ultimate goals:	
Symptom-relief:	Symptom-relief probably not attainable without fairly radical relief of "antisocial," i.e., paranoid, attitudes.
Difficulties expected:	It would be very difficult for me to keep warmly and sympathetically aware of his real distress, and I would fortify myself with photographs or other mementos to be brought by the patient.
Focus:	Primarily, hope of developing satisfaction in action, probably exhibitionistic pleasure in skills—maybe chess or checkers, maybe puzzle solving.
Dangers:	Very likely to quit treatment and see another doctor when his poverty of enthusiasm is clearly revealed.
Areas to be avoided:	After initial opener comment on "exasperated or maybe resentful," I would lay off hostile emphasis as *his,* and try to approach situationally.
Behaviors to be encouraged:	Yes (see focus).
Behaviors to be discouraged:	Antisocial philosophizing.
Strictness vs. permissiveness:	I'd try to be fair, rather than *permissive* or indulgent, but very, very *considerate.*
Clues:	Many (see comments in work sheet).
Course of transference:	Suspicious, hostile, usually polite, but nasty-polite.
Approach to transference:	If one remains passive with this patient, nothing will happen therapeutically, but active interventions should be carefully chosen, quickly inserted, without rancor, or quibbling, and not "huckstered" to him.
Activity vs. passivity:	
Free association:	Discourage.
Ego strength:	Too little evidence.
Anxiety:	A fair amount.
Insight:	Very little.
Emotional maturity:	Fairly immature—at childhood or late infantile level.
Social adjustment:	Very inadequate.
Degree of disturbance:	Seriously disturbed.
Degree of therapeutic change attempted:	Much change needed, little change likely.
Prognosis without therapy:	Remain about the same.
Prognosis with therapy:	Somewhat unfavorable or very unfavorable.
Recommendations:	0
Attitude toward patient:	Ambivalent (from very strong positive to very strong negative).

Reasons: The world is full of injustice; therefore, I feel
                            quite sympathetic; but "there ain't no justice
                            nohow" so quit the griping.

EVALUATION OF FILM THERAPIST

Adequacy: Reasonably adequate.
  Reason: 0
Activity vs. passivity: Somewhat too passive or much too passive,
                            sometimes inappropriately.
Support: 0
Life history data: About the same.
Attitude toward therapist: Somewhat positive, except when he makes
                            "dumb questions." These seem to me "dumb"
                            because he misses chances to express (by gesture
                            or otherwise) a sympathetic understanding of
                            patient's attitude.

FILM RESPONSES

1. How do you do? You asked to see me. (Move hand to chair.)
2. 0
3. 0 (Any comment, other than quizzical gesture, will put patient on defensive here.)
4. 0 (or lift eyebrow).
5. "Yes" (very promptly).
6. You speak of being hemmed in, not only as if it were uncomfortable, but also I take it you feel it's unfair.
7. 0
8. Have you found any means, by yourself, sometimes for successfully breaking this circle?
9. 0
10. You tell me now in what ways you can keep up the vicious circle. How can it be interrupted?
11. When she *keeps on talking*, do you feel hemmed in?
12. 0 (but look intensely interested).
13. Antisocial, you mean . . . (trail off).
14. This does make a problem, doesn't it?
15. Were you able to work in those days? . . . Where? That kept you away from the trouble through the day?
16. "Afraid," or "hemmed in?"

17. 0 (I couldn't catch the latest remark of patient).
18. Yes, of course. When you picture being well, what time in your life do you remember when you really felt fine and functioned okay?
19. 0
20. Oh?
21. Again we have the matter of "injustice" coming up. As you say, three strikes against you at the start.
22. Would your brother have shared the responsibility with you? What was *his* attitude about mother then?
23. Well, not quite before, rather as if you misjudged the first pitch. And have felt overwhelmed ever since. And maybe exasperated or resentful.
24. Your brother was not very cooperative?
25. That seems to be a very hard lesson to learn. Sometimes negative learning is very painful.
26. Was your father a fair and just person? . . . How did he show it? . . . What might he do now, for your justice?
27. So?
28. I see how you have become concerned in this way.

COMMENT

Clinical Assessments: This psychiatrist, aged 60, a recognized leader in the field, observes painstaking care in making his thinking clear. I believe his formulations may serve as a model of deep and genuine professional concern. The patient's problem is never approached lightly or flippantly; there is a simple seriousness and task-orientation, from which pomposity is utterly lacking. This, too, is the respondent's approach to the experiment and the questionnaire.

He sees the patient as seriously disturbed, and while he counsels long-term therapy, he is not optimistic about its outcome. There is no question but that his judgments emerge from a rich context of pertinent experience with similar patients. He declines to advance a formulation of the patient's dynamics, but many revealing comments bearing on this topic are interspersed in his remarks. His distinction between fairness and permissiveness is illuminating: he stresses considerateness rather than permissiveness or indulgence. He also recognizes his difficulty in keeping warmly and sympathetically aware of the patient's real distress; the statement about his ambivalent feelings is honest and dispassionate. While he recognizes the patient's hostility, his formulations are devoid of counterhostility or rancor. He seems thoroughly realistic.

Film Responses: This interviewer sees the need for a greeting and indicates where the patient is to sit. He then proceeds to listen and guards against putting the patient on the defensive. In Response 6 he anticipates the patient's feelings of blame, injustice, and accusation which are elaborated in the second half of the filmed interview. Response 8 inquires whether the patient has ever been able to deal with his problem constructively; Response 10 again focuses on reality. Its formulation is challenging, yet respectful. Response 14 conveys simple acceptance that a problem exists (compare this statement with the responses of many therapists who seem to dispute this fact). In Response 18, unlike many respondents, the therapist turns attention to the patient's emotional assets rather than liabilities, thereby reinforcing the patient's expressed desire to get well. In Response 23 the patient is accepted as he is, without condemnation or moralistic judgment; nonetheless there is no indication that the therapist sides with the patient or that he considers his feelings appropriate or desirable. In Response 25 the therapist speaks as an expert and authority; he also conveys reassurance through gentle support. At the end, one might expect this interviewer to formulate a plan of action and perhaps he would have done so had the film not ended somewhat abruptly; as it is, he merely states that he understands the patient's plight. And since he seems to be sincere, this may mean a great deal.

In sum, the therapist leads the patient very effectively but he never dominates or overpowers him. He alternates between investigative questions and support. He maintains a friendly, warm, and understanding attitude but makes it clear that he does not succumb to the patient's rationalizations. His sensitivity, ability to recognize and respond to the patient's feelings, and modest self-confidence are truly impressive not only to the outsider but very probably to the patient as well. Indeed, the interview seems like a promising beginning for psychotherapy.

CODE: 22

BIOGRAPHICAL INFORMATION

Code:	22
Age:	59 years.
Sex:	Male.
Professional affiliation and status:	Psychiatrist.
Psychoanalytic training:	No training; no plans.
Personal analysis:	0
Experience in psychotherapy:	15 years; a great deal.
Type of therapy:	(Coded as analytical, but item was left blank.)
Type of patients:	Psychoneurotics.
Theoretical orientation:	If any, then Sullivan.

CLINICAL ASSESSMENTS

Diagnosis

Dominant personality type:	Anxiety; paranoid.
Formulation of dynamics:	Repetition of creating the same situation of being hemmed in as he was with his mother.

Treatment plans

Form of treatment:	Individual psychotherapy followed by group therapy.
Treatment goals:	Make him realize that he is his own worst enemy and how this came about. And that he is creating the insufferably enmeshing situations.
Frequency of sessions:	?
Length of treatment:	6 months.
Intermediate goals:	
Ultimate goals:	
Symptom-relief:	6 weeks.
Difficulties expected:	Some difficulty to establish good rapport. Increased anxiety attacks, perhaps forgetting the treatment.
Focus:	Home situation; relation to mother.
Dangers:	His mysteriousness and sensitivity.
Areas to be avoided:	Sexual history.
Behaviors to be encouraged:	Real self-confidence; aggressiveness, more than just verbal.
Behaviors to be discouraged:	Self-pity.
Strictness vs. permissiveness:	Rather strict.
Clues:	His coolness toward others; his vicious, groping gestures; his conceit, and lack of confidence; his delight in speaking of ambivalent behavior.
Course of transference:	Quite uneven.
Approach to transference:	As a way opens itself.
Activity vs. passivity:	Rather active.
Free association:	I don't know yet.
Ego strength:	Relatively little.
Anxiety:	A fair amount.

Insight:	Very little.
Emotional maturity:	Fairly immature.
Social adjustment:	Very inadequate.
Degree of disturbance:	Seriously disturbed.
Degree of therapeutic change attempted:	Fairly extensive change.
Prognosis without therapy:	Get a little worse.
Prognosis with therapy:	Somewhat favorable.
Recommendations:	He will find it himself, but may then need some support.
Attitude toward patient:	Somewhat positive.
Reasons:	As for any person who works like . . . (?) and cannot find himself.

EVALUATION OF FILM THERAPIST

Adequacy:	Very adequate.
Reason:	It was possible to bring out rather clearly the characterological structure, some important points of the illness and the dynamics and historical facts.
Activity vs. passivity:	Somewhat too passive.
Support:	Neither too much nor too little.
Life history data:	About the same.
Attitude toward therapist:	Neutral.
Reason:	He impressed me as a man who knows his job and an expert, just as I would have expected.

FILM RESPONSES

1. (Wait for the next statement of the patient.)
2. ?
3. What makes you remember this incident so clearly?
4. Yes, I see!
5. Yes, but how actually do you feel then?
6. Once too often? How do I understand this?
7. Are you worried about your physical health?
8. Hm, hm, pressure, yes!
9. Health?
10. Pity?
11. (Nod and wait.)
12. How did they begin?
13. Antisocial?
14. How do you feel about your mother?
15. (Could not understand exactly what was said?)
16. (Wait.)
17. Tell me about your wife.
18. Have you told your mother how you feel about the situation?
19. Are you the only child?
20. (Offer him a cigarette.)
21. To fight?
22. It seems you didn't like it.
23. Then what did you do?
24. You had no cooperation, you say!
25. No friendly feelings, anywhere?
26. No, not quite.
27. The sensations made you, not the other way, you think.
28. No, this will not happen.

COMMENT

Clinical Assessments: The therapist is keenly aware of those attitudes in the patient which might readily evoke counterhostility ("his coolness toward others; his vicious, groping gestures; his conceit and lack of confidence; his delight in speaking of ambivalent behavior"). However, he himself does not appear to react to them; in fact, he gives his attitude as somewhat positive, referring to the patient's futile efforts to extricate himself from his neurotic conflicts. He judges the prognosis as somewhat favorable, sees the patient as fairly anxious and seriously disturbed, but expects therapeutic results in relatively short order. This appears somewhat remarkable in view of his emphasis on the patient's paranoid features. He disadvises focus on the sexual area. Treatment seems designed to foster some insight. Unlike most experienced therapists, he is lenient and even complimentary in his evaluation of the film therapist. Responses on the whole are rather brief, although reasonably precise.

Film Responses: As in his questionnaire responses, the therapist does not waste words on the patient. His communications are concise yet respectful and occasionally even sympathetic (Response 25). It is somewhat difficult to assess the emotional tone of Response 28 ("No, this will not happen"), but it may be a useful antidote to the patient's obsessive thinking, although in the absence of information about the patient's physical health one may question the wisdom of making the statement.

It appears that his recommendations for strictness and activity are carried out in the first interview. He seems friendly but sparing in communicating his feelings. In keeping with his recommendation for short-term therapy, he seems goal-oriented and intent upon achieving his therapeutic objective in the shortest time possible.

CODE: 23

BIOGRAPHICAL INFORMATION

Code:	23
Age:	53 years.
Sex:	Male.
Professional affiliation and status:	Psychoanalyst.
Psychoanalytic training:	Completed training but never presented paper before society.
Personal analysis:	Completed analysis.
Experience in psychotherapy:	20 years; a great deal.
Type of therapy:	Psychoanalysis, psychoanalytically oriented therapy when suitable.
Type of patients:	Schizophrenics, young homosexuals, marital problems, anxiety hysteria and paranoids.
Theoretical orientation:	Sullivan.

CLINICAL ASSESSMENTS

Diagnosis

Dominant personality type:	Anxiety, hysteria with paranoid trends.

Formulation of dynamics:	Rejection in early childhood rationalized by memories he can recall; the hatred thus engendered has been converted into bodily ailments and anxiety.

Treatment plans

Form of treatment:	Psychoanalysis with a very passive warm therapist who understands analysis of psychotics.
Treatment goals:	The immediate goal is some resolution of his psychosomatic complaints—enough for him to function a little better in society and then a greater change toward projection. Real resolution of these difficulties would take years and years.
Frequency of sessions:	3 to 5 times a week.
Length of treatment:	
Intermediate goals:	With the right doctor several months might be necessary for some easing of his physical complaints, but years for the ultimate goal.
Ultimate goals:	0
Symptom-relief:	3-6 months at 3-5 times a week.
Difficulties expected:	Criticism about fear of getting too dependent and too long period of treatment.
Focus:	Work and immediate family.
Dangers:	Insight might come too quickly with too much interpretation if too little rapport existed.
Areas to be avoided:	0
Behaviors to be encouraged:	0
Behaviors to be discouraged:	0
Strictness vs. permissiveness:	0
Clues:	Yes; heavy woman (on chest), jealousy of brother, i.e., father.
Course of transference:	Great dependency as a child for mother and great hostility about homosexual drives.
Approach to transference:	He needs much warmth and love for a long time and then gradual interpretation of reality of this dependence.
Activity vs. passivity:	Vary active and passive to suit needs of an essentially basic underlying psychosis.
Free association:	Encourage.
Ego strength:	A great deal.
Anxiety:	A great deal.
Insight:	A fair amount.
Emotional maturity:	Fairly immature.
Social adjustment:	Very inadequate.
Degree of disturbance:	Seriously disturbed.
Degree of therapeutic change attempted:	Fairly extensive change.
Prognosis without therapy:	Get much worse.
Prognosis with therapy:	Somewhat favorable.

Recommendations: Not now, but gradually as insight is gained through treatment.

Attitude toward patient: Somewhat positive.

    Reasons: I like him because of his strong determination and wish to see things through. He has some "guts" and the right therapist could help him. He is on his way.

EVALUATION OF FILM THERAPIST

   Adequacy: Reasonably adequate.

     Reason: He comforted patient somewhat but not enough. Did not build up anything for next visit.

Activity vs. passivity: Somewhat too passive.

Support: Somewhat too little.

Life history data: Somewhat more time.

Attitude toward therapist: Somewhat positive.

     Reason: (0 ?) Here is a man who wants help and I feel I could give it to him.

FILM RESPONSES

1. Tell me what is troubling you.
2. 0
3. Anything like feelings you had in dreams?
4. 0
5. You seem to have a lot of resentment.
6. How would you describe these emotions?
7. I am not clear what you mean by insight.
8. What is your wife like? Is your mother living? Have you any sisters?
9. What other stuff? How do you feel you can regain your health?
10. You stress these feelings so much. What about your past experiences, childhood and adolescent?
11. Is your disposition anything like your mother's, generally speaking?
12. You would like to have some of this allayed.
13. You feel money is the root of all evil.
14. Hm . . . Dignified way?
15. You seem to stress your physical complaints a great deal. How about how she affected you?
16. This must have been very disturbing to you.
17. You seem to be aware of a lot of resentment. Does this relate to your physical symptoms?
18. What made your mother that way? Are you happily married?
19. Did your mother prefer girls to boys? What sex instruction did you receive?
20. Dad sort of babied mother, didn't he? Were you at all jealous of this?
21. Tell me your earliest childhood memories.
22. Then it was he who was favored. Was he older or younger than you?
23. I'm not too sure about that.
24. What about this keeping up with the Joneses? Did your father live beyond his means?
25. That is hard to say. It doesn't sound very practical.
26. (Could not hear) 0.
27. Do you feel this an act of fate or do people work against you? Dislike you?

28. Has anyone ever told you that
the sensations are probably caused
by your emotions? Some relief of
your feelings with people might
prevent any danger of harm to
you physically.

COMMENT

Clinical Assessments: The respondent, a highly experienced analyst of 20 years' experience, gives "anxiety hysteria with paranoid trends" as his diagnosis. He feels the patient needs a very passive, warm therapist who understands analysis with psychotic patients. He sees the patient as being in need of much warmth and love for a long time as a therapeutic approach to the patient's underlying psychosis. While he considers the patient as seriously disturbed, he judges the prognosis somewhat favorable and infers a great deal of ego strength. His recommendations for treatment are quite specific; while some symptom relief may be expected in several months, years would be required for a thorough resolution of the difficulties. It is noteworthy that despite the momentous expenditure of therapeutic effort which is considered necessary, the respondent foresees a successful outcome; his optimism seems based not on the judgment of a mild disturbance but rather on the intensity of the therapeutic effort. The recommendations appear to flow from a great deal of experience with psychotic or borderline patients. He cautions against premature interpretations, particularly in the absence of insufficient rapport (compare this recommendation with the tactic of direct confrontations advocated by other therapists!).

Film Responses: The therapist opens the interview by inviting the patient to tell about his troubles. The reference to dreams in Response 3 appears somewhat premature. In Response 5 he proceeds to label an important component of the patient's feelings which becomes elaborated later in the interview. While he seeks to obtain additional data, he is sensitive to the patient's striving for health (Responses 9 and 12). Response 7 indicates that the interviewer does not tacitly accept undocumented generalizations. Significant departures from more conventional communications may be noted in Responses 19, 24, and 25. Response 25 in its implied discouragement of acting out resentment seems quite realistic, a tendency which is also apparent in the final comment, which cannot fail to reassure the patient at least to some extent.

In sum, the therapist conveys warmth, support and understanding; at the same time he pursues an investigative approach. He appears experienced, confident, and reassuring.

CODE: 24

BIOGRAPHICAL INFORMATION

Code:	24
Age:	39 years.
Sex:	Male.
Professional affiliation and status:	Psychiatrist.
Psychoanalytic training:	0
Personal analysis:	Completed in 1951; 400 hours.

Experience in psychotherapy:	A great deal; 10.0 years.
Type of therapy:	Analytically oriented at times; interpersonal at times.
Type of patients:	Neurotic; mild character or immaturity problems with many symptoms.
Theoretical orientation:	Whitehorn.

CLINICAL ASSESSMENTS
Diagnosis
Dominant personality type:	Obsessive.
Formulation of dynamics:	Ambivalent feelings toward mother (and her personality). Lack of adequate father figure.

Treatment plans
Form of treatment:	Group.
Treatment goals:	I would not treat him.
Frequency of sessions:	0
Length of treatment:	I have at times seen such patients for 2-6 times to see if any available ego strength could be mobilized.
Intermediate goals:	0
Ultimate goals:	0
Symptom-relief:	Temporary; a few times but not for long-anticipated period for cures.
Difficulties expected:	Intellectualization (as resistance), stopping treatment, possibly psychotic episode.
Focus:	At beginning, anything positive I could find, even if only interest in baseball.
Dangers:	Precipitating psychotic episode (schizophrenic), homicidal tendencies.
Areas to be avoided:	Early: avoid fantasies.
Behaviors to be encouraged:	Ask about positives.
Behaviors to be discouraged:	No; not at danger of getting into fighting with his character defenses.
Strictness vs. permissiveness:	Rather permissive.
Clues:	Looking at his fingers. Touching things on desk.
Course of transference:	Easily negative, unless therapist could offer patterns acceptable to this patient for imitation.
Approach to transference:	Hope that I could accomplish second.
Activity vs. passivity:	Rather active.
Free association:	Discourage it.
Ego strength:	A fair amount: negatively, his sick persistence; relatively little by standard meaning.
Anxiety:	A fair amount.
Insight:	Very little.
Emotional maturity:	Very immature.
Social adjustment:	Very inadequate.
Degree of disturbance:	Moderately disturbed.
Degree of therapeutic change attempted:	Relatively little change.

Prognosis without therapy:	Probably remain the same.
Prognosis with therapy:	Somewhat unfavorable.
Recommendations:	No.
Attitude toward patient:	Somewhat negative.
Reasons:	I do not enjoy stubborn negativism, with the hostility so close to the surface.

EVALUATION OF FILM THERAPIST

Adequacy:	Reasonably adequate.
Reason:	Helpful material came out and he also (in a way) tested this man's level of hostility and anxiety.
Activity vs. passivity:	Somewhat too passive.
Support:	About right.
Life history data:	Would devote considerably more time.
Attitude toward therapist:	Somewhat negative.
Reason:	Too stiff, and nagging; relied too much on his own defenses of repeating the patient's own words.

FILM RESPONSES

1. 0 (Sit down myself, after invitation.)
2. 0 (I'd settle back comfortably, not ask questions at this point, unless patient was uncomfortable and blocked.)
3. 0 (Nothing at this point. I would already want to know, "Why now" after 20 years' fear, and would wait for appropriate time to ask.)
4. What makes you mad now?
5. 0 (I'd wait for time for me to be more active and ask why so many (intellectual) words. I'd try to get him to relax, not allow him to get so riled up.)
6. Same as above.
7. 0 (I'd not be parroting his words. Same as 5 and 6.)
8. 0 (Offer him a cigarette and take one myself.)
9. Have you gone to other (and many) doctors and what have they told you?
10. (Shift off present. Start with past history. Already I would have formed feelings not to treat him, but would check myself with information.)
11. 0 (Hard not to smile.)
12. Boy, you sure got troubles! (Lean back. I hope I wouldn't be sleepy.)
13. 0
14. (Either nothing or) *So what*. (Back to 13, mental status, I should like to get at some time.)
15. 0
16. ("Been afraid," etc.) You haven't died yet! (Perhaps) Why hard to relax now, telling me?
17. 0
18. How much have you been reading about these things?
19. What do *you* do for fun?
20. 0
21. (Either) If so, why do something now? (or) What was the best time in your life?
22. 0
23. What was the check ($35) for?
24. 0
25. (Ask specific questions about how he got even, what he didn't want to discuss.)

26. 0. "Three strikes . . ." You seem to like baseball.
27. Won't bother me if you cry.

28. What difference would it make if I said yes or no? (Perhaps I might go on, not antagonistically, to explain that's not the problem.)

COMMENT

Clinical Assessments: It is significant that this therapist, after having observed the patient for 10 to 15 minutes, notes that he has already formed feelings not to treat him (see film responses). In his evaluations he sees the patient as an obsessive who might be precipitated into a schizophrenic episode with homicidal tendencies. The prognosis is unfavorable and the therapist's attitude "somewhat negative." His reason: "I do not enjoy stubborn negativism, with the hostility so close to the surface." His focus in therapy would be on any positive aspects he could find in the patient's living; he anticipates difficulties from the patient's hostility unless the therapist succeeded in offering patterns acceptable for imitation; if the therapist became involved in fighting the character defenses, the patient might leave therapy or become psychotic; the therapist should be active and discourage free association. Clearly, the therapist has a strong aversion to the patient, of which he is aware.

Film Responses: Quite early in the interview the therapist focuses on the patient's anger (Response 4). Simultaneously he observes that he would try to get the patient to relax and not allow him to get so riled up. It seems doubtful, however, that the approach would be conducive to this result. Response 12, together with the aside about sleepiness, is an unvarnished expression of hostile rejection. The sarcasm is continued in Response 16 ("You haven't died yet"), Response 19 ("What do you do for fun?"), when the patient is recounting a significant aspect of his childhood, Response 21 ("If so, why do something now?") and Response 28 ("What difference would it make if I said yes or no?"). The last two comments, in particular, seem to communicate: Why bother me with your troubles? Response 27, which might sound warmly accepting in a different context, here merely seems to reflect disinterest.

If the therapist's objective is to discourage the patient from entering therapy with him, few approaches would be more effective. There are mitigating circumstances in the respondent's open refusal to treat the patient, but it would seem that a modicum of considerateness, courtesy, and respect may be rightfully expected from any professional person.

CODE: 25

BIOGRAPHICAL INFORMATION

Code:	25
Age:	45 years.
Sex:	Male.
Professional affiliation and status:	Psychiatrist.
Psychoanalytic training:	No training; no plans.
Personal analysis:	No analysis; do not expect to undertake it.

Experience in psychotherapy:	A great deal; 20.0 years.
Type of therapy:	0
Type of patients:	Neuroses.
Theoretical orientation:	Eclectic; Meyer.

CLINICAL ASSESSMENTS

Diagnosis

Dominant personality type:	Anxiety symptomatology; personality is more inadequate.
Formulation of dynamics:	Immature, unassertive personality who was overly conscious about the responsibilities thrust upon him.

Treatment plans

Form of treatment:	Supportive therapy and sedation. The use of hypnosis is indicated.
Treatment goals:	(1) A very limited goal. (2) A sense of acceptance by the therapist. (3) A gradual appreciation of his need to do things his own way (free from responsibility).
Frequency of sessions:	Once or twice weekly.
Length of treatment:	
Intermediate goals:	To ever attain freedom from the major complaints will be a matter of 3-5 years (300+ hours).
Ultimate goals:	0
Symptom-relief:	1 hour weekly or two weeks, same time. 3 to 5 years.
Difficulties expected:	Marked resistance to any disagreement that the world owes him a living and mother is the cause of it all.
Focus:	I would treat him as if he were a paranoid patient with a fixed delusional system.
Dangers:	Avoid promising any cure.
Areas to be avoided:	Avoid a feeling of being misunderstood and of not being accepted.
Behaviors to be encouraged:	I would develop a therapeutic *folie à deux* so he would think that I'm in full agreement.
Behaviors to be discouraged:	Not for a long time would I venture to be critical.
Strictness vs. permissiveness:	Rather passive.
Clues:	His hostility is great and requires much support.
Course of transference:	A marked positive relationship (clinging), masking a desire to prove that I never knew how sick he really is.
Approach to transference:	A strong attempt to make him feel I really understand him.
Activity vs. passivity:	Rather active.
Free association:	Neither encourage nor discourage.
Ego strength:	Very little.

Anxiety:	A great deal.
Insight:	Very little.
Emotional maturity:	Very immature.
Social adjustment:	Very inadequate.
Degree of disturbance:	Moderately disturbed.
Degree of therapeutic change attempted:	Very little change.
Prognosis without therapy:	Probably remain about the same.
Prognosis with therapy:	Very unfavorable.
Recommendations:	0
Attitude toward patient:	Somewhat negative.
Reasons:	True suffering is not colored by marked hostility.

EVALUATION OF FILM THERAPIST

Adequacy:	A reasonably adequate job.
Reason:	There were times when the repetition of the patient's words sounded a bit moronic.
Activity vs. passivity:	Somewhat too passive.
Support:	About right.
Life history data:	Would devote about the same time.
Attitude toward therapist:	Neutral.
Reason:	0

FILM RESPONSES

1. What brought you to see me?
2. Go ahead . . .
3. So?
4. And then?
5. Cornered?
6. You sure sound like you have taken a beating.
7. Tell me about the dizziness.
8. What else?
9. Tell me more about these *sensations* . . .
10. And?
11. You sure have had a tough time of it, haven't you?
12. Tell me *more* about that?
13. Social attitudes? or 0.
14. And then after your mother left?
15. 0
16. So, or 0.
17. Tell me about this.
18. 0
19. You sound more grown-up in this early age than your mother.
20. And you felt that your father . . . ?
21. You feel you never did get a square deal or a fair start . . .
22. Uh huh, or 0.
23. And then?
24. Cooperation? or 0.
25. Why can't you? (or How did you learn it?
26. 0
27. I see . . . you never really had a chance.
28. With your good luck, you're going to live and suffer.

COMMENT

Clinical Assessments: Treatment goals are seen as very limited, but they include a sense of acceptance by the therapist and a gradual appreciation by the patient of his need to do things his own way (refusal to accept responsibility).

The prognosis is judged as being very unfavorable but reconstruction of the patient's personality is considered at least possible. The respondent's attitude is described as "somewhat negative" ("True suffering is not colored by marked hostility"). A great deal of anxiety is said to be present but the personality is "inadequate." Supportive therapy, drugs, and hypnosis are recommended. A rather unusual procedure is suggested: "I would develop a therapeutic *'folie à deux'* so he would think that I'm in full agreement." He would treat him as if he were a paranoid patient with a fixed delusional system; avoid instilling a feeling of being misunderstood and of not being accepted. Not for a long time would he venture to be critical. He sees the patient's hostility as great and requiring much support (see, however, below!).

Film Responses: After a polite introduction and a few minimal questions the therapist, in Response 6, delivers himself of an observation whose colloquial quality sounds a bit crude. Response 11, in the same vein, seems somewhat more sympathetic. Responses 19 and 27 might be considered supportive. Most communications, however, seem curt and rather brittle. It seems highly doubtful that Response 28 can be said in a friendly tone of voice; it is more likely an expression of the therapist's own hostility; its effect on the patient must be equivalent to a slap in the face.

It seems that this therapist made up his mind early in the interview that the patient was not "really" suffering, that he was a hostile-dependent and therefore unworthy person, and the therapist then reacts in nongiving, unfriendly, and hostile fashion.

CODE: 26

BIOGRAPHICAL INFORMATION

Code:	26
Age:	45 years.
Sex:	Male.
Professional affiliation and status:	Psychoanalyst.
Psychoanalytic training:	Completed training.
Personal analysis:	Completed analysis that lasted at least 800 hours.
Experience in psychotherapy:	10 years; a great deal.
Type of therapy:	Analysis; analytically oriented therapy.
Type of patients:	Psychoneurotic.
Theoretical orientation:	Psychoanalytically oriented (general).

CLINICAL ASSESSMENTS

Diagnosis

Dominant personality type:	Hysteria.
Formulation of dynamics:	1) Conflicts concerning his relationship with his mother. 2) Rivalry. 3) Passivity and dependency.

Treatment plans

Form of treatment:	Trial interviews to see how he gets along.

Treatment goals: 1) Ventilation and exploration of his feelings about mother and wife. 2) Deeper study of events going on with origin of phobias, i.e., 1st time. 3) Symptomatic relief.

Frequency of sessions: 2-3 times a week.
Length of treatment:
  Intermediate goals: Symptomatic relief in 6 months to a year. Character formation—can't say.
  Ultimate goals:
Symptom-relief: 6 months to 1 year at 1-2 times a week.
Difficulties expected: Displacements, over-intellectualizations, demandingness and projections.
Focus: Relations with wife and mother. Work relations.
Dangers: Avoid intellectualizations and getting lost in details.
Areas to be avoided: No.
Behaviors to be encouraged: No.
Behaviors to be discouraged: Psychological reading and theorizing.
Strictness vs. permissiveness: No more strict or permissive than with others.
Clues: Slip about father's death—calling it mother's—his constant reiteration of being enclosed, hemmed in seem to be related to unconscious feminine identification.

Course of transference: Hostile, demanding, distrustful.
Approach to transference: By interpretation.
Activity vs. passivity: Rather active.
Free association: Encourage it.
Ego strength: Relatively little.
Anxiety: A great deal.
Insight: Very little.
Emotional maturity: Very immature.
Social adjustment: Very inadequate.
Degree of disturbance: Seriously disturbed.
Degree of therapeutic change
  attempted: Very extensive.
Prognosis without therapy: Remain about the same.
Prognosis with therapy: Very unfavorable.
Recommendations: He needs to be helped to help himself.
Attitude toward patient: Neutral.
  Reasons: My slight contact with him.

EVALUATION OF FILM THERAPIST
  Adequacy: Somewhat inadequate.
    Reason: He let the patient ramble too much. He asked too many detail questions about particular phobias person used. Missed chances to get history.
  Activity vs. passivity: Much too passive.
  Support: Neither too much nor too little support.

Life history data: Considerably more time.
Attitude toward therapist: Somewhat negative.
Reason: 0

FILM RESPONSES

1. Have a seat. Name? Age? Address? Occupation?
2. 0
3. 0
4. 0
5. Whom do you support?
6. 0
7. How else are you bothered?
8. 0
9. Tell me about your life history, childhood, parents.
10. ("Sorrowful . . .") What are your sorrows?
11. 0
12. What worried you in high school?
13. How were you getting on with mother then?
14. How did she come to live with you in the first place?
15. What was mother like when you were a small child?

16. Tell me about your brother or were there other children besides?
17. What had you in mind when you came to see me?
18. 0
19. How do you feel about your mother?
20. 0
21. Tell me about your jobs.
22. 0
23. ("Antisocial.") What antisocial attitudes?
24. 0
25. 0
26. 0
27. Seems as though you have to have your own way.
28. No. These are only the effects of things you don't understand within yourself.

COMMENT

Clinical Assessments: The therapist is a psychoanalyst, with a good deal of experience and rather extensive personal analysis. His diagnosis is "hysteria," which is usually associated with a somewhat favorable outlook. This therapist, however, regards the prognosis as very unfavorable, a judgment the reasons for which are not evident from the remainder of his responses. He is impressed with the patient's intellectualizations, demandingness, rivalry, and projections as well as his unconscious feminine identification. He is uncertain about ultimate treatment outcomes, but considers symptom-relief feasible. The suggested avenues are ventilation and exploration of his feelings about mother and wife, and eventually a deeper study of events surrounding the origin of his phobic fears. He is cautious in his recommendations and suggests trial interviews. His attitude toward the patient is given as "neutral," the reason being "my slight contact with him." He is critical of the film therapist.

Film Responses: The interview is introduced in business-like fashion, and a no-nonsense approach is sustained throughout. One gets the impression the therapist is doing a job and he is trying to do it conscientiously. He is respectful, serious, but not supportive, at least not in an overt way. His communications are concise questions dealing with interpersonal relations, particularly in the past. Notice the rather frequent silences. In Response 17, since the purpose of the interview had not previously been established, he asks—appropriately, it seems—why the patient came to see him. In Response 27 ("Seems as though you have to have your own way") he ventures a deeper interpretation which may be construed by the patient as criticism or rejection. His final response is unequivocal and correct; however, it gives but little support and may be experienced by the patient as quite inadequate (as would, of course, be true of any response since no therapist can possibly fulfill the patient's immense unconscious demands).

The therapist says elsewhere he would be rather active, which seems borne out by his film responses. His neutral, business-like attitude is also evident in his communications. It is difficult to penetrate his rather distant and impersonal approach. He seems withdrawn, aloof, and possibly critical of the patient. Certainly, he is averse (incapable?) to communicating warmth, friendliness, or kindness. His seriousness and respect, however, are unexceptionable.

CODE: 27

BIOGRAPHICAL INFORMATION

Code:	27
Age:	49 years.
Sex:	Male.
Professional affiliation and status:	Psychoanalyst.
Psychoanalytic training:	Completed training.
Personal analysis:	Completed analysis of 550 hours.
Experience in psychotherapy:	23 years; a great deal.
Type of therapy:	Psychoanalysis; analytically oriented therapy.
Type of patients:	Neuroses; psychosomatic; character disorders.
Theoretical orientation:	Freudian psychoanalysis (orthodox only).

CLINICAL ASSESSMENTS

Diagnosis

Dominant personality type:	Anxiety; passive-inhibited character neurosis.
Formulation of dynamics:	A passive-inhibited character neurosis—resenting being called upon to be active and responsible man and regressing to the agoraphobic and claustrophobic state.

Treatment plans

Form of treatment:	Active psychotherapy, keeping a tight rein on the tendency to regress into a dependent relationship with doctor.
Treatment goals:	1) Relieve his somatic anxieties. 2) Insight into the meaning of his regressive and aggressive trends.
Frequency of sessions:	2-3 times a week.
Length of treatment:	
Intermediate goals:	3 months.
Ultimate goals:	1½ to 2 years.
Symptom-relief:	2-3 times a week for 3-4 months.

Difficulties expected:	To get him to work and pay for his treatment.
Focus:	On his feelings about his mother, father, their relationship to each other and his brother.
Dangers:	To avoid the emphasis on his symptoms.
Areas to be avoided:	Yes, in his various complaints.
Behaviors to be encouraged:	To ventilate his feelings about the important people in his life.
Behaviors to be discouraged:	Yes, continual repetition and recital of complaints.
Strictness vs. permissiveness:	Rather permissive.
Clues:	His anger at the world, his anger about having to be an adult.
Course of transference:	A passive demanding one (you owe me something).
Approach to transference:	Yes, after several months, reassurance about his symptoms through interpretation.
Activity vs. passivity:	Rather active.
Free association:	Encourage it.
Ego strength:	Relatively little.
Anxiety:	A fair amount.
Insight:	Very little.
Emotional maturity:	Fairly immature.
Social adjustment:	Fairly inadequate.
Degree of disturbance:	Seriously disturbed.
Degree of therapeutic change attempted:	Relatively little change.
Prognosis without therapy:	Remain about the same.
Prognosis with therapy:	Neither favorable nor unfavorable.
Recommendations:	? I don't know enough about it at present time.
Attitude toward patient:	Neutral (?).
Reasons:	I have sympathy for his lot, but do not admire his regressive and evasive solution.

EVALUATION OF FILM THERAPIST

Adequacy:	Very inadequate.
Reason:	There was no real contact between patient and doctor.
Activity vs. passivity:	Much too passive; he wasn't even there!!!
Support:	Much too little support; I would not call him supportive.
Life history data:	Considerably more time.
Attitude toward therapist:	Somewhat negative.
Reason:	Because he failed miserably to make contact with his patient.

FILM RESPONSES

1. Tell me your problem.
2. What about your mother and this fear?
3. Can you give me other examples of this feeling of being hemmed in? And what is it that you fear in this situation?

4. (Up to now the interviewer is too vague and indefinite.) Tell me about your brother.
5. (I would have asked the above right after he mentioned his brother.)
6. 0 (I am critical of the doctor's vague, monosyllabic questions.)
7. What do you think your disease is? You say you have been reading about your ailment.
8. You say it brings on your fear. Fear what? What do you think will happen?
9. Which other stuff?
10. 0 (Except to wait for spontaneous remarks.)
11. How are you able to support mother and not work? How did you feel with father's death?
12. (Nothing at this break but this) Father's death.
13. How much time and interest would mother show in you during your childhood? Why seven times?
14. It's not unusual to have angry feelings about mother. Did you have any? Like what?
15. (The doctor succeeds in eliciting too many somatic complaints. I would draw out more of his negative feelings toward mother.)
16. Afraid of what?
17. (At such a blank moment) What are you thinking about right now?
18. Did it ever occur to you that being ill now, unpleasant as it is, has some value for you?
19. (A very weak doctor!!!)
20. (It is long past time to get a history and picture of *mother, father, siblings* and his feelings about them.)
21. You feel that you got a dirty deal in life.
22. What do you think your life would be like if mother died?
23. How did mother react to this check incident, being fired, etc.?
24. Why *damn* government? Were you really happy about all this responsibility dumped into your lap?
25. Get even? For example?
26. What do you mean the world owes you a living? Do you miss your dad? Do you think about him much?
27. If you had your choice, how would you live your life?
28. No, your physical symptoms will not harm you. But it is important to understand what they do *for* you.

COMMENT

Clinical Assessments: The formulations of this highly experienced psycho-analyst seem knowledgeable and sound. He feels the therapist should be rather active and keep a tight rein on the patient's tendency to regress to a dependent relationship with the doctor. Although he declines to judge the prognosis, he formulates a rather positive treatment program. There is considerable self-confidence and sureness in his evaluations, constructions, and inferences, and he is realistic throughout. He describes his personal attitude toward the patient as neutral, and his "reasons" encompass a human as well as a therapeutic reac-tion ("I have sympathy for his lot, but do not admire his regressive and evasive solution"). Thus, he recognizes the patient's suffering as well as the provocative aspects of his defenses; he is likewise aware of the demands of the therapeutic task. He can accept the patient as a human being in distress; but, to him, sym-pathy does not imply satisfying the patient's neurotic needs. He does not con-demn his "solution," nor does he admire it; he simply sees it as a therapeutic problem.

• He is critical of the film therapist, particularly with respect to his failure to establish rapport and to give support.

Film Responses: The therapist attempts a systematic exploration of the patient's life situation, showing a good deal of initiative in this quest. In Response 14 ("It's not unusual to have angry feelings about mother. Did you have any?") he refers to the commonality of human experience and, in effect, gives the patient "permission" to have angry feelings about his mother. Response 18 highlights the secondary gains of incapacitation; while provocative, the formulation is respectful and does not attack the patient's defenses frontally. Response 21 is a nondirective clarification, not frequently used by psychiatrists. Response 22, inquiring about the patient's life if mother died, may be experienced as quite anxiety-provoking. In the responses that follow the therapist refuses to accept the patient's formulations about blame and revenge; he is trying valiantly not to become enmeshed in the patient's framework, and seeks to penetrate it. Response 28 meets the patient's challenge head-on, but simultaneously suggests that there are "reasons" for the patient's plight which serve an important function in his psychic economy. The first part of this reply may be experienced as reassuring; the second is probably too intellectual and beyond his understanding, especially when considered in the context of the high emotional pitch.

The therapist seems to be at ease, confident, and experienced; he covers a lot of ground. At first, he is perhaps asking too many questions, but as the interview proceeds he becomes more supportive even though not particularly warm. He interacts with rather than reacts to the patient, asks thought-provoking and searching questions, and at times mobilizes his anxiety. Obviously, the respondent is aware of the symptoms' adaptive function and refuses to accept and operate upon their surface meaning. He seems well-equipped to establish a collaborative relationship.

CODE: 28

BIOGRAPHICAL INFORMATION

Code:	28
Age:	61 years.
Sex:	Male.
Professional affiliation and status:	Psychoanalyst.
Psychoanalytic training:	Completed training.
Personal analysis:	Completed analysis of 200 hours.
Experience in psychotherapy:	31 years; a great deal.
Type of therapy:	Psychoanalysis; analytically oriented therapy.
Type of patients:	0
Theoretical orientation:	Psychoanalytically oriented (general).

CLINICAL ASSESSMENTS

Diagnosis

Dominant personality type:	Psychopathic.
Formulation of dynamics:	0

Treatment plans

Form of treatment:	Occasional interviews.
Treatment goals:	Short, practical goals.
Frequency of sessions:	0
Length of treatment:	0
Intermediate goals:	
Ultimate goals:	
Symptom-relief:	0
Difficulties expected:	(See diagnosis.)
Focus:	0
Dangers:	0
Areas to be avoided:	0
Behaviors to be encouraged:	0
Behaviors to be discouraged:	0
Strictness vs. permissiveness:	No more strict or permissive than with others.
Clues:	0
Course of transference:	0
Approach to transference:	0
Activity vs. passivity:	No more active or passive than with others.
Free association:	Discourage it.
Ego strength:	Relatively little.
Anxiety:	Relatively little.
Insight:	Relatively little.
Emotional maturity:	Fairly immature.
Social adjustment:	Very inadequate.
Degree of disturbance:	Seriously disturbed.
Degree of therapeutic change	
attempted:	Very little change.
Prognosis without therapy:	Remain about the same.
Prognosis with therapy:	Very unfavorable.
Recommendations:	0
Attitude toward patient:	Neutral.
Reasons:	0

EVALUATION OF FILM THERAPIST

Adequacy:	Somewhat inadequate.
Reason:	0
Activity vs. passivity:	Somewhat too passive.
Support:	0
Life history data:	Considerably more time.
Attitude toward therapist:	Neutral.
Reason:	0

FILM RESPONSES

1. 0
2. What is your economic condition?
3. Any physical examination?
4. 0
5. 0
6. (Father's behavior and reaction to patient.)
7. When did all this start?
8. Comparable to any experience in dreams?

9. 0
10. An everyday experience?
11. (Father's behavior and reaction to patient.)
12. How long has wife been sick?
13. Antisocial tendencies?
14. Mother and wife?
15. (Mother's attitude and reaction when patient was a child.)
16. Continue about mother.
17. (More mother expression in patient. Continue with mother.)
18. 0

19. Any positive trends in mother?
20. Brother older or younger?
21. Do you really think so? Feel it?
22. (To mention the slip?)
23. (To have him continue, saying nothing.)
24. (Back to the grandparents—the corrupting factor? Delinquency.)
25. 0
26. (More factual material.)
27. (To try to get the patient away from his descriptions about his feelings and sensations.)
28. (The same.)

COMMENT

Clinical Assessments: The respondent, an older analyst with many years of experience, considers the patient "psychopathic," judges the prognosis as very unfavorable, and in keeping with his diagnosis, perceives little anxiety in the patient; nevertheless he evaluates the disturbance as serious. His treatment goals are described as "short, practical goals," and he would strive for "very little change"; his replies to the questions pertaining to strictness vs. permissiveness, activity vs. passivity, and personal attitude are answered in noncommittal fashion. His lack of interest in the patient, the experimental task, or both, are amply documented by his responses which inform anyone that he is not going to exert himself.

Film Responses: A similarly negative attitude permeates the communications to the patient. The questions seem routine and almost reflex-like. He is searching for factual material and more factual material; there is no indication that he regards the patient as a living person who struggles, gropes for a solution, and fails. The diagnosis of psychopath neatly summarizes this attitude: he is considered a person lacking in human sensitivity and responsibility, who blithely transgresses the rules of social conduct when it suits his whims, who has no moral scruples and no conscience. He is an enemy of society and deserves its scorn; the way to deal with him is to punish him for his asocial and antisocial behavior.

Instead of reacting to the patient with open counterhostility this therapist seems to convey nonverbally that he wishes to have nothing to do with him. Overtly, he is gathering data (facts) for a purpose, but what is the purpose? He makes no effort to establish rapport. His attitude, which is given as neutral, might be described more accurately as distant and cold.

CODE: 29

BIOGRAPHICAL INFORMATION

Code: 29
Age: 60 years.
Sex: Male.

Professional affiliation and status:	Psychoanalyst.
Psychoanalytic training:	Completed training.
Personal analysis:	Completed analysis of about 200 hours.
Experience in psychotherapy:	30 years; a great deal.
Type of therapy:	Psychoanalysis and psychoanalytically oriented psychotherapy.
Type of patients:	Those with psychoneuroses, character disorders, borderline cases and psychosomatic disorders.
Theoretical orientation:	Psychoanalytically oriented (general).

CLINICAL ASSESSMENTS

Diagnosis

Dominant personality type:	Paranoid.
Formulation of dynamics:	Could see clearly, only, the frustration at time of father's death. Mother further frustrated his passive and dependent longings. Hostility noted, probably was reaction to this.

Treatment plans

Form of treatment:	I would complete the evaluation first before formulating a plan.
Treatment goals:	I would complete the evaluation before attempting to answer the question.
Frequency of sessions:	0
Length of treatment:	See above under form of treatment.
Intermediate goals:	0
Ultimate goals:	0
Symptom-relief:	Temporary relief of symptoms probably would come within a short period of time but recurrences would be expected.
Difficulties expected:	Attempts to control the treatment, demands for help other than that pertaining to self-understanding.
Focus:	First, on the reality of his uncomfortable (i.e., need for guidance) situation at the time of his father's death, then support of those ego functions which are not in the service of regression.
Dangers:	Dangers of acute paranoid schizophrenic psychosis if he is confronted too suddenly by his passive homosexual wishes or if he is pushed too quickly to accept full responsibility as a man.
Areas to be avoided:	His sexual life, his corrupt ego ideals (to be dealt with later in therapy).
Behaviors to be encouraged:	Whatever tends to move him away from regression and infancy.
Behaviors to be discouraged:	The attitude of blaming someone in the past or in the present for his distress.
Strictness vs. permissiveness:	From the beginning I would not promise to "heal" his symptoms, but would express the hope that, with better understanding, they

Clues:

probably would subside. I would support realistic needs, including those dependent needs appropriate to the doctor-patient relationship. Yes; his mentioning the big woman that sat next to him—smothering fantasy—probably connected with his hostile dependence on the mother. His description of claustrophobia and agoraphobia suggest specific psychodynamics in relation to mother.

Course of transference:

Hostile dependence, defended against by aggressive attempts to control the therapist; inclinations to regress to an oral dependent level.

Approach to transference:

From the beginning would find out what he expects from therapy and let him know that the therapist is not all-powerful.

Activity vs. passivity: Rather active.
Free association: Discourage it.
Ego strength: Very little.
Anxiety: A great deal (but most of it repressed).
Insight: Very little.
Emotional maturity: Very immature.
Social adjustment: Very inadequate.
Degree of disturbance: Seriously disturbed.
Degree of therapeutic change
  attempted: Too little evidence.
Prognosis without therapy: Get much worse.
Prognosis with therapy: Too little evidence.
Recommendations: Would wait until further evaluation.
Attitude toward patient: Somewhat negative.
Reasons:

He does not impress me as sincere. Unless hospital facilities are near at hand, psychotherapy, here, would be largely on a research basis because of the patient's poor capacity for reality testing. He does not seem sincerely to want to look within.

EVALUATION OF FILM THERAPIST

Adequacy: Somewhat inadequate.
  Reason: He seemed to lack confidence in obtaining a dynamic awareness.

Activity vs. passivity: Much too passive.
Support: Much too little support (regarding the need to obtain data other than the patient's description of symptoms).

Life history data: Considerably more time.
Attitude toward therapist: Somewhat negative.
  Reason: He gave the impression of entering into a treatment situation before obtaining more specific information about onset, about history, etc.

FILM RESPONSES

1. 0
2. In what way did economic conditions affect you?
3. How far back does this go, this feeling of being hemmed in?
4. Were you crowded in your home when you were a child? Is that what you referred to a moment ago?
5. Is your brother older or younger?
6. 0
7. When did this fear of going outside begin?
8. When you have these sensations, what do you think might happen to you? What do these sensations mean to you?
9. 0
10. Did you think those physical aspects of anxiety would harm you in some way?
11. What is talked about at the table?
12. Tell me more about that period when you were in high school.
13. What attitudes were you speaking of?
14. 0
15. What does your mother "gripe" about?
16. Is there more?
17. What traits of character?
18. 0
19. Tell me about your father's work.
20. 0
21. What kind of work do you do?
22. When did your father die?
23. Did anyone at the bank treat you unfairly?
24. What responsibilities did you assume then?
25. 0
26. How old were you when father died?
27. When your father died, you really were not ready to take care of others. Weren't you then only a child in age, actually needing to be taken care of yourself?
28. In what way do you believe I can help you? What do you expect to gain from treatment?

COMMENT

Clinical Assessments: The respondent asserts he would defer formulating a treatment plan pending the completion of an evaluation, and he criticizes the film therapist for entering into a treatment situation before obtaining more specific information about onset, history, etc. Nevertheless, his hesitancy is not a reflection of an inability to observe keenly and to integrate the limited data at his disposal. The contrary is true. His formulations, while cautious, are more complete and insightful than those of many other respondents. He points out the danger of an acute schizophrenic episode if the patient is confronted too suddenly with his passive homosexual wishes or if he is pushed too quickly to accept full responsibility as a man. His comments speak for themselves and reveal an earnest, dispassionate, and thoughtful therapist. He seems impressed by the seriousness of the patient's problem, the patient striking him, however, as insincere and poorly motivated for psychotherapy. He admits to a somewhat negative attitude. Clearly, he is pessimistic about the patient's future.

Film Responses: In accordance with his recommendation to obtain more complete clinical data, he follows a largely investigative approach. His questioning is respectful, nonjudgmental, and conveys a restrained, friendly interest. Response 23, for example, is focused on the patient's feelings rather than the therapist's interpretation of the check-writing episode. Response 27 reveals greater warmth than preceding communications, and Response 28 extends a helping hand, without being effusive or smothering. It seems thoroughly honest, sincere, and reality-oriented. Judges had no difficulty in rating his approach as empathic.

The therapist may not have any great personal liking for patients of this kind, but nowhere does he permit this attitude to intrude. A high degree of self-awareness permeates his therapeutic operations, which seem extraordinarily lucid. He is goal-oriented, at ease in the situation, and obviously honest with himself and the patient. There is no pretense, no stuffiness, no duplicity. Another first-rate interviewer!

CODE: 30

BIOGRAPHICAL INFORMATION

Code:	30
Age:	52 years.
Sex:	Female.
Professional affiliation and status:	Psychoanalyst.
Psychoanalytic training:	Completed training.
Personal analysis:	Completed analysis of 700 hours.
Experience in psychotherapy:	10 years; a great deal.
Type of therapy:	Psychoanalysis, psychoanalytically oriented therapy.
Type of patients:	Neurotic and psychosomatic.
Theoretical orientation:	Psychoanalytically oriented (general).

CLINICAL ASSESSMENTS

Diagnosis

Dominant personality type:	Obsessive.
Formulation of dynamics:	Narcissistic anxiety on a deeply repressed sexual conflict, with much rivalry and hostile retreat.

Treatment plans

Form of treatment:	Psychotherapy.
Treatment goals:	Develop a rapport first by trying to discuss with him the present-day circumstances. Frequency: about 2 times a week. Consider social service assistance if reality situation is as bad as he says. Very little uncovering of deep material. More rationalizing and development of identification with therapist.
Frequency of sessions:	2 times a week.
Length of treatment:	Depends upon reality resources—2-3 years.
Intermediate goals:	0
Ultimate goals:	0
Symptom-relief:	6 months.
Difficulties expected:	Increases of anxiety, perhaps paranoid tendencies, some depression and angry outbursts.
Focus:	Present-day—job, marriage and friends. .

Dangers:	He could become paranoid and perhaps suicidal.
Areas to be avoided:	Sexual conflicts, especially homosexual.
Behaviors to be encouraged:	Has he kept on trying? If no, encourage that. Find his assets and work on them.
Behaviors to be discouraged:	Can't answer yet.
Strictness vs. permissiveness:	Firm and encouraging but realistic.
Clues:	The slip of the tongue I mentioned. The relationship with the brother and with the educated relatives. The hand gestures—flicking the end of the table even when not angry. The oral facial movements.
Course of transference:	Demanding of answers and taking over by the therapist—something he wanted the father to stay alive to do. This would be followed by competition and patient's desire to take over and be independent.
Approach to transference:	Answer when I could but help him to find his own answers. I probably would not "interpret" the transference in its repetition of the past, but in unreasonable present sense with me.
Activity vs. passivity:	Rather active.
Free association:	Discourage it.
Ego strength:	Too little evidence.
Anxiety:	A fair amount.
Insight:	Relatively little.
Emotional maturity:	Fairly immature.
Social adjustment:	Too little evidence.
Degree of disturbance:	Seriously disturbed.
Degree of therapeutic change attempted:	Relatively little change.
Prognosis without therapy:	Get much worse.
Prognosis with therapy:	Neither favorable nor unfavorable.
Recommendations:	Don't know enough about his present mode of living.
Attitude toward patient:	Neutral.
Reasons:	No.

EVALUATION OF FILM THERAPIST

Adequacy:	Very inadequate.
Reason:	Too little information of present-day situation with which we have to work. Too much passive acceptance of "theme song."
Activity vs. passivity:	Much too passive.
Support:	Much too little support.
Life history data:	Considerably more time.
Attitude toward therapist:	Somewhat negative.
Reason:	I put myself in patient's position and would have felt a lack of interest, an aloofness, and apparent ineptitude that would not make sense to me. I would think he was "dumb."

FILM RESPONSES

1. 0
2. Tell me how old you are and more about your mother.
3. 0 (disagree with therapist's focus on this feeling of being hemmed in; it becomes an argument).
4. 0 ("Encased.")
5. I can understand what you are describing, but let's find out more about your early life. Are you married?
6. Anything else than the streetcar experience make you feel hemmed in recently?
7. Mm-hm (or) I see.
8. Let's talk about the circumstances at home when this trouble began.
9. Tell me about other illnesses in your life.
10. Do you ever get angry? What kinds of things make you angry?
11. Mm . . . naturally! (Wife encephalitis) How old is she? Any children?
12. Tell me about your high school experiences.
13. You feel you have never had enough to manage on?
14. Mm . . . Tell me something about your father.
15. Let's talk about your jobs . . . from the bank on . . .
16. Mm . . . We have to try to work out the causes and try to do something about them.
17. For example . . . (Note slip of tongue: Father away from work, from house, but say nothing to patient).
18. I can well understand that. What does your wife say?
19. 0
20. Give an example of what your mother would tell your father.
21. How do you support yourself now?
22. Mm-hm . . .
23. Then what did you do?
24. A difficult situation . . . but this happened 30 years ago. You said you were married. Tell me about that.
25. Tell me about the getting even. Maybe we can figure out some other things to do.
26. Mm-hm. Are you a father too? Army? Tell me what happened there? Did you talk with a psychiatrist there?
27. What happened after you left the service? (Question regarding sensations) Have you talked to psychiatrists lately?
28. No, they will not damage you. They are a result of a lot of piled up feelings, and if we can get them straightened out, I think we can help you.

COMMENT

Clinical Assessments: The respondent notes the patient's obsessive personality features, his narcissistic anxiety based on a deeply repressed sexual conflict, his rivalry, and hostile retreat. She is noncommittal about the prognosis and states her attitude as neutral; she declines to speculate why she feels this way. Her emphasis in treatment is on the development of rapport, encouraging constructive moves, amelioration of the reality situation, and dealing with present-day concerns. She envisages the possibility of a paranoid psychosis and acting out of suicidal tendencies. One gathers that she disadvises investigative psychoanalytic therapy, at least in the early stages, and her reasons are clear. She regards the patient as seriously disturbed and feels he might get much worse if no therapy were undertaken. Her focus on present-day reality also emerges in her criticisms of the film therapist. It is interesting to note that, unlike many of her colleagues, she attempts to put herself in the patient's position to assess the effects of the film therapist's technique. From this vantage point, she experiences him as lacking in interest, aloof, and inept. She follows the majority in judging the amount of support as inadequate.

Film Responses: The therapist makes it clear from the start that *she* is conducting the interview, that she is interested in obtaining specific data, and that she knows what she is after and how to get it. At the same time, there is a good deal of warmth communicated in her explorations; she never dominates, condemns, or criticizes, nor does she approve or condone. Quite early in the interview (Comment on Response 3) she foresees the danger of the interview degenerating into an argument. Notice that from the start the interview is conceived as a *collaborative* enterprise. She speaks in terms of "we" and "us," and this device alone seems to convey a good deal of support. Slips of the tongue (Responses 17 and 22) are noted, but, in keeping with the therapist's objective to allay rather than to mobilize anxiety, not responded to. Responses 16, 24, 25, 26, and 28 are genuinely warm, sincere, and forthright. Response 25 displays remarkable empathic skill in its attempt to deal with the patient's resentment by directing it into more constructive channels. She also sees the need to give some direct reassurance in Response 28; here again there is an impressive simplicity and directness, together with a constructive recommendation for the future.

In sum, the therapist is warm, mature, friendly, and eager to help. At the same time, she has in mind a specific plan of action which she pursues with considerable determination. These qualities are exceptionally well balanced and integrated. The result is an interview conducted with consummate skill.

11

GROUP IV:

CLIENT-CENTERED THERAPISTS

This section presents the records of 10 psychotherapists (psychologists) who described their theoretical orientation as "client-centered" (followers of Carl Rogers). Nine of the respondents were affiliated with the Counseling Center of the University of Chicago, and one therapist (the most experienced) was a psychologist employed by the Veterans Administration. The protocols are arranged in ascending order of the therapist's experience in psychotherapy.

No attempt has been made to comment on each therapist's performance. While the reader will undoubtedly detect qualitative differences in the application of the reflection-of-feeling technique used rather consistently by all respondents, the author did not consider critical evaluations of individual protocols within his province. For a discussion of rather pronounced group differences between client-centered therapists and those following the psychoanalytic viewpoint (broadly defined), the reader is referred to Chapter 7. With reference to the therapists' communications, the following observations appear to apply to most of the records in this section:

1. The technique of reflecting the patient's feelings is followed almost to the complete exclusion of any other mode of verbal communication. Nevertheless, different therapists focus on different feelings at particular junctures.

2. "Silent" responses are used rather infrequently. In other words, the therapist responds readily to the invitation (built into the experimental procedure) to respond to stopping points in the film.

3. Since client-centered therapists specifically disavow attempts to

formulate the nature of the patient's problem or to pursue a treatment goal other than that suggested by the patient's phenomenal
self, each reflection of feeling typically refers to the segment immediately preceding the therapist's comment. The therapist asks himself: What is the predominant feeling here being communicated?
and then responds to it.

4. In keeping with the client-centered theory, therapists never
question, investigate, or cast doubt upon a formulation presented by
the patient. Whereas a number of psychoanalytically oriented therapists, for example, seek to dislodge the patient's belief that "the
world owes me a living" by registering doubt about the adequacy
of his viewing reality in this fashion, the client-centered therapist
typically accepts the patient's structure of his internal world, through
empathy with his feelings as well as sympathy for his lot. (It is safe
to say that many analytically oriented therapists would strongly
disadvise this procedure on the grounds that it fuels the patient's
paranoid and obsessive ruminations; rather than paving the way to
an understanding of his own contribution to the problem, this approach would merely augment his resentment and play into his
projective defense mechanisms.*)

5. The communications of nearly all client-centered therapists
disclose a marked predilection for the vernacular, a "folksy" flavor,
and the use of a number of stock phrases. Examples include: "You
feel like. . . ."; "that *really* seems like. . . ."; "just seems like.
. . ."; "I guess you felt. . . ."; "sort of. . . ."; "fed up"; "damned";
"mess"; "lousy circumstances"; "kind of. . . ."; "screwed up"; etc.

6. In response to the patient's intense plea for reassurance (expressed with particular urgency at the end of the interview), client-
centered therapists typically continue steadfastly to reflect the domi-

---

* This raises the important issue whether it is ever therapeutically advisable to "take
the patient's side" against circumstances and other people. The Rogerian therapists
here represented would unquestionably assert that their technique is designed to
communicate the therapist's understanding, empathy and "unconditional positive
regard." Rather than experience it as such, the patient may come to feel, however,
that the therapist is commiserating and showing condescension—an unfortunate result
for any neurotic patient whose self-esteem, self-respect, and self-acceptance are usually
markedly impaired. Surely, there are many ways for the therapist to show respect,
understanding, and acceptance of the patient as a person, of which the reflection-of-
feeling technique is merely one. Indeed, the thesis may be defended that respect,
understanding, and acceptance—certainly cornerstones of all systems of modern psychotherapy—are most effectively communicated *nonverbally*, by genuine interest, attentive
listening, impartiality, firmness, punctuality of appointments, etc.

nant feeling. In other words, they consistently follow the therapeutic role as they conceive of it, unlike numerous other therapists
who at this point either gave direct assurance or made suggestions
for possible courses of external action (physical examination, etc.).

CODE: 1R

BIOGRAPHICAL INFORMATION

Code:	1R
Age:	31 years.
Sex:	Male.
Professional affiliation and status:	Psychologist.
Psychoanalytic training:	(Client-centered; 1½ years.)
Personal analysis:	Plans for (client-centered).
Experience in psychotherapy:	A fair amount; ½ year.
Type of therapy:	Client-centered.
Type of patients:	Psychoneurotics.
Theoretical orientation:	Rogers (client-centered therapy).

CLINICAL ASSESSMENTS

Diagnosis

Dominant personality type:	Anxiety.
Formulation of dynamics:	A domineering, demanding mother-child relationship. Client unable to function by himself, yet constantly faced with responsibilities that overwhelm him.

Treatment plans

Form of treatment:	An accepting, empathically understanding therapist who can move along with the client so that he can understand his feelings and give expression to them.
Treatment goals:	Goals more apt to be that which client himself sets up as we move along. My goal would be to be with him. Hope, but will not demand or expect, a more integrated self and accepting understanding.
Frequency of sessions:	Tend to prefer two interviews per week, but inclined to let client decide.
Length of treatment:	Can't say; 50-75 hours.
Symptom relief:	Can't say; maybe 25 sessions or less? more?
Difficulties expected:	Don't know.
Focus:	Client determines this; suspect it may center on his mother, wife, brother and father.
Dangers:	No.
Areas to be avoided:	No. Client determines movement generally.

Behaviors to be encouraged:	No. Client's own experimenting and exploring determines movement generally.
Behaviors to be discouraged:	Not *discourage* but clarify and understand and accept.
Strictness vs. permissiveness:	Rather permissive.
Clues:	Question of masculinity—but not that I would use it. Am sure he will get to it himself; if not, then it may not have been important.
Course of transference:	Don't emphasize this—probably mother?
Approach to transference:	Acceptance, understanding, clarifying.
Activity vs. passivity:	Rather active (?)
Free association:	Encourage.
Ego strength:	Relatively little.
Anxiety:	A great deal.
Insight:	Relatively little.
Emotional maturity:	Fairly immature.
Social adjustment:	Fairly inadequate.
Degree of disturbance:	Moderately disturbed.
Degree of therapeutic change attempted:	Very little change; client at his own pace.
Prognosis without therapy:	Remain about the same.
Prognosis with therapy:	Somewhat favorable.
Recommendations:	No. Client decides himself as he gets to a better understanding of self.
Attitude toward patient:	Somewhat positive.
Reasons:	Probably more a desire to help, feeling and understanding with him. Seems a good client to work with.

EVALUATION OF FILM THERAPIST

Adequacy:	Very inadequate.
Reason:	Probing, but especially almost ignoring what client is saying or has said.
Activity vs. passivity:	Too active at wrong times, dearth of responses; question doesn't fit my way of looking at it.
Support:	Much too little support.
Life history data:	Considerably less time.
Attitude toward therapist:	Somewhat negative.
Reason:	(Criticizes technique of therapist, and rather cold handling of client's feelings.)

FILM RESPONSES

1. Won't you sit down here?
2. Something about this experience on the street car which reminded you or brought to you a fear which in some way you feel related to your mother?
3. Something about being hemmed in by this large, big woman that caused you to feel anxious.
4. Being hemmed in by this big woman sort of reminded you of being hemmed in by all kinds of things, economic, etc., sort of squished and hamstrung?

5. Never feeling free to do what you would like, always various pressures upon you, sort of cornered always.

6. Forces beyond your control or means to ward off and do what you would want?

7. Sort of needing your wife to be with you to help or protect you out in the streets all the time. Now feeling you can go out without her but now there's a dizzy feeling?

8. Sensing this feeling makes for more anxiety or fears?

9. Uh, huh, the other sort of goes away?

10. Tell me a little more about it.

11. Her personality is such you just can't stand to have her live with you. She sort of upsets you, I sense you're saying.

12. Your mother even upsets your wife and part of it is because she is so involved in other people's affairs?

13. Uh, huh. All this moving around sort of upset you.

14. Awful as she may be, she's still my mother; sort of?

15. She gets you angry and anxious, sort of makes you feel completely drained out.

16. Kind of fearful to go outside?

17. Kinda angry in finding in yourself some of the same characteristics your mother has which you don't like.

18. Really would like to overcome these feelings which affect so strongly.

19. Something about nonmasculine characteristics that annoy you?

20. Angry and wanting to leave home —sort of resented this "tattle-tale" behavior of your mother.

21. Everything in your life seems unpleasant or painful that you feel that you started life with everything against you.

22. She made your brother completely irresponsible and you responsible for everything?

23. Sort of doing that caused you to lose everything, your job, position in society, etc.

24. You felt this was your responsibility but just didn't feel you could handle it or was ready for this, especially in view of your mother's demand and lack of cooperation from them.

25. Sort of feeling you just weren't given a fair break, that you sort of feel resentful and wanted to get back at them or it, as you say?

26. Sort of just my tough luck not to have had a father to carry out things so normally.

27. As if to say why me, of all people. I have enough problems myself, never had a chance to really live your own life, I sense you saying?

28. They hit you so hard that it demoralizes you so you have run home. Here it is safe but yet even here it may come upon you too? Then you feel you just have to face it, take it?

CODE: 2R

BIOGRAPHICAL INFORMATION

Code:	2R
Age:	36 years.
Sex:	Female.
Professional affiliation and status:	Psychologist.

Psychoanalytic training:	None; no plans.
Personal analysis:	In analysis; completed 25 hours.
Experience in psychotherapy:	Very little; ¾ of a year.
Type of therapy:	Client-centered.
Type of patients:	Children, adults, college students, self-referrals not likely to be hospitalized.
Theoretical orientation:	Rogers (client-centered).

CLINICAL ASSESSMENTS

Diagnosis

Dominant personality type:	Anxiety.
Formulation of dynamics:	He feels trapped; this is expressed in psychosomatic symptoms, which circularly make him feel more trapped.

Treatment plans

Form of treatment:	Psychotherapy.
Treatment goals:	I wouldn't set goals in way I think this means.
Frequency of sessions:	Would let him decide; would offer possibility of 2 or 3 times a week.
Length of treatment:	Think he would be possible client for short-term therapy such as we are currently doing research on. 10 weeks at twice a week, 10 weeks off, 10 weeks twice a week available again.
Symptom relief:	?
Difficulties expected:	I think he might expect the therapist to take over for him.
Focus:	I would focus on the feeling expressed without reference to area of living.
Dangers:	No.
Areas to be avoided:	I would not be choosing the areas, would leave this to him.
Behaviors to be encouraged:	Be trying to understand the feelings expressed —and communicating this—I suppose I would be encouraging him to express his feeling life.
Behaviors to be discouraged:	No.
Strictness vs. permissiveness:	Rather permissive.
Clues:	No—except inasmuch as such clues make me more understanding of this person, and so more sensitive to his experiences at any given time.
Course of transference:	I think he would see me as another authority (parental) and might want me to take over for him in a protecting way.
Approach to transference:	I would try to communicate understanding of his wish to be taken care of, but would try to value him as a person, without making demands or taking over for him.
Activity vs. passivity:	Rather active.
Free association:	Neither encourage nor discourage it.
Ego strength:	A fair amount.

Anxiety:	A great deal.
Insight:	Too little evidence to make a judgment.
Emotional maturity:	Very immature.
Social adjustment:	Very inadequate.
Degree of disturbance:	Too little evidence to make a judgment.
Degree of therapeutic change attempted:	0
Prognosis without therapy:	Too little evidence to make a judgment.
Prognosis with therapy:	Somewhat favorable.
Recommendations:	No; I don't make such recommendations.
Attitude toward patient:	Somewhat positive.
Reasons:	0

EVALUATION OF FILM THERAPIST

Adequacy:	Very inadequate.
Reason:	He became just one more prober.
Activity vs. passivity:	Somewhat too passive.
Support:	Much too little support.
Life history data:	Considerably less time.
Attitude toward therapist:	Somewhat negative.
Reason:	Too fidgety, too probing.

FILM RESPONSES

1. Sit down also (in way to make him feel comfortable).
2. The fear that you've always had came back at that time.
3. You were so hemmed in then, you couldn't stand to stay there.
4. You felt like maybe you couldn't push out of this one.
5. You feel trapped by this, and all so unfair.
6. It seems so unnecessary—this hemming in—and this time was too much.
7. You can move away from a little more, but it still doesn't feel okay.
8. You just can't break out of it.
9. You can ignore the problems that worry you, but the physical symptoms are too much.
10. These feelings of anxiety hit your whole body.
11. Having her around you would be unbearable.
12. When your mother's around you feel anxious — with her busybodiness.
13. Uh-hmm.
14. You feel like you have to put up with her somewhat, but want to get her away when you can.
15. You feel empty and torn when she's around you.
16. Uh-humm.
17. You really don't like to be told you're like her.
18. You've had so many strikes against you, but now you want to push your way out of it.
19. It was terribly embarrassing.
20. Felt like you had to take it, but you really wanted to smash things.
21. Seems right now like you're already licked.
22. The whole thing was on your shoulders.
23. They just wouldn't see your side of it; you caught the brunt of it.
24. It felt good to be the head, but you didn't get any cooperation from them.
25. You've been hurt so much that you want to get even. You try, but even that doesn't work.

26. You really needed him.
27. You feel so cheated by it, and so full of feeling that can't come out.

28. These feelings get so strong. You're afraid they may really damage your body.

CODE: 3R

BIOGRAPHICAL INFORMATION

Code:	3R
Age:	25 years.
Sex:	Male.
Professional affiliation and status:	Psychologist.
Psychoanalytic training:	None; no plans.
Personal analysis:	Completed 70 hours; expect it to last 100 hours.
Experience in psychotherapy:	A fair amount, 1 year.
Type of therapy:	Client-centered therapy.
Type of patients:	Psychoneurotic men and women.
Theoretical orientation:	Rogers (client-centered).

CLINICAL ASSESSMENTS

Diagnosis

Dominant personality type:	Anxiety, hysteria, obsessive.
Formulation of dynamics:	All I could say to this is that they go way way back.

Treatment plans

Form of treatment:	Psychotherapy, if he wanted it.
Treatment goals:	To set up a free and warm and close relationship, in which he could freely explore and feel himself and his experiences (intermediate). Mature patient (ultimate).
Frequency of sessions:	As often as he likes within practical limits (although probably not more than three times weekly).
Length of treatment:	Not too long for immediate goals for a relationship. Perhaps just an hour or two. But quite some time (a year perhaps, or more) for a profound change in him.
Symptom relief:	Not too long for temporary symptom-relief (20 hours would probably do well).
Difficulties expected:	An aggressive and persistent demand for concrete help from therapist.
Focus:	His "self" living.
Dangers:	None. He appears well aware of his own weaknesses and situation.
Areas to be avoided:	No.
Behaviors to be encouraged:	Very gently, if at all, encourage self-expression.
Behaviors to be discouraged:	Can't think of any, except personal violence.
Strictness vs. permissiveness:	Rather permissive.

Clues:	That life really is down on him right now. That he wants to please the therapist (shined shoes and meek demeanor).
Course of transference:	Quite aggressive with the therapist in the film. A little, but very transient, with a therapist of my ideal.
Approach to transference:	As with all other expressions of client.
Activity vs. passivity:	No more active or passive than with others.
Free association:	Neither encourage nor discourage it.
Ego strength:	A fair amount.
Anxiety:	A fair amount.
Insight:	Relatively little.
Emotional maturity:	Fairly immature.
Social adjustment:	Fairly inadequate.
Degree of disturbance:	Seriously disturbed.
Degree of therapeutic change attempted:	Fairly extensive change.
Prognosis without therapy:	Probably get a little better.
Prognosis with therapy:	Very favorable.
Recommendations:	No. I feel that he is capable of making such a decision.
Attitude toward patient:	Somewhat positive.
Reasons:	His honesty and vigor and humannness make me feel positive. I am somewhat disconcerted, though, by his *very negative* feeling toward society.

EVALUATION OF FILM THERAPIST

Adequacy:	Very inadequate.
Reason:	He was defensive, unresponsive, lost any number of feelings of the patient, shied away from patient.
Activity vs. passivity:	Neither too active nor too passive; about right.
Support:	Somewhat too little support.
Life history data:	Considerably less time.
Attitude toward therapist:	Somewhat negative.
Reason:	That he was very tense and closed up. Yet he tried and is trying to do better.

FILM RESPONSES

1. 0 (sit down and wait).
2. 0 (or if the patient stops, a comment on the strangeness and pervasiveness of his fear).
   Doctor: Hemmed in? (definitely would not have said this).
3. 0 (or same as above).
   Doctor: 2 or 300 pounds. (Would not have said this either.)
4. You feel terribly caught and trapped.
5. "My God! I am unfairly trapped by a lot of lousy circumstances."
6. I have *never* been free.
7. The panic was so severe you were crippled for days and now that that's gone you are frightened by being dizzy (don't like this too well) or 0.

8. 0 or "very helpless."

9. Your awful feelings that are im-´portant right now.

10. Your anxiety is what you want to deal with here.

11. It would be a pretty bad situation to live with your mother. She is so upsetting.

12. "I am now and have *always* been an anxious and scared person."

13. 0

14. Even though you don't like her and she has hurt you, there is the blood relation that still counts.

15. Uh-uh (nodding). (I want to catch the track he is on, or wants to be on again.)

16. The terrific panic and dizziness scare the daylights out of you, they don't belong to you somehow.

17. There's another troubling thing (didn't catch all of the movie).

18. Sick and tired of being crippled so badly.

19. She annoyed you in so many little ways.

20. You wanted to run away and get angry very much. Somehow your father helped you feel somewhat better.

21. "I am angry and, well, sad, about my whole life. I just haven't had a chance."

22. 0

23. This made you hate people, and it was more than enough to do that to anyone.

24. You are just so *angry*. It has been a very dirty deal.

25. You have gotten a few good licks in.

26. You would have liked it a lot to have had him around a bit more.

27. You are so sad that you want to cry right now.

28. They are horrible enough in themselves, but what you would also like to know from me is: "Will they somehow disfigure me or harm me permanently?"

CODE: 4R

BIOGRAPHICAL INFORMATION

Code:	4R
Age:	28 years.
Sex:	Male.
Professional affiliation and status:	Psychologist.
Psychoanalytic training:	None; no plans.
Personal analysis:	Completed analysis (25 hours).
Experience in psychotherapy:	Very little; two years.
Type of therapy:	Client-centered therapy.
Type of patients:	Mild neurotics.
Theoretical orientation:	Rogers (client-centered).

CLINICAL ASSESSMENTS

Diagnosis

Dominant personality type:	Anxiety.
Formulation of dynamics:	Need to maintain a flattering self-concept in the face of environmental trauma has led to symptoms caused by those aspects of himself that he has denied to awareness.

Treatment plans

Form of treatment:	Psychotherapy.
Treatment goals:	None. I would hope therapy moved in the direction of the patient's aims, i.e., symptom-relief and greater comfort with his environmental circumstances.
Frequency of sessions:	As often as he wanted within the limits of my schedule.
Length of treatment:	Anywhere from 30 to 100 interviews.
Symptom relief:	No idea, really. Probably at least 20 hours.
Difficulties expected:	He seemed a rather demanding person and I would imagine his pleading might be at times difficult to deal with.
Focus:	Whichever seemed important to him. That is, whatever he focused on.
Dangers:	None, except for lapses in my own understanding.
Areas to be avoided:	None.
Behaviors to be encouraged:	None other than self-exploration.
Behaviors to be discouraged:	None.
Strictness vs. permissiveness:	No more strict or permissive than with others.
Clues:	None.
Course of transference:	I expect that he might develop a number of strong feelings toward me and would not expect any part.
Approach to transference:	Understand it, accept it, and try to communicate this to him.
Activity vs. passivity:	Rather passive.
Free association:	Neither encourage nor discourage it.
Ego strength:	A fair amount.
Anxiety:	A great deal.
Insight:	Relatively little.
Emotional maturity:	Very immature.
Social adjustment:	Too little evidence to make a judgment.
Degree of disturbance:	Moderately disturbed.
Degree of therapeutic change attempted:	Very little change. (Whatever patient would attempt.)
Prognosis without therapy:	Probably get a little worse.
Prognosis with therapy:	Somewhat favorable.
Recommendations:	No. I have neither the knowledge nor the desire to intervene to this extent in a patient's life.
Attitude toward patient:	Somewhat positive.
Reasons:	He was very expressive and quite easy to understand. The only thing I didn't like was the pleading quality of his voice.

EVALUATION OF FILM THERAPIST

Adequacy:	Somewhat inadequate.
Reason:	His responses to the patient seemed to contribute to rather than reduce his defensiveness.

Activity vs. passivity:	Not too active nor too passive; about right.
Support:	Somewhat too little.
Life history data:	Somewhat less time.
Attitude toward therapist:	Neutral.
Reason:	I felt sorry for him. He seemed ill at ease and as though he were trying awfully hard to cover his own discomfort in the situation.

FILM RESPONSES

1. 0 (say nothing, but sit down).
2. You've been afraid and anxious for a long time.
3. Um, hm.
4. You've felt emeshed in things all your life. Kind of tied up.
5. Um, hm.
6. Just reached the point you felt you couldn't take it any more.
7. 0
8. Once it starts there doesn't seem any way out. Just get more and more stirred up.
9. It's the *physical* sensations that really bother you. The other isn't important.
10. 0
11. 0
12. You've felt anxious for a long time.
13. Um, hm.
14. You feel like you owe her *something* since she's your mother.
15. Um, hm.
16. Um, hm.
17. (Nod my head.)
18. You'd really like to do something about these symptoms.
19. It makes you squirm to think of them even now.
20. Um, hm.
21. Feel like you never had a chance.
22. 0
23. That really seems like about as bad a beginning as a person could have.
24. At first it really felt good to have this responsibility.
25. You're not so proud of some of the things you've done.
26. Recently you've wished he had lived longer so it wouldn't have been so tough on you.
27. Just seems so unfair, that you feel almost like crying about it.
28. I guess you're worried about what damage these feelings will do to your body.

CODE: 5R

BIOGRAPHICAL INFORMATION

Code:	5R
Age:	31 years.
Sex:	Male.
Professional affiliation and status:	Psychologist.
Psychoanalytic training:	None.
Personal analysis:	Completed 300 hours, expect to complete 400 hours.
Experience in psychotherapy:	A fair amount, two years.
Type of therapy:	Nondirective.

Type of patients:	Middle-range, with a few hospitalized.
Theoretical orientation:	Rogers (client-centered).

CLINICAL ASSESSMENTS

Diagnosis

Dominant personality type:	Don't know.
Formulation of dynamics:	Major feelings: no chance; not his fault.

Treatment plans

Form of treatment:	Wouldn't recommend; would tell him about the availability of psychotherapy.
Treatment goals:	Would set up none.
Frequency of sessions:	2-3 times.
Length of treatment:	200 hours.
Symptom relief:	Unknown.
Difficulties expected:	Resentment and passive clinging.
Focus:	Wouldn't.
Dangers:	Medical check-up.
Areas to be avoided:	No.
Behaviors to be encouraged:	No.
Behaviors to be discouraged:	No.
Strictness vs. permissiveness:	No more strict or permissive than with other patients.
Clues:	No.
Course of transference:	A clinging hostile dependency.
Approach to transference:	Like any other feeling he would have at the moment.
Activity vs. passivity:	Rather active.
Free association:	Neither encourage nor discourage it.
Ego strength:	A fair amount.
Anxiety:	A great deal.
Insight:	Relatively little.
Emotional maturity:	Very immature.
Social adjustment:	Very inadequate.
Degree of disturbance:	Seriously disturbed.
Degree of therapeutic change attempted:	0
Prognosis without therapy:	Probably get much worse.
Prognosis with therapy:	Somewhat favorable.
Recommendations:	No; would seriously interfere with therapy.
Attitude toward patient:	Somewhat positive.
Reasons:	Seems a lot of interesting emotional flow.

EVALUATION OF FILM THERAPIST

Adequacy:	Very inadequate.
Reason:	Blocked the patient.
Activity vs. passivity:	Somewhat too passive.
Support:	Neither too much nor too little; about right.
Life history data:	Considerably less time.
Attitude toward therapist:	Somewhat negative.
Reason:	Keeps stopping the patient from developing his feelings.

FILM RESPONSES

1. 0, or, Won't you sit down?
2. "This felt like an old and familiar fear."
   Pt.: "I was in a hurry." Dr.: "It was a life and death matter to get off."
3. 0
   (Pt.: "Anyone would feel hemmed in.") Anyone would feel this way.
4. You've had this feeling everywhere in your life.
5. You've felt squeezed by everything that's happened to you.
6. You've just gotten squeezed too often.
7. It's about as bad now as it was before.
8. There's no way of breaking out of this thing.
9. It's the way that you're always feeling that bothers you.
10. There's no getting away from it.
11. You wouldn't get along with her.
12. You've always felt this way and it's something that's always been a part of you.
13. You can see what caused all your anxieties.
14. You feel you owe her something.
15. 0
16. Always afraid.
17. You get mad whenever anybody pushes words at you.
    (Pt.: "I was anxious before I started out.") You didn't have a chance.
18. You *really* want to stop this business.
19. She got on your nerves as far back as you can remember.
20. Your Dad was okay with you?
21. You've never had a honest chance.
22. 0
23. They just kicked you around.
24. You could have done it with an even break.
25. You would have liked to get even and I gather you don't feel very happy about it.
26. 0
27. Never had a chance to live like you would like.
28. You really feel that they might have a permanent physical effect.

CODE: 6R

BIOGRAPHICAL INFORMATION

Code:	6R
Age:	29 years.
Sex:	Male.
Professional affiliation and status:	Psychologist.
Psychoanalytic training:	None, but "Practicum" training series at Counseling Center.
Personal analysis:	Completed "analysis" of 120 hours.
Experience in psychotherapy:	A fair amount; three years.
Type of therapy:	Client-centered.
Type of patients:	People who are functioning but under great internal pressure.
Theoretical orientation:	Rogers (client-centered).

CLINICAL ASSESSMENTS

Diagnosis

Dominant personality type: 0
Formulation of dynamics: 0

Treatment plans

Form of treatment: Acceptance of his feelings of sorrow for himself and of his feelings of helpless "stuckness" and oppression which he is expressing now.

Treatment goals: Other than his own goals as they develop, I would try to allow him to come to feel his feelings fully.

Frequency of sessions: Twice a week.
Length of treatment: I have no idea. 10-60 hours.
Symptom relief: 0
Difficulties expected: He would be likely to stick to a view of helplessness and try to force me to fix him, probably whenever he can't continue the flow of feelings or it isn't accepted at some moments.

Focus: 0
Dangers: Not to accept his assumptions (example: "I had to step in and carry the family") or to resent them myself, but to allow him to see and feel them: e.g., "You felt you had to."

Areas to be avoided: Any which he doesn't himself raise or intend to show at least somewhat.

Behaviors to be encouraged: His feelings, whatever their object might be, as most strongly expressed *now, here.*

Behaviors to be discouraged: 0
Strictness vs. permissiveness: No more strict or permissive than with others.
Clues: 0
Course of transference: 0
Approach to transference: I stay visibly *myself* and consistent, so that he can feel all projected ways about me and still sense my real person responding to him, as well.

Activity vs. passivity: No more active or passive than with others.
Free association: I always allow the person to guide himself and respond as fully as possible to his feelings and to the intention of the procedure he develops.

Ego strength: 0
Anxiety: 0
Insight: 0
Emotional maturity: 0
Social adjustment: 0
Degree of disturbance: 0
Degree of therapeutic change
    attempted: 0
Prognosis without therapy: Probably get a little worse.
Prognosis with therapy: 0

Recommendations:	No. That would only focus him even more on the situation and away from his feelings as well as agreeing with his attitude of helpless entrapment rather than allowing him to discover his freedom of action.
Attitude toward patient:	Somewhat positive.
Reasons:	I can feel the person in his predicament and his urges to change and his fears and insistent way of perceiving his situation. I suppose I feel positive toward a person, the more I feel I understand him.

EVALUATION OF FILM THERAPIST

Adequacy:	Somewhat inadequate.
Reason:	I would have responded to the man's feelings, instead of asking for information and then having to pick the conversation up again myself where I had interrupted it by not responding, as he did in the film. Also this person will expect positive advice or direction, because he has not yet experienced the relief of surprising flow of expression which often obviates passive expectancy at the start.
Activity vs. passivity:	0
Support:	Much too little.
Life history data:	0
Attitude toward therapist:	Somewhat negative.
Reason:	. . . Also the film's therapist acted, looked and sounded as if he found the person incredible and amazingly weird.

FILM RESPONSES

1. 0
2. You've been scared a lot in your life and you know this about yourself and why.
3. You felt *trapped* and that always scares you.
4. That feeling of being hemmed in is familiar to you from lots of situations—sort of helpless.
5. Jumbled up . . . helpless and trapped . . . that's what scares you.
6. It's been piling up, this being stuck, helpless.
7. You were afraid of what would happen in your body. . . . Someone sitting on me . . . like being suffocated.

8. It's more frightening than you can stand and the fear brings it on too. . . . Hell for you . . . you can't get out.
9. It's not the situation but how it feels inside you.
10. You feel you *know* the piled-up feelings that can bring this on.
11. 0
Your mother's personality was always too much to take.
12. That's what caused it and you've known it inside yourself ever since then. Years . . . so you know why you might be anxious.

13. Lots of your attitudes come from them (did he say his antisocial attitudes, I'm not sure I heard it right).
14. You can't be too hard on *her* but you *do* resent what it did to you.
15. She just keeps you that way continually.
16. You've been so afraid you couldn't do anything, so you're *stuck* but she can get around.
17. To think you'd be like her really gets you. Heart attack . . . you started out with all this from her.
18. You're really sick of all that, and you want *out* of it! ("Artificial . . .") she made it hard for you to be manly.
19. She often made you mad. Tear down the house . . . you could really explode but you swallowed it down.
20. You were supposed to just take it and be pleasant about it. ("Quit") It's been so complete that you really don't wonder.
21. You feel like it's just *fated* that everything will go wrong for you. Somehow you had to worry about everything.
22. You had to step in and take over the family.
23. No wonder, you mean, that they're angry and resentful. ("Responsibility . . .") How did all that drop on you, hunh. (" . . . support your mother") You felt like you *had* to and couldn't get around it.
24. You were just left stuck in it.
25. You sure felt like hitting *something* back, but it doesn't work.
26. Feel like his death really forced you into this. ("Me . . . myself.") It was *unfair. Why you?*
27. You really *feel* for the person that's trapped in this and couldn't help it.
28. Will they finally get you some way and destroy you? This is where you want help.

CODE: 7R

BIOGRAPHICAL INFORMATION

Code:	7R
Age:	33 years.
Sex:	Male.
Professional affiliation and status:	Psychologist.
Psychoanalytic training:	No analytic training; no plans.
Personal analysis:	Completed personal therapy of 300 hours.
Experience in psychotherapy:	A fair amount; 4 years.
Type of therapy:	Client-centered.
Type of patients:	Primarily neurotic.
Theoretical orientation:	Rogers (client-centered).

CLINICAL ASSESSMENTS

Diagnosis
Dominant personality type: 0
Formulation of dynamics: No real masculine pattern developed.

Treatment plans
Form of treatment: Psychotherapy, individual at first.
Treatment goals: None. He's almost ready to discover his own.

Frequency of sessions:	Twice per week.
Length of treatment:	Two years, twice per week.
Symptom relief:	20 Hours.
Difficulties expected:	Frustration at my not taking care of him. His direction, sympathy, etc. He looks pretty easy though. Highly motivated.
Focus:	Let him focus on what he wishes.
Dangers:	No.
Areas to be avoided:	No, that is, I would feel no need to steer him away from anything.
Behaviors to be encouraged:	Hell, no. He's beginning to . . . .
Behaviors to be discouraged:	No.
Strictness vs. permissiveness:	Rather permissive.
Clues:	There are plenty of clues, but I wouldn't "make a note" of them, except as they deepened by empathic feeling for him.
Course of transference:	Highly dependent, then petulant, then rather a good deal of hostility.
Approach to transference:	1) Understand. 2) Communicate understanding. 3) Communicate respect.
Activity vs. passivity:	Rather active.
Free association:	Neither encourage nor discourage it.
Ego strength:	A fair amount.
Anxiety.	A great deal.
Insight:	A fair amount.
Emotional maturity:	Fairly immature.
Social adjustment:	Fairly inadequate.
Degree of disturbance:	Seriously disturbed.
Degree of therapeutic change attempted:	Fairly extensive change.
Prognosis without therapy:	Probably remain about the same.
Prognosis with therapy:	Very favorable.
Recommendations:	Not enough evidence.
Attitude toward patient:	Somewhat positive.
Reasons:	0

EVALUATION OF FILM THERAPIST

Adequacy:	Very inadequate.
Reason:	1) No understanding communicated. 2) Threatened by situation. 3) Not sensitive.
Activity vs. passivity:	Neither too active nor too passive; about right.
Support:	Neither too much nor too little support; about right.
Life history data:	Considerably less time.
Attitude toward therapist:	Somewhat negative.
Reason:	Only because of his ineptness, which I assume is due to inexperience. He's probably a nice enough person.

FILM RESPONSES

1. 0
2. You've always been pretty frightened of life, but this was a kind of new fear sensation—on the bus, I mean.
3. It really was a panic, then. You were just sort of paralyzed at first. Then you *had* to get out.
4. You've always felt just trapped . . . by things over which you've no control.
5. (Before therapist said, "How does it make you feel?") You've never had a chance to be really free.
6. It was the last straw this time, eh?
7. You had to have someone along to protect you, sort of. And that's kind of hard to talk about, I guess.
8. Like a spiral, kind of. Or a vicious circle. And where does it come from, eh? ("Fulfill the bill for you.") Like a trapped animal, almost?
9. They are the real worries right now, eh?
10. Your whole body just seems to do the wrong things for you. Is it kind of like that?
11. She's a real thorn in your side. In fact, you just can't stand her to be around.
12. Your mother really screwed you up—right from the start.
13. Money seems to be the big problem—now and as far back as you can remember. And it's around a lot of feelings against people and society.
14. You can almost hate her, but yet you feel something positive toward her. (After "eviscerated.") Your guts are just gone.
15. And that's just one of the feelings she brings on.
16. You're really in pretty bad shape, eh? Do you see it that way?
17. Your wife nettles you too, somewhat.
18. You're kind of at the end of your patience with this business. Now you want to do something—but fast.
19. So many, many things—even the little ones—that she did, just irked the hell out of you.
20. Your father was a pretty nice guy, eh? I'll bet you looked forward to coming home.
21. You just can't remember anything good, and you were licked before you started.
22. 0 ("I just got fired for that, see.") Pretty damned unjust, eh?
23. I'll bet it just felt like no one cared a damn for you. ("Without ones.") Everything shoved on you before you were ready—mature.
24. Nobody gave you any help, eh? If they had, you could have done all right, maybe.
25. Sounds like you did a few things you're kind of ashamed of—even though the whole situation justifies them. But you can get away with them.
26. Yes, I believe so. ("Bill Smith.") Why the hell should it be dumped on me? ("Different.") If mother had died instead of dad, what a difference that would have been!
27. It's just so damn hopeless and unfair, sometimes you feel tears welling up in you and you want to cry—like a child who's alone and lost.
28. And this added burden—you want to be assured that you won't be damaged by all this.

CODE: 8R

BIOGRAPHICAL INFORMATION

Code:	8R
Age:	38 years.
Sex:	Male.
Professional affiliation and status:	Psychologist.
Psychoanalytic training:	0
Personal analysis:	Completed therapy of about 60 hours.
Experience in psychotherapy:	A fair amount; 5 years.
Type of therapy:	Client-centered therapy.
Type of patients:	Neurotics.
Theoretical orientation:	Rogers (client-centered).

CLINICAL ASSESSMENTS

Diagnosis

Dominant personality type:	Anxiety.
Formulation of dynamics:	0

Treatment plans

Form of treatment:	Would recommend a good therapist rather than a variety of therapy.
Treatment goals:	1) Be receptive and acceptant in attitude. 2) Understand conscious communicative intent. 3) Convey both of above to patient.
Frequency of sessions:	Two to three times a week.
Length of treatment:	60 hours.
Symptom relief:	30 hours.
Difficulties expected:	None particularly. However, I would expect patient to understand therapy only in terms of symptom.
Focus:	None.
Dangers:	No.
Areas to be avoided:	Would leave this to patient.
Behaviors to be encouraged:	No.
Behaviors to be discouraged:	No.
Strictness vs. permissiveness:	No more strict or permissive than with other patients.
Clues:	Anger and frustration. Would not exploit therapeutically.
Course of transference:	Would try to avoid developing a transference relationship. Form would be demanding dependence.
Approach to transference:	Reflect feelings shown.
Activity vs. passivity:	Participative communicant.
Free association:	Neither encourage nor discourage it.
Ego strength:	A fair amount.
Anxiety:	A fair amount.
Insight:	Relatively little.
Emotional maturity:	Very immature.

Social adjustment: Fairly inadequate.
Degree of disturbance: Moderately disturbed.
Degree of therapeutic change
  attempted: Very little.
Prognosis without therapy: Probably get a little better.
Prognosis with therapy: Very favorable.
Recommendations: No. This sort of behavior develops transference
                              and this I don't like to do.
Attitude toward patient: Somewhat positive.
  Reasons: Apparently he is caught in a vicious circle. Ap-
                              parently his environment is and has been
                              against him.

EVALUATION OF FILM THERAPIST

Adequacy: Somewhat inadequate.
  Reason: Seemed wooden, uncomprehending, arbitrary
                              in selections.
Activity vs. passivity: Somewhat too active (not amount but place).
Support: Neither too much nor too little support; about
                              right.
Life history data: Considerably less time.
Attitude toward therapist: Neutral.
  Reason: Seemed lifeless.

FILM RESPONSES

1. I'm Dr. _____. Please sit down there.
2. You look at yourself as a pretty anxious person then? (with a rising inflection).
3. You had a deep panic reaction and just had to get out of there (response to first part of passage only).
4. Always felt surrounded by something that was too much for you.
5. Never could do what you wanted to do and somewhat unjustly too, although you'd like to help mother.
6. You feel like you've been deprived of too much.
7. You're feeling a little better but you're still afraid to function.
8. It sort of feeds on itself, huh? Your fear brings more fear until you're overwhelmed.
9. It just seems like there's no way out and you want out.
10. M'mhm (encouragingly).
11. Your mother's way of living and yours just don't go together, is that right?
12. M'mhmm (encouragingly).
13. Mother made it difficult before you were married and after . . . of her personality. And on top of that she's an economic load on you.
14. She's still your mother but there's a lot about her you don't like.
15. You resent her a lot even though she is your mother (picking up first part only).
16. Mhm.
17. Not only are you afraid but you're afraid that your fear will leave you unable to support yourself and to meet your responsibilities.
18. It angers you to feel that she influenced your personality in ways that you don't like. Your personal troubles began with her.

19. You've had enough of being a football for your feelings. Her behavior when you were a kid made you feel angry and ashamed, is that right?
20. Dad was a pretty good guy, huh?
21. No matter where you look, life has been bad for you. You feel you never really had a chance.
22. Mhm.
23. No one ever helped you or gave you a break. Is that the way you feel about it?
24. You feel that you were overlooked and mother just made it harder

by being irresponsible and not cooperating.
25. You were doing the best you could and your brother was goofing off. It made you feel like getting even.
26. You wish your father would have lived; you might have had a better break.
27. Looking back on it, you feel you were too weak and unprepared to take on such a load and it just seems unfair.
28. What you feel afraid of is that these symptoms might hurt you and you just haven't been able to get evidence that they won't.

CODE: 9R

BIOGRAPHICAL INFORMATION

Code:	9R
Age:	41 years.
Sex:	Female.
Professional affiliation and status:	Psychologist.
Psychoanalytic training:	None; no plans.
Personal analysis:	Completed client-centered therapy of 150 hours.
Experience in psychotherapy:	A fair amount; 5 years.
Type of therapy:	Client-centered.
Type of patients:	Don't think of clients as "types."
Theoretical orientation:	Rogers (client-centered).

CLINICAL ASSESSMENTS

Diagnosis

Dominant personality type:	Anxiety.
Formulation of dynamics:	0

Treatment plans

Form of treatment:	Client-centered therapy.
Treatment goals:	I would let the client set the goals.
Frequency of sessions:	I'd discuss this with him and together arrive at a conclusion. I would prefer twice a week.
Length of treatment:	0
Symptom relief:	0
Difficulties expected:	Resistance.
Focus:	0
Dangers:	0
Areas to be avoided:	0

Behaviors to be encouraged: 0
Behaviors to be discouraged: 0
Strictness vs. permissiveness: Permissive.
Clues: 0
Course of transference: Some hostility and dependence.
Approach to transference: Make responses to let him know I understand his feelings and respect his right to have them.
Activity vs. passivity: No more active or passive than with others.
Free association: Neither encourage nor discourage it.
Ego strength: 0
Anxiety: A great deal.
Insight: Relatively little.
Emotional maturity: Very immature.
Social adjustment: Very inadequate.
Degree of disturbance: Moderately disturbed.
Degree of therapeutic change
  attempted: 0
Prognosis without therapy: Probably get a little worse.
Prognosis with therapy: Somewhat favorable.
Recommendations: No. I'd leave this up to him.
Attitude toward patient: Somewhat positive.
  Reasons: He is suffering. He seems to have the courage and desire to do something about it.

EVALUATION OF FILM THERAPIST

Adequacy: Somewhat inadequate.
  Reason: Since the client verbalized so freely, questions seem particularly out of place—often asking for information already given.
Activity vs. passivity: Somewhat too passive.
Support: 0
Life history data: Considerably less time.
Attitude toward therapist: Somewhat negative.
  Reason: Felt he was somewhat inadequate and at times almost naive in his responses. My reaction at times: "Such a stupid question!"

FILM RESPONSES

1. How do you do.
2. You feel you have been a fearful person . . . and that somehow it is connected with your mother.
3. You felt a real panic and wanted to get away from this hemmed in space.
4. You've always felt hemmed in by things.
5. You've felt, "Why did I have to accept these responsibilities?"
6. Earning a living has seemed to hem you in, and this incident seemed like the last straw.
7. Uh-huh.
8. There's a feeling of pressure, then fear.
9. Your real concern is the sensations.
10. Sorrow seems to bring on the sensations.
11. Uh-huh.

12. Both of you are too much upset by your mother to have *her* around.
13. Getting money has been a problem.
14. She was your mother, but you certainly resented her.
15. Being with your mother makes you feel angry and anxious and sort of empty inside.
16. Uh-huh.
17. You're feeling angry about this.
18. Seems as though you've been terribly anxious all your life, and now you're really fed up with this feeling.
19. There was something about your mother's ways that made you so darned disgusted and annoyed!
20. Uh-huh.
21. Life has seemed one big mess with everything against you, you didn't have a chance.
22. Uh-huh.
23. It made you so mad that such a little thing should have such big effects in your life.
24. All the things you felt obligated to do just seemed like too much for you, because no one helped.
25. There are some things you are so disgusted about—you just don't want to talk about them.
26. If only your father had lived a bit longer, life wouldn't have been so tough for you.
27. You feel, "Why was I picked on like this?" And I guess you feel so bad you could almost weep.
28. Seems as though you've had more than you can bear, and you're so worried that your sensations will hurt you beyond repair—maybe even kill you.

CODE: 10R

BIOGRAPHICAL INFORMATION

Code:	10R
Age:	41 years.
Sex:	Male.
Professional affiliation and status:	Psychologist.
Psychoanalytic training:	None; no plans.
Personal analysis:	None yet.
Experience in psychotherapy:	A fair amount; 8 years.
Type of therapy:	Nondirective therapy.
Type of patients:	Patients who can be expected to leave the hospital within a year or so.
Theoretical orientation:	Rogers (client-centered).

CLINICAL ASSESSMENTS

Diagnosis

Dominant personality type:	Anxiety.
Formulation of dynamics:	Too early to say. Obviously the mother-son relationship is quite important.

Treatment plans

Form of treatment:	Prolonged psychiatric therapy.
Treatment goals:	Insight into feelings toward mother, father and wife.

Frequency of sessions:	Two times a week.
Length of treatment:	1-2 years at two hours a week.
Symptom relief:	Six months.
Difficulties expected:	Resistance to any interpretation other than "economic" causes. Hostility toward father figure.
Focus:	Relationships with parents and wife.
Dangers:	He knows the lingo and can intellectualize.
Areas to be avoided:	0
Behaviors to be encouraged:	His sense of responsibility.
Behaviors to be discouraged:	Attitude toward economic factors as cause of his difficulty.
Strictness vs. permissiveness:	No more strict or permissive than with others.
Clues:	Some masturbatory movement. Some twitching, sucking-like movements of the mouth.
Course of transference:	At first negative, then positive—pleading for father to help him.
Approach to transference:	Interpret what I think it means.
Activity vs. passivity:	Rather active.
Free association:	Encourage it.
Ego strength:	Relatively little.
Anxiety:	A great deal.
Insight:	Very little.
Emotional maturity:	Very immature.
Social adjustment:	Too little evidence to make a judgment.
Degree of disturbance:	Moderately disturbed.
Degree of therapeutic change attempted:	Too little evidence to make a judgment.
Prognosis without therapy:	Probably get much worse.
Prognosis with therapy:	Too little evidence to make a judgment.
Recommendations:	With more evidence, I might suggest vocational counseling.
Attitude toward patient:	Somewhat positive.
Reasons:	Bright enough to express himself; wants help and needs help.

EVALUATION OF FILM THERAPIST

Adequacy:	Reasonably adequate.
Reason:	Established a good atmosphere, permissive and accepting.
Activity vs. passivity:	Neither too active nor too passive; about right.
Support:	Neither too much nor too little; about right.
Life history data:	About the same time.
Attitude toward therapist:	Somewhat positive.
Reason:	0

FILM RESPONSES

1. (Sit down and wait for patient to begin.)
2. Uh, huh.
3. You felt better when you got off?

4. Uh, huh.
5. Cornered?
6. Things seemed to come to a head?
7. Dizzy?
8. *You* bring on the sensation?
9. What other stuff?
10. Your *feelings* are causing this trouble?
11. Uh, huh.
12. You felt this way as a child?
13. The troubles are economic?
14. You feel some responsibility toward her, but she does cause you trouble.
15. Your mother's presence caused you to be anxious?
16. Afraid?
17. Your wife compares you to your mother?
18. You'd like to do something about it now?

19. Her behavior annoyed you quite a bit?
20. You felt your dad didn't understand what was going on?
21. You feel you've gotten a pretty raw deal?
22. You had to bear the burden for everyone.
23. You can feel pretty angry at these people who treated you this way.
24. You weren't really made to feel that you were the *man* of the family.
25. You can't fight the world always?
26. You wish now your father could be here to help you?
27. Economic? (indicate some disbelief by gesture).
28. You're afraid something pretty bad will happen if this keeps up.

PART III

Toward the Comparative Study
of Psychotherapeutic Techniques

12

A SYSTEM FOR ANALYZING
PSYCHOTHERAPEUTIC TECHNIQUES

The system of analysis to be described in this chapter was in-
spired by a realization which in recent years has gained momentum
among researchers, namely, that ways and means must be found to
isolate common denominators in the techniques of therapists adhering to different schools as well as to document unique differences. So far it has not been possible to make objective comparisons
between the techniques of, say, an orthodox Freudian and a neo-
Freudian, an Adlerian and a Jungian, and so forth. As will become
clearer in the following discussion, one of the major difficulties is
that of specifying criteria which cut across the various systems of
psychotherapy as set forth by their respective proponents. Yet, this
appears to be a first step in taking an objective look at the operations
of therapists differing in theoretical orientation, level of experience,
and the like. The common denominators which an investigator
chooses to define *a priori* may not be the dimensions which will ultimately be most relevant to the enterprise of psychotherapy, but such
preliminary efforts may help to bring some order to the complexity
of data and perhaps indicate other lines along which more fruitful
approaches might be sought.

To elaborate the last point: the present system of analysis was
developed initially for the purpose of comparing the techniques of
different therapists or the techniques of a single therapist in a series
of interviews (see Chapters 13 and 14). When the system was subsequently applied to the data collected in the course of the investigation described in Part I of this volume, it emerged that

differences in the degree of empathy shown by the therapist-respondents appeared to be a considerably more fruitful indicator of their total approach than structural differences, to which the system gives major emphasis. As a result, greater attention is being devoted in future researches to the exploration of attitudinal and personality variables in the therapist.

The system of analysis is a methodologic tool for abstracting and measuring selected aspects of therapeutic technique, aspects which are considered relevant to any psychotherapeutic procedure which stresses the development of insight on the part of the patient and emotional understanding of his difficulties in living. The uses to which the resulting indices are put are dictated by the research objectives, which, in turn, help to determine the value of the measures. Inevitably, the present system will be superseded by others yielding more precise and more sensitive measures, but technique measures of some kind must play a part in the comparative evaluation of therapeutic results. Before the effects of two drugs can be evaluated it is indispensable to specify their respective ingredients. Similarly, before the merits of two forms of psychotherapy, say, psychoanalysis and intensive psychotherapy based on psychoanalytic principles, can be assessed, it will be necessary to specify the "ingredients." (I am ignoring here other experimental controls which are equally necessary.) This achievement, unfortunately, lies far in the future. But this much is clear: it is doing scant justice to the complexities of the situation to compare "psychoanalysis" with "eclectic psychotherapy," as has been done in the past (see, for example, Eysenck, 1952) without a more adequate description of the similarities and differences in the two techniques.

BACKGROUND

Almost twenty years ago Edward Glover (1940, printed 1955a) surmised that analysts, despite the presumed similarity of their training, might differ in their therapeutic practices, and that many differences seemed to be obscured by what he called "the psychoanalytic *mystique*." He designed a rather comprehensive questionnaire on technique, and solicited the responses of 29 British analysts. From the replies of 24 respondents it became apparent that on only 6 out of 63 points raised was there unanimous agreement, and that only one of the 6 points—the importance of analyzing the transference—could be regarded as fundamental. Among the areas of disagreement, the subject of interpretation loomed large. There was a lack of agreement concerning almost all aspects of interpretation, including mode, length, timing, and depth. I shall not go into the details of this very illuminating survey, but it is noteworthy that a pioneer attempt was made, that it yielded valuable results despite the smallness of the sample, and that it highlighted considerable divergences of opinion on both theoretical and practical issues. If it is further remembered that Glover dealt with *opinions* which his respondents were willing to commit to paper—probably after a good deal of soul-searching—rather than the actual *therapeutic data,* it seems likely that the degree of agreement was overstated rather than understated.

In more recent years, Glover (1955b, pp. 375-376) has continued to challenge the assumption that psychoanalysts "hold roughly the same views, speak the same technical language . . . [and] practise approximately the same technical procedures and obtain much the same results, which incidentally are, by common hearsay, held to be satisfactory." He states unequivocally that "without some reliable form of standardisation of technique there can be no science of psycho-analysis, for if we cannot standardise the behaviour of the patient, we must at least be able to standardise the behaviour of the analyst," and that this is a problem for research and not for discussion at a symposium (1955b, p. 283).*

Glover's concern is shared by many American analysts. Marmor (1955, p. 505) summarizing a symposium held by the American Psychoanalytic Association, states that "one of the most important scientific tasks facing psychoanalysis today is that of attempting to find the *common denominators* that underlie the varying data and the therapeutic successes of these different schools of thought. Toward this end, tolerance toward dissident viewpoints, the elimination of semantic differences, the efforts at presentation of concepts in common everyday language, the breaking down of barriers toward free communication between differing groups, and the fostering of more interdisciplinary contacts and group research, are all steps which need to be strengthened and furthered."

One of the stumbling blocks which has delayed progress is the question of how to evaluate the basic data of psychoanalysis and psychotherapy. With the advent of improved methods of sound recording and a greater willingness on the part of therapists to participate in research studies, there is a potentially large pool of data which

---

* There is now preliminary evidence—at least with regard to initial interviews—that an attempt to standardize the therapist's interventions leads to notable invariance or stability of certain interaction patterns. See Saslow, Matarazzo, and Guze (1955).

await the ingenuity of the researcher. It is on the methodologic side that psychologists during the past 10 to 15 years have made notable contributions. While these studies have rarely dealt specifically with *psychoanalytic* case materials, they provide a starting point for the investigation of the more intense forms of psychotherapy.*

Of primary interest in this connection are those investigations which have attempted to deal systematically with the *therapist's* verbal communications. The general procedure has been to abstract certain relevant characteristics from the therapist's verbal behavior, to rate or to classify communications on the basis of operationally defined criteria, and to use the resulting frequencies or proportions as indices of the therapist's activity. Working within Rogers' "nondirective" framework, Porter (1943) set up a system consisting of some twenty categories—for example, defining the interview situation, bringing out and developing the problem situation, developing the client's insight and understanding, and so on. Despite his use of Rogerian terminology, Porter was careful to strive for a descriptive rather than an evaluative scheme. Another widely used system by a nondirectivist, Snyder (1945), subtly confounds description with evaluation. Both of these systems have been applied primarily to the data of client-centered therapy, for which they were originally constructed. They are in principle applicable to other forms of therapy, but since they stress aspects of technique which are more or less specific to the client-centered framework, they are not sufficiently analytical for other purposes.

Bales' (1950) 12-category system of interaction process analysis, intended as a general-purpose framework for analyzing social interaction, has been used in a number of investigations having as their objective some problem pertaining to psychotherapeutic technique. This system has the advantage of not being encumbered by any theoretical predilections relative to psychotherapy, but it is relatively limited in its applicability to therapeutic data because of its overinclusiveness and generality. Built on the conception of social interaction as a problem-solving sequence, it does not go beyond characterizing a communication as a question, interpretation, restatement of the patient's content, and the like. Nevertheless, it has been useful in preliminary investigations.†

---

* For a comprehensive review of content-analysis studies of psychotherapy, see Auld and Murray (1955).

†. For examples of analyses using the Bales system with reference to psychotherapy, see Strupp (1955a, 1955b, 1955c).

Collier's (1953) scale of depth of interpretation attempts an objective assessment of one important dimension of the therapist's activity. It fulfills the requirement of being theoretically neutral, hence applicable to the operations of therapists regardless of their theoretical preferences, and, more important, it objectifies a common denominator of diverse therapeutic operations. A variation of this scale has recently been described (Harway *et al.*, 1955).

Like any scientific instrument, a system of content analysis must be *objective* and *reliable*—that is, the measurement units must be operationally defined, and the observations must be repeatable by independent observers with a high degree of accuracy. The most crucial requirement, however, is that a system of analysis be *valid*.* Validity is to some extent a matter of definition, and the schemes mentioned above are undoubtedly valid for the purposes for which they were constructed. Porter's system is valid—that is, relevant—to the Rogerian form of psychotherapy; Bales' system is relevant to problem-solving behavior in small groups; neither system may be valid for, say, intensive psychotherapy, and, indeed, no such claim has been advanced by their authors. It appears that there is at present no system of analysis which would permit the *comparative analysis of diverse therapeutic techniques*. Minimally, such a system should meet the following criteria:

(1) It should take cognizance of the purpose and aims of psychotherapy as a unique form of social interaction and respect its complexities; it should show particular recognition of the therapist's role in the therapeutic process.

(2) While being anchored to therapeutic operations, it should be sufficiently general to be applicable to the techniques of therapists whose theoretical positions may be divergent. In other words, it should stress the *common denominators* of different therapeutic approaches.

(3) It should be primarily descriptive and nonvaluative, on the assumption that the relative effectiveness of therapeutic techniques must be evaluated on the basis of external rather than internal criteria.

(4) It should meet the requirements of objectivity, reliability, and system.

---

* For a clear statement of the technical requirements for content analysis systems, see Berelson (1952).

THE PROPOSED SYSTEM

In its present form the system here proposed comprises two sets of categories and three intensity scales. It is intended to be sufficiently general to cut across the various theoretical orientations, while at the same time being relevant to the purposes of psychotherapy. It views each communication by the therapist as a multidimensional datum, on which five simultaneous assessments are made. It takes advantage of some features of previously developed content systems and combines them into a single conceptual framework. Since the system was constructed with psychotherapy specifically in mind, it is inevitable that it reflects certain assumptions about the therapeutic process, personality change, and, above all, the role of the therapist. It is hoped that the assumptions underlying the formulation of the concepts are relatively noncontroversial and generally acceptable so that the bias which may determine the results from this source is minimal.

For present purposes, psychotherapy may be viewed as a controlled interpersonal relationship which is integrated for the purpose of effecting changes in the patient's feelings, attitudes, and behavior through the systematic application of psychological techniques. With regard to the therapist's role in the interpersonal process, the following implications of this definition may be stressed:

(1) Psychotherapy is a planful interpersonal relationship between a trained professional person (the therapist) and a person seeking help for his difficulties in living (the patient). It is a personal relationship within an impersonal framework. It is further implied that the relationship is integrated for the patient's benefit and that the totality of the therapist's activity throughout treatment is oriented toward this goal; thus, it precludes any participation or intervention in the patient's living which is not therapeutic in character.

(2) It is hypothesized that the patient's difficulties in living are a function of emotional conflicts, of whose existence, significance, and consequences he is insufficiently aware, and that the application or institution of certain technical operations by a trained professional person (the therapist) in an interpersonal setting is peculiarly suited to bringing about a lasting amelioration of the patient's problems.

(3) The uniqueness of psychotherapy derives from the application of psychological techniques, based upon scientific principles, in a controlled interpersonal setting. Irrespective of the ways in which

the nature of the conflict is conceptualized, the following technical operations seem to be common to the major theoretical viewpoints:

(a) The therapist listens and attempts to "understand" the patient's verbal (and nonverbal) message. In contrast to the more usual forms of social interaction, he pays close attention to the connotative or symbolic content of the communications, which typically he explains in terms of certain theoretical conceptions.

(b) Sooner or later the therapist communicates to the patient some part of this "understanding." He may verbalize the feelings expressed by the patient or he may express a conjecture concerning the implicit meanings of the patient's message. In either event, he states a hypothesis or an inference, commonly called an "interpretation." The function of this activity is to increase the patient's self-awareness and to point out to him dynamic relationships which, it is hypothesized, have a bearing on the central emotional conflict or on one of its derivatives. Which aspects of the patient's communication are singled out for interpretive activity depends on the therapist's theoretical leanings, his objectives, and the techniques considered most appropriate to achieve a desired therapeutic result.

(c) There are numerous technical operations which may be considered subsidiary to the interpretive function. Thus, the therapist may often consider it necessary to ask more or less specific questions to gain fuller information on a point, sometimes as a preamble to an interpretation. At other times, he may judge the patient's line of verbalization "unproductive" and deliberately change the focus by directing the patient's attention to an area which he thinks to be more promising therapeutically. Sometimes he may feel it necessary to alleviate a patient's anxiety by a word of reassurance or support; or, contrariwise, he may wish to precipitate anxiety by being deliberately cold, aloof, or even sarcastic. Sometimes he has to explain something about the procedure, the goals, and the function of psychotherapy; on rare occasions, he may express an opinion or suggest a course of behavior or activity outside of therapy.

Ideally, there is always a rationale for the therapist's activity, so that, depending on the context, one approach is more desirable, therapeutically speaking, than another. In other words, some criterion of therapeutic effectiveness is implicit in what is considered the preferred technique. If it were true, as some maintain, that the relationship between patient and therapist is more "important" than the verbal exchange, it would be futile to speak of therapeutic techniques or to try to study them. If technique does make a difference, then presumably one technique is more effective than another. This is partly the *raison d'être* for the various schools of therapy which attempt to explain a set of similar phenomena in different terms and advocate different therapeutic approaches. From the point of view of empirical science, a first step would be to describe what techniques are actually practiced and to specify the conditions under which they are used. Such an exploratory survey might in itself suggest new hypotheses and leads, and pave the way for a comparative evaluation in addition to a comparative description. This reasoning is reflected in the scales and categories of the system proposed here, which attempt to provide specific answers on the following points:

What *kinds* of technique does the therapist employ? Does he primarily use questions, interpretive statements, authoritative opinions, and so on?

To what extent is his therapeutic behavior characterized by *inferential* operations? Are his hypotheses closely related to what the patient is expressing, or does he propound hypotheses which go far beyond the available data?

What is the *focus* of his therapeutic interventions? Does he try to stay within or close to the patient's frame of reference, or does he introduce and operate within a frame of reference of his own or that of his "school"?

Does he leave the *initiative* for structuring the content of the therapeutic hour with the patient, or does he assume the initiative for directing the patient's verbalization into a given channel? To what extent does he do either?

Are his communications predominantly emotionally "neutral," or does his attitude express *warmth* or *coldness*?

The scales and categories provide systematic information on each of the above questions for all verbal communication by the therapist.

The Scales and Categories

Type of Therapeutic Activity. These categories, presented in Table 16, appear to be the minimum number necessary to characterize most therapeutic communications without duplicating information obtained from other components. They are intended to represent meaningful abstractions from the therapist's intervention and are predicated upon commonly recognized differences in technique. They are based upon the general hypothesis that the techniques of therapists adhering to varying theoretical schools show specific differences.

The major categories and subcategories were developed empirically by analyzing a variety of therapeutic protocols; they are objective and essentially nonvaluative—that is, ratings are largely independent of the rater's theoretical outlook and his conceptions of what constitutes effective psychotherapy; and they are mutually exclusive.

TABLE 16

Type of Therapeutic Activity

(00) *Facilitating Communication* (*Minimal activity*)
    (01) Silence.
    (02) Passive acceptance, acknowledgment.

(10) *Exploratory Operations*
    (11) Simple questioning: asking for further information, clarification, examples, elaborations; simple probes, case history questions; accenting by repeating one or more words.
    Focal probes (with hypothesis), questioning to stimulate the patient's curiosity, encouraging self-exploration.

(20) *Clarification* (*Minimal interpretation*)
    (21) Reflection of feeling, restatements for purposes of clarification (may include "?").
    (22) Summaries (essentially noninterpretive).

(30) *Interpretive Operations*
    (31) Interpretations, analysis of defenses, establishing connections, definitions of the patient's problem (interpretive).
    (32) "Reality Model": any operation by which the therapist's communication asserts the patient's rights, needs, and so on, and represents a reasonable model of reality (usually interpretive).
    (33) Summaries (essentially interpretive).

(40) *Structuring*
    (41) Structuring the therapeutic situation, describing the functions and tasks of therapy in general terms.
    (42) Discussions about theory (relatively abstract).
    (43) External arrangements, time, place, fees, and so on.

(50) *Direct Guidance*
    (51) Direct suggestions for activity within the therapeutic framework.
    (52) Direct suggestions for activity outside the therapeutic framework.
    (53) "The therapist as an expert": Giving information, stating an opinion, answering direct questions, speaking as an authority. Such communications may seem primarily objective, but they may also convey reassurance (warmth) or rejection (coldness).

(60) *Activity Not Clearly Relevant to the Task of Therapy*
    (61) Greetings, small talk, endings, and so on.

(70) *Unclassifiable*

Depth-Directedness. This scale, shown in Table 17, embodies the conception that any communication by the therapist, so long as it fulfills the requirement of being therapeutic (see the definition), carries with it an implication about, first, the patient's "problem" (as conceptualized by the various schools), and, second, the method of procedure best designed to bring about its alleviation or resolution.* This applies to the therapist's silences, probing questions, reflections of feeling, interpretations, summaries, or what not. Depending upon his theoretical orientation, he may deal with any of a number of levels implicit in the patient's communications, using the technique he deems most appropriate.

The concept of *depth-directedness* refers to these levels. By this definition, a therapist's comment which operates upon the manifest meaning of the patient's communication is at the surface, whereas one that propounds a hypothesis, inference, conjecture, or interpretation is deep. Along this continuum, defined by the extremes, all therapeutic remarks find their place. The essential element in this conception is that inference is part and parcel of every therapeutic communication. Whatever differences occur are differences of degree, not of kind. Inferential depth is, perhaps, the most important single characteristic of psychotherapeutic communications.

The present scale differs from a similar one proposed by Harway and his co-workers in that it is not restricted to one class of therapeutic communications, usually labelled "interpretations," which these investigators define as "any behavior on the part of the therapist that is an expression of his view of the patient's emotions and motivations—either wholly or in part" (Harway *et al.* 1955, p. 247). A second difference refers to the relational definition of depth— "Depth of interpretation is a description of the relationship between

---

* This formulation may throw some light on the often-heard remark by therapists, "That's funny—*my* patients never bring up that kind of material!" (Marmor 1955, p. 504), or on the Rogerians' disregard of defenses and transferences. To some extent, at least, the patient's productions soon reflect the theoretical framework within which the therapist operates. Because of the reflexive nature of the therapeutic situation, in which the activities of both participants become almost inextricably interwoven, it is difficult to make observations that are not immediately influenced by the interaction itself, including the theoretical framework of the therapist through which his observations are filtered.

The Rogerian therapist is no different from other therapists in this respect, his claims of nondirectiveness notwithstanding, for his reflection-of-feeling technique is thoroughly interpretive in this sense. Certainly, the particular feeling that is singled out for "reflection" is a very definite inference in terms of the therapist's orientation. (See also Kramish (1954).

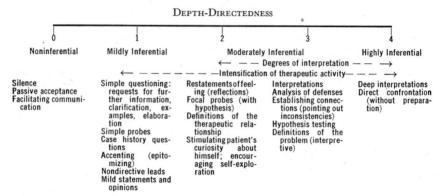

TABLE 17

Depth-Directedness

0	1	2	3	4
Noninferential	Mildly Inferential	Moderately Inferential	Highly Inferential	

← — — Degrees of interpretation — — →
← — — — — — —Intensification of therapeutic activity— — — →

| Silence
Passive acceptance
Facilitating communi-
cation | Simple questioning:
requests for fur-
ther information,
clarification, ex-
amples, elabora-
tion
Simple probes
Case history ques-
tions
Accenting (epito-
mizing)
Nondirective leads
Mild statements and
opinions | Restatements of feel-
ing (reflections)
Focal probes (with
hypothesis)
Definitions of the
therapeutic rela-
tionship
Stimulating patient's
curiosity about
himself; encour-
aging self-explo-
ration | Interpretations
Analysis of defenses
Establishing connec-
tions (pointing out
inconsistencies)
Hypothesis testing
Definitions of the
problem (interpre-
tive) | Deep interpretations
Direct confrontation
(without prepara-
tion) |

the view expressed by the therapist and the patient's awareness"
(Harway *et al.*, 1955, pp. 247-248). While this definition seems
useful, there is reason to believe that depth is more invariant and
not solely dependent on the patient's current level of understanding.

There are five scale points, which are defined on an *a priori* basis
rather than on the basis of empirical judgments. Raters are encouraged to use intermediate scores such as 1+ or 2—, which are
statistically treated as half steps.

Dynamic Focus. The definition of psychotherapy as a planful and
goal-directed enterprise implies some kind of theoretical orientation
or framework which provides guidelines as to how the therapeutic
relationship is to be structured, what goal or goals are to be pursued,
and what technical procedures are to be utilized to achieve these
objectives. The therapist's understanding of the therapeutic process,
in keeping with the particular theoretical formulations to which he
subscribes, tells him what is "important" in the therapeutic situation
and what is not, what he should focus on at a particular moment,
and what is of no dynamic relevance, what is to be dealt with now
rather than later, and so on. The way in which a therapist "sees" a
situation is already an interpretation in terms of his particular
framework—as well as a function of more personal factors.

To cite some examples: An orthodox Freudian may be expected
to pay a great deal of attention to transference phenomena, manifestations of resistance, and the analysis of dreams and other fantasy
productions, and to interpret the patient's productions in terms of
infantile conflicts. Whether he accepts or rejects the libido theory,
his emphasis will be on the *genetic* determinants.

A neo-Freudian, on the other hand, may be somewhat more
concerned with *current* interpersonal conflicts. Instead of being

primarily interested in genetic or historical antecedents, he may pay more attention to the ways in which past experience distorts the patient's contemporary interpersonal relations.

While both orientations stress the analysis of transference and resistance, their relative emphases might be expected to differ (see Wolstein, 1954).

A client-centered therapist of the school of Carl Rogers will focus on the patient's phenomenal self as it reveals itself in the therapeutic relationship. The dynamic concepts of transference and resistance are de-emphasized and interpretations are shunned as "directive."

Examples could be multiplied, but the point is clear. Depending on his theoretical position, the therapist may be expected to engage in therapeutic activities congruent with his theoretical framework. An analysis of his focus alone may lead to an operational testing of his theoretical allegiance.

The concept *dynamic focus,* as shown in Table 18, refers to the frame of reference adopted at a particular juncture, by which the therapist structures the operational field and often elicits a particular content from the patient. Basically, the therapist can do one of two things: he can accept a patient's formulation as it is presented (Sector A), or he can introduce or superimpose a different frame of reference (Sector B). In the first instance, he may be silent, show

TABLE 18

DYNAMIC FOCUS

Sector A	Sector B
Therapist accepts the patient's formulation (minimal interference) without introducing a new frame of reference: Passive acceptance, facilitating communication, repeating word or phrase, reflections of manifest feeling	Therapist directs the patient's communication into a different channel and/or introduces a new frame of reference:
	B–1 Indications that additional information, clarification, examples, elaboration, and so on are needed to further the therapeutic operation
	B–2 Focus on *dynamic* events in the *past*
	B–3 Focus on *dynamic* events in the *present*
	B–4T Focus on the dynamics of the *therapist-patient relationship* (analysis of the transference)
	B–4 Focus on the *therapist-patient interaction* (therapist emerging as a person, authority, or expert)

interest, encourage the flow of communication, nod approval, reflect the feelings conveyed in the patient's communication, and the like. In the second instance, he may do a number of things: He may feel that further information is needed before a meaningful therapeutic intervention—perhaps in the form of an interpretation—can occur (category B-1). He may focus on dynamic events in the patient's past which may have a dynamic bearing upon his current difficulties (B-2). He may focus on dynamic events in the present, such as interpersonal relations with contemporaries (B-3), and as a special case, with the therapist (transference) (B-4T). It also seems desirable to distinguish a class of communications in which the therapist responds to the patient by asserting his own role as an expert who states an authoritative opinion, expresses a value judgment, or something of the kind (B-4).

Dynamic focus, as defined here, is not a continuum but a set of categories which bear a meaningful relationship to the over-all heading. Two major sectors serve to differentiate whether the therapist is "going along" with the patient (A), or whether he introduces a different focus (B). Communications assigned to Sector A are not broken down further, but those assigned to Sector B are further analyzed with respect to the subcategories outlined in the preceding paragraph. Categories B-2, B-3, and B-4T are concerned with problems of function, in that they operate on the general hypothesis that the study of the patient's interpersonal performances, past or present, is effective therapeutically. In contradistinction, category B-1 is relatively static in its emphasis; the theoretical meaning of category B-4 is presently not clear. The rating on dynamic focus thus reflects the manner in which the therapist focuses the therapeutic spotlight.*

Initiative. Consider the following statements addressed to a patient:

Mmmh.
Can you tell me more about that?
Earlier in the hour you talked about your father. How did you get along with him?
Now this is one of the ways this thing started. But the more insidious thing was that it kept up. When you see this clearly, you can do something about it.

In each statement the therapist gives a certain measure of direction to the patient and indicates the avenue along which he desires the patient to proceed. In the first remark the therapist is merely com-

---

* Eugene Pumpian-Mindlin's "frames of reference" seem to be closely related to this conception (Marmor, 1955, pp. 498-499).

municating: "I hear you; go ahead." In the last one, he outlines to the patient what is to be done in order to achieve a given result. Many fine shadings of directiveness can find their way into a therapist's remarks; in some cases the direction is clear, in others it is less

TABLE 19

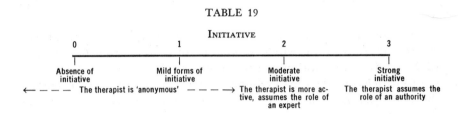

INITIATIVE

0	1	2	3
Absence of initiative	Mild forms of initiative	Moderate initiative	Strong initiative
← – – – The therapist is 'anonymous' – – – →		The therapist is more active, assumes the role of an expert	The therapist assumes the role of an authority

apparent; but, typically, direction, guidance, or steering are never absent. Such guidance is even implied in deliberate silence in response to a patient's question, which says in effect: "If you ask direct questions, I am not going to answer them, at least until we find out the reasons. Communicate along different lines." This attribute of the therapist's communications may be called *initiative*, and defined as the extent to which he accepts responsibility for directing the patient's verbalization in a given channel.

By definition, all therapeutic activity is directed toward a goal. The goal as well as the techniques for reaching the goal, may differ; but ideally all activities by the therapist guide the patient in a goal-directed channel. For present purposes, then, the concept *initiative* has a specific meaning which is related to goal-directedness or therapeutic directiveness. In intensive psychotherapy with reconstructive goals, the therapist assumes the initiative by directing the patient toward self-exploration, self-understanding, abandonment of defensive systems, and so on. In other forms of therapy, the therapist may focus on a specific problem (sector), the phenomenal self, and so on. Less frequently will he take the initiative in the sense of telling the patient how to conduct his life. While he may assume the role of an authority or expert, he will usually not interfere with the patient's autonomy and will safeguard the patient's right to make his own decisions. Whether the patient welcomes this is another matter.

If initiative is an important component of the therapist's communications, it should be possible to make distinctions concerning the *degree* of initiative present in a particular statement or sequence of statements. The operational scale proposed in Table 19 is built

upon the hypothesis that there is a continuum along which therapist
communications may be arranged. Therapeutic statements may be
regarded as ranging from a zero point (absence of initiative) through
an area of mild and moderate initiative to an extreme of strong or
authoritarian directiveness. The intensity of the therapist's initiative, rather than its quality, is the measurement attempted by this
scale.*

Therapeutic Climate. This dimension hypothesizes an attitudinal-
emotional continuum, which should be of considerable importance
in the study of psychotherapeutic processes. There is a growing consensus which considers the existence of a warm, accepting relationship
the *sine qua non* of effective psychotherapy. It is said that the
therapist must be a warm, tolerant, accepting, and understanding
person who is capable of integrating a relationship with the patient
in which respect for the latter's personality is uppermost. The
rationale for this assertion derives from the conception of the therapist as a more tolerant, reliable, and rational model of reality than
was provided by the significant persons with whom the patient
identified in his childhood. The presence of a climate of warmth,
love, and understanding would thus constitute a precondition for
the exploration and living through of painful experiences, which is
often necessary for emotional growth.

TABLE 20

THERAPEUTIC CLIMATE

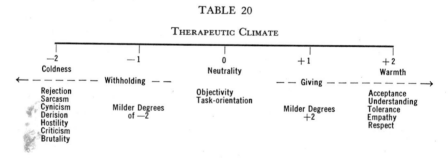

−2 Coldness	−1	0 Neutrality	+1	+2 Warmth
← − − − − − − Withholding − −			− − Giving − − − − − − − →	
Rejection Sarcasm Cynicism Derision Hostility Criticism Brutality	Milder Degrees of −2	Objectivity Task-orientation	Milder Degrees +2	Acceptance Understanding Tolerance Empathy Respect

The judgment of warmth or coldness transcends the symbolic
structure of the communication and deals with its feeling tone.
Admittedly, the measurements neglect to some extent the ways in
which a therapeutic climate is fostered nonverbally; nevertheless, it

---

* Notice that initiative is *not* defined as a function of the particular technique being
used, nor is it asserted that interpretations are directive and reflections of feeling are
nondirective. It should be apparent that the scale is not intended to perpetuate the
time-worn controversy between so-called directive and nondirective therapy, which
has been notably unproductive.

is believed that, despite this restriction, useful inferences about the therapeutic climate can be made by considering simultaneously the structure of the verbal communication and its emotional overtones.

The bipolar scale shown in Table 20 ranges from a neutral position to an extreme of acceptance, warmth, and the like in one direction, and to an extreme of rejection, hostility, coldness, and so on in the other.

THE SYSTEM IN ACTION

Materials

The scoring of therapist responses obtained in the major investigation reported in this book represents a somewhat unusual application of the system; however, the procedures which were followed in quantifying the responses, summarizing them, and testing rater agreement are quite illustrative of more general uses. In the following sections an attempt is made to set forth the procedures which would be followed in applying the system to typical therapy protocols. It is assumed that a sound recording as well as a typescript of the therapeutic hour to be scored is available, although Chapters 13 and 14 show that it is quite feasible to work from typed or printed materials. Nevertheless, voice quality, intonation, pitch, and so on, often provide valuable clues to the scoring, particularly as far as *therapeutic climate* is concerned; indeed, here they are almost indispensable.

Unit of Analysis

The single therapist communication occurring between two patient statements is treated as the common unit of analysis. This seems realistic since experience indicates that therapist communications are usually brief and concise. Moreover, even longer communications usually are devoted to the discussion of a *single* theme. In rare cases, it may be necessary to subdivide a therapist communication into two or three units.

The Rating Process

In scoring a single treatment hour, the rater is guided by the history of the therapist-patient interaction as it has evolved up to that time. The background should be provided by studying the actual therapeutic proceedings rather than by reading a summary prepared by the therapist, which may be biased in unknown and unpredictable ways. Therapist communications should never be scored out of context.

Before embarking upon the ratings proper, the observer should listen to a sound recording of the treatment hour, perusing a typescript simultaneously. In case of doubt, he may refer to the sound recording later on. He will then begin the systematic scoring, taking one set of categories or dimensions at a time. This seems to have the advantage that it avoids constantly having to change one's frame of reference while considering a single scoring unit. It also tends to insure greater independence of the ratings on the several categories and scales.

The Rater's Role

The rater's vantage point is that of a 'generalized therapist.' He stands outside but midway between therapist and patient, and attempts to understand the patient's communications from the point of view of a therapist. Unlike the participating therapist, he need not be concerned with the effect of his activity upon the patient, which assures a greater measure of distance and—hopefully—objectivity. At any particular point, he must ask himself a number of questions which are systematically posed by the requirement of a score on the categories and scales. These determinations concern aspects of the communication itself as well as inferences relative to the therapist's intent expressed in the message. In order to score objectively, the rater must, as far as possible, divorce himself from his own theoretical predilections and attempt to empathize with the therapeutic goals of the therapist whose procedures he is observing. Nevertheless, he can never abandon the general conceptions of psychotherapy, which are basic to his understanding of the interactive process. He must be critical of the therapist's technical procedures, but not from the point of view of what he, the rater, would have done at a given juncture.

This is a difficult assignment, in view of the strong tendency to regard one's own procedures as the only true and effective ones. In some respects the rater's job is similar to that of a supervising therapist: he is to observe and to evaluate the treating therapist's techniques in the context of the ongoing interaction—that is, in terms of the therapist's personality and his modes of relating to people, rather than to assert how he, the supervisor, would have proceeded.

Objective criteria, definitions, and examples, compiled in a manual, are intended to maximize the objectivity of the observations, and the rater's familiarity with them should minimize his personal biases. However, in the final analysis it is the rater's self-knowledge, integrity, intellectual honesty, and technical competence which determine the usefulness of his observations. Even a precision tool is useless in unskilled hands; and this system is considerably less than a precision tool.

Rater Qualifications

It is apparent that a rater must not only have a familiarity with the characteristics of the system, which can be acquired relatively easily, but he must be thoroughly conversant with and sensitized to the phenomena of psychotherapy. Preferably, he should have experience as a therapist. Above all, he must have a solid grasp of the major technical operations used in therapy and their respective rationales. He should also have a working knowledge of the varying emphases of the major theoretical writers and schools.

Training of Raters

Following a study of the system and its components the rater must score a number of sample protocols and discuss points of difficulty with a more experienced person. Finally, it is necessary to conduct reliability studies to test intra- as well as inter-rater agreement.

STATISTICAL TREATMENT OF RESULTS

A simple technique for summarizing the ratings is that applied in Chapters 13 and 14. It essentially consists of adding the frequencies obtained in each category and at each scale point. These totals may then be expressed as a proportion or as a percentage of the total number of interventions during an interview. In this way a profile of the therapist's activity for a given interview or series of interviews may be obtained. Comparisons between interviews may then be made by appropriate statistical techniques. The method for comparing groups of therapists, illustrated in Part I, is substantially identical to this procedure.

With regard to two continua (*depth-directedness* and *initiative*), mean ratings may be obtained for each interview. A series of interviews may then be compared by analysis of variance technique, *t*-tests, and so on. For some purposes it may be more useful to deal only with the high-intensity (extreme) ratings, and to note their frequencies. This is advisable because the means tend to be heavily influenced by the low-level ratings, which are typically found to preponderate. With reference to *therapeutic climate,* it is almost indispensable to concentrate on nonzero scores, which are usually very few in number. A mean in this case is almost totally devoid of meaning.

If a comparison of interviews is desired on the categories (*type of dynamic focus*), the chi square technique appears to be the method of choice.

The foregoing suggestions pertain only to simple over-all analyses, designed to answer such questions as: What is the therapist's typical profile? How does his activity vary between initial interviews, the middle phase of treatment, and the terminal stage? To what extent does his activity differ with different patients? In what respects does therapist A differ from therapist B? In other instances, the method of analysis of course depends on the hypothesis being tested.

Rater Agreement

The data presented in Tables 2 and 22 indicate that the system is highly reliable in the hands of trained raters. It may be appropriate, however, to append some general comments on techniques of testing for rater agreement.

An incisive analysis of rater agreement must deal with the ratings of independent judges on a unit-by-unit basis. In this way it becomes possible to determine whether raters agree on a given unit, and the possibility of compensating errors—frequently obscured in a comparison of totals—is excluded. Such estimates are conservative and will not indicate spuriously high agreement.

For the intensity scales which yield fairly large variance (*depth-directedness* and *initiative*), the product-moment coefficient of correlation appears adequate. The correlation between two independent raters, computed on a unit-by-unit basis, is a good index of their agreement. Concerning *therapeutic climate,* the preponderance of zero scores precludes this index. Although a zero score may be seen as a judgment, like a $+1$ or -2 score, the usual techniques are not applicable. One solution is to deal with totals of all plus and minus scores per interview.

With reference to the discrete categories (*type* and *dynamic focus*), a simple but useful index is provided by determining the over-all per cent agreement, which is an index based upon the number of units on which two independent raters agree. If the agreement exceeds chance at a specified level, the result may be considered satisfactory. Obviously, this merely defines a lower bound. For a system to yield useful and usable results, the agreement must be considerably better than chance—just how much is a matter of judgment. A refinement is provided by analyzing the agreement for each category. This procedure indicates not only that two raters show a certain percentage of over-all agreement, but identifies the categories which are rated reliably and the ones which are not. By relating actually obtained agreement to agreement expected by chance one again obtains a lower bound as a basis for comparison.

LIMITATIONS

Finally, it seems appropriate to make explicit certain limitations and cautions which apply to the present as well as to similar systems of content analysis:

(1) Since the system is restricted to the *therapist's* activity, it provides only a one-sided picture of the interaction. The information must, therefore, be supplemented by data on the patient's behavior. The interactive elements are taken into account in coding the therapist's verbalizations, but the resulting measures must always be considered in context. This illustrates the desirability of devising a parallel system for analyzing patient communications along similar lines, a task which seems quite feasible.

(2) In its focus on the single communication the system is atomistic and disregards the idiosyncratic communication content. Therein lie both its strengths and weaknesses. On the positive side, it yields objective assessments of each intervention as it occurs, and is thus quite analytical. On the negative side, it does not throw light on the larger units of therapeutic interaction, such as themes and phases of the therapeutic work. Additional descriptions of the therapeutic process in terms of its idiosyncratic content undoubtedly mitigate this shortcoming, and are indeed indispensable. In this respect, the information yielded by this analysis is the direct antithesis of the typical case history found in the psychoanalytic literature, which stresses the larger sweep of dynamic events, but usually disregards the single interaction units. The two kinds of approaches may complement and supplement each other.

(3) The analysis is relatively time-consuming, requiring two to four hours for a typical therapeutic hour, and it requires highly qualified and trained raters.

(4) Since the system is primarily descriptive and essentially non-valuative, it makes no qualitative distinctions. Thus it provides no information as to whether an interpretation is 'correct' or 'incorrect,' whether the therapist uses precise language, whether an intervention

is properly timed, whether a remark is appropriate or anxiety-provoking, and so on. Such evaluations are contingent upon adequate external criteria.

(5) The system is restricted to the analysis of verbal symbolic messages and their emotional overtones; it largely omits from consideration nonverbal forms of interaction. This is not to deny their importance, but points up the need for developing further special methodologies.

(6) There is an elusive but significant limitation which derives from the assumptions in any quantitative analysis. It is assumed that each unit of analysis (therapist intervention) is equivalent to every other unit, that the units are additive, and that frequency of occurrence is an important heuristic indicator.

APPLICATIONS

In conclusion, the system may prove useful in many research operations requiring a quantitative measure of the therapist's verbal communications. This volume incorporates (1) comparisons between various groups of therapists, (2) comparisons between a series of interviews conducted by a single therapist (Chapter 13), and (3) comparisons between two therapists adhering to different theoretical orientations (Chapter 14). Additional uses might include: intratherapist analyses, e.g., longitudinal studies of single cases for the purpose of analyzing and comparing variations in technique as a function of the patient's current problems, stage of therapy, therapeutic aims, diagnosis, etc.; the testing of specific hypotheses in process studies, e.g., reactions by the patient to, say, "deep interpretations, focus on transference feelings toward the therapist, variations in the therapist's attitude, "warmth," etc.

Needless to say, there is nothing "final" about the scales and categories proposed here. They are little more than heuristic guidelines which eventually should be modified as refinements can be made.

13

AN APPLICATION OF
THE SYSTEM TO A THERAPY CASE

In the preceding chapter attention has been called to the need for comparative studies of psychotherapeutic techniques and a system of analysis for abstracting and measuring certain relevant aspects of therapeutic communications has been presented. The following is an attempt to apply this method to a case treated by short-term psychotherapy based on psychoanalytic principles. The objective is to illustrate this approach and to indicate some of its potentialities.

The case history to be analyzed was published by Wolberg (1954, pp. 688-780)* and comprises nine treatment sessions, which are transcribed and fully reported, minor changes having been made only for the purpose of concealing the patient's identity. In addition to the therapist-patient communications, the transcript includes comments by the therapist.

By way of introduction, Wolberg states:

> The type of treatment employed was insight therapy with re-educative goals. The problem for which therapy was sought was a "run-of-the-mill" type of situation often encountered in practice. I was happy that the psychopathologic material elicited in this case was not so startling as to excite concentration on psychodynamics. In teaching therapy there is so often a temptation to focus on the spectacular, to wallow so in symbolic representations of conflict and in the manifold defenses that the human mind employs in seeking surcease from turmoil, that one may fail to emphasize what is really important in treatment: the study of the relationship that develops between the patient and the therapist. I felt that the case I chose would permit us to explore such aspects as the conduct of an initial interview, the establishment of a working relationship with the patient, the techniques for arriving at the dynamics of a neurosis, the promotion of activity toward therapeutic change, and the termination of therapy (pp. 688-689).

---

* All references in this chapter are to this source, unless otherwise indicated.

And further:

> The case was chosen not for its dramatic interest—since there was nothing spectacular about the involved dynamics—but because it delineates within the nine sessions that comprised the total treatment period, important processes observed in the opening, middle and terminal phases of therapy (p. 688).

According to this rationale, the case should be equally well suited for our present purposes because it yields a useful profile of the therapist's activity at various stages of treatment. By the same token, it should disclose clear-cut differences in therapist activity correlated with the dynamic events of each therapeutic hour. To be sure, the profile mirrors Wolberg's technique, which may or may not be representative of other therapists' procedures. This question will remain unanswered until analyses of comparable therapeutic sessions conducted by other therapists provide additional data.

While no summary can adequately convey the richness of the actual therapist-patient interaction, it is impossible to reproduce here the case history in its entirety. It has been necessary to condense radically the happenings during each therapeutic hour, but interested readers may refer to the original source.

Seven of the nine interviews were scored jointly by two raters from the transcript; two interviews were rated independently by the same raters to obtain a measure of rater agreement. Editorial remarks were disregarded as far as possible in an effort to base the analysis upon the interaction itself. Since the original sound recording was not available, it is conceivable that some nuances were lost.

Before presenting the case history, I will discuss the quantitative measures used, in order to highlight the kinds of information yielded by the multidimensional analysis. Subsequently, the reader can judge for himself to what extent these results gain in meaning when the totality of the interaction is considered.

DISCUSSION OF RESULTS

Type of Therapeutic Activity

Figure 9 presents a profile of the therapist's verbal communications for the nine interviews in regard to *type* (statistical data are given at the end). The breakdown is by major categories, the frequencies for each interview having been converted to percentages. The total number of interventions over the nine interviews was 1,075. Considering the regular interview time, the frequencies ranged from 79 (in the second interview) to 154 (in the last interview), with a median of 114. (The N of 174 in the fourth interview was due to the fact that this session ran overtime, but the therapist had noted the point at which the regular time was up.)

Minimal activity (category 00, including such verbalizations as "Mm-hm," "I see," and so on) ranged from about 2.5 per cent in the second interview to 24.7 per cent in the ninth, with a median of about 13 per cent. The frequencies of all other activities ranged, in absolute numbers, from 75 to 151, with a median of 97. Assuming the typical session to last about 50 minutes, this would mean approximately two interventions per minute—a fairly high level of verbal activity.

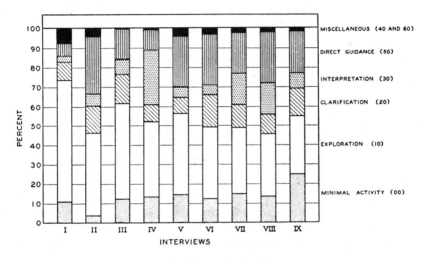

FIG. 9. Analysis of Therapeutic Communications in Terms of *Type*.

Exploratory operations (category 10) ranged from 31.5 per cent in Interview VIII to 64.8 per cent in the initial interview. With the exception of the first interview, in which the therapist asked a great many exploratory questions, the 'exploratory level' remained fairly constant throughout treatment, comprising somewhat better than a third of all communications.

Clarification (category 20), which includes reflections of the patient's feelings, restatements of content, and noninterpretative summaries, was used rather sparingly. It comprised approximately 10 per cent of all interventions.

With respect to interpretive operations (category 30), there were sharp fluctuations: interpretations ranged from less than 2 per cent in the initial interview to 28.1 per cent in Interview IV. There was a gradual rise from Interview I to Interview IV, a sharp drop for the two succeeding interviews, and another increase (beginning with Interview VII), which was maintained, with minor changes, until termination. The data for *depth-directedness* will further elucidate this finding.

Structuring (category 40) made up 5.6 per cent of the communications in Interview I but occurred so infrequently thereafter that it was lumped with other miscellaneous communications (greetings, small talk, and so on) in category 60.

Category 50 which, for lack of a better term was labeled "direct guidance," includes communications in which the therapist emerges as an expert or authority, states opinions, gives approval, provides reassurance, and so on (see also category B-4, under *dynamic focus*). This type of activity was used minimally in Interview I (6.5 per cent) and reached its peak in Interview II (27.8 per cent), with Interviews V, VI, and VIII following closely. It is the frequency of this form of activity which typifies this therapist's approach as re-educative. It is also interesting, in this connection, that Interview IV, which showed a spurt in interpretive communications, had a concomitant decline in category 50. In other words, interpretive and re-educative techniques alternated, to some extent at least.

Depth-Directedness

In order to give a graphic presentation of the relative depth of the therapist's communications, three levels were distinguished. Level 1 includes communications scored 1+ or less on the five-point scale; Level 2 comprises the range of 2— to 2+; and Level 3 is made up of interventions rated 3— or higher. Figure 10 shows the relative frequency of each level within an interview.

It is readily apparent that Level 1 exceeded 80 per cent in Interviews I, V, and VI, with Interviews II and IX not far removed; in other words, most therapist communications in these interviews were rather close to the 'surface' and relatively noninferential. By contrast, Interview VII showed the highest proportion of inferential communications, followed by Interview IV. Intermediate depth occurred in relatively higher proportions in these two interviews as well. The bar diagrams also point to an increase in inferential activity from Interview I through Interview IV, a sharp decline for Interviews V and VI, another spurt in Interview VII, and again a decline to the end of treatment.

The *mean depth* for each interview has been plotted in Figure 11. This analysis follows closely the trend of Figure 10, although the means are heavily depressed by the preponderance of low scores;

nevertheless, the gradual increase, the two peaks at Interviews IV and VII, the sharp drop in the middle phase, and the gradual decline at the end clearly emerge.

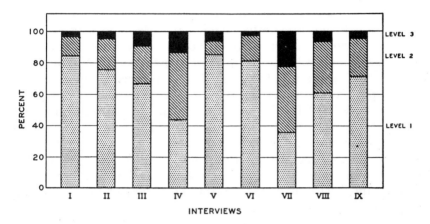

FIG. 10. Analysis of Therapeutic Communications in Terms of *Depth-Directedness*.

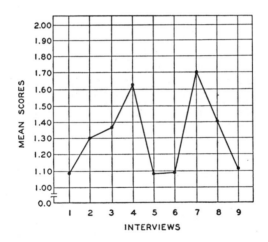

FIG. 11. Distribution of Mean *Depth-Directedness* Scores.

Dynamic Focus

Figure 12 presents a breakdown of therapist communications in terms of *dynamic focus*. Sector A (no shift in dynamic focus) accounted for some 22 per cent in Interviews II and IV, at its lowest, and for 46.7 per cent in Interview IX, at its highest, for the remaining interviews, the rate was fairly constant—in the neighborhood of 30 per cent.

Requests for additional information (B-1) ranged from 14.9 per cent in Interview IV to 50 per cent in Interview I, and a sizeable proportion of the activity in most interviews was taken up by this particular focus, with a median of 28.2 per cent.

Greater interest attaches to the focus of communications commonly called interpretations. Here, the therapist's interpretive efforts were concerned primarily with dynamic events in the *present;* focus on dynamic events in the patient's past occurred only in Interview IV (8.6 per cent), Interview I (3.7 per cent) and Interview VI (1.2 per cent); transference dynamics were minimally dealt with in Interviews III, VIII, IV, VII, and V (in descending order, percentages ranging from 3.7 to .8). Dynamic interpretations of the patient's contemporary interpersonal relations accounted for 42.5 per cent of all therapist interventions in Interview IV and 28.1 per cent in Interview VII—the most 'interpretive' interviews.

In all interviews, with the possible exception of the two highly interpretive ones, the therapist introduced a fair measure of guidance into the situation. Category B-4, which is closely related to category 50 under *type* accounted minimally for 6.5 per cent of all interventions in Interview I, and maximally for about a third in Interviews II and VIII.

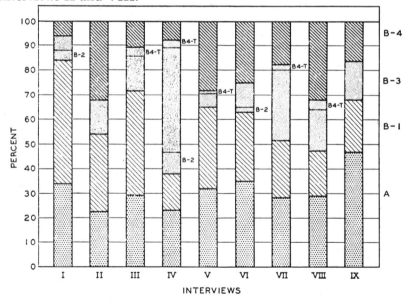

FIG. 12. Analysis of Therapeutic Communications in Terms of *Dynamic Focus.*

Initiative

The data presented so far suggest that the therapist was quite active in his participation, that his interpretations were phased, and that he favored the current-interpersonal focus. However, regardless of technique, to what extent did he assume the initiative in guiding the patient's communications into a goal-directed channel? Figure 13 presents a tabulation of *initiative* scores, which have been grouped into three levels: Level 1, scores of 1+ and below; Level 2, scores of 2— through 2+; and Level 3, scores of 3— or above.

Mild initiative was displayed to a rather variable degree, ranging from 28.9 per cent in Interview VII to 72.2 per cent in the initial interview. It was outweighed, however, by moderate and high scores in Interviews II, IV, and VII. Extreme scores showed a steady increase to Interview V, a level which was maintained, with minor fluctuations, throughout the remainder of treatment.

A somewhat dissimilar picture is conveyed by the mean scores (Figure 14). Here, the plateau is worthy of note, as are the valleys in Interviews I, III, and IX, indicating that the therapist's initiative was relatively low in these sessions. Again, the mean scores are greatly influenced by the high proportion of low scores. For this reason, it may be instructive to consider the *absolute* number of extreme (Level 3) scores and to relate them to comparable scores on *depth-directedness*. This has been done in Figure 15.

It is seen that both *depth* and *initiative* rose concomitantly to the middle of treatment, but that the former reached its peak in Interview IV—already identified as the first highly interpretive one—whereas *initiative* did so in the following hour, in which depth sharply dropped. Interview VI was characterized by relatively low *depth* and *initiative*. From then on, the plots diverge: *depth* showed another peak in the second highly interpretive interview (Interview VII), whereas the plateau of *initiative* was maintained. To pursue his goals, the therapist used *both* interpretation and initiative—exemplified by re-educative techniques—which seemed to implement each other. The observed differences in phasing may be of more than passing interest.

Therapeutic Climate

The relative absence of nonzero scores, augmented perhaps by the procedure of scoring from the printed page, presented difficulties and contributed to a certain tenuousness of results on this component. There was never any question concerning minus scores, which were clearly not present; but with respect to positive scores, differentiations between scores of $+1$ and $+2$ were not feasible. In absolute numbers, Interview V ranked lowest, with 3 positive scores, and Interviews II and IV highest, with 8 positive scores. Even so, there is little question but that the therapist was accepting, sympathetic, warm, and benevolent.

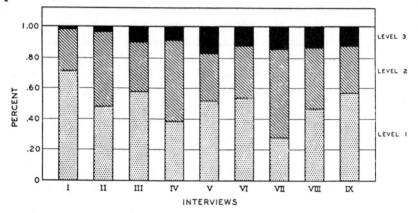

FIG. 13. Analysis of Therapeutic Communications in Terms of *Initiative*.

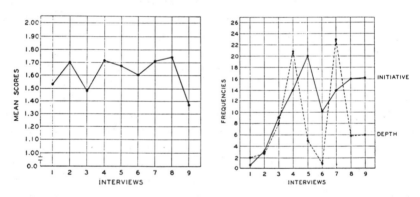

FIG. 14. (*left*) Distribution of Mean *Initiative* Scores.
FIG. 15. (*right*) Distribution of Extreme (Level 3) Scores on *Depth-Directedness* and *Initiative*.

Summary of the Analysis

The quantitative analyses make it abundantly clear that the therapist's techniques showed systematic variations over the course of this short-term therapy. The initial interview was largely devoted to an exploration of the patient's problem; the next two interviews revealed an intensification of therapeutic activity, both in terms of inferential operations and initiative; Interviews IV and VII emerged as deeply interpretive ones, the intervening ones appearing as less 'dramatic;' data for the remaining sessions pointed to a phasing out of interpretive activity, but initiative was maintained at a relatively high level. The therapist's interpretive operations were geared to the dynamics of the patient's current interpersonal relations, and transference analysis and focus on genetic antecedents were generally de-emphasized. Throughout the course of treatment, but especially in the second half, the therapist stood out as a person who, in the role of an expert, gave guidance, stated opinions, and engaged in procedures which are best characterized as re-educative. He was clearly more active than passive, both in terms of frequency of interventions and in directing the course of therapy. The aptness of Wolberg's descriptive label—"insight therapy with re-educative goals"—is certainly corroborated by the quantitative analysis. The most noteworthy single result is perhaps the *phasing* of therapeutic activity, which is reflected so clearly in the tabulations. It seems that the therapist gradually prepared the patient for deeper interpretations, which he advanced in the fourth session. Then he waited for the consolidation of insights before renewing his interpretive endeavors in Interview VII. Thereafter, he diminished his interpretive activity, while maintaining a degree of therapeutic pressure until the end.

SYNOPSIS OF THE CASE HISTORY

It is now appropriate to take a look at the interactive events in this case history, with emphasis upon those facets which might illuminate the quantitative analysis. In order to minimize possible biases of my own, I shall rely mostly on the therapist's comments and summaries. Wolberg relates the background in these words:

> I received a telephone call from a former patient who asked if I could see a friend of hers in consultation. Her friend, a retired business woman, had, during the past two years, become progressively more depressed, and in the past six months had retreated from her customary social contacts. An attractive widow, and comfortably situated financially, there was no objective reason why she should act in this manner. She had tried to convince her friend to seek therapy six months previously, but the reaction to this suggestion was a bad one. However, her friend had telephoned her this morning and had asked to be referred. My comment was that I would want to see her friend in consultation before I could decide whether I was the best person to treat her particular problem. If she would ask her friend to call me, I would be pleased to give her an appointment. That afternoon the patient telephoned me and I set up an appointment for an initial interview (p. 690).

Interview I. The initial interview was designed to establish rapport, to make a tentative diagnosis, to get an idea of the psychodynamics which were involved, to evaluate the feasibility of treatment, and to make arrangements for therapy. The therapist decided to accept the patient for treatment, asked a fairly large number of diagnostic questions, and made the tentative diagnosis of a "psychoneurotic depression engrafted on a personality disorder" (p. 699). He felt that "the involved psychodynamics were unclear, but a number of elements were suggested, namely, the possibility of having experienced shattered security and self-esteem due to maternal neglect, the need to submit herself to exploitation as evidenced in her relationship with her husband, the low estimation of herself along with self-neglect, and the blocking of her ability to relate to people" (p. 699).

Interview II. The therapist structured the therapeutic situation by explaining the procedures and goals of therapy. The patient provided further data on her history and touched upon her need to help people who in turn seemed to exploit her.

Interview III. Toward the end of the interview, in which the patient had shown resistance, as evidenced by her demands on the therapist to supply her with "answers" and by self-recriminations, the therapist summed up the events in these words:

> T. *[89]:* So, as a child you were unhappy, and you married to get away from it; but you were still unhappy. Then you met the middle man, and you put everything into that relationship, but it ended. You took care of an orphan and that ended tragically for you, too. You married John and felt exploited and used. And with the last man, too, things ended by your feeling that you got little out of it. That's quite a series of depriving incidents. *[90]* No matter what you did and gave, it ended as if you had nothing to give (pp. 718-719).*

In his comments about the interview the therapist wrote:

> As tension accumulates in the interview, she comes out with suppressed and partially repressed material, with some catharsis. She attempts to act-out an impulse to be exploited in the transference, which I circumvent. She continues to try to force me into a directive role, and finally she becomes aware of her intent. At the end she seems to accept my structuring of the therapeutic situation. We seem to be entering into the middle phase of treatment (p. 720).

Interview IV. In his comments on this interview, the therapist noted:

> In this session the patient has arrived at several insights. She sees a pattern weaving through her life and connects it with what happened to her in her

---

* The numberings *89, 90,* and so on which appear in this section were given the therapist's communications for the purposes of the present study.

childhood. She realizes the values of her neurotic patterns, but also appreciates their destructive effects. At the end of the session she challenges her need to pursue the pattern of her giving presents to be loved (pp. 732-733).

The tenor of the therapist's interpretive activity is epitomized by the following quotation:

> *T. [57]:* Maybe you feel people wouldn't like you unless you did.
> *P.:* Unless I would do something.
> *T. [58]:* If this is so, how do you think this would make you feel?
> *P.:* Terrible, feeling always they won't like me.
> *T. [59]:* That they'd reject you. And, if this is so, isn't it possible that if you have to keep doing things to keep people liking you, you would either want to run away from the relationship or else continue to have to do things for the person over and over? (p. 724).

The following samples illustrate the therapist's re-educative techniques:

> *T. [76]:* It is possible for you to find many things in your life that you don't like. All people do things about which they may have shame. You can catalogue all the bad things you have done and make testimony that sounds overwhelming, but when you compare your life to any person's life, your sins will probably compare to theirs. So far, you haven't told me a thing that would justify your feeling the way you do (p. 725).
> *T. [168]:* The important thing is to understand your patterns of living thoroughly, see how they cross you up, why they occurred and are still occurring, and then challenge them (p. 732).

Interview V. The therapist noted:

> In this session the patient begins to make positive plans for the future. An attempt to deal with deeper unconscious material is revealed in a dream; however, the patient resists this effort and seeks to keep the interview on her immediate environmental situation. I act more directive in suggesting a positive course of action (pp. 741-742).

(These encouragements concern a course in antiques, in which the patient has expressed an interest.) It seemed that the patient had assimilated the therapist's previous interpretations to some extent.

Interview VI. The therapist commented, "This session is illustrative of sessions in which not much seems to be happening. The working-through process may be going on nevertheless" (p. 742). To the patient, the therapist put the matter in this way:

> *T. [53]:* There is one thing you may have to watch for when you meet a worthwhile person. In the face of this man's apparent good qualities, you may say to yourself, "Well, gosh, he'll never see anything in *me*. Why should I get myself messed up over him? If he sees something in me, it's because he just wants sex, or because he wants to take advantage of me, or something like that; it isn't likely that he respects me for myself." And after that, you won't give him a chance; you'll just run like a deer. Now you've got to build up this

estimate of yourself, if things are to be different. We have a fairly good idea of the origin of this bad estimate of yourself in your early upbringing. But this has produced in you an extremely insidious situation, in which you keep on despising yourself, in which you feel you have no inherent qualities, in which you feel that you can only be loved for what you can do for people, and not for yourself. Now these patterns keep messing you all up (p. 747).*

In his remarks about this hour, the therapist called attention to the presence of deeper unconscious conflicts which he suspected that

---

* The direct quotations given in this section were chosen to provide convenient summaries of a particular session or to illustrate certain aspects of Wolberg's technique; they are not necessarily representative of his technique throughout treatment. It may be of interest, in this connection, to quote Wolberg on what he considers to be the essentials of his therapeutic approach in general:

"The particular kind of therapy that I utilize is psychoanalytic therapy. This varies from formal psychoanalysis on a four- or five-times-a-week basis, with an establishment of a transference neurosis, to an approach on a once-a-week basis in which there is face-to-face interviewing. While in the latter approach a transference neurosis is avoided as much as possible, therapy, even on a once-a-week basis, depends on an adequate dealing with transference and resistance. Dreams are employed constantly and, in my opinion, are the most effective medium of approach to the unconscious. I find that from time to time I modify my methods, employing, on the one hand, supportive devices when the individual is extremely sick and manifests symptoms of adaptational collapse or impending psychosis and, on the other hand, devices to expedite awareness of unconscious material through hypnoanalysis. . . .

"I would say that my therapeutic system breaks down into four essential parts. The first deals with the development of a working relationship with a patient. In this phase, we work through characterologic resistances that prevent the individual from relating to me. Essentially, analytic techniques are employed here, and I am more or less active until I am certain that I have a good relationship with the patient. Once this relationship is assured, the second phase of therapy begins, which involves investigation of the sources of the individual's problems. Here I employ dream analysis, the investigation of the current life situation, the verbal associations of the patient, and any transference manifestations that he exhibits in his relationship with me. The third phase of therapy consists of translating insight and understanding into action. The final phase involves terminating the treatment process and handling dependencies that may exist. This framework might rightfully be called eclectic since it utilizes concepts derived from various disciplines, including psychoanalysis, psychobiology, casework, and psychological counseling. The objective of this framework is reconstruction of the personality, although there is recognition of, and allowance for, the fact that this goal may have to be scaled down in instances where motivation is lacking or there is diminutive ego strength.

"Both directive and nondirective approaches are utilized, depending on the needs of the patient and the specific phases during therapy. For instance, I am more inclined to be directive at the start of therapy, at the time when the working relationship is being set up. During the explorative phases of therapy, passivity is the keynote. In handling resistances of the patient, particularly toward activity and change, much greater activity may be required. Finally, in the terminal phases of therapy, a more nondirective approach is mandatory." (Quoted by Werner Wolff; 1956, pp. 114-115.)

the patient was unwilling to explore. He decided to strive for limited therapeutic goals, because of her age.

Interview VII. This interview was characterized by a further exploration of the patient's neurotic patterns and the therapist's suggestion that she participated in their perpetuation more than she had realized. The therapist felt that the patient was more hopeful and less self-defeating, but that she evinced reluctance to "go deeper." The patient seemed exceptionally cooperative and task-oriented.

Interview VIII. The therapist considered this session typical of the middle phase of treatment (p. 760) and called attention to the patient's growing insight in the direction of change (p. 769). Her insight was tested and challenged repeatedly, but she asserted herself by making constructive plans for her life.

Interview IX. In this, the final interview, the patient announced her decision to terminate treatment in what appeared to be a confident tone. The therapist accepted her plans, but warned of recurrences of her difficulties, which might necessitate further therapy. He appeared to encourage her newly won self-confidence, and helped her to consolidate her gains.

In his final comment, Wolberg emphasizes that good results were achieved in an unusually short time, and he attributes this to the patient's motivation for therapy, the relative lack of resistance, and the fact that there was no strong secondary gain. Concerning his technique, he mentions that the work proceeded almost entirely on a characterologic. level, and that the effect of treatment was mostly of a re-educative nature despite his dealing with resistance, and, in a few instances, with transference (pp. 779-780).

This very brief summary of the treatment history may give some glimpse of the interactive events upon which the quantitative analysis was based. It lies outside the scope of this comparison to relate specific incidents of the case history to the quantitative indices, although such a task would be quite feasible. My main purpose has been to show that the profiles bear a meaningful relationship to dynamic events in psychotherapy and that they help to characterize both the kinds of technique which are used throughout as well as their ebb and flow from hour to hour.

At this point the critical reader may well ask, "What does this quantitative analysis add to my knowledge? After all, if I want to learn something about this patient, her problem, and the therapist's techniques, all I have to do is to read the transcript and come up with the same answers. I will be able to tell that interpretive techniques are used in conjunction with re-educative measures, that the therapist is quite active in his approach, that he seems benevolent and supportive, and so on. And I might even tell you that Interviews IV and VII are more interpretive than the initial or the terminal interview. Aren't you just demonstrating the obvious? Besides, you haven't said a word about the effectiveness of this particular therapeutic technique. Isn't it conceivable that identical or more beneficial results would have been achieved had the therapist employed different methods?"

I would reply that these criticisms are quite cogent as far as this particular case history is concerned. But suppose the investigative task is to compare the therapeutic techniques of two, three, or more therapists with comparable patients. How could one make such comparisons without being able to say that Therapist A is using more of this and less of that at various stages of therapy than Therapist B? And how could one place any confidence in the accuracy and objectivity of one's observations unless one used some kind of a calibrated measuring instrument? I would concede that the present tool is a far cry from a precision instrument, as precision is thought of in the physical sciences. But at least it permits the investigator to conduct a systematic inquiry and to make observations which can be closely approximated by independent observers. The fact that the results seem to corroborate information obtained by less rigorous means, instead of detracting from the quantitative measures, attests to their potential validity.

As for the second stricture, concerning the absence of qualitative judgments, my answer would be that this avoidance is deliberate. I believe that a concerted effort must be made to separate descriptions from value judgments; once it is possible to specify, with increasing accuracy, the relevant aspects of therapeutic interactions, one can turn to external criteria of effectiveness—such as 'cures,' improved adjustment, or better functioning—and relate them to internal measures, as obtained by the present system of analysis. If it becomes further possible to achieve better control over such elusive variables as the initial degree of disturbance, the personality of the therapist, the intervention of influences outside the therapeutic framework, and the like, questions as to the relative effectiveness of different techniques may come nearer solution. The strife among the warring factions represented by the different schools of psychotherapy is fueled by the continuing lack of adequate quantitative criteria, and it may not be expected to subside unless and until a measure of scientific rigor can be brought to bear upon the exceedingly complex phenomena within their domain.

STATISTICAL INDICES

Rater agreement. In order to estimate reliability of the scoring system, two of the nine interviews were analyzed independently by two raters. The indices presented in Table 21 are based upon a unit-by-unit analysis; agreement on a unit (therapist communication) means that both raters assigned it to the same category (on *type* or *focus*, respectively), or that they gave it an intensity score (on *depth-directedness* or *initiative*, respectively) no more than one-half step apart. For the last mentioned scales, product-moment coefficients of correlation were computed, in addition.

TABLE 21

AGREEMENT BETWEEN TWO INDEPENDENT RATERS

System Component	Interview VII $N = 114$	Interview IX $N = 154$
Type	80.7%	80.5%
Depth-Directedness	86.0% $(r = .86)$	94.0% $(r = .885)$
Dynamic Focus	80.7%	85.7%
Initiative	87.7% $(r = .87)$	93.5% $(r = .93)$
Therapeutic Climate	Agreement on 7 out of 9 nonzero scores	Agreement on 3 out of 5 nonzero scores

All percentages are significant beyond the .01 level.
All correlation coefficients are significant beyond the .01 level.

TABLE 22

LEVELS OF SIGNIFICANCE

Figure	Type of Analysis	Result	Degrees of Freedom	p Level
9	Chi square	$x^2 = 142.08$	32	< .001
10	Chi square	$x^2 = 171.73$	16	< .001
11	Analysis of variance	$F = 20.45$	26	< .001
12	Chi square	$x^2 = 231.83$	24	< .001
13	Chi square	$x^2 = 79.20$	16	< .001
14	Analysis of variance	$F = 8.17$	26	< .001

Correlation between depth-directedness and initiative. Since the two scales appear to be interrelated, it seemed desirable to investigate whether they may be regarded as independent measures. Accordingly, product-moment correlation coefficients were computed for three selected interviews, V, VII, and IX. The respective r's were .13, .61, and .63. While the reliability of the two scales is high, it appears that in certain interviews the two scales yield rather similar information; nevertheless, even with an r of .63, only slightly more than a third of the variance is accounted for. In other interviews, the two scales do not co-vary to any appreciable degree. It must be concluded that *depth-directedness* and *initiative,* as measured by the two scales, is often fairly highly correlated, but that this is not always the case. Experience indicates that deeply interpretive communications usually are rated high on *initiative* also, but that the converse is not necessarily true.

Significance levels. Table 22 presents the levels of significance for the analyses which have been presented in the body of this chapter.

14

A COMPARISON
OF THERAPIST ACTIVITY
IN TWO CASES

The analysis of therapeutic protocols has occupied the time of researchers for some years, but rarely has an attempt been made to go outside a school of thought and to compare the techniques of, say, a nondirectivist with those of an analyst. Yet, such comparisons will inevitably play a part in future attempts to evaluate the relative effectiveness of competing approaches to psychotherapy.

This chapter presents a preliminary descriptive analysis of two varieties of psychotherapeutic techniques: insight therapy with re-educative goals based on psychoanalytic principles, and client-centered therapy. The analysis is mediated by the multidimensional system previously described. The data obviously do not permit an evaluation of the respective merits of short-term analytic and client-centered therapy.

THE TWO CASE HISTORIES

The first case history is the one discussed in the preceding chapter. The second case history is that of Mary Jane Tilden, counseled by Rogers in a series of eleven interviews (Snyder, 1947, pp. 128-203).

Miss Tilden was described as a 20 year old, attractive young woman brought to the clinic by her mother, who complained that the patient was sleeping all the time, brooding, and ruminating. Miss Tilden seemed to be withdrawing progressively; she had given up her job and lost interest in her social life. Miss Tilden was treated by nondirective therapy. Rogers felt that the eleven counseling hours were followed by a period of improved adjustment; nevertheless, the evaluation of final outcome remained somewhat in doubt since, shortly after a year had elapsed, there seemed to be a recurrence of the earlier symptomatology.*

PROCEDURE

Seven of the nine Wolberg interviews and three representative interviews from the Miss Tilden case were scored jointly from the printed scripts by two raters.

RESULTS

The Wolberg case

The therapist's activity, as mirrored by the multidimensional system of analysis, has been presented in the preceding chapter. The most noteworthy single result is perhaps the *phasing* of therapeutic activity. It seems as if the therapist gradually prepares the patient for the more inferential formulations which he advances in the fourth session. Then he waits for a consolidation of insight before renewing his interpretive efforts in Interview VII. Thereafter, he diminishes his interpretive activity while maintaining a degree of therapeutic pressure till the end.

The case of Miss Tilden

The analysis comprises three selected interviews; they are, however, separated in time and presumably represent different stages of therapy.

Reference to Figures 16, 17, 18, and 19 indicates that the profiles of therapist activity are quite similar from interview to interview. As might be expected, reflections of feeling account for a large percentage of all interventions (75%); interpretations are virtually absent; explorations are used minimally in the initial session and are almost nonexistent later on; direct guidance is equally rare. The data on *Depth-directedness* and *Initiative* corroborate these findings: neither maximal *Depth-directedness* nor maximal *Initiative* is used to any appreciable degree, but the initial interview is rela-

---

* Although one cannot be sure, this case may pertain to that period in the evolution of client-centered therapy in which Rogers (1946) detects "vestiges of subtle directiveness."

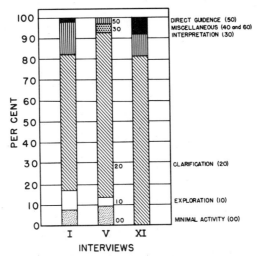

FIG. 16. Analysis of Therapeutic Communications in Terms of *Type*. (Interviews: $T, N = 57$; $V, N = 23$; $XI, N = 53$. Total number of therapist interventions: N: 133.)

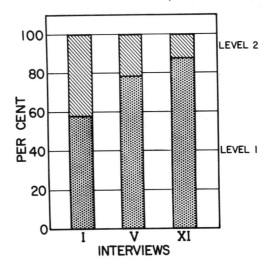

FIG. 17. Analysis of Therapeutic Communications in Terms of *Depth-Directedness*.

tively more inferential than the final one. (In this instance, chi square exceeded the .01 level of probability; all others failed to reach the .05 level.) In most of his interventions, the therapist accepts the patient's focus; only very rarely does he assume the role of an expert or an authority.

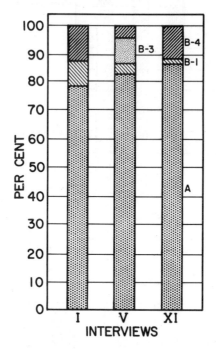

FIG. 18. Analysis of Therapeutic Communications in Terms of *Dynamic Focus*.

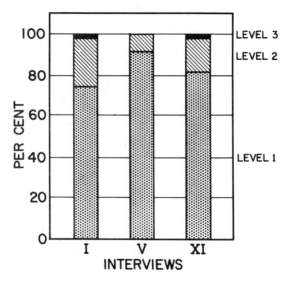

FIG. 19. Analysis of Therapeutic Communications in Terms of *Initiative*.

Intertherapist comparisons

While the preceding analyses have shown that Wolberg's technique varies systematically over the course of treatment whereas Rogers' does not, the question may still be asked, how do the two therapists compare at different stages of therapy? To explore this problem, three interviews from the beginning, middle, and terminal phases of the Wolberg series were selected and compared with the Miss Tilden case. Since the distributions of the categories within *Type* and *Dynamic Focus* vary so greatly for the two therapists. the only meaningful comparisons concern the continua of *Depth-directedness* and *Initiative*. The results of this analysis are presented in Table 23.

In the case of *Depth-directedness*, a significant chi square indicates that Wolberg's technique is significantly more inferential than Rogers'; with respect to *Initiative,* Wolberg exerts stronger guidance in the middle and terminal interviews, but not in the initial one. The latter finding is accounted for by the fact that Wolberg employs a great many exploratory questions of a diagnostic character in his first session, which in terms of *Initiative* receive scores similar to the reflection-of-feeling technique, which Rogers employs throughout.

TABLE 23

Chi Square Comparisons of Therapist Activity in Initial,
Middle, and Terminal Interviews

	Wolberg I ($N = 108$) vs. Rogers I ($N = 57$)	Wolberg IV ($N = 174$) vs. Rogers V ($N = 23$)	Wolberg IX ($N = 154$) vs. Rogers XI ($N = 53$)
Depth-directedness	19.32***	9.39**	4.66*
Initiative	.19	22.79***	9.85**

* Significant between the .02 and .05 level.
** Significant at the .01 level.
*** Significant at the .001 level.

DISCUSSION

The system of analysis has been applied to the therapist's communications in two forms of therapy in an effort to measure aspects which may be common to both. With respect to the Miss Tilden case, the system of analysis yields data which are substantially in agreement with other analyses which have been performed on interviews conducted by nondirective counselors. By and large, these results also agree with Rogers' recommendations on therapeutic technique. Wolberg's technique, too, is in agreement with his descriptive account but, to my knowledge, no comparable quantitative studies have been published. While not crucial, such evidence attests indirectly to the validity of this system of analysis. Of at least equal importance, however, is the tentative demonstration that the method facilitates the comparative treatment of therapeutic techniques—a treatment which is quantitative and highly objective and which does not prejudge a particular communication as desirable or undesirable on *a priori* grounds.

To be sure, the present two case histories are comparable only in superficial respects and they do not lend themselves to a rigorous evaluative comparison. However, they suggest a number of questions which appear to be basic to all psychotherapy research. Consider the following two points.

We know that both patients entered psychotherapy seeking alleviation of their emotional problems. Did their difficulties have any common basis? What was the relative degree of their disturbance? Even if both had been diagnosed as "depressed," or given any other label, we would know but little about the common denominators of the underlying dynamics. As Kubie (1956) has pointed out, the time is ripe for fresh attempts to identify the common principles of the "neurotic process." It is clear that studies in which patients are matched with experimental "controls" remain largely meaningless unless this Herculean research task can be accomplished.

Secondly, what transpired in the therapeutic sessions that led both therapists to evaluate the outcome as "successful"? Both therapists are highly experienced men in their field; both had a rationale for their respective procedures which, on the evidence of this study, differed quantitatively (*Depth-directedness* and *Initiative*) and perhaps qualitatively (*Type* and *Dynamic Focus*). Rogers, in keeping with his theory, consistently reflected the patient's feelings, whereas Wolberg, combining analytic principles with re-educative techniques, attempted to effect therapeutic changes in his patient mainly by means of interpretation and guidance. But even if the patients could be equated, it would not be possible to attribute differences in therapeutic outcome (whose measurement is another staggering problem) to variations in technique as long as relevant factors in the therapist's personality are left out of account. Certainly, Wolberg was more "directive" (by Rogerian standards). But both therapists conveyed an attitude of respect for their patients and implied their right to self-direction; both appeared to be warm, accepting, and noncritical; both encouraged the patient's expression of feeling; and both, by their therapeutic performance, seemed to engender a feeling of greater self-acceptance in their patients. These attitudes on the part of the therapist—he may have them in common with the mature person who can also be a good parent*—are as yet largely unexplored by objective research, but they may be the touchstone of all therapeutic success, regardless of the theory.† Given the "basic therapist personality" it may still be possible that some therapeutic techniques or combinations of techniques catalyze the therapeutic process, whereas others are relatively "inert"; contrariwise, no amount of training in technique may compensate for deficiences in the therapist's "basic attitudes." To approach these problems by research is difficult, but by no means impossible.

It seems that altogether too little attention has been paid by researchers to the therapist and his contribution to the therapeutic process. In keeping with this conviction, I have focused upon one facet, the therapist's techniques, and attempted to abstract common denominators from the therapist's verbal operations. The isolation and measurement of common denominators in varying therapeutic techniques appears to be a needed research task which must be expanded by research on the therapist's personality, from which technique seems to be inseparable.

The primary implications of this comparison relate to the comparative study of therapeutic techniques, which is considered one of the most important frontiers of research in psychotherapy. The

---

* I have in mind Fromm's (1947) "productive character."

† There is increasing evidence that the therapist's attitude may "cut across" theoretical orientations. For a comprehensive statement of the client-centered position, see Rogers' discussion (1950, pp. 19-64). On the other hand, Wolberg's transcript offers evidence that respect for the patient, his capacities, his right to self-direction, and his worth as a human being can be conveyed even when the therapist makes interpretations. Fiedler's studies (1950a, 1950b, 1951) suggest that "experts," irrespective of whether they subscribe to the analytic, Adlerian, or client-centered viewpoint, create highly similar "ideal therapeutic relationships," but, as Bordin (1955, pp. 115-116) has pointed out, Fiedler's findings cannot be regarded as evidence for or against the question of the importance to be attached to differences among theories.

isolation and measurement of common denominators in the techniques of therapists adhering to different schools should lead to more definitive studies of the therapist's personality, particularly of those attitudes which, wittingly or unwittingly, he brings to bear upon the therapeutic interaction.

PART IV

The Therapist and Research
in Psychotherapy

15

TOWARD AN ANALYSIS OF
THE THERAPIST'S CONTRIBUTION
TO THE TREATMENT PROCESS

In this chapter an attempt will be made to explore further the hypothesis that the therapist's contribution to the therapeutic process is an important determinant of its course and outcome. The therapist's personality has long been recognized as a potent factor in therapeutic action, but the mainstream of psychoanalytic thinking has tended to characterize this influence as nonanalytic, preliminary, subordinate, or even antagonistic to interpretive operations which traditionally have been considered the hallmark of psychoanalytic psychotherapy. In more recent years, partly as a result of the work of Sullivan, Horney, and other exponents of the "cultural" school, some of whose ideas were anticipated by Rank and Ferenczi, the totality of the therapist's personality and the reality aspects of the therapeutic situation have received increasing attention. In keeping with these newer formulations I shall elaborate on the notion that the therapist's personality, attitudes, and values are very much in the picture at all times, and that they color and influence the direction and quality of his therapeutic operations.

Earlier in this volume, guided by certain experimental findings, I was led to assert that the therapist's contribution is both a *personal* and a *technical* one. The personal contribution was seen as uppermost, although technical procedures might materially further the therapeutic endeavor; on the other hand, in the absence of a favorable emotional matrix, no amount of expert technique would be capable of shifting the psychodynamic balance in the direction of therapeutic growth. My purpose is not to add another argument or opinion but, hopefully, to stimulate systematic and controlled research which might cast further light on the issues. Such investigations may help to sort out the various influences impinging on the interpersonal process called psychotherapy and eventually permit the assignment of relative weights—statistical or practical—to the relevant variables. At present, there is no precise knowledge of what makes psychotherapy effective or ineffective with certain therapists or patients; furthermore, experimental designs which would produce such incontrovertible evidence probably lie far in the future.

In addition to theoretical considerations, certain practical implications are perhaps of greater and more immediate relevance. I am referring to the ubiquitous but insufficiently realized effects of the therapist's attitudes as they permeate and color his clinical observations and judgments as well as the structure and feeling tone of his communications to the patient. As a sensitive human being the therapist is a highly complex scientific instrument, whose operational characteristics are in great need of exploration and specification. It is a truism by now that the objectivity of information gathered about a patient in the social interaction of psychotherapy is at best relative, because it is partly filtered through and affected by the social interaction which itself is a function of the therapist's underlying personality structure. I have presented preliminary experimental evidence that the quality of the therapist's perceptions, evaluations, judgments, predictions, and interventions is subtly affected by his own unwitting emotional reactions.*

This, coupled with an accumulating body of observations, leads to an increased realization that in psychotherapy, perhaps more than in most areas of scientific investigation, the participant observer becomes subject to the principle of indeterminacy since it is impossible to make observations in the interpersonal field without altering that field in potentially important ways. To the extent that the therapist is clearly aware of the alterations he introduces, he may in some measure adjust and correct for his biases; to the extent that he is unaware of the ways in which he influences the interpersonal process, he is at the mercy of unknown forces and he may merely observe

---

* Stone addresses himself to this point as follows: "In no other field, save surgery, to which Freud frequently compared analysis, is the personal equation so important. It is up to us to know our capacities, intellectual and emotional, if we cannot always know one another so clearly in this respect. Again, special predilections, interests, emotional textures may profoundly influence prognosis, and thus—in a tangible way—the indications" (1954, p. 592).

and record events which his very operations have brought about. The adverse effects of gross distortions resulting from "blind spots" in the therapist were recognized early by Freud (1953a, p. 289), and the requirement for a didactic or training analysis was an ingenious step toward reducing therapist bias from this source. Considerably less attention has been accorded the more subtle variables influencing the therapist's mental processes, techniques, and theoretical predilections, such as temperamental, attitudinal, and cultural factors underlying his modes of perceiving the outside world.

This chapter has two interrelated foci: on the one hand, an attempt will be made to restate certain well-known ideas relative to the therapist's emotional contribution as a potentially crucial variable in the effectiveness of reconstructive psychotherapy; on the other hand, reference will be made to certain operational aspects of the therapist's attitudes and personality as they affect his thinking about and his interventions in the therapeutic process.

BACKGROUND

The dynamics of the therapist-patient relationship are the *sine qua non* of psychoanalytic psychotherapy, and all major contributions have taken as their point of departure Freud's revolutionary conceptions of transference and countertransference. The historical evolution of these concepts is clearly beyond the scope of this chapter. Moreover, major trends have been reviewed with admirable clarity by Orr (1954) and Thompson (1950); Wolstein's (1954) trenchant analysis represents another attempt to view current thinking in historical perspective. It is clear that under the impact of operationism in science certain modifications have occurred since the time of Freud. In general, there is an increasing tendency to deal with the dynamics of the therapeutic situation in process terms, to think of transference and countertransference as phenomena along continua instead of regarding them as either "positive" or "negative." Furthermore, greater emphasis is being placed on the here-and-now experience in the therapeutic relationship. J. Rioch's formulation may serve as an example of this trend:

> The therapeutic aim in this process is not to uncover childhood memories which will then lend themselves to analytic interpretation. . . . Psychoanalytic cure is not the amassing of data, either from childhood or from the study of the present situation. Nor does cure result from a repetition of the original injurious experience in the analytic relationship. What is curative in the process is that in tending to reconstruct with the analyst that atmosphere which

obtained in childhood, the patient actually achieves something new. He dis-
covers that part of himself which had to be repressed at the time of the
original experience. He can only do this in an interpersonal relationship
with the analyst, which is suitable to such rediscovery. . . . Thus, the transference phenomenon is used so that the patient will completely re-experience
the original frames of reference, and himself within those frames, in a *truly,
different relationship with the analyst,* to the end that he can discover the
invalidity of his conclusions about himself and others (Rioch, 1943, p. 151).
(Emphasis supplied.)

In this view the therapist is *more* than a sympathetic listener who
interprets the patient's transference distortions, nor are his interpretations regarded as the only or the most effective factor in
therapeutic success. He makes a significant emotional contribution,
which is positive if it succeeds in creating the kind of emotional
atmosphere in which the patient's re-experiencing can take place.
By the same token, "countertransference" reactions are interferences
with this positive emotional contribution, that is, instances in which
the therapist's own personality and unresolved emotional problems
impede the full realization of the therapeutic goal.

When Freud introduced the term "countertransference" in 1910,
he revised his earlier view of the analyst as an impersonal mirror by
recognizing that "blind spots" in the analyst's personality structure
might interfere with his usefulness as a therapist (1953a, p. 289).
The emphasis of Freud's original formulation and that of subsequent
elaborations has been on *interferences* with the analytic process
introduced by deficiencies, shortcomings, and characterological distortions of the analyst. This led to recommendations about dangers
to be avoided, attitudes to be discouraged, and so on. The objective
was to keep the analytic field clean and uncontaminated, by minimizing unwarranted intrusions and involvements of the analyst in
the patient's transference maneuvers. There is no doubt that this
did much to augment the objectivity of observations in the analytic
situation and to decrease the possibility of influencing the phenomena under scrutiny. It furthermore approximated a definition
of the analytic situation as a laboratory situation for studying and
modifying interpersonal processes—an achievement of the first magnitude, many of whose implications still remain to be realized.

It is instructive to note that in the earlier formulations countertransference was defined in relation to transferences of the patient,
with little regard for the healthy or realistic aspects of the therapist's
personality and his attitudes. Even today, as Orr (1954, p. 647)
points out, there is widespread disagreement as to what the term

comprises. For example, distinctions have been made between positive and negative countertransferences; some writers insist that all feelings of the therapist should be included; others differentiate between whole and partial responses to the patient; still others restrict the term to the therapist's unconscious reactions (Orr, 1954, pp. 646-657). Berman, writing in 1949, suggests a distinction between countertransference in the classic sense and the therapist's reasonable and appropriate emotional responses which he calls "attitudes" (Berman, 1949, p. 159). He also addresses himself to certain contradictions in Freud's writings, and reasons that, "The answer could simply be that the analyst is always both the cool, detached, surgeon-like operator on the patient's psychic tissues, and the warm, human, friendly, helpful physician" (Berman, 1949, p. 160). The rest of his paper is devoted to an enlightening discussion of the therapist as a human being whose attitudes are characterized by the term "dedication."

According to orthodox analytic principles, the therapist must not influence the transference situation by any means other than interpretations, which thus become the primary therapeutic agent. Furthermore, it has been denied that differences in the analytic atmosphere created by the analyst's personality exert an influence upon the transference situation and the therapeutic results. According to this view, "the" transference neurosis evolves more or less automatically provided the therapist does nothing to interfere with its development. The question of whether the therapist's personality does or does not influence the transference situation is, of course, an important problem for careful empirical research.

In his last formulation, Freud viewed the analyst as a new superego, who corrects errors in the patient's early upbringing.* Strachey,

---

* Freud states: "The new superego now has an opportunity for a sort of after-eduation of the neurotic; it can correct blunders for which his parental education was to blame." But then Freud immediately proceeds to sound a warning against the therapist's educational influence, disavowing that this is a legitimate part of his activity: "However much the analyst may be tempted to act as a teacher, model and ideal to other people and to make men in his own image, he should not forget that this is not his task in the analytic relationship, and indeed that he will be disloyal to this task if he allows himself to be led on by his inclinations. He will only be repeating one of the mistakes of the parents, when they crushed their child's independence, and he will only be replacing one kind of dependence by another. In all his attempts at improving and educating the patient the analyst must respect his individuality. The amount of influence which he may legitimately employ will be determined by the degree of inhibition in development present in the patient. Many neurotics have

writing in the same vein, observes:

> The principal effective alteration consists in a profound qualitative modification of the patient's superego, from which the other alterations follow in the main automatically. . . . This modification of the patient's superego is brought about in a series of innumerable small steps by the agency of mutative interpretations, which are effected by the analyst in virtue of his position as object of the patient's id impulses and as auxiliary superego. The dosed introjection of good objects is regarded as one of the most important factors in the therapeutic process (Strachey, 1934, p. 159).

Bibring recognizes that the therapist makes a positive contribution through his own personality, but considers this to be essentially "non-analytical":

> . . . the therapeutic changes which take place in the superego are effected by purely analytical means, i.e., by demonstrating contradictions in structure and development and by making an elucidation of them possible. . . . In my opinion the analyst's attitude, and the analytical atmosphere which he creates are fundamentally a reality-correction which adjusts the patient's anxieties about loss of love and punishment, the origin of which lies in childhood. Even if these anxieties later undergo analytical resolution I still believe that the patient's relationship to the analyst from which a sense of security emanates is not only a pre-condition of the procedure but also effects an immediate (apart from an analytical) consolidation of his sense of security

remained so infantile that in analysis too they can only by treated as children" (Freud, 1949, p. 67).

There seem to be several contradictions in this passage, which apparently flow from these assumptions: (1) Analysis and "after-education" are separate and distinct processes: analysis is the essence of therapy; after-education is at best a tolerable by-product. (2) The analyst is not or should not be a model or a teacher because such people make men in their own image, crush the child's independence and fail to respect his individuality. None of these things are *ipso facto* true of education in the best or in the literal sense of the word. Rather, the analyst and educator appear to have much in common, a fact which Freud recognized when in a different context he says: "psychoanalytic treatment is a kind of re-education" (Freud, 1935, p. 392).

Wolstein, too, draws a sharp line between "analysis" and "re-education." The danger of the latter is said to be that the therapist by making suggestions may exploit his position of authority "as a magical source of truth." "The aim of constructive analysis is definitely not re-education. The goal is to find, by inquiring into transference distortions, what has blocked the patient's way to whatever re-educational sources he wishes in order to pursue his goals" (Wolstein, 1954, p. 78).

The point of view developed here is that re-education and analysis are not antithetical and that both are integral aspects of the therapist's functions. The therapist really has no choice in the matter: either he will be a good model of reality or he will be a poor one, but in either event he will be more than the analytic operator (see later). This appears to be true even though the patient's transference reactions may emerge relatively independently of the therapist's personality.

which he has not successfully acquired or consolidated in childhood. Such an immediate consolidation—which, in itself, lies outside the field of analytic therapy—is, of course, only of permanent value if it goes along with the coordinated operation of analytic treatment (Bibring, 1937, pp. 182-183).*

One may wonder whether the atmosphere created by the therapist in which a "reality-correction" takes place is in fact separate and distinct from the (interpretive) essence of analytic treatment. It may be that both are integral parts of analytic psychotherapy and that they operate conjointly as therapeutic factors. To tease out their relative contribution is a research task of the first magnitude, and one which may approach a solution of the question of what is effective in psychotherapy.

THE EMOTIONAL CONTEXT OF THE THERAPY SITUATION AND THE THERAPIST AS REALITY MODEL

It is a truism that in order to be effective psychotherapy must be an emotional experience; likewise, intellectual understanding per se does not produce therapeutic change although it frequently is a byproduct or an accompaniment of emotional insight. This emotional experience, to use Alexander's term, must be a corrective one. The therapist's foremost task is to create an appropriate context for this emotional experience, and the success of therapy may depend largely on the achievement of this aim. Consequently, his activity (including his attitudes and communications) must be placed in its service. This appears to be one of the cardinal reasons for strict adherence to the tenet that no communication between therapist and patient is inconsequential, because extraneous communications or interventions which are unrelated to the therapeutic objective potentially complicate and distort the field of interaction and becloud the therapeutic context. What makes the therapist's task so enor-

* In a more recent article Bibring (1954) delineates five groups of basic therapeutic techniques: (a) suggestive; (b) abreactive; (c) manipulative; (d) clarifying; and (e) interpretive, and makes an important distinction—difficult though it may be to define it operationally—between "technical" and "curative" applications of these principles. He asserts that in psychoanalysis proper all therapeutic principles are employed; however, "insight through interpretation is the principal agent and all others are—theoretically and practically—subordinate to it" (Bibring, 1954, p. 762). He also notes a contemporary shift in emphasis from insight through interpretation to "experiential manipulation," exemplified in the approach of Alexander and French. The formulations advanced in this paper would appear to correspond to Bibring's conception of "influence through experience."

mously difficult is the patient's tenacious unconscious opposition to unlearning inappropriate patterns and learning new, less conflictual ones. The fundamental problem for therapeutic technique is the search for optimal procedures to effect lasting modifications of the patient's personality structure. The patient must be shown, clearly and unequivocally, *what* he has to change and *how* he can change it. Opinions differ whether he also has to be presented with substitute solutions, or whether the spontaneous growth or reparative processes, aided by the patient's conscious strivings, can take over.*

In interpersonal relationships all of us operate on more or less unconscious assumptions or hypotheses about the other person, particularly with regard to the question of whether he represents a threat to our security. Realistically, the other may be a threat to our security or he may not; however, a serious problem arises when, as a result of unfortunate life experience, we are unable to make this discrimination. We are then treating the other person as though he were a representation of our past, and our reactions to him will be determined by the kinds of assumptions or hypotheses we were forced to adopt at that time rather than by the reality of the present situation. It seems to make little difference whether such distortions are called transference or parataxis; the process remains the same.

It is the therapist's job to demonstrate to the patient how he distorts current situations in terms of his past, and how such distor-

---

* Dr. Benjamin Wolstein (personal communication) makes the following cogent observations:

"Perhaps we have to distinguish between patients for whom social adjustment or adequate functioning is a worthwhile task, since they are so disturbed and maladjusted; and patients who not only seek but require the goal of personality change, who are not able to accept Freud's early goal of "transforming neurotic misery into ordinary unhappiness." Many of the grey, bored, 'dead' people who now seek analysis do so just because they are no longer satisfied with 'ordinary unhappiness.'

"Thus the effect of analysis may appear to be 'corrective'; the aim of analysis, however, must now be taken as reconstructive, as a basic change in personality structure. And it would follow, then, that if analysis, as distinct from the nondirective therapies, has something to offer patients, we have to go beyond social adjustment as this is ordinarily understood; and we have to see the analytic relationship not as nonjudgmental, accepting, etc., but as a highly organized and concentrated effort to find out what is wrong. I think it inevitable that such be the case in view of the fact that undertaking an analysis—the decision by the patient—already contains a firm value judgment. . . . It is not the resultant performance—its appropriateness or inappropiateness—or the profession—its goodness or rightness—which tell the tale; rather, it is the actual living concern with being human which is not always evident in performance or profession. Except in cases of severe social maladjustment, I do not see the value of equating goal-oriented functioning with human-oriented living."

tions tend to complicate his interpersonal relations with his adult
contemporaries. The stereotypy and rigidity of the patient's emotional reactions and behavior patterns must be analyzed and understood. This may come about most effectively if the patient's current
experience with the therapist contrasts the inappropriateness and
the futility of his past performances. The patient must be enabled
to make meaningful comparisons between the present and the past,
to the end of opening to his own questions his assumptions or
hypotheses about other people and their reactions to him. In this
framework the totality of the patient's defenses emerge and become
subject to analysis. The point is that the patient's emotional
experience (interaction) with the therapist must be sufficiently
different from previous interpersonal experience to highlight the
patient's own contribution; yet, paradoxically, the emotional
context must have common elements with the past to form a bridge.
The emotional context created by the therapist *is* contemporary
reality and it provides the backdrop against which the patient's
distortions eventually stand out in bold relief. Thus, in general, it
may be hypothesized: the sharper the experiential contrast, the
greater the likelihood of constructive personality change.

How does the therapeutic situation provide a new emotional context? The essential ingredients have often been described; they are
summed up in Fromm-Reichmann's key phrase: the therapist listens
(Fromm-Reichmann, 1950, p. 7). The therapist bends all his ener-
gies upon the task of understanding the patient's communications,
particularly their emotional implications and undercurrents. His
attitude is respectful, accepting, nonvaluative, noncondemning, non-
criticizing, and thus invariably in contrast to the patient's experiences
with significant adults in his early life. The therapist, unlike
significant people in the patient's past and present life, minimizes
his own emotions, feelings, and needs and maximizes the patient's.
Usually for the first time in his life, the patient has the unique
experience of hearing himself, of experiencing himself. The importance of the therapist's attitude, as communicated nonverbally or by
minimal verbal cue, can hardly be overestimated. The magnitude of
the divergence between present and past, as experienced by the
patient, may become a sensitive indicator of the degree of damage or
injury to his self-esteem, and thus of the seriousness of his disturbance. The message to the patient is that of simple acceptance and
worthwhileness as a person and as a human being, regardless of his
symptoms and personality characteristics about which the patient

and/or others (including the therapist) may have misgivings or regrets. In this way the therapist helps the patient toward greater self-acceptance and self-esteem. ("If the therapist is tolerant and noncondemning, perhaps I can accept myself better, too.")

The therapist's basic acceptance provides a powerful impetus for therapeutic movement because of its security-giving aspects. In a profound sense, the patient becomes attached and forms a meaningful interpersonal relationship to the therapist, not on the basis of his irrational and unreasonable expectations but on the basis of the *reality of the situation.** It is an experience with a human being who is "different," who can be trusted, irrespective of the content of the patient's disturbing feelings or impulses. The character of this basic relationship must be maintained throughout therapy, through each session, through each minute; it must never be shaken. In consequence, the only serious danger to the therapeutic relationship could come from an actual breach of the unspoken contract, or from real or unreal, consciously or unconsciously determined misunderstandings of the therapist's veracity, honesty, or respect. If the patient can feel assured deep within himself of the reality of the relationship, errors in technique, including premature or erroneous interpretations, should be less of a threat to the therapeutic enterprise.

The security-giving aspects of the therapist's attitude must be experienced and felt by the patient; they cannot be communicated effectively by verbal means, reassurances, and effusiveness of warmth, joviality, etc. This does not mean that the therapist's verbal communications, questions, and comments are unsuited to reflect his basic attitude of respect; the opposite is true; but essentially the patient must work through to the realization that this attitude exists, that it is genuine, sincere, and reliable.

---

* When Freud spoke of transference as "the best instrument" of cure, he addressed himself exclusively to the *irrational* elements in the patient-therapist relationship. He did not recognize that apart from transference feelings the patient may have reality-based feelings about the therapist, and that these may play a part in the curative effort. To the last, Freud viewed the patient's positive transference, i.e., his infantile, irrational, and distorted investments in the therapist as the true motive force for the patient's collaboration and the strongest factor operating in the therapist's favor (Freud, 1949, p. 66; p. 77).

In contrast, Anna Freud states: ". . . so far as the patient has a healthy personality, his real relationship to the analyst is never wholly submerged. With due respect to the necessary strictest handling and interpretation of the transference, I feel still that we should leave room somewhere for the realization that analyst and patient are also two real people, of equal adult status, in a real personal relationship to each other" (Anna Freud, 1954).

The therapist thus comes to serve as a *new model of reality*. He does this by the time-proven method of setting an example, which enables the patient to compare his approach to his feelings and attitudes with that of the therapist and note the differences. Gradually the patient perceives that feelings and actions are not identical, that he condemns himself equally for both, and that the critical and punitive attitudes which he had attributed to others are really his own. At the same time the therapist does not take sides with the patient against people in the latter's environment; he implies that understanding is more important than blame; that the past is no longer subject to change; that the patient has within himself the capacity to grow, to place a more positive evaluation on himself, to exercise a choice, and so on. The therapist attempts to be an objective and dispassionate observer and encourages the development of similar attitudes in the patient, who thus gains greater distance from himself (the "splitting of the ego" in analytic terminology).

As a new model of reality the therapist represents reality in its constructive aspects. This means, among other things, that the therapist treats the patient as an adult capable of making his own decisions who must assume and discharge adult responsibilities. While the therapist respects the patient he does not pamper him. Nor is acceptance of the patient's feelings tantamount to approval or approbation; feelings are neither "good" nor "bad"—they are simply data whose significance in the patient's living is to be studied and understood. Similarly, recognizing and accepting the patient's dependency needs does not mean that the therapist aids and abets them or that he participates in their perpetuation. This applies with equal force to the patient's need to please, to manipulate, or to gain attention. Thus the therapist sets realistic limits.* As the patient

---

* This function of the therapist's role is often misunderstood and mismanaged. In Rogers' (1957) recent formulation, for example, the requirement of "unconditional positive regard" for the patient, of prizing him, is extolled as a prerequisite for therapeutic movement. The emphasis, however, of entering completely the patient's phenomenologic field, which operationally means taking his side, often *against* the outside world, neglects the important therapeutic need for realism. The patient must be enabled to see himself in perspective; he must experience his feelings and especially his irrational needs and expectations in relation to a realistic model of reality, not an all-loving and all-giving mother image which has no existence outside the therapy room. The therapeutic situation is unique in many ways; but the relationship to the therapist must become the prototype and model of human relationships. Hence, Sullivan's dictum that to the extent that the patient is able to untangle the complications in his relationship with the therapist he is able to have less complicated relations with people in the outside world.

comes to experience the full intensity of his unreasonable demands on the therapist who accepts them but does not satisfy them, which is really the unconscious expectation prompting their emergence, the patient reacts with profound disappointment, resentment and rage. But, as he gains a more realistic appreciation of the therapist's unwavering position as a reality model, he is gradually able to relinquish some of his intense demands and to channel others in more productive, and in the long run more satisfying, ways.

While the patient must experience the therapist's trust, maturity, and integrity, the therapist must be *sparing* in verbally communicating his interest, understanding, and respect, in accordance with the rationale that the patient must work out his own solutions. He gains strength through his own efforts, and his achievements will be more thorough and lasting if he feels that they are his own. A parent who promptly rushes to the aid of the child whenever he is trying to master a problem is not doing the child a service because the child comes to feel—if this parental attitude is a persistent one—that solutions to life's problems will always be presented on a silver platter. By analogy, the patient must be permitted to work on his problems at his own speed without interference or pushing from the therapist. This speed may at times appear excruciatingly slow to the participant observer, and his temptation to accelerate it may be strong. If he succumbs to the temptation, he may seemingly speed up the therapeutic process but in actuality he may be instrumental in fostering the patient's dependent needs instead of analyzing them. Contrariwise, if he has sufficient patience and maturity, he helps the patient work through to a sense of unsuspected strength and to a realization that he can endure, survive, and integrate painful feelings. In this way, too, the therapist teaches by example that achievements are commensurate with the expended effort; besides, he fosters self-confidence, self-reliance and independence.

The therapist's attitude conveys his unfaltering willingness to help the patient in constructive efforts to master his problems; yet, he does not solve them for him, nor does he do the work of therapy. While the therapist is giving, he is not all-giving. Rather, in contrast to the patient's early life experience, he teaches the patient that he too can give, that his gifts can be worthwhile, and that others do not necessarily or invariably reject the giver. The patient's giving is fostered through the injunction to communicate all of his thoughts, fantasies, feelings, and wishes. By withholding them he tends to repeat infantile patterns which, as Freud has so clearly elaborated, may have originated in early interpersonal experiences, e.g., attitudes

surrounding toilet training. The pleasure of withholding is frequently a conflictual one, reflecting the patient's attitude toward his
mother: "I am punishing or fighting you by holding on to my
thoughts, feelings, and feces. In this way, I gain power over you.
I give you nothing." It is evident that a therapist who indiscrimi-
nately showers the patient with the gifts of human kindness does not
succeed in evoking the patient's retentive and negativistic attitudes,
thus depriving himself and his patient of the opportunity of understanding them in all their ramifications.

From everything that has been said, it is clear that therapy, like
any educational process, requires long periods of time. The extent
to which the growth process may be accelerated by interpretations
and other techniques is a major question for research in this area.
The attitudes which have been mentioned may rank among the most
important catalysts available.

EMOTIONAL CONTEXT, THERAPIST'S ATTITUDES, AND COUNTERTRANSFERENCES

In the foregoing an attempt has been made to delineate some of
the important aspects of the emotional context created by the therapist's attitude. This matrix is hypothesized to be the essence of the
therapist's positive contribution and the *sine qua non* for basic
psychotherapeutic change. While here-and-now experiences with the
therapist have been stressed, no attempt has been made to deal
systematically with etiologic factors or the technical operations of
psychotherapy, including the analysis of transference distortions; *nor
should anything in this chapter be construed as minimizing the
importance or the potential effects of analytic interpretations.*

The phenomena usually classed under the heading of countertransference appear to be relatively gross deviations of the therapist from
his role as an objective participant observer and creator of a new
reality model. Perhaps these deviations are viewed more fruitfully
not as a class of phenomena by themselves but as extremes of a continuum or of continua underlying the emotional context of therapy.*
When the therapist responds to the patient's transference behavior in

* Jackson (1956), in a provocative paper suggesting the need for a broader definition
of countertransference, proposes the term palintropic processes to describe "all those
processes which make up the sum total of happenings between two people" (Jackson,
1956, p. 236).

terms of the patient's distorted expectations rather than in terms of a new reality model, he has abdicated his therapeutic role and minimized his usefulness to the patient. The therapist's distortions may be instigated by and represent a response to the patient's transference behavior; frequently, perhaps, this is the case. On the other hand, they may be distortions which the therapist would exhibit relatively independently of the patient's distortions. Furthermore, it appears that most deficiencies in the therapeutic emotional context created by the therapist are not the gross phenomena which have traditionally been grouped under the heading of countertransference but rather more subtle shortcomings in the therapist's contribution. The experimental evidence supports the contention that the therapist's unconscious attitudes may subtly color his "technical" thinking about a case, his diagnostic formulations, prognostic estimates, therapeutic plans, goals, and ultimately the character of his communications or the neurotic process itself. Thus, conscious or unconscious rejecting attitudes on the part of the therapist may find their way into his therapeutic interventions, and have a detrimental effect on the therapeutic enterprise.* These attitudinal distortions may be particularly insidious if the therapist is firmly convinced of the "objectivity" of his thinking when actually he is projecting feelings and attitudes onto the patient which have little relation to the clinical material under consideration. Such projections may be exemplified as follows:

The therapist may feel that he "ought" to be stricter with a patient who is likely to make great demands on him. Similarly, he may feel that he should be more active with such a patient, and discourage the free expression of feelings. He may feel that the prognosis is

---

* Fromm-Reichmann gives the following examples: "The emanation of the psychiatrist's general system of ethical values is not the only example of the possibility of inadvertent communication of his viewpoints and its influence on the course of treatment. The emanation of the psychiatrist's evaluation of and judgment about the symptomatology of his patients may turn out to be of equally great importance. One of the most impressive examples illustrating this fact presents itself in the history of the psychiatric evaluation of the symptom of stool-smearing. In the old days, stool-smearing was considered to be a symptom of grave prognostic significance in any psychiatric patient. Since psychiatrists have learned to approach this symptom in the same spirit of investigating its psychopathology and its dynamics as they approach any other symptom or mode of expression, it has lost its threatening aspects. In other words, stool-smearing patients of previous periods in psychiatric development were sometimes destined to deteriorate and become incurable. This was not because of the inherent gravity of the symptom but because of the atmosphere of awe, disgust, and gruesomeness which it evoked in their moralistic, pedagogically minded psychiatrists and which they unwittingly conveyed to the patients" (Fromm-Reichmann, 1950, p. 36).

poor, which may provide a "justification" for a lack of interest on his part and be concomitant with his feeling that the patient is not worth helping, that the great expenditure of energy and interest which is required for creating a favorable emotional context for psychotherapy is a "waste of time," and so on. He may feel inclined to recommend brief psychotherapy instead of more intensive treatment, or rationalize that the patient is not really in need of psychotherapy. He may consider it "appropriate" to manipulate the transference relationship by making recommendations to the patient on how to lead his life. He may counsel the avoidance of certain topics in therapy, focus on others, and in general take a more active part in changing the patient than he normally would if his emotional reactions were less aroused. A consciously felt disinclination to treat such a patient, resulting in a referral elsewhere, would appear to reflect an honest solution of the impasse.

Again, the therapist's choice of words in diagnosing and describing the patient's emotional dynamics may reflect a subtle (moral) value judgment about the patient. A diagnostic "label" assigned to a patient may carry with it a trace of disapproval which may have a pervasive influence on succeeding therapeutic interactions; such terms as "psychopathic," "paranoid," "character disorder," may be more revealing of the therapist's attitude than of the patient to whom they are assigned.

How do the therapist's attitudes express themselves in his communications to a patient, even in an initial interview? In the investigation reported in the preceding chapters, the results suggested a distinction between therapists who seemed to function in the role of a professional helper and those who were deficient in creating a potentially constructive emotional context for psychotherapy:

The first group of therapists tended to recognize the existence of an emotional problem and communicated such understanding to the patient somewhere in the interview. They recognized with the patient that at least he had overcome his resistance to change by seeking help, that there was a relationship between his physical symptoms and his emotional conflicts which could be elucidated in psychotherapy, and that the resulting clarification might lead to constructive personality change. They attempted to alleviate the patient's discomfort in the interview by putting him at ease and allaying some of his anxiety, by instilling some hope for the future, and by refraining from threatening his self-esteem. They felt the need to communicate to the patient something about treatment plans, on the assumption that the patient had a right to expect such a statement from the interviewer as an expert. They gave evidence of listening to the patient, of being respectful, nonderogatory, noncritical, and nonjudgmental in a moral sense. Their questioning was designed to facilitate the patient's self-exploration rather than to expound their own views or hypotheses based on fragmentary data.

Therapists of the second group either failed to make a positive contribution or gave evidence of reacting to the patient's communications in ways which appeared antithetical to the therapist's role. Most common seemed to be reactions in which the therapist responded to the patient's anger and demanding attitudes with anger on his part, which in turn led to accusations, criticisms, or direct interpretive attacks on the patient's defenses. Oftentimes the therapist's negative attitudes toward the patient expressed themselves in relatively indirect ways which, in the experimental situation under discussion, were highlighted because of their contrast to the performance of other therapists. Such attitudes seemed to be exemplified by coldness, distance, extreme impersonality, and by treating the patient as a "specimen." Needless to say, these distinctions are schematic and probably overdrawn; nor can one be sure of what may be desirable, "therapeutic," or appropriate in a given set of circumstances; however, it is doubtful whether a patient who comes to perceive the interviewer as a cross-examiner whose sole purpose appears to consist in exposing the patient's "weaknesses" is likely to develop an attitude leading to the eventual relinquishment of defenses, if indeed he remains in therapy.

Deficiencies in empathic understanding* may reflect not only "blind spots" in the therapist's personality but they may be intertwined with attitudes fostered by the culture of which the therapist as well as the patient are a part. Whereas the culture of nineteenth century Vienna dictated the suppression and repression of sexual matters, contemporary American culture is more intolerant of overtly expressed hostility, arrogance, antagonism, and signs that an adult male, for instance, is dependent, "immature," passive, weak, and helpless. Certainly, the therapeutic task is contravened if the therapist reacts to these manifestations in the patient with anger and rejection instead of bringing them into the open where they can be understood in terms of the patient's emotional dynamics.

Clearly, intensive research effort must be applied to the scrutiny

---

* The concept "empathy" has numerous and often fuzzy meanings. The operational criteria I used in judging its presence or absence have been spelled out previously (see ch. 4).

of the therapist's attitudes, whether determined by the culture or his own personality. What the therapist perceives as ongoing processes between himself and the patient, the manner in which he evaluates his perceptions, and the therapeutic actions he takes as a consequence—these are to an important degree a function of his own personality and his culture which partly determine not only what shall be "objective" in the outside world but dictate the course of action and the fate of the therapeutic interaction.

THE FUNCTION OF INTERPRETATIONS

What function do verbal communications serve in the therapeutic interaction? Proceeding from the hypothesis that the essence of the psychotherapeutic process is the interaction within the emotional context created by the two participants, it follows that verbal communications must be placed in the service of this interaction and parallel it. Verbal communications are therapeutic to the extent that they coincide with the interaction of emotional contexts. The patient is encouraged to put his feelings into words, an assignment which poses considerable difficulties for any person who has developed great skills in keeping words and feelings apart. The therapist, in turn, attempts to understand the patient's emotional context, which is typically at variance with his verbal communications. When the therapist, with the help of a variety of clues (verbal and behavioral), succeeds in identifying an emotional, attitudinal or behavioral sequence which is inappropriate to or incongruous with the realities of the situation as the therapist sees it, he may attempt to put this discrepancy into words. An interpretation, then, is an attempt to describe by means of verbal symbols an emotional reaction or a behavior pattern exhibited by the patient in relation to the therapist, of whose interpersonal or dynamic significance the patient is unaware or insufficiently aware. The meaning and significance of such patterns is recognized by the therapist because his training and experience have alerted him to their occurrence, and secondly because he perceives them as incongruous responses to what he knows is going on in the therapeutic situation. The interpretation is properly timed and potentially successful if the patient is emotionally ready to recognize with the therapist the inappropriateness of his performance. Interpretations may relate to other interpersonal situations of the patient, but they are most dramatic and probably most effective if they refer to the here-and-now of the therapeutic situation. Freud observed that "the patient never forgets again what he has experienced in the form of transference" (Freud, 1949, p. 70). This learning refers to the emotional experience and only secondarily to its verbal counterpart. Verbal symbols aid and promote the process of achieving emotional understanding and insight, but they cannot take the place of the emotional experiences. On the other hand, verbal symbols play an important part in binding the emotional experience to the patient's cognitive structure: mastery is achieved over emotional experiences if they can be put into words and adequately described.

Interpretations are considered particularly effective if they refer to here-and-now experiences in the patient-therapist relationship; contrariwise, intellectual reconstructions of the past which are not accompanied by appropriate affect are said to remain sterile. Typically, the patient's defenses pertain to emotional contexts of the past which made the emergence of defenses inevitable. The task of therapy is to recreate the emotional conflict of the past in the present in order to open the door for new solutions. The patient can only be made to undergo these painful emotional experiences again if there is sufficient security in the present situation to render a better solution more probable. This security in the present, which was absent or misperceived in the past, is provided by the therapist in his role as a new model of reality.

GENUINENESS OF THERAPIST'S ATTITUDE

A question arises concerning the genuineness of the therapist's attitude, his spontaneity, and freedom of self-expression. The argument runs something like this. If the therapist is "himself," spontaneous, natural, relaxed, and unself-conscious—qualities stressed by numerous writers—he is not in a favorable position to be an objective and dispassionate observer. Contrariwise, if he attempts to be a "scientist," by controlling his verbal communications, by appraising and anticipating their possible effects, he interferes with his spontaneity as a therapist and thereby damages the free give-and-take of the interaction. It has also been asserted that the ideal therapeutic attitude of acceptance, permissiveness, noncriticalness, and imperturbable equanimity is unattainable, and that the therapist who purports to carry it out is dissimulating and is insincere and dishonest with himself.

It is certainly true that society has erected specific limits for the therapist's behavior which cannot be transcended even if it were therapeutically desirable. Secondly, the goal of scrutinizing the interpersonal relationship between therapist and patient demands that the field be kept as "clean" as possible in order to evaluate the respective contributions of patient and therapist. If the therapist fails to impose controls over himself and his communications, this goal is almost impossible to achieve. This is indeed a basic scientific requirement: not to let the process of observation interfere with the phenomena under scrutiny. Finally, certain aspects of the therapist's role are by definition "artificial"; so is the essence of the therapeutic situation as a laboratory situation for studying the patient's personality in interaction with another human being.

I believe that the imposition of procedural rules does not preclude a genuine interest on the therapist's part to help and to understand. The value of the emotional experience is not lessened by the fact that the patient pays for the therapist's time and thus for his interest and effort. The limitations of reality notwithstanding, the therapist can be genuinely interested in his task of studying and understanding interpersonal processes, he can respect the patient as a person, without compulsion to "love" him, to side with him, or to spoil him. The patient must learn to get along with minimum essentials from other people, and this to a very important extent is part and parcel of the therapeutic experience. He may have had an excess of pampering in his childhood, or he may have suffered from sore neglect, but he has never had the experience of being accepted simply as a human being.* This experience the therapist can and must provide. The patient soon realizes that the therapist has a life of his own, that he has family and friends, and so on, but these facets enter as little as possible into the interaction. The therapist does not become "artificial" by keeping his private life out of the picture, any more than an executive at a conference is "artificial" if he devotes himself undividedly to the task at hand without talking about the weather or his hobbies.† In time, the patient comes to appreciate the therapist's unwavering attention during the therapeutic hour to the understanding of the patient's interpersonal processes. Just as his parents may have never taken him seriously, so he has never taken

---

* I am not referring here to the superficial "hail-fellow-well-met 'acceptance,'" typically extended in our culture to most strangers.

† A flaw in this analogy is that the executive, unlike the therapist, arouses no expectations of an intimate personal relationship, i.e., the ambiguity of the therapeutic situation is lacking (see Bordin, 1955).

himself seriously. The therapeutic session is perhaps the first situation in which someone takes him seriously, which in turn permits him to assume a similar attitude toward himself. The therapist who has mastered the therapeutic role does not feel constricted by it, and in time the patient will accept the reality of the situation and use it to advantage.

TOWARD AN OPERATIONAL ANALYSIS OF THE THERAPIST'S ATTITUDE

In concluding this admittedly sketchy analysis, an attempt will be made to enumerate major determinants of the therapist's attitude. If one were to take a cross-section of the therapist's behavior at a given point in therapy, such an analysis would help to answer the question as to antecedent variables and their relative influences, and aid in providing more precise knowledge about therapeutic principles. The crux is to tease out, from the total fabric of the interaction, particularly the therapist's operations, those variables which are "active ingredients" in the therapeutic process and to assay their relative importance.

It appears that the therapist's attitude toward a patient consists at least of the following components, which, to complicate matters, undoubtedly interact:

(a) The therapist's customary or characterological attitudes, by which are meant organized and perduring personality patterns, ways in which he relates to people "in general." Thus, he may be outgoing, reserved, spontaneous, stilted, and so on. The most important feature of these attitudes is that they are largely beyond conscious manipulation. For example, a therapist may have a life history of early rejection by significant adults; he may have come to understand the implications of these vicissitudes through his personal analysis and have developed a considerable degree of self-awareness; however, he will continue to meet strangers with a certain reserve even though he consciously knows that they are less "dangerous" than the significant adults of his past. These basic attitudes shade imperceptibly into temperament, from which they may at times be indistinguishable.

(b) A second component relates to the personality structure of the patient with whom he is interacting. The therapist may react warmly toward schizoid patients, coldly toward paranoid ones, and so forth. These patterns may reflect attitudes which he holds toward himself or significant people in his early life, or which significant people in his early life held toward him. Depending on the therapist's degree of self-knowledge and self-awareness, these attitudes may play an important part in coloring his clinical evaluations of, and his willingness and ability to do therapy with, certain patients.

(c) The patient's station in life, his socioeconomic status, intellect, sex, age, color, and so forth, may evoke attitudes in the therapist which are conditioned by the culture of which both are a part. The degree to which these attitudes influence or distort the therapist's perceptions is again a function of his self-knowledge. Cultural values may also partly determine the meaning and "clinical significance" which the therapist will attach to attitudes and behaviors of the patient, such as anger, hostility, dependency, weakness, "immaturity," and so on.*

(d) Fourthly, a set of conscious or preconscious attitudes pertain to the therapist's conceptions of therapy, therapeutic goals, and techniques; they also comprise the therapist's understanding of his role in the therapeutic undertaking, which partly dictates the attitude he adopts toward a given patient. He may accept the notion of the therapist as an "objective mirror" and structure his behavior accordingly; or, he may feel that the therapist should be relatively spontaneous, "giving," warm, and so on, and pattern his behavior vis-a-vis the patient in accordance with this conception. Most of these "conscious" attitudes may be ego-syntonic and thus interact with the unconsciously determined attitudes mentioned before. To some extent, then, the therapist's idea of the "optimum" attitude represents a rationalization, in that he purports to behave in the way he *must* behave or in the manner in which he feels most comfortable. There is reason to believe that the therapist's choice of theory and technique is determined, to some extent, at least, by these factors, which have never been systematically explored.

(e) It may be necessary to differentiate further the therapist's reaction to what he perceives to be the patient's needs at the moment and on a long-range basis. With regard to the latter, the therapist's attitude may reflect his consciously formulated therapeutic goals, which in turn may be based on his therapeutic philosophy and

---

* Cholden (1956), addressing himself to the psychotherapy of schizophrenics, observes that "the therapist is reacting to both the real and the imagined person seen before him. The patient's response, too, results from the real and imagined person he perceives. The unreal aspect of the relationship, as determined by past attitudes on the part of both, co-determines the relationship" (Cholden, 1956, p. 240). Cholden, too, believes that in the final essence, the attitude of the therapist is the major treatment tool.

theory; with regard to the former—the patient's momentary needs —theoretical considerations are perhaps usually present, but so are unconscious factors which may produce serious distortions in the therapist's perceptions, evaluations, and attitude, and determine the character of his intervention, not excluding silence. Thus, counter-transference reactions would be operations in which the therapist relinquishes his defined therapeutic role in order to pursue the covert gratification of his own needs instead of adhering to his avowed therapeutic objectives.

(f) Additional fluctuations in the therapist's attitude are of course a function of day-to-day variations and hence due to "chance," which merely means that it is difficult to bring them under scientific control.

How can an operational analysis of the therapist's attitudes be carried out? Methodologically, one can rely on the therapist's conscious report, the patient's report, and/or observations by external observers. Or, one can approach the problem indirectly, by studying the therapist's perceptions, evaluations, and clinical judgments, and determining their relationships to his attitudes, however these may be measured. In its barest essentials, the therapist's attitude toward a patient is either positive or negative, approaching or withdrawing, adient or abient. This is not to minimize the enormous subtlety and complexity of interaction patterns which undergo many shifts throughout any therapeutic hour. But, as research efforts succeed in analyzing this composite and mapping out meaningful relationships to other variables, there should result increased understanding, improved control, and greater predictability of the therapeutic process.

In making these recommendations, I am fully aware of a rather painful disparity between avowed aims and the methodologies currently at our command. Unfortunately, I have no dazzling solutions to offer. I am deeply convinced, however, that research techniques must be found to deal more meaningfully with the configurational aspects of the therapeutic situation. By this, I mean that atomistic approaches (e.g., those focusing on single patient or therapist communications or studies of the kind described in this volume) may extend the frontiers of knowledge, but I am afraid there are definite limits. Eventually, better ways must be found to deal objectively with the broad sweep of the clinician's mental processes, particularly his ability to detect unconscious dynamic patterns in the patient's free associations and to construct on their basis a coherent picture of the "problem," a conceptual "map" which guides the therapeutic operations and, hopefully, leads to therapeutic change.

16

SOME COMMENTS
ON THE FUTURE OF RESEARCH
IN PSYCHOTHERAPY

You know that we have never been proud of the fullness and finality of our knowledge and our capacity; as at the beginning, we are ready now to admit the incompleteness of our understanding, to learn new things and to alter our methods in any way that yields better results.

SIGMUND FREUD (1919)
(Collected Papers, Vol. II, p. 392.)

There is a growing consensus today which says that the future of psychotherapy is that of a scientific discipline. In recent years this point of view has been advanced by numerous writers, who add that any other course would tend to relegate psychotherapy to a doctrine, a faith, or a gospel.* While Freud often spoke of psychoanalysis as a "movement" and a "cause," he never conceived of it as anything but a science. Moreover, he feared greatly that institutionalization would lead to stagnation and the emergence of a cult rather than to scientific development. This apprehension, it must be conceded, has not been altogether groundless, but fortunately there is a counter-trend; and it is this countertrend with which many of the foremost thinkers in the area ally themselves. I am referring to the increasing emphasis on controlled research and experimentation, that is, the application of the scientific method to furthering our understanding of the psychotherapeutic process. During the past fifteen years the quantity as well as the quality of research contributions has grown, and there is every reason to believe that the coming decades will see an intensification of this effort. Has research exerted a demonstrable influence on the theory and practice of psychotherapy? In my

---

* See, for example, Kardiner, 1958, p. 125; Kubie, 1956.

opinion, the influence has been slight, and I propose to examine some of the reasons for this seemingly pessimistic conclusion. I am also prompted by the belief that, somehow, we should be able to do better.

First, it will be necessary to clarify what "research contribution" is intended to mean in this context. The term "research" is broad indeed and connotes very different things to different people. To American psychologists and social scientists schooled in the tradition of empiricism, positivism, and operationism the meaning is fairly clear; basically, it means the formulation and testing of a hypothesis to aid in building a theory. The ground rules for this process are often intricate and complicated, but the insistence is always on empirical evidence for any assertion and an explicit statement of the means by which knowledge is derived. Such knowledge is public rather than private; it is demonstrable, reproducible, and communicable. These stipulations are those of any science, and they must be adhered to insofar as psychotherapy aspires to the status of a scientific discipline.

To Freud and those working in the psychoanalytic tradition, "research" had a similar but not identical meaning. To be sure, Freud diligently searched for empirical evidence; he was concerned with making explicit the procedures by which knowledge was acquired; he recognized the need to replicate findings; and he strove for a distinction between clinical findings and the theoretical formulations he devised to explain them. Nevertheless, he was far less rigorous in his investigations than contemporary researchers—if also, let it be noted, infinitely more productive. Certainly, one of Freud's greatest and probably most lasting achievements is that of having devised a novel and unique method of investigation (the psychoanalytic situation) and having incisively explored its essential ingredients. Psychoanalytic research was and largely continues to be done in the clinical setting; this setting led to the emergence of the cardinal principles upon which psychoanalysis as a therapeutic technique is built; this setting, too, by its very nature imposes serious restrictions on the rigor which is part and parcel of the scientific method. True, it has its built-in "controls"; it defines the therapeutic situation as well as the role of the analyst (within rather broad limits); it seeks to maximize the patient's contribution to the situation while holding the analyst's constant; it imposes relatively strict rules upon the role behavior of the analyst; but it fails to insure that the analyst's observations (and the inferences he draws therefrom) are *reliable,* that is, more than purely subjective experience.*

Limiting the discussion to the American scene, it may be noted that knowledge about the psychotherapeutic process is enriched from two major sources: (*a*) analysts working in the tradition of Freud, and (*b*) research workers whose approach is more eclectic. The former group, largely on account of the restrictions imposed on psychoanalytic training, consists principally of analysts whose background training has been in medicine; the second group consists primarily of psychologists whose training and experience has been in clinical psychology. With the rise of clinical psychology as a science and profession during the last decade, and as a result of the increased contact of psychologists with psychoanalytic principles and techniques, research workers bring to bear upon their investigations a vastly greater understanding and appreciation of the subject matter, problems, and concerns of psychoanalysis than was true before 1940.†

Psychoanalysts, on the other hand, have begun in some instances to seek the collaboration of psychologists whose training has stressed research design and methodology as well as clinical experience in psychotherapy. In short, there seems to be a tendency for psychoanalysts to know more about research (in a rigorous sense) and for research workers to know more about the dynamics of psychotherapy as an interpersonal process. Consequently, there is an expanding meeting ground, and hence greater possibility for communication and collaboration.

This statement is not intended to suggest that the millennium has arrived. The cleavage between the two kinds of research contributions, with a few notable exceptions, continues to be a rather sharp one. On the one hand, there is a plethora of papers which, while usually starting with clinical observations, pile inference upon inference and arrive at conclusions which, typically, are not capable of verification. On the other hand, there are numerous investigations

---

* Not long ago a British follower of Melanie Klein reported that she was "shocked" to learn from a conversation with an American analyst that he and most practicing analysts in this country do very little research. As she saw it, *every* case at her institute is a "research" case. A similar comment was made to the writer by a British child analyst trained by Anna Freud. There are indications that the younger generation of American analysts, perhaps as a result of more extensive training in the natural and social sciences, tend to use the term "research" in a stricter sense.

† A comprehensive survey prepared in 1943 (Sears, 1943) revealed a widespread preoccupation with "validating" psychoanalytic concepts and principles through methods then current in academic psychology. Significantly, Sears dispensed with reviewing "a few studies . . . of the psychoanalytic process itself . . . since none of these was designed to test any theoretical point" (Sears, 1943, p. x) .

whose attention to matters of methodology, sampling, quantitative assessment, and statistical control is reasonably adequate, but which fall short of illuminating the phenomena they purport to clarify. It is noteworthy that by and large the first kind of contribution tends to appear in "psychoanalytic" journals, the second kind in "psychological" ones. It is a hopeful sign that in papers of the first kind there is increasing emphasis on scientific rigor; with respect to researches of the second kind there is greater stress on meaningfulness and relevance. Very probably, the future will bring even greater rapprochement, and perhaps an eventual amalgamation of the two approaches. At present, however, it remains true that the former studies focus on the individual case, stressing longitudinal development, idosyncratic richness, and depth; the latter place greater confidence in the cross-sectional approach, in which one or a few variables are systematically investigated in a sample of patients, therapists, etc. Here the individuality of the single case is subordinated to considerations of experimental design and statistical inference.

This problem is familiar to all who have witnessed the battle over psychometric vs. projective tests, and it seems hardly necessary to belabor the issue. Although new statistical techniques (which are still not very widely employed) have opened new vistas for the study of the individual case, the problem remains with us. Let it be conceded without further discussion that both sides have a contribution to make and that a scientific discipline of psychotherapy can and does profit both from exhaustive studies of individual cases and from cross-sectional researches. The one may suggest hypotheses which can be more conclusively investigated by the other, and in general there is little danger that either approach will soon have to be abandoned for lack of problems.

At the same time, it is clear that the development of psychotherapy tends in the direction of greater specificity, explicitness, and precision. This movement is inescapable if psychotherapy is to be taught, described, and explicated. It is becoming an axiom that concepts must be defined more stringently and that the vagueness inherent in the subject matter must be diminished. The demands for operational definitions, or at least demonstrable empirical referents, can hardly be sidestepped. These desiderata are expounded with considerable vigor at scientific meetings, but, with the exception of a small minority of researchers, most practicing clinicians and psychotherapists are none too mindful of these injunctions. And, in a sense, rightly so; they cannot suspend their clinical work until such time as research sharpens their tools; they must go ahead, meet the vast clinical demands, and do their best under existing conditions.

The increasing split between the clinical function and the research function is undoubtedly due to many complex reasons, of which the technical difficulty of combining scientific rigor with therapeutic objectives is merely one. By contrast, it is interesting to note Freud's assertion that, in psychoanalysis, therapy and research always go hand in hand. Indeed, he considered this one of the distinctive features of the method. To him, each individual patient was the proving ground for his previous theories and the *fons et origo* of new clinical discoveries, which were then woven into subsequent formulations. He found it impossible to divorce research from the process of therapy, and conceived of himself more as a scientist than as a "healer." In fact, he came to the final conclusion that the possibilities of psychoanalysis as a research tool far overshadowed those of a treatment technique. To Freud, "research" meant *clinical* research, i.e., the painstaking study of individual patients. However, he applied the scientific method and, through the study of new cases, tested his hypotheses in an approximate way, without however achieving strict experimental control. In some instances, his observations led Freud astray, but it is a tribute to his genius that he succeeded in making valid generalizations on the basis of exceedingly small samples. At any rate, he found the roles of scientist and therapist quite congenial, and the thought of applying a therapeutic technique routinely was utterly alien to him. Nevertheless, as he envisaged the future of psychoanalysis, he foresaw a growing group of analysts who were primarily practitioners rather than researchers and who would rely on others to forge and refine the tools needed for clinical work.*

Furthermore, Freud held the view that research on psychoanalysis (as a therapeutic instrument) could *only* be conducted in the psychotherapeutic situation; at least, he did not foresee other possibilities. Even today a strong belief is held in many quarters that in order to do research on the psychotherapeutic process, particularly long-term, analytically-oriented psychotherapy, it is mandatory to leave the therapeutic situation undisturbed, even though various research techniques may be used as long as they do not interfere with the therapeutic situation proper. Another group of researchers seems to

---

* Rogers (1955), on the other hand, feels that he cannot simultaneously function in both roles; if, in the clinical situation he attempts to be a scientific observer, he feels his empathic abilty suffers. He considers the two roles diametrically opposed and essentially irreconcilable.

feel that relevant and meaningful research can be conducted experimentally or quasi-experimentally. The first group, harking back to Freud, asserts that the analytic situation represents a specific method of investigation and that *psychoanalytic* research cannot be performed without this method; the latter group, without questioning the value of the method for therapeutic and other purposes, believes that other approaches, too, may yield fruitful and provocative data, which, eventually, may find their way back into the treatment situation.

So far, I have tried to indicate that essentially there are two kinds of research approach to the psychotherapeutic process: the clinical, used preponderantly by practicing analysts and therapists; and the experimental, exemplified chiefly by clinical research psychologists. While changes are gradually taking place, it appears that clinical penetration and scientific rigor have varied inversely. Furthermore, the two approaches undoubtedly reflect the temperaments of the proponents. If the advances of psychoanalysis as a therapeutic technique are compared with the experimental research contributions, there can be little argument as to which has more profoundly enriched the theory and practice of psychotherapy. To make the point more boldly, I believe that, up to the present, research contributions have had exceedingly little influence on the practical procedures of psychotherapy. This, in view of the advocacy of more and more research, the expansion of facilities and the greater availability of federal and private financial support, is a deeply disquieting state of affairs and one requiring closer scrutiny. Why is this so? Why have research contributions had so little impact? Is it that they have nothing to teach the practicing therapist? Are therapists so impervious to scientific findings that they are unable to profit from them? Is our knowledge of the subject matter so rudimentary that, at this stage, research cannot possibly be expected to have left its mark on clinical practices? I raise these questions, not as a therapeutic nihilist but as a researcher who feels that important answers should come from research. But I must confess that I am not fully convinced that they will. A closer look at the contemporary scene may not enable one to discern trends to forecast the future but it may help to clarify the schism that divides practicing therapists and investigators doing research on the therapeutic process.

The therapist-clinician might speak as follows: Psychotherapy, first and foremost, is a clinical art, not a science. My task is to aid and promote personality growth, or, more accurately, to help a troubled human being in his struggle with his emotional difficulties. I assume that the patient is fully capable of steering his own life course once the obstacles which stand in his way are removed. My task is to aid him in this process. I don't "handle" a case, I don't "manipulate" a person, I don't apply a "technique." My whole effort is concentrated upon *understanding* this person and his difficulties in living. If I am a psychoanalyst or an analytically oriented therapist, I follow certain technical rules (based on such concepts as transference, resistance, defense, etc.) which mediate the therapeutic process. From this vantage point, I don't see how it would help me to know that persons having certain psychological characteristics are better candidates for intensive psychotherapy than persons having some other characteristics; that interpretations of a certain kind tend to produce resistance in certain kinds of patients at a certain stage in therapy; that under certain conditions the therapist's personal problems tend to interfere with the therapeutic process; that certain patterns of personality characteristics in a therapist are more conducive to progress in therapy than certain others; that interpretive techniques are more effective in the hands of certain therapists with certain kinds of patients under certain circumstances, etc. How do such findings help me to understand my patient, Joe Smith, whom I am seeing three times a week, who relates to me, a particular therapist, in a particular way, who tells me about his anxieties in highly specific situations and whose stye of life, defensive patterns, life goals, fantasies, wishes are a unique constellation? True, there are important clinical papers which have influenced me deeply; they are the papers of a host of sensitive therapists, not the kinds of investigations which are based on a sample of patients, often treated by student therapists, which report results at the .05 or .01 level of statistical confidence. I am in sympathy with the point of view which says that we must achieve greater clarity about our concepts and our operations, but I doubt whether an experimenter standing *outside* the therapeutic situation can deepen my understanding of patients *qua* living human beings.

The researcher-scientist might speak thus: I fully recognize that the major contributions to the theory and practice of psychotherapy are based on careful observations of perceptive clinicians. Freud and those who followed in his footsteps have revolutionized our thinking about psychic conflicts and have developed a unique method for effecting fundamental and lasting personality change. Certainly, clinical observation and painstaking efforts by individual therapists have taught us most of what we know about the principles of psychotherapy and psychotherapeutic technique. It is possible that these insights will not be equaled or even approached in another century. However, we must not lose sight of the fact that Freud considered psychoanalysis a *science,* and he strove until his dying day to preserve the scientific attitude which formed the basis of his most notable discoveries. Unlike some of his followers, he did not consider his formulations as final pronouncements or immutable truths. To be sure, his methods were relatively uncontrolled, nor was he able to marshal the scientific rigor that is demanded of investigations today; but he applied the scientific method as clearly and unmistakably as an experimental psychologist who runs rats through a maze or a physiologist who measures the contractions of muscle. The differences are quantitative rather than qualitative.

Furthermore, it must be recognized that our knowledge of psychotherapy is at a very rudimentary stage. As Kubie (1956) points out, we stand at the threshold of a new era; discoverers like Freud have pointed the way, but it remains for others to systematize his insights, to document the wealth of his observations, to sift, discard, build, and revamp. Reluctant as the clinician may be to bring the searchlight of dispassionate and objective research to bear upon his clinical operations, no other course is open. It may be a long time before our knowledge is reorganized in revolutionary ways, and, compared to the sweeping discoveries of Freud, the patient and laborious investigations of the researcher may appear pedestrian, obsessive, and even picayune. Nevertheless, they are needed and may surely be counted upon to advance the frontiers of knowledge. Possibly none or very few of the current research investigations provide principles which *radically* change therapeutic technique or even have a marked influence on clinical practice. But neither have clinical insights during the last decades led to momentous changes in therapeutic technique. Progress in this area has been slow, although by no means negligible. Besides, the clinician's attitude of respect, empathy, and understanding has nothing to do with what research has to contribute; however, the greater specificity which will come from research will strengthen and illuminate the clinical framework of his practical operations and gradually enable him to be of better help to his patients.

These arguments, based as they often are on emotional commitments, have a familiar ring. They underlie the nomothetic-ideographic controversy; they are mirrored in the fundamental differences between the *geisteswissenschaftliche* approach of German psychology and the naturalistic-positivistic approach of American psychology; they have recently been revived in existentialist thinking and *Daseinsanalyse* (May, Angel and Ellenberger, 1958); and they are rooted in the subject-object schism of Western philosophy. These basic philosophic convictions determine one's view of psychology as a science, the methods by which knowledge is acquired about psychological processes, as well as one's conception of psychotherapy and of the role and function of the psychotherapist.

It is instructive to note that after having lived with Freud's discoveries for half a century, with a view of the individual patient as the battleground of impersonal forces shaping his destiny, we are still largely ignorant of the nature of the therapeutic action, but renewed attention is being focused on the psychotherapist as a *person*, who, some suspect, plays a larger part in the therapeutic endeavor than has hitherto been acknowledged or made explicit.* Working with widely different methods of investigation, theoretical orientations, and therapeutic objectives, numerous investigators appear to converge on this point. Alexander (1958), after a lifetime of experience in psychoanalysis, refers to "the most opaque area of psychoanalysis: the question of the therapist's influence on the treat-

---

* In one of his last papers Freud (1952) makes this highly significant point: "Amongst the factors which influence the prospects of an analysis and add to its difficulties in the same manner as the resistances, we must reckon not only the structure of the *patient's* ego but the personal characteristics of the *analyst*." ... The analyst ... because of the peculiar conditions of his work, is really impeded by his own defects in his task of discerning his patient's situation correctly and reacting to it in a manner conducive to cure. So there is some reason in the demand for a comparatively high degree of psychical normality and correct adjustment in the analyst as one of his qualifications for his work. And there is another point: he must be in a superior position in some sense if he is to serve as a model for his patient in certain analytic situations and, in others, to act as his teacher. Finally, we must not forget that the relationship between analyst and patient is based on a love of truth, that is, on the acknowledgment of reality, and that it precludes any kind of sham or deception" (Freud, 1952, pp. 351-352). As in earlier papers, the emphasis rests on those aspects of the therapist's personality which might create an impediment to therapy; however, Freud also recognizes that the therapist must be "in a superior position in some sense if he is to serve as model for his patient. ...." Unfortunately, one is left to guess what is meant by "superior position," but I wonder whether Freud meant that the therapist has to be somewhat of a *Persönlichkeit*. If in the passage immediately following he expressed doubts that the candidate would acquire the "ideal qualifications" for his work *solely* in his personal analysis, he clearly had the removal of "blind spots" in mind, but perhaps he also questioned whether the candidate could ever become a *Persönlichkeit solely* through his personal analysis unless his analyst in turn embodied the "model qualities" which Freud alluded to.

ment process by the virtue of being what he is—an individual personality, distinct from all other therapists." Frank (1959), speaking as a researcher concerned with experimental controls, sees as a chief problem "to distinguish the effects of the therapist's personality or attitude, from the effects of his technique." Furthermore, he considers the therapist as the most important, but least understood, "situational" variable in psychotherapy research. Elsewhere Frank (1958) considers the possibility that the patient's faith and trust in the therapist may be the single most important variable in therapeutic change. Rogers (1957) speaks of the therapist's "genuineness in the relationship," his "unconditional positive regard," and "empathy." He views the therapeutic relationship "as a heightening of the constructive qualities which often exist in part in other relationships, and an extension through time of qualities which in other relationships tend at best to be momentary"(Rogers, 1957, p. 101). In the same paper, Rogers comes to the conclusion that "the techniques of the various therapies are relatively unimportant" (p. 102) and, stressing the overriding importance of the therapist's attitudes:

> Any of the techniques may communicate the fact that the therapist is expressing one attitude at a surface level, and another contradictory attitude which is denied to his own awareness. Thus one value of such a theoretical formulation as we have offered is that it may assist therapists to think more critically about those elements of their experience, attitudes, and behaviors which are essential to psychotherapy, and those which are non-essential or even deleterious to psychotherapy (p. 103).

On the basis of the research results reported in this volume I have come to conceive of the therapist's contribution to the treatment process as both personal and technical (see Chapter 6).

There appears to be, then, a growing disenchantment with psychotherapy as a "technique," American preoccupations with technology notwithstanding. The keynote of this development was perhaps sounded by Freud himself. His attention to the technical aspects of psychoanalytic therapy declined toward the middle and end of his career, and, contrary to his theoretical revisions in other areas, he had relatively little to add to his earlier papers on technique. While he considered the therapist's personal attributes important, he stressed their potentially noxious influence, leaving the positive aspects largely unformulated (Freud, 1952). True, at one time he conceived of psychoanalysis as a kind of "after-education" but later on expressed a distaste for the conception of the therapist as an "educator" or "mentor" (see, in this connection, Burchard, 1958). He feared that the therapist might make similar mistakes as the patient's parents in "indoctrinating" him with a set of values and rules which would impede his free development and self-direction. In the 1920's and '30's much emphasis was given to interpretations, their timing, correctness, and adequacy. Concomitantly, the person making the interpretations tended to be lost sight of, and under Freud's impetus the essence of psychoanalytic therapy was seen as the resolution of the transference neurosis through appropriate interpretations—a process, one surmised, which would reel off, regularly, automatically, and inexorably if the "correct" technical procedures were but followed. This is not the place to trace subsequent developments except to draw attention to a trend culminating in the "rediscovery" of the therapist as a person, whose attitudes, personality, and values presumably play an exceedingly important, if not crucial, part in the therapeutic process. Concomitantly, it is being realized that increasing effort must be expended to elucidate his personal influence, which may far transcend his technical contribution (see Chapter 15).

Could it be that we have come full circle? Starting from the age-old view of the potentially beneficial effects of love, friendship, and acceptance on one's emotional well-being, we seem to have traversed an era in which a highly technical procedure (psychoanalysis) came to the ascendancy. Here the therapeutic task was conceived as an effort to bring about a reconciliation of impersonal forces, to help the ego come to terms with an irrational id and an unreasonable, overly severe superego. Moving along a spiral, the developments of ego psychology have stressed a conception in which the ego's autonomy and integrative functions again came to the fore. Contemporaneously, the psychotherapeutic situation is again seen as an encounter between two *persons*. The patient is regarded as an individual with problems in living, but also as a human being striving to realize his potentialities. The therapist is viewed not as an analytic manipulator or technician but as a human being who, aided by technical training *and* experience in living, attempts to *understand* the patient as a person. This understanding is to be accomplished through emotional participation in living with the other person over an extended period of time, to the end that the therapist's influence conduces to constructive personality growth. The focus is upon the experiential components of the situation, to which everything else becomes subordinate, including the technical operations by which the experience is facilitated. Consequently, the operations of psychotherapy are not simply to be explained by rules which tell the novice when to interpret and what; rather, they presuppose a deep understanding of the principles governing the whole gamut of human collaboration. Aware of this complexity, though speaking in a different context, Freud (1953) said:

> He who hopes to learn the fine art of the game of chess from books will soon discover that only the opening and closing moves of the game admit of exhaustive systematic description, and that the endless variety of the moves which develop from the opening defies description; the gap left in the instructions can only be filled in by the zealous study of games fought out by master-hands (Freud, 1953b, p. 342).

This analogy illustrates a point, but like all analogies it has its limitations. It asserts that (a) there *are* rules governing the conduct of psychotherapy; (b) these rules are explicit and communicable, hence teachable; (c) there is an over-all strategy in psychotherapy as there is in chess, i.e., there is a specific objective; (d) while knowledge of the basic rules is a prerequisite, it does not, in and of itself, enable one to play the game with any degree of skill; in other words, the general rules must be applied in highly specific and concrete situations, and once a measure of skill is acquired, the basic rules seem to recede into the background so that the player is largely unaware that he is employing them; (e) one learns the skill by watching and studying closely the operations of experts; in doing so, one learns to avoid pitfalls and refines his technique, which ultimately becomes interwoven with one's personality. One of the important shortcomings of this analogy is that the rules of psychotherapy are established empirically, not, as in chess, *a priori*. Furthermore, they are modifiable in the light of empirical findings, that is, their validity is to be established by reference to an external criterion. As the analogy suggests, the expert is more "successful" in playing the game than a novice, as evidenced by the fact that he wins more games. Is the expert psychotherapist more "successful" than the novice? This is a purely empirical question, which so far as I know has not been answered to anyone's satisfaction. One of the important reasons that it has not been done is the difficulty of *comparing* the performance of an expert with that of a novice, under rigidly specified conditions, and to note differences in outcome. Such a comparison presupposes the definition and measurement of dimensions which are hypothesized to make a difference (maturity, technical skill, for example). In all probability, the expert does differ in his therapeutic performance from the novice, but this must be demonstrated unequivocally, beyond a reasonable doubt. One approach might be to study the therapeutic behavior of a group of experts to see what they have in common. One might then search for the same common characteristics (therapeutic ingredients) in a group of beginners and determine whether differences exist. If so, they should lead to predictably different outcomes. If not, the results may be due to other factors yet to be defined. Freud attributes the results of psychoanalysis primarily to certain technical operations on the therapist's part; Rogers is inclined to search for them in the area of the therapist's "unconditional regard"; Frank hypothesizes a series of nonspecific factors, such as faith and trust. I suspect that salient characteristics of the therapist's personality interact with technical skill to make possible a new emotional experience, cognitive learning, and the gradual acquisition of attitude patterns based on identification with the therapist.

Preoccupations with psychotherapeutic technique have increasingly come under criticism in recent years. In this country, Rogers has been an eloquent spokesman for the view that *understanding* the patient is the therapist's first and foremost task. In Europe, the rise of existential psychotherapy has brought with it a further deemphasis of technique. In explicating this point of view to American readers, May states: "Existential analysis is a way of understanding human existence, and its representatives believe that one of the chief (if not *the* chief) blocks to the understanding of human beings in Western culture is precisely the overemphasis on technique, an overemphasis which goes along with the tendency to see the human being as an objective to be calculated, managed, 'analyzed' " (May, Angel and Ellenberger, 1958, p. 76). The central issue is "whether the human being is an object to be analyzed or a being to be understood" (p. 81). However, the emphasis on the here-and-now relationship neither obviates technical training nor should it discourage research on problems of technique. In May's words, this relationship

> . . . is in no way an over-simplification or short-cut; it is not a substitute for discipline or thoroughness of training. It rather puts these things in their context—namely, discipline and thoroughness of training directed to understanding human beings as human. The therapist is assumedly an expert; but, if he is not first of all a human being, his expertness will be irrelevant and quite possibly harmful. The distinctive character of the existential approach is that understanding *being human* is no longer just a 'gift,' an intuition, or something left to chance; it is the 'proper study of man,' in Alexander Pope's phrase, and becomes the center of a thorough and scientific concern in the broad sense. The existential analysts do the same thing with the structure of human existence that Freud did with the structure of the unconscious—namely, take it out of the realm of the hit-and-miss gift of special intuitive individuals, accept it as the area of exploration and understanding, and make it to some extent teachable (pp. 82-83).

Thus, it is of little avail to investigate whether psychotherapy "works," or even whether one technique is more "effective" than another. Rather, one must ask: Is this particular therapist, by virtue of being a particular person, capable of creating the kinds of conditions in which a given technique or techniques can attain their maximum usefulness? The question of the relative effectiveness of techniques still has to be answered, but the primary focus is on the *person* of the therapist by whom a particular technique is used. Can he understand the patient as a human being struggling with life's problems? Can he communicate this understanding, to the end that the patient feels deeply understood? For methodologic reasons, research may emphasize one aspect or the other, but the totality of therapist and technique in interaction with a particular patient cannot be ignored.

There appears to be a serious danger in overemphasizing either relationship or technique at the expense of the other. To avoid these pitfalls, it would appear that ways and means must be found to conduct investigations which do justice both to the demands of scientific rigor and the depth and breadth of the therapeutic undertaking. To this end, researchers must become better and more insightful clinicians, and clinicians must develop a greater awareness of the ideals which the scientist espouses. Among other things, such a rapprochement may result in a larger number of research contributions which are meaningful and relevant to the therapist. Similarly, it may inspire that tentativeness, caution, and respect for error in human observation which is still lacking in many clinicians.

The subject-object split which continues to pervade the science of psychology seems a particularly grave obstacle to the interpenetration of clinical practice and research in psychotherapy. Russell (1948), quoted by Szasz (1957), has eloquently dealt with this issue and defined psychology as a science dealing with essentially private experience. Among psychologists, Allport (1955) has taken issue with the prevailing behaviorist tendency to regard the human person as "empty." In the area of psychotherapy, the investigations of Rogers and his students (Rogers and Dymond, 1954) are perhaps the best illustration that fruitful research on the process of psychotherapy can be done, while retaining something of the uniqueness of the persons participating in the process. These are but beginnings, but they seem important beginnings in studying objectively the subjective experiences of patient and therapist in interaction.

Erwin Straus's (May, Angel and Ellenberger, 1958, p. 145) dictum that, "Whatever is related to my particular existence lessens and obscures knowledge," seems to strike at the core of an important dilemma in research on psychotherapy. In order to expand scientific knowledge of the therapeutic process, it is necessary to objectify essentially subjective experiences, but as one succeeds in doing so, one runs the danger of sacrificing the essence of what one is studying. Therefore, the obverse of the quotation likewise appears to be true: Knowledge lessens and obscures whatever is related to my particular existence. This, of course, is precisely what science attempts to do in all areas of investigation. Is psychotherapy an exception? If so, it can hardly become a science. If not, the search for invariance amidst change must go forward; common elements must be abstracted; and the unique aspects of the therapeutic encounter may have to go by the board. In one sense, I seem to have suggested that the future *may* bring the development of techniques for *simultaneously* achieving both objectives. This is a hope which may never materialize. We may find that we can't "have our cake and eat it." In that event, the therapist and the researcher in psychotherapy may move further apart, unless the clinician abandons his commitments, which seems to be as doubtful as that the researcher will forsake the ideals of science.

Among other things, it will be fruitful to learn how a particular patient is perceived, experienced, and reacted to by a particular therapist and *vice versa*. But if "objective" knowledge in psychotherapy is possible we must also learn more about what patient and therapist are "really" like, as seen by *external* observers. Some evidence has been presented earlier to suggest that preconceptions on the therapist's part (e.g., notions about the treatability or nontreatability of certain "conditions") may blind him to the patient's potentialities and assets. Of course, the therapist should develop maximal self-awareness of all factors which might adversely affect his therapeutic attitudes. But, important as the study of subjective elements and biasing factors may be, it must not overshadow the thorough scrutiny of interpersonal processes (e.g., transference manifestations) *qua* objective facts which, as every analyst knows, usually emerge in the treatment process irrespective of the therapist's unique personality characteristics, even though they may be colored by the latter. And, to continue arguing on this side of the fence, it seems that the latter-day emphasis on "encounter," "here-and-now experience," "understanding," etc., does scant justice to the painstaking and prolonged process of "working through," a highly *technical* operation which is considered an integral part of all fundamental personality change achieved through intensive psychotherapy. Difficult as controlled research on these problems will be, I am sure the limits have not been tested. However, I am not fully convinced that it will be possible to reconcile successfully scientific rigor with the richness and subtle complexity of interpersonal dynamics.

The questions raised at the beginning of this chapter still loom large. It is disquieting to contemplate the large discrepancy between clinical and philosophical insights, on the one hand, and research accomplishments, on the other. As researchers, we seem to lack methods for making greater inroads on the phenomena with which psychotherapy deals: the broad spectrum of human experience. For instance, how do we assess and measure such qualities in the therapist as: respect for the patient's struggle toward self-realization and self-direction; capacity for empathy; warmth; acceptance of the humanness of another person; depth of one's *Weltanschauung* and life experience; emotional maturity; ability to serve as a model of reality; and so forth,* all of which undoubtedly play an important role in determining the extent to which the therapist can participate in and collaborate with the patient's striving for realizing his human potentialities. By contrast, the quantitative and comparative analyses of technique, formidable as they are, appear like child's play.

The fact that techniques for measuring significant personality attributes are in their infancy does not mean that they are doomed to remain there. The fact that so far the contributions from researchers to psychotherapeutic theory and practice have been relatively slight need not remain an immutable truth and omen for the future. The task poses a challenge to our imagination as researchers; we must show greater penetration in forging our research tools and refuse to purchase precision in measurement at the expense of shallowness of concepts. If we agree to the proposition that psychotherapy's future is that of a scientific discipline, we have no choice but to undertake the laborious and painful drudgery of checking the empirical value of brilliant clinical insights glimpsed by intrepid pioneers and to sharpen our research instruments that they may become adequate to deal with the phenomena in our domain. It is just barely possible that a few crumbs of insight left over by the giants may be the reward of the patient researcher, not to mention the gratification of demolishing along the way some hypotheses which contemporaneously enjoy the status of a creed.

---

* We need to specify those qualities of character which give the therapist stature as a mature personality and model of reality. Compare the statement of Freud's position (Freud, 1952).

REFERENCES

Alexander, F.: Unexplored areas in psychoanalytic theory and treatment. Behavioral Sc. *3:* 293-316, 1958.

Allport, G. W.: Becoming: Basic Considerations for a Psychology of Personality. New Haven: Yale University Press, 1955.

Auld, F. Jr., and Murray, E. J.: Content-analysis studies of psychotherapy. Psychol. Bull. *52:* 377-395, 1955.

Bakan, D.: A reconsideration of the problem of introspection. Psychol. Bull. *51:* 105-118, 1954.

————: Clinical psychology and logic. Am. Psychologist *11:* 655-662, 1956.

Bales, R. F.: Interaction Process Analysis. Cambridge, Addison-Wesley, 1950.

Berelson, B.: Content Analysis in Communication Research. Glencoe, Ill., Free Press, 1952.

Berman, L.: Countertransference and attitudes of the analyst in the therapeutic process. Psychiatry *12:* 159-166, 1949.

Bibring, E.: Symposium on therapeutic results of psychoanalysis. Internat. J. Psycho-Analysis *18:* 170-189, 1937.

————: Psychoanalysis and the dynamic psychotherapies. J. Am. Psychoanal. A. *2:* 745-770, 1954.

Bordin, E. S.: Ambiguity as a therapeutic variable. J. Consult. Psychol. *19:* 9-15, 1955.

————: Psychological Counseling. New York, Appleton-Century-Crofts, 1955.

Burchard, E. M. L.: The evolution of psychoanalytic tasks and goals. Psychiatry *21:* 341-357, 1958.

Cholden, L. Observations on psychotherapy of schizophrenia. *In* Fromm-Reichmann, F. and Moreno, J. L. (Eds.) Progress in Psychotherapy 1956. New York, Grune & Stratton, 1956, pp. 239-247.

Collier, R. M.: A scale for rating responses of the psychotherapist. J. Consult. Psychol. *17:* 321-326, 1953.

Eysenck, H. J.: The effects of psychotherapy: an evaluation. J. Consult. Psychol. *16:* 319-324, 1952.

Fenichel, O.: The Psychoanalytic Theory of Neurosis. New York, Norton, 1945.

Fiedler, F. E.: The concept of an ideal therapeutic relationship. J. Consult. Psychol. *14:* 239-245, 1950a.

————: A comparison of therapeutic relationships in psychoanalytic, nondirective, and Adlerian therapy. J. Consult, Psychol. *14:* 436-445, 1950b.

————: Factor analyses of psychoanalytic, nondirective, and Adlerian therapeutic relationships. J. Consult. Psychol. *15:* 32-38, 1951.

———: Quantitative studies on the role of therapists' feelings toward their patients. *In* Mowrer, O. H., *et al:* Psychotherapy: Theory and Research. New York, Ronald Press, 1953, pp. 296-315.

Frank, J. D.: Some effects of expectancy and influence in psychotherapy. *In* Masserman, J. H., and Moreno, J. L. (Eds.) : Progress in Psychotherapy. New York, Grune & Stratton, 1958, Vol. 3, pp. 27-43.

———: Problems of controls in psychotherapy. *In* Rubinstein, E. A., and Parloff, M. B. (Eds.): Research in Psychotherapy. Washington, D. C., American Psychological Association, 1959, pp. 10-26.

Freud, A: The widening scope of indications for psychoanalysis. J. Amer. Psychoanal. A. *2:* 607-620, 1954.

Freud, S.: A General Introduction to Psychoanalysis. New York, Liveright, 1935.

———: An Outline of Psychoanalysis. New York, Norton, 1949.

———: Analysis terminable and interminable. *In* Collected papers. London, Hogarth Press, 1952, Vol. V, pp. 313-357.

———: The future prospects of psycho-analytic therapy. *In* Collected papers. London, Hogarth Press, 1953a, Vol. 2, pp. 285-296.

———: Further recommendations on the technique of psychoanalysis. *In* Collected papers. London, Hogarth Press, 1953b, Vol II, p. 342.

Fromm, E.: Man for Himself. New York, Rinehart, 1957.

Fromm-Reichmann, F.: Principles of Intensive Psychotherapy. Chicago, University of Chicago Press, 1950.

Gitelson, M.: The emotional position of the analyst in the psychoanalytic situation. Internat. J. Psycho-Analysis *33:* 1-10, 1952.

Glad, D. D.: Operational Values in Psychotherapy. New York, Oxford University Press, 1959.

Glover, E.: Common technical practices: a questionnaire research. *In* The Technique of Psycho-Analysis. New York, International Universities Press, 1955a, pp. 261-350.

———: Therapeutic criteria of psychoanalysis. *In* The Technique of Psycho-Analysis. New York, International Universities Press, 1955b, pp. 274-386.

Harway N. I., Dittmann, A. T., Raush, H. L., Bordin E. S., and Rigler, D.: The measurement of depth of interpretation. J. Consult. Psychol. *19:* 247-253, 1955.

Hoch, P. H., and Zubin, J. (Eds.) : Current Problems in Psychiatric Diagnosis. New York, Grune & Stratton, 1953.

Holt, R. R., and Luborsky, L.: Personality Patterns of Psychiatrists. New York, Basic Books, 1958.

Jackson, D. D.: Countertransference and psychotherapy. *In* Fomm-Reichmann, F., and Moreno, J. L. (Eds.) : Progress in Psychotherapy 1956. New York, Grune & Stratton, 1956, pp. 234-238.

Kardiner, A.: New horizons and responsibilities. Am. J. Psychoanalysis *18:* 115-126, 1958.

Kramish, A. A.: Problems in the non-directive therapist's reflection of feeling. J. Social Psychol. *39:* 201-209, 1954.

Kubie, L. S.: Some unsolved problems of psychoanalytic psychotherapy. *In* Fromm-Reichmann, F., and Moreno, J. L. (Eds.): Progress in Psychotherapy 1956. New York, Grune & Stratton, 1956, pp. 87-102.

Marmor, J.: Symposium on validation of psychoanalytic techniques. J. Am. Psychoanal. A. *3:* 496-505, 1955.

May, R., Angel, E., and Ellenberger, H. (Eds.): Existence: A New Dimension in Psychiatry and Psychology. New York, Basic Books, 1958.

Orr, D. W.: Transference and countertransference: a historical survey. J. Am. Psychoanal. A. 2: 621-670, 1954.

Porter, E. H., Jr.: The development and evaluation of a measure of counseling interview procedures. Educational and Psychological Measurement 3: 105-126; 215-238, 1943.

Raines, G. N., and Rohrer, J. H.: The operational matrix of psychiatric practice. I. Consistency and variability in interview impressions of different psychiatrists. Am. J. Psychiat. 111: 721-733, 1955.

Rapoport, A.: Operational Philosophy. New York, Harper, 1953.

Reich, W.: Character-Analysis (3rd ed.). New York, Orgone Institute Press, 1949.

Rioch, J. M.: The transference phenomenon in psychoanalytic therapy. Psychiatry 6: 147-156. 1943.

Rogers, C. R.: Significant aspects of client-centered therapy. Am. Psychologist 1: 415-422, 1946.

———: Client-Centered Therapy. Boston, Houghton Mifflin, 1951.

———, and Dymond, R. F. (Eds.): Psychotherapy and Personality Change. Chicago, University of Chicago Press, 1954.

———: Persons or science: a philosophical question. Am. Psychologist 10: 267-278, 1955.

———: Client-centered therapy: a current view. In Fromm-Reichmann, F., and Moreno, J. L. (Eds.): Progress in Psychotherapy 1956. New York, Grune & Stratton, 1956, pp. 199-209.

———: The necessary and sufficient conditions of therapeutic personality change. J. Consult. Psychol. 21: 95-103, 1957.

Russell, B.: Human Knowledge: Its Scope and Limits. New York, Simon & Schuster, 1948.

Sargent, H.: Intrapsychic change: methodological problems in psychotherapy research. Unpublished manuscript, 1959.

Saslow, G., Matarazzo, J., and Guze, S.: The stability of interaction chronograph patterns in psychiatric interviews. J. Consult. Psychol. 19: 417-430, 1955.

Sears, R. R.: Survey of Objective Studies of Psychoanalytic Concepts. New York, Social Science Research Council, 1943.

Siegel, S.: Nonparametric Statistics for the Behavioral Sciences. New York, McGraw-Hill, 1956.

Snyder, W. U.: An investigation of the nature of non-directive psychotherapy. J. Gen. Psychol. 33: 193-223, 1945.

——— (Ed.): Casebook of Non-Directive Counseling. Boston, Houghton Mifflin, 1947.

Stone, L. S.: The widening scope of indications for psychoanalysis. J. Am. Psychoanal. A. 4: 567-594, 1954.

Strachey, J.: The nature of therapeutic action of psychoanalysis. Internat. J. Psycho-Analysis 15: 127-159, 1934.

Strupp, H. H.: An objective comparison of Rogerian and psychoanalytic techniques. J. Consult. Psychol. 19: 1-7, 1955a.

———: Psychotherapeutic technique, professional affiliation, and experience level. J. Consult. Psychol. 19: 97-102, 1955b.

———: The effect of the psychotherapist's personal analysis upon his techniques. J. Consult. Psychol. 19: 197-204, 1955c.

————: A multidimensional system for analyzing psychotherapeutic techniques. Psychiatry *20:* 293-306, 1957a

————: A multidimensional analysis of technique in brief psychotherapy. Psychiatry *20:* 387-397, 1957b.

————: A multidimensional analysis of therapist activity in analytic and client-centered therapy. J. Consult. Psychol. *21:* 301-308, 1957c.

————: The psychotherapist's contribution to the treatment process. Behavioral Sc. *3:* 34-67, 1958a.

————: The performance of psychoanalytic and client-centered therapists in an initial interview. J. Consult. Psychol. *22:* 265-274, 1958b.

————: The performance of psychiatrists and psychologists in a therapeutic interview. J. Clin. Psychol. *14:* 219-226, 1958c.

————: Toward an analysis of the therapist's contribution to the treatment process. Psychiatry. In press.

————: Some comments on the future of research in psychotherapy. Behavioral Sc. (In press) .

Szasz, T. S.: Pain and Pleasure: A Study of Bodily Feelings. New York, Basic Books, 1957, ch. 2.

————: The problem of psychiatric nosology: a contribution to a situational analysis of psychiatric operations. Am. J. Psychiat. 114: 405-412, 1957.

Thompson, C.: Psychoanalysis: Evolution and Development. New York, Hermitage House, 1950.

Tolman, R.: Virtue rewarded and vice punished. Am. Psychologist *8:* 721-733, 1953.

Whitehorn, J. C., and Betz, B. J.: A study of psychotherapeutic relationships between physicians and schizophrenic patients. Am. J. Psychiat. *110:* 321-331, 1954.

Wolberg, L.: The Technique of Psychotherapy. New York, Grune & Stratton, 1954.

Wolff, W.: Contemporary Psychotherapists Examine Themselves. Springfield, Ill., Charles C Thomas, 1956.

Wolstein, B.: Transference: Its Meaning and Function in Psychoanalytic Therapy. New York, Grune & Stratton, 1954.

NAME INDEX

Alexander, F., 294, 318, 327
Allport, G. W., 323, 327
American Psychoanalytic Association, 72
Angel, E., 318, 322, 323
Auld, F., Jr., 245n, 327

Bakan, D., 3, 327
Bales, R. F., 245, 327
Berelson, B., 246n, 327
Berman, L., 292, 327
Betz, B. J., xi, 330
Bibring, E., 294, 327
Bordin, E. S., 246, 251, 252, 285n, 306n, 327, 328
Boring, E. G., x
Burchard, E. M. L., 319, 327

Cholden, L., 308n, 327
Collier, R. M., 246, 327

Dittmann, A. T., 246, 251, 252, 328
Dymond, R. F., 323, 329

Ellenberger, H., 318, 322, 323, 329
Eysenck, H. J., 243

Fenichel, O., 119, 327
Ferenczi, S., 288
Fiedler, F. E., 285n, 327, 328
Finesinger, J. E., 10
Frank, J. D., vii, 100, 121n, 319, 322, 328
French, T. M., 294n
Freud, A., 297n, 312n, 328
Freud, S., ix, 5, 289n, 290, 291, 292, 297n, 305, 310, 311, 314, 316, 317, 318n, 319, 320, 321, 322, 328
Fromm, E., 285n, 328
Fromm-Reichmann, F., 116n, 296, 301n, 328

Gitelson, M., 119n, 328
Glover, E., ix, 243, 244, 328

Harway, N. I., 246, 251, 252, 328
Holt, R. R., xi, 328
Horney, K., 288

Jackson, D. D., 300n, 328

Kardiner, A., 310n, 328
Klein, M., 312n
Kramish, A. A., 251n, 328
Kruskal, W. H., 38, 70
Kruskal-Wallis one-way analysis of variance by ranks, 38, 70
Kubie, L. S., 284, 310n, 317, 328

Luborsky, L., xi, 328

Mann, H. B., 38, 70
Mann-Whitney U Test, 38, 70
Marmor, J., 244, 251n, 254, 328
May, R., 318, 322, 323, 329
Murray, E. J., 245n, 327

Orr, D. W., 119n, 290, 291, 329

Porter, E. H., Jr., 245, 329
Powdermaker, F., 10
Psychotherapeutic Interviewing Series, Part V, A Clinical Picture of Claustrophobia, 10
Pumpian-Mindlin, E., 254n

Raines, G. N., 38, 329
Rank, O., 288
Rapoport, A., viii, 329
Raush, H. L., 246, 251, 252, 328
Reich, W., 120, 329
Rieger, R. E., 74
Rigler, D., 246, 251, 252, 328
Rioch, J. M., 121, 290, 329
Rogers, C. R., 95, 107, 115, 116n, 117, 120, 121, 253, 279, 280, 283, 284, 285, 298n, 314, 319, 322, 323, 329
Rohrer, J. H., 38, 329
Russell, B., 5, 323, 329

Sargent, H., 3n, 329
Sears, R. R., 312n, 329
Siegel, S., 37, 329
Snyder, W. U., 245, 279, 329
Stekel, W., 5
Stone, L. S., 289n, 329
Strachey, J., 292, 329
Strauss, E., 323
Strupp, H. H., vi, xiii, 245n, 329, 330
Sullivan, H. S., 4, 288, 298n
Szasz, T. S., 5, 103, 323, 330

Thompson, C., 290, 330
Tolman, R., 5, 330

United World Films, 10

Veterans Administration, 10
Veterans Administration Film Library, 10

Wallach, M., 125
Wallis, W. A., 38, 70
Whitehorn, J. C., xi, 330
Whitney, D. R., 38, 70
Wolberg, L. R., 263, 271ff., 274n, 275, 280, 283, 284, 285, 330
Wolff, W., 274, 330
Wolstein, B., 253, 290, 293n, 295n, 330

SUBJECT INDEX